# ENTRIES & EXITS

Founded in 1807, John Wiley & Sons is the oldest independent publishing company in the United States. With offices in North America, Europe, Australia, and Asia, Wiley is globally committed to developing and marketing print and electronic products and services for our customers' professional and personal knowledge and understanding.

The Wiley Trading series features books by traders who have survived the market's ever-changing temperament and have prospered—some by reinventing systems, others by getting back to basics. Whether a novice trader, professional, or somewhere in-between, these books will provide the advice and strategies needed to prosper today and well into the future.

For a list of available titles, please visit our Web site at www.WileyFinance.com.

# ENTRIES & EXITS

## VISITS TO SIXTEEN TRADING ROOMS

# DR. ALEXANDER ELDER

WILEY

John Wiley & Sons, Inc.

Published by John Wiley & Sons, Inc., Hoboken, New Jersey.
Published simultaneously in Canada.

For general information on our other products and services or for technical support, please contact our Customer Care Department within the United States at (800) 762-2974, outside the United States at (317) 572-3993 or fax (317) 572-4002.

Wiley also publishes its books in a variety of electronic formats. Some content that appears in print may not be available in electronic books. For more information about Wiley products, visit our Web site at www.wiley.com.

**Library of Congress Cataloging-in-Publication Data**

Elder, Alexander, 1950–
   Entries & exits : visits to sixteen trading rooms / Alexander Elder.
     p.  cm. — (Wiley trading series)
   Includes bibliographical references.
   ISBN-13: 978-0-471-67805-2 (cloth)
   ISBN-10: 0-471-67805-8 (cloth)
   1. Investment analysis.   2. Stocks.   3. Futures.
I. Title: Entries and exits.   II. Title.   III. Series.
   HG4529.E46 2006
   332.64′20922—dc22
                                                2005029249

Printed in the United States of America

10  9  8  7  6  5  4  3  2  1

*In memory of Eddie Ching,*
*my best friend Patricia's kid brother,*
*who on September 11, 2001,*
*went to a business meeting at the World Trade Center*
*and vanished from our lives.*

# CONTENTS

# ENTRIES & EXITS

# INTRODUCTION

You are about to meet 16 private traders. Some trade for a living, while others are still at a semiprofessional level, clawing their way to the upper rung. These men and women live in different countries, trade different markets, and use different methods, but all share several traits—most importantly their dedication to trading. They are utterly serious about their work, while most amateurs, who supply the bulk of their winnings, are chasing the excitement of an adrenaline rush.

The people you are about to meet have generously agreed to describe their methods and show their actual trades. Why would they do that? Why would a person who knows how to trade talk to anyone instead of keeping his or her mouth shut and grinding out profits in silence?

The secret of trading is that there is no secret. There is no magic formula you can buy or steal and plug into your computer to automatically make money. Success is based on discipline, hard work, and a bit of flair. These traders know that their success will not be diminished by the success of others, which is why they are willing to show you what they do. Also, many have traveled a hard road and feel kind toward beginners.

Trading is an immensely rich field, and no one can become an expert in all aspects of it, just like a doctor cannot be an expert in every field of medicine. Many beginners spread themselves painfully thin between investing and day-trading, between stocks, futures, and options. You're about to see that almost all successful people find one area that appeals to them and specialize in it.

People become successful when they focus on what they love to do. In reading this book you will probably come across a trading vehicle you like or a concept that appeals to you. Once you find it, stay with it and mine that area for its rich deposits. I wrote this book to help you break out of isolation, learn from others, pick up ideas that suit your style, and return to your trading room a better, more confident trader.

## HOW I MET THESE TRADERS

Eight years prior to writing this book, I went on a Caribbean vacation and by the end of the week felt thoroughly bored. The blue sky, the warm beach, and the rich food became a little repetitive after a few days. I realized that my favorite vacation was a working trip during which I could alternate work with sightseeing. I thought there must be others with similar tastes, and the following winter scheduled my first Traders' Camp. Eighteen traders signed on, and we went to the Dominican Republic for a week. We ran on the beach every morning, had classes from 9 AM to 1 PM and again from 5 to 6:30 PM, spent several hours around the pool after lunch, and partied every night. The group loved the classes, the resort, and the company. They told their friends about our Camp, and people started calling and asking to join. From then on we ran Traders' Camps several times a year on islands in the Caribbean, Pacific, and Mediterranean.

After working and playing together for a week, many campers became friends and kept in touch. I started having monthly campers' meetings in my apartment in New York. Many campers returned to subsequent Camps for refresher courses. After watching their progress over the years, I knew who I wanted to interview for this book. They included Sherri Haskell, Sohail Rabbani, Ray Testa, Mike McMahon, Michael Brenke, Kerry Lovvorn, and Diane Buffalin. I would have interviewed several more, but we could not mesh our schedules.

I always invited at least one guest instructor to every Camp to offer a greater diversity of views. I taught in the mornings, and they taught in the afternoons. Four people in this book—Fred Schutzman, Gerald Appel, David Weis, and Martin Knapp—taught in two or more Camps. I kept inviting them back because traders loved their lessons. As soon as I began working on this book, I knew I wanted to interview them.

I had been hearing of Bill Doane for several years and invited him for an interview to expand outside the camper circle. I ran into Peter Tatarnikov in Moscow and was impressed by the maturity and depth of this very young man; we conducted an interview in his securely locked office a few days before I flew back to New York.

**MALE OR FEMALE?**

Almost every nonfiction writer faces this dilemma—which pronoun to use. He? She? He or she?

Male traders outnumber women, although the ratio is rapidly becoming more balanced, as more and more women come into the markets. I find that the percentage of successful traders is higher among women. They tend to be less arrogant, and arrogance is a deadly sin in trading. The male ego—that wonderful trait that has been bringing us wars, riots, and bloodshed since time immemorial—tends to get heavily caught up in trading. A guy studies his charts, decides to buy, and now his self-esteem is involved—he has to be right! If the market goes his way, he waits to be proven even more right—bigger is better. If the market goes against him, he is tough enough to stand the pain, and waits for the market to reverse and prove him right—while it grinds down his account.

Women traders, on the other hand, are much more likely to ask a simple question: *Where's the money?* They like to take profits and avoid losses instead of trying to prove themselves right. Women are more likely to bend with the wind and go with the flow, catch trends, and hop off a little earlier, booking profits. When I tell traders that keeping records is a hugely important aspect of success, women are more likely to keep them than men. If you are looking to hire a trader, all other factors being equal, I'd recommend looking for a woman.

Still, there are many more male than female traders. The English language being what it is, "he" flows better than "he or she" or even jumping between the two pronouns. To make reading easier, I'll use the masculine pronoun throughout this book. I trust you understand that no disrespect is intended towards women traders. I want to make this book easier to read for everybody, of any gender, anywhere in the world.

*Adapted from Come into My Trading Room*

After reading my books, several traders approached me with very thoughtful questions and showed me their work, which was extremely serious and instructive. I enjoyed swapping ideas with them, and in the process of writing this book, invited them to be interviewed—Andrea Perolo from Italy, Damir Makhmudov from Latvia (he signed up for our Camp later), and Pascal Willain from Belgium.

Finally, there were several traders with whom I explored the possibility of an interview, but it never materialized. There were two campers who made massive amounts of money, moved offshore to tax havens, and did not want the visibility of an interview. There were also a few people with whom I discussed a possible interview—they talked a good talk but could not provide documentation of their trades.

I visited some of these traders, while others flew to New York to meet with me, and a few came to see me in Sicily and Amsterdam when I traveled in Europe. These days, with readily available Internet access, a trader's office is wherever he can put down a laptop.

# HOW THIS BOOK IS ORGANIZED

At the start of each chapter I'll introduce you to a trader and tell you about his or her background and method. Each person will show you two trades, and I will comment on both entries and exits. I will conclude each chapter by discussing an important theme or topic arising from that interview. In addition, I invited each trader to write a personal statement after our interview. Some described their personal development, while others sent more technical e-mails.

The entry into each trade will be shown on the right-hand page, with charts looking exactly how they did when that trader made his or her decision to go long or short. Do not rush to turn over that page—study the charts to decide whether that trade is likely to be a winner or a loser. Review the trader's comments on his or her charts. Ask yourself whether you agree or disagree with that trader's reasoning. Once you've made your decision, turn the page to see how the trade came out. Review the exit charts and read my comments on both the entry and exit. Proceed to the second trade and repeat the process.

Several traders wanted to show how their trades looked a month or two after the exit. I let them do it, but did not encourage such "hindsight charts." All of us are smart after the fact, with buy and sell signals plainly visible in the middle of the chart. The closer we get to the right edge, however, the murkier it becomes. Since we have to make our decisions there, I wanted the charts in this book to look as close as possible to the real thing. The middle of every chart looks easy, but we have to do our job at the right edge.

I want you to focus on the work of traders I visited, but since I comment on every single trade, I want to make my approach clear to you. I will begin this book by offering a very brief outline of my method.

It always shocks me to pick up a technical book without a bibliography. Any author of such a book must be a genius who doesn't owe thanks to anybody. You will see not one but two bibliographies in this book. First, there is a list of books mentioned during the interviews. Second, I asked every trader to give me their recommended reading list—they all did, and some added comments to their picks.

While I was working on this project, a steady stream of questions came in from campers and webinar participants. I saved some of their e-mails and included them, along with my answers, in the Q&A boxes throughout this book.[1]

---

[1]This might be the right place to mention that I have no "technical support person" for my books. I am the only trader in my office. My manager receives a steady stream of questions for me, but unfortunately, I cannot answer most of them for sheer lack of time. I answer questions from campers or participants in my private webinars, and also reply to e-mails from serious traders—which is how I met Andrea, Damir, and Pascal.

We are embarking on a journey together. It took me more than a year to create this book, and the people interviewed spent years rising to their current level. Slow down and do not rush—take your time, keep notes while you read, and study the charts. The more you put into this project, the more you'll get out of it.

# WARNING: OBJECTS IN THE MIRROR ARE FARTHER AWAY THAN THEY APPEAR

Most of us like to brag about our successes and hide our failures. Traders in this book have broken the mold—they will show you losing as well as winning trades. You are about to see real trades, made with real money. Still, there are several caveats you should keep in mind.

It is human nature to select especially attractive winners and relatively innocent losers when showing one's trades. I would think that most winning trades are not quite as great as what you see here, and many losing trades are a lot worse. Success is always a little farther away than it seems, while the risk of failure is a little closer than we imagine. To paraphrase the warning car companies engrave on side-view mirrors—objects in the mirror are farther away than they appear.

You'll meet several traders who are already famous, but most are unknown to the public. I have known almost everyone interviewed here for several years and feel sure that some of them will rise to prominence as money managers or analysts. At the same time, it would be unlikely for all 16 to remain successful. Markets are harsh, and some people inevitably fail. Please keep in mind that this book does not offer an unlimited lifetime endorsement of any interviewee.

Yet another word of caution is about my own comments. They express my opinion about each trade, its pluses and minuses, its strengths and weaknesses. At the same time you have to keep in mind that all of these comments were written after the fact—after each trade was already closed. All of us are smart after the fact. Being smart about the future is much harder. Hindsight offers a terrific advantage.

It is easy to see good trades in the middle of the chart, but the closer you get to the right edge, the more confusing the markets are. There is a big difference between exploring a battlefield after a fight and making decisions amidst what the great military historian John Keegan calls "the fog of war." This is why the level of clarity you see in these comments would be difficult to achieve in the middle of a trade.

To achieve clarity in your own thinking, you must keep good trading records. Make an entry in your diary after putting on each trade, paste up the charts, mark up their signals, and write down your reasons for going long or short. After exiting a trade paste up an updated chart, mark up its signals, write down your reasons for exiting, and analyze the pluses and minuses of that trade. When your own diary gets to be as thick as this book, you'll be well on your way towards becoming a successful trader.

# ON THE MENU

In recent years I've developed a friendly working relationship with the people who own and run Intershow, the largest conference company for traders and investors in the United

States. They often invite me to Traders' Expos and Money Shows to conduct day-long intensive workshops.

Speaking at their conferences allows me to meet hundreds of traders, many of whom have taken my classes repeatedly. I notice massive differences in what traders at various levels of development try to take home from the workshops. Several dozen people sit shoulder to shoulder and listen to the same talk, but each tries to capture something different.

Beginners scramble for hot tips, writing down any symbol that comes up. We often find a few good tips; the problem is that after a while these tips will play themselves out, and then what? Intermediate traders ask about indicator parameters and crane their necks to copy my numbers from the screen. They appear suspicious when I tell them there are no magic numbers and that the exact settings are not that important. Experienced traders sit back and watch, taking a few notes. They keep telling me the best part of the class is seeing a professional trader make decisions in real time in front of a live screen and explain how he makes them.

After hearing those comments I restructured my presentations—less lecturing, more sharing. This approach has carried over into my writing. Instead of lecturing you, I want to show you how professionals go about making decisions. Traders in this book share a wealth of information; what you take home is entirely up to you.

## MY METHOD

Since you will be seeing my comments on every trade in this book, I need to outline my own approach to the markets. This is an extremely brief overview because I do not want to repeat my previous books. To learn more about my views on trading psychology and technical analysis, please read *Trading for a Living*. For an in-depth review of my trading techniques, money management rules, and record-keeping practices, please read *Come into My Trading Room*. There is very little overlap between the two books; if you're going to read both, start with the first, but if you're going to read only one, read the second.

I believe that successful trading is based on three M's—Mind, Method, and Money. Mind is your trading psychology; Method is how you analyze markets and make trading decisions; Money is risk control. An ironworker client told me he renamed this formula the three B's—Balls, Brain, and Bankroll. The 3 M's are like the legs of a three-legged stool: If any one is missing, a person will end up on the floor.

Beginning traders, especially those with scientific or engineering backgrounds, tend to underestimate the importance of psychology. It always surprises them that the methods they tested so well on paper fail when they start trading real money (see Chapter 8). Those who survive come to realize that when the level of emotion goes up, the level of intelligence goes down—and this doesn't apply only to trading. I could lecture you for hours on the need to be cool, calm, and collected, but you are likely to forget everything within five minutes of sitting in front of a live screen, with prices ticking up and down in front of your eyes. The best way to remain calm and preserve discipline is to keep good records. Write down your plan for the day ahead, put it next to the keyboard, and follow it. Do not change your plan during trading hours.

## THE 2% RULE

Beginners are easily seduced by technical indicators, but successful traders know that money management is equally important. The two pillars of risk control are the 2% and the 6% Rules. The 2% Rule states that you may never risk more than 2% of your account equity on any single trade. People often misunderstand this rule and wonder why a person with a $100,000 account may only buy $2,000 worth of a stock. You may buy a lot more, but you are not allowed to risk more than $2,000. If you know your entry price, stop level, and permitted risk, it is easy to calculate the maximum number of shares you may buy or sell short. Let's say you're buying a $12 stock with a $10 stop. Since you're risking $2 per share and your maximum permitted risk is $2,000, you may buy up to 1,000 shares. You can buy a smaller position if you wish, but never go over the 2% limit.

## THE 6% RULE

The 6% Rule limits the risk in your account as a whole by stating you may never expose over 6% of your account equity to the risk of loss. For example, if you trade a $100,000 account and risk $1,000 on every trade, you may not have more than 6 open trades at any given time. Suppose you lose money on two trades—now you are not permitted to have more than four open trades. You've already lost 2% and have only 4% open risk available for the rest of the month. This rule allows you to have more trades when you're on a roll, but slows you down when you are starting to lose money.

A good trade begins with a money management question: *Does the 6% Rule allow me to trade? Do I have enough available risk in my account?* If the answer is yes, you can analyze the stock using your method. Then, if you find an attractive trade, just before putting it on, return to money management and ask: *Based on the 2% Rule, how many shares may I buy or sell short?*

## TRIPLE SCREEN

Between these two money management questions lies the vast field of market analysis. These interviews will expose you to a variety of analytic methods. My own approach is based on the Triple Screen trading system that I developed in the 1980s and continue to improve to this day. Since every market can be analyzed in several timeframes, Triple Screen insists that you begin by defining your favorite timeframe. Once you know what it is, do not look at it! You must first go to the timeframe one order of magnitude higher, make your strategic decision there, and return to your favorite timeframe only to make a tactical decision—where to buy or sell, going in the direction given by the longer timeframe. Since my favorite timeframe tends to be the daily, I use weekly charts to make my strategic decisions, and return to dailies to implement them. The weekly and daily charts are my first two screens. The third screen is the entry method, for which you can use either an intraday chart or simply place a standing order using a daily chart.

Fundamentals drive long-term economic trends, and I like to know something about them, but the bulk of my work is in technical analysis. I tend to stay away from classical charting because it is too subjective; I prefer to use computerized indicators.

In choosing technical tools I believe that less is more, just as in many other areas of life. Many programs for technical analysis have 200 or more indicators. All of them juggle the same few bits of data—open, high, low, close, volume, and, for futures, open interest. My rule of "five bullets to a clip" limits the number of indicators to the number of bullets in a century-old army rifle. You will see my favorite five on the charts—two moving averages, an envelope, MACD Lines with MACD-Histogram, and the Force Index. Let us take a quick look at each of these indicators, as well as a system that combines two of them—the Impulse system.

# MOVING AVERAGES

Each price is a consensus of value at the moment of a trade. A moving average (MA) reflects an average consensus of value in its time window. If price is a snapshot, a moving average is a composite photograph. It provides two important messages to traders. First, its slope identifies the direction of change in the public's mood. A rising moving average reflects growing optimism (bullish), while a falling MA reflects growing pessimism (bearish).

Another important role of the MA is differentiating between what I call "value trades" and "greater fool theory" trades. If you buy near the moving average, you're buying value. A person who buys well above the moving average is in effect saying—"I'm a fool, I'm overpaying, but I hope to meet a greater fool down the road." There are very few fools in the financial markets, and a person who keeps buying above value is not likely to win in the long run. He may get lucky once in a while, but buying near value is a much more sensible strategy. I like using two exponential moving averages (EMAs) on my charts, one showing a longer-, another a shorter-term, consensus of value. I call the area between them "the value zone."

There are several types of moving averages, but I always use exponential ones. EMAs are more sensitive to incoming prices and less sensitive to old prices. I only use EMAs on my charts, although several people interviewed for this book were perfectly comfortable with simple MAs.

# ENVELOPES OR CHANNELS

One of the very few scientifically proven facts about the markets is that prices oscillate above and below value. You could say that markets are manic-depressive—rising too high and falling too low, only to swing back.

There are several types of channels, and my favorite is a straight envelope—the lines above and below the EMA, both parallel to it. A well-drawn channel fits like a good shirt, covering the body of prices, with only the most extreme prices—the neck and the wrists—sticking out. Amateurs love to buy breakouts, but professionals tend to look for buying opportunities near the lower channel line and shorting opportunities near the upper channel line.

Some traders like to use standard deviation channels, often called Bollinger bands, which expand and contract in response to market volatility. They are only useful for options traders because volatility is a key factor in option pricing. If you trade stocks, futures, or forex, you are better off with straight envelopes.

# MACD LINES AND MACD-HISTOGRAM

Moving Average Convergence-Divergence (MACD) is an indicator invented by Gerald Appel (Chapter 7). Its fast line represents the short-term consensus of value, and the slow line the long-term consensus. When the fast line rises above the slow line, it shows that bulls are dominant, and when the fast line is below the slow line, the bears are in charge.

MACD-Histogram measures the power of bulls and bears by tracking the difference between the two MACD lines. When their spread increases, it shows that the dominant market group is becoming stronger—it is a good time to trade in that direction. Divergences between peaks and bottoms of MACD-Histogram and price may be the strongest signals in technical analysis.

MACD-Lines and MACD-Histogram are derived from three exponential moving averages of closing prices. Gerald Appel used 12-day, 26-day, and 9-day MAs. Those settings—12, 26, and 9—have migrated into trading software and have become default settings in many packages. In writing my books, I used those settings to illustrate this indicator.

What settings should you use? Well, if you want to use the same ones as everyone else, use 12, 26, and 9, because the crowd is basically lazy and uses the default values. You can also choose settings that are a little faster or a little slower. It depends on whether you want to receive your signals a little ahead or a little behind the crowd. Think about it and experiment with the values, or use the defaults.

# FORCE INDEX

Everybody watches prices, but it is volume that moves them. Volume reflects the intensity of traders' commitment, the heat of their exuberance, and the depth of their fear. Instead of looking at a plain plot of volume, I use Force Index, which links volume with price changes. On one hand, divergences between Force Index and prices tell me when a trend is becoming weak and ready to reverse. On the other hand, new highs or lows of Force Index tell me that the trend in force is strong and likely to continue.

Prior to the computer age I used to calculate Force Index by hand and still remember how excited I felt by its signals, which no other trader had. I also remember my inner struggle whether to reveal this indicator in my first book. My friend Lou Taylor, to whom *Trading for a Living* is dedicated, encouraged me to write about it, and I am grateful for his advice. The indicator continues to work just fine since I published that book.

# THE IMPULSE SYSTEM

This system identifies bullish and bearish phases in any market and timeframe by combining two indicators. The slope of the moving average identifies the inertia of the market, while the slope of MACD-Histogram identifies the push of the bulls or bears. The Impulse system gives a buy signal when both the EMA and MACD-Histogram rise, and a sell signal when both decline. The two indicators get in gear during especially bullish or bearish periods. Just as importantly, the Impulse shows when bulls or bears start slipping, and a trend starts growing weaker.

One of my campers, a brilliant programmer named John Bruns, programmed the Impulse system for several popular software packages, coloring each bar in accordance with the Impulse system. When the EMA and MACD-Histogram rise at the same time, the market is in gear to the upside and the bar is green. When both fall, bears are in control and the bar is red. When the two indicators point in opposite directions, the bar is blue.

| Impulse system | Slope of EMA | Slope of MACD-Histogram | Trading message |
|---|---|---|---|
| Green | Up | Up | Long or stand aside; no shorting |
| Red | Down | Down | Short or stand aside; no buying |
| Blue | Up | Down | Either long or short |
| Blue | Down | Up | Either long or short |

At first I tried using the Impulse system as an automatic trading method, but discovered that it worked best as a censorship system. When the Impulse is green, you may buy or stand aside but absolutely no shorting is permitted. When the Impulse is red, you may go short or stand aside but buying is prohibited. I wait for the Impulse system to go "off green" before shorting and "off red" before buying.

Some programs do not allow users to change the color of their bars on the basis of conditional formatting, but you can still identify green or red Impulse by noticing the slope of the EMA and MACD-Histogram. Coloring the bars is a convenience, and I am so used to it that I apply the Impulse to all my charts.

Name: Sherri Haskell
Lives: Sausalito, CA
Previous profession: Fundraiser for technology companies
Trades: Stocks and futures
How long: Since 1985, full time as of 1999
Trading account: Medium ($250k–$1m)
Software: www.stockcharts.com, TC2005, eSignal
Traders' Camp: St. Maarten, January 2003

# CHAPTER 1

# SHERRI HASKELL

## A LOGICAL WAY OF LOOKING AT THINGS

I met with Sherri twice while writing this chapter—first in 2003 when I was just planning to write this book, and again a year later. Sherri kept excellent records—in 2004 she could pull out the trades we had discussed a year earlier as easily as the trades from the previous week. These two interviews, held 12 months apart, offer a glimpse into how a serious trader's approach can change within a year.

In October 2003 I flew to a conference in San Francisco one day early in order to visit Sherri, who lives in Sausalito. I took a shuttle from the airport, crossed the Golden Gate Bridge, and got off on the other side of the bay. The air smelled of eucalyptus trees. Sherri was waiting for me in her sporty Lexus two-seater. When we arrived at her hillside house, a Mercedes convertible was parked in the driveway—Sherri liked her cars small and nimble, much like herself.

We had a campers' meeting that night, and the following morning Sherri picked me up at the hotel and brought me back to her trading room. Wall-to-wall windows overlooked the expanse of the bay and the hills on the other side. A table underneath the windows that ran the length of the room was crammed with computers, screens, and other gear. An exercise bike and a weight-lifting rack stood against the back wall. Sherri's fat cat, whom she did not have the heart to put on a diet, kept wandering in and out through the open windows, onto her trading desk, and back into the garden.

Sherri complained to me about what she called her poor performance. "I am up 90% this year," she said. "But the year is not over yet; I'll push to do better." I laughed and said, "Lay off a bit, relax—your results are fantastic, way outside of the envelope. You're at the upper edge of the top one percent of traders." Sherri did not think so. "I'm not good enough because I see stocks that go up 400% and I only make 90%," she said. "At the end of this year I want to be up 200%."

She told me that pushing for more had different meanings for men and women. Sherri always felt compelled to push extra hard to succeed in a male world. She had done very well in two traditionally male areas of business—medical equipment sales and fund raising for start-ups. Now she was just as determined to do well in trading.

I asked Sherri to tell me about her trading and show me two recent trades—one winning and another losing. She opened a hard-bound notebook, its pages full of scribbles. "I trade a couple of different ways—one way is following breakouts. I troll at night, looking for consolidating stocks with unusual volume. Something that hasn't moved very much but has big volume—that tells me momentum is building and it may bust out."

Sherri's notebook had four columns, and I read several lines. Some symbols, such as EWT and SNIC, were highlighted in yellow.

| Symbol | Comment | SafeZone | Stop |
|--------|---------|----------|------|
| ABAX | Looks OK but ADX turned down | 15.23 | 15.69 |
| ATYT | Really tight—clear to 16.5 | 14.94 | 14.87 |
| EWT | RSI < 70, MACD-lines getting ready | 11.09 | 11.32 |
| SNIC | Nice tight range | 14.62 | 17.74 |

I jot down ideas every evening—the yellow markings mean the stock looks wonderful and I put those into my eSignal alert system. When a stock is yellow, it usually hits my mark within a day. I have no problem finding stocks or understanding technicals. My problem is deciding where to add to positions and where to set stops. I am still refining that.

Every night I go over all my positions—this morning I have 13, on most days I have about 8, but even that is too many. I write a note on each position every night and then the chart image stays in my mind, so I do not need to look at charts intraday, but simply watch price levels.

I do my initial review in Stockcharts or TC2000, then track my list using eSignal in real time. End-of-day Stockcharts are the easiest to read—I do not want to pay extra for intraday real time, and 20-minute delayed quotes are useless. I put the symbols of the stocks that I selected in Stockcharts into eSignal, which lets me know when a symbol hits my price. It sends me an alert by phone, an e-mail, or a pop-up window, which is what I prefer because I am in the office most of the time.

Sherri writes herself notes in eSignal, attaching them to each ticker. All notes are dated and she cleans out old notes once a week. When Sherri likes a stock a lot, she marks it with a star, and when she does not like it, she writes **Watch!** next to it. "When the page is mostly stars, the market is bullish. When it's mostly 'Watches', it is more bearish. Before I enter a trade, I check that stock's volume—if it is strong, I go. If it is 50% above the normal daily level, it is a sure buy; otherwise I think the move has no staying power."

## TRADE 1 | SHERRI'S ENTRY

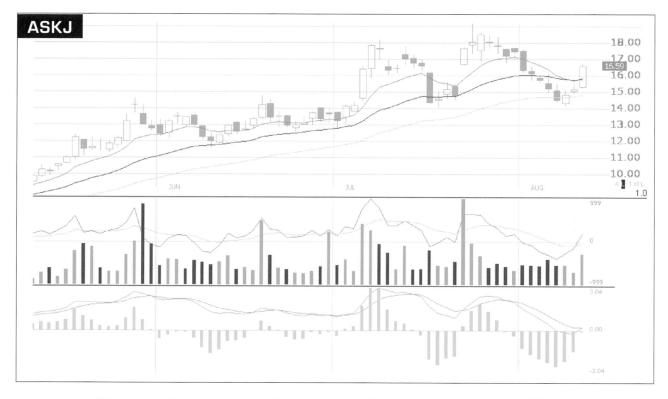

| | |
|---|---|
| **Upper pane:** | Candlestick chart (daily) and three exponential moving averages—10, 28, and 50 days |
| **Middle pane:** | Bar chart of volume (green = rising price day, purple – dropping price day); grey line—14-day TSV (time-segmented volume); blue line—a 10-day simple moving average of volume |
| **Lower pane:** | MACD Lines and MACD-Histogram |

### ASKJ

My initial buy was on 8/12/03 at $16.21. At that time several indicators were giving simi-
lar signals, confirming each other. The RSI had just crossed above 50, the price was moving up on strong volume, MACD-Histogram and both MACD Lines were rising, crossing
above the zero. Stochastic was turning up from below 20. How nice! The indicators were
screaming to buy, and I happened to be listening.

will this
trade make
or lose money?

# TRADE 1 | SHERRI'S EXIT

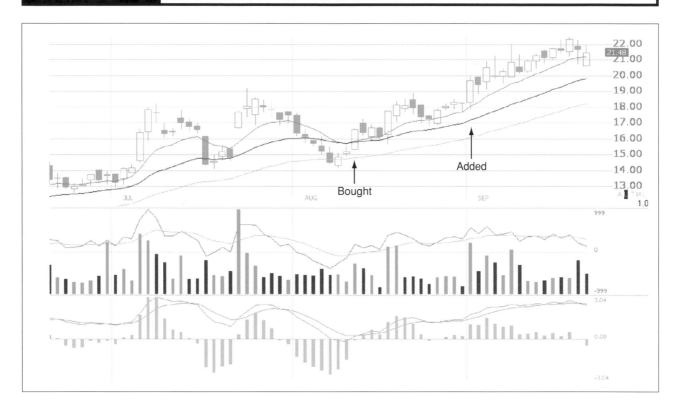

I added to my long position on 9/2/03. The stock had been moving up nicely, then developed a lateral consolidation. After four trading days, it broke out of its consolidation on extremely strong volume. RSI was advancing, MACD was strong, and Stochastic was continuing to climb. The most important factor was the breakout from the consolidation pattern on such strong volume, while all the indicators supported my action.

I sold on 9/22/03 at $20.74. The stock had been moving up for a couple of weeks, but the volume was gradually diminishing, and that got my attention. On 9/19 the price traced a *doji*, a bearish candlestick pattern. That set off an alarm, especially since the doji was on a much higher volume. I thought the price was topping out. While the price was going up, MACD-Histogram started falling off. The combination of all these factors was my cue to get out, saving my profit. I exited the next day at $20.74, just as MACD lines crossed on their way down and MACD-Histogram crossed below zero. It was time to bail out. My timing of the exit was fortunate, as the stock has continued to tumble since that day.

## ▲ TRADE SUMMARY

Long ASKJ 8/12/03 @ $16.21

Added 9/2/03 @ $19.30

Sold all 9/22/03 @ $20.74

Profit = $4.53 per share on the first position,
$1.44 per share on the second position

# TRADE 1—ENTRY COMMENT

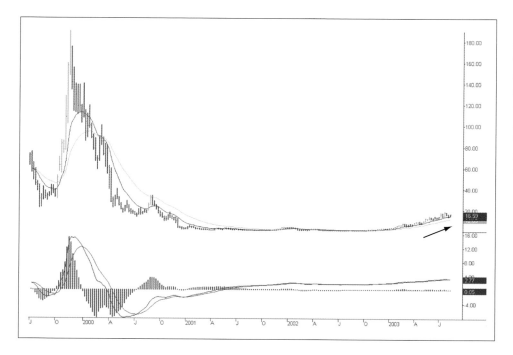

Whenever I load up the file of a stock I have not seen for a long time, I begin by compressing its weekly chart until the entire history fits into a single screen. This allows me to tell whether that stock is cheap or expensive relative to its lifetime history.

The history of ASKJ reveals that the stock had been sold to the grateful public in an IPO at approximately 70 (split-adjusted) and ran up above 190 in a final dizzying vertical rally in 1999. From there it crashed and then ground down to a low of 75 cents in 2001. Any stock that falls more than 99% from its peak, like ASKJ, has every right to die. But this puppy decided to live. ASKJ lay quietly on the bottom in 2001 and 2002, just trying to breathe, and in 2003 it lifted its head and started getting up, climbing into double digits. At the right edge of the weekly chart, both moving averages are trending higher, confirming the bullish trend and allowing us to buy.

**THE MOST EXPENSIVE $50**

I told Sherri about a client who had consulted with me a few years earlier. He had been trading stock index futures and after a long stretch of very poor performance started making money. At that point he set the goal of $1,000 profit per day. One day he entered a long position just right and soon was up $1,950. He decided to hold until that trade netted him a round $2,000 and took it overnight, overriding his technical rules. That day happened to have been the top of the 1999 bull market! Soon his gain shrunk to $1,000, then down to zero. He continued to hold, determined to reach his new $2,000 goal, while his trade went negative. Trying to recoup it, he doubled his position and then doubled again. By the time he threw in the towel and closed out that trade, his account had been reduced from almost $100,000 to $14,000. He then had to go to his father and ask for money, opening a whole new can of worms. —AE

*When the weekly charts give a buy signal, I turn to the dailies. There I decide to go long or stand aside, depending on the message of the daily charts. One thing I will never do is go short if the weekly charts tell me to buy. I will not trade against the message of the weekly Impulse system.*

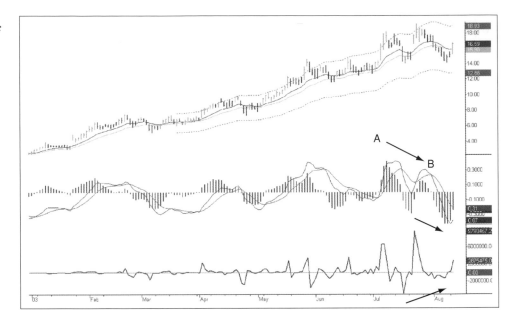

The extreme bar at the right edge of the daily chart is green—the Impulse system is giving a bullish signal. This occurs when both MACD-Histogram and the EMA are trending higher. This means that market inertia, reflected in the slope of EMA, is on the side of the bulls, and those bulls are becoming even stronger, as reflected in the rising slope of MACD-Histogram. An even better buy signal occurred a day earlier, when the color of the daily bar had changed from red to blue. When the bars stop being red, they indicate that the bears are starting to lose their power and the bulls are about to take control.

This chart is bullish, but it is not the best-looking daily chart. There are a few troublesome signs, including the bearish divergence of MACD-Histogram that occurred just before the decline near the end of the chart, which gave an extra powerful sell signal. Declines that follow bearish divergences tend to persist. A fresh multi-month record low of MACD-Histogram also points to the strength of bears.

Trading for my own account, I probably would have skipped this trade; at the same time I would not have argued with Sherri had she told me she was going to take it. Still, a serious trader like Sherri never asks anybody before making a trade. I am mentioning this only to show that different people trade differently. This is certainly a "legal" trade from the point of view of the Impulse system.

# TRADE 1—EXIT COMMENT

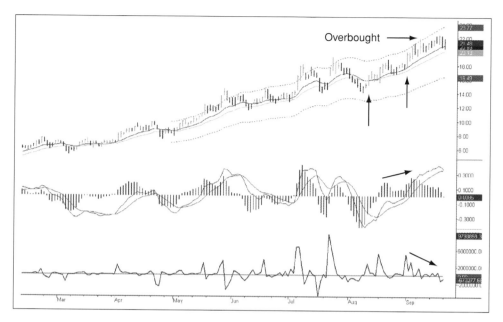

Overbought →

*Notice how the first pull-back at the end of August had returned prices to their value zone, and a few days later they returned to kiss that red line. This fast moving average represents the upper border of value. It is a measure of Sherri's skill that she was able to add to her longs on that slight pullback.*

Sherri caught a beautiful Impulse trade, capturing an eruption from the bottom of a sharp decline, added on a slight pullback, and jumped off as the trend began to weaken. This trade felt iffy for the first two weeks, as prices remained stuck below $20 and the daily bars alternated between green and blue. Then a breakout, confirmed by new peaks of MACD-Histogram and Force Index, confirmed that the bulls were becoming stronger.

In early September, the bulls became especially strong. On September 4, 5, and 9, they drove prices to the upper channel line. Those contacts with the upper channel line confirmed the strength of the bulls, but afterwards, even as the rally continued, prices could not come up to that line. That was a sign that the bulls were starting to run out of steam. MACD-Histogram started sloping down and Force Index drew a broad and ominous bearish divergence, illustrating the weakness of the bulls. At that point, prices continued to rise simply out of inertia.

It is a reflection of Sherri's experience as a trader that when prices started pulling back into the sweet zone between the moving averages she sold instead of buying. Same signal, different action! Sherri did not catch the bottom of the move, nor did she nail its top. Instead, she accomplished the goal of every serious trader—she took a massive chunk out of the middle of a big move.

**ACCOUNTABILITY**

Sherri was the only trader I interviewed twice for this book. When the folks at Intershow first asked me to speak in San Francisco, I took the opportunity to schedule an interview with Sherri who lived just across the bay. When they invited me to return a year later, I called and asked Sherri to schedule a monthly traders' meeting to coincide with my visit. It felt only natural to schedule another interview and see what had changed during that year.

The one thing that absolutely did not change was Sherri's sharp focus on performance and results. She is determined to succeed in everything she does, and extremely serious about her trading. One of the best reflections of her focus on results is the quality of her records. Sherri can tell you with total precision when she traded any stock or future and why she traded it, how it looked on entry, how it looked at the exit, the result of the trade, and the lessons she learned.

Keeping good notes introduces an essential learning loop into a trader's performance. Whenever you put on a trade, you have two goals. The first is to make money; the second is to become a better trader. You may or may not reach your first goal in any given trade, but you must always reach the second. You can learn from your winning trades as well as from your losing ones. If you fail to reach that goal, the trade has been wasted.

Markets change, and good traders change with them. At the time of our first interview in October 2003 the stock market had been rising in a pretty straight line for much of the year. Sherri's account was fully committed to stocks, often going on margin. The following year was very hard for stock traders, as the market was essentially flat, with no sustainable trades, faking out both bulls and bears. When I saw Sherri in October, I learned that she did not stick around to take the punishment the way most people did. She did independent research, discovered that many futures were starting to rally from multi-year bases, and shifted her attention to those markets. She studied and traded them so seriously that by the time we met a year later, she was sending her daily spreadsheet to several friends.

There was another notable change during the year between our meetings. I could see how Sherri's charts had become cleaner and less cluttered. Beginning and intermediate traders almost always use too many tools—partly because they are just learning and partly because of a common fantasy that more tools lead to better analysis. Accomplished traders tend to use just a small number of analytic techniques, distilled by experience.

I look forward to my next visit to San Francisco, another look at Sherri's latest trades, and another visit with her traders' group. Perhaps next time I will get enough courage to go on a horseback ride with her!

—AE

# TRADE 2 | SHERRI'S ENTRY

## GRMN

I bought GRMN on 6/19/03 at $44.49 and it turned into one of those lessons I get for being a little too confident. I had been talking to another camper about GRMN—we both liked the stock and had made decent money on it. Tony persuaded me that this was a good time to buy back in—the stock was in a lateral consolidation, but it would surely break out to the upside.

The stock got hit earlier in the week but looked like it was getting ready to rebound; MACD-Histogram was turning up. It looked like we'd get a jump on the rally and opted to do that instead of being patient and waiting for a confirmation. This went against my better judgment; had I been more prudent, I would have seen RSI below its centerline and not moving up, MACD lines headed down, and Stochastic below 50 and falling.

Those were clear signals to sit on my hands. The day I bought that stock it closed below its 50-day moving average for the first time in over six months.

Will this trade make or lose money?

## TRADE 2 | SHERRI'S EXIT

Bought

I sold on 6/23/03, two trading days later, at $43.36. That day the price dropped on very high volume. RSI fell below 30, MACD-Histogram dropped, confirming a growing bearish momentum, and Stochastic was falling as well. I got out as fast as I could, kicking myself for a sloppy trade.

Tony sucked me in, but I ran and he stayed and got really burned. I kept saying to him, "Don't try to be cute, don't try to be in front of the trade."

## ▼ TRADE SUMMARY

**Long GRMN 6/19/03 @ $44.49**
**Sold 6/23/03 @ $43.36**
**Loss = $1.13 per share**

# TRADE 2—ENTRY COMMENT

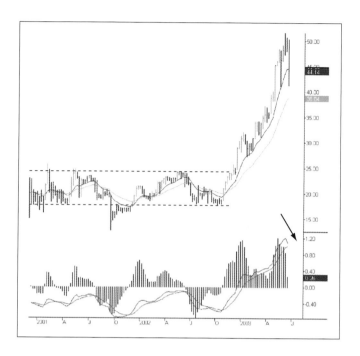

At the right edge of the weekly chart GRMN had fallen into its value zone, a potential buying area. Still, I would not trade it from the long side until its MACD-Histogram stopped declining. Its uptick would confirm that the decline was over and it would be safe to go long. The fact that it is still above zero and falling indicates that there is plenty of room on the downside.

GRMN had spent 2001 and much of 2002 in a flat trading range, between approximately $16 and $24, before breaking out. For several months following the breakout, it had a beautiful steady uptrend.

The stock's character began to change in May 2003, and that change provided an important warning for the bulls. Prior to that month, the weekly bars were neat and orderly, averaging about $3 in height. In May 2003 speculators started pouring in hot and heavy, as reflected by extraordinarily tall weekly bars, which reached up to $7 per week, both on the way up and on the way down. This sharp increase in the height of the weekly bars often marks the final hysterical stages of an upmove. Such tall bars often precede reversals, and I prefer to use them for taking profits rather than entering fresh positions.

**HOW TO HANDLE A LOSING TRADE**

One of the key differences between winners and losers is how they handle trades that go against them. Nobody wins in every trade—everybody has to take a loss every once in a while. Winners take their losses very quickly, while losers keep hoping and waiting for a trend to turn and bail them out. They keep finding excuses and explanations for why a stock should turn just about now, while it continues to go against them, grinding down their equity and sapping their morale. There is a saying on the floor—"If you hope, you're a dope." Both Sherri and her friend went "fishing for a bottom" and failed. They made the same mistake, but there was a huge difference in how they handled a bad trade. Sherri ran quickly and got away with a small loss; her friend kept holding and hoping until he took the full measure of the decline. —*AE*

The daily chart of GRMN shows a strong bearish divergence between the May and June peaks. In June prices rose to a new high while MACD–Histogram rose to a much lower peak, showing that below the surface the bulls were becoming weaker. Markets run on a two–party system, and when the bulls become weak, the other party is ready to take control.

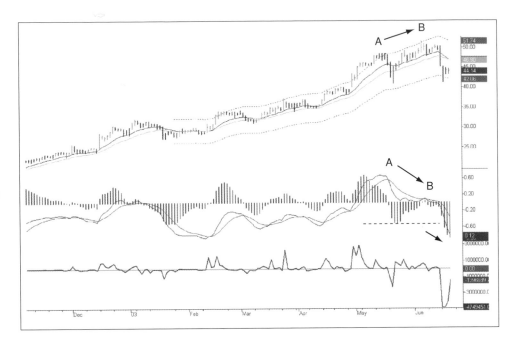

At the right edge of the daily chart MACD-Histogram is falling to a new low. The record deep bottom shows that the bears are exceptionally strong and the corresponding bottom in price is likely to be retested or exceeded. Force Index is also giving a bearish message. Its new record low, lacking any sign of a bullish divergence, fully confirms the short-term downtrend.

Prices at the right edge are near the lower channel line. This means it is too late to sell short, even though a new low in MACD-Histogram shows that further bearish action is likely ahead. I would much rather be shorting near the upper channel line than at this low level. GRMN looks dangerous to me at this stage, and I would stand aside at this time.

# TRADE 2—EXIT COMMENT

The message of the daily indicators, which were making fresh new lows and calling for lower prices ahead, turned out to be right. Prices tumbled to a new low. At the right edge of the chart they fell below their lower channel line, proving once again that channel boundaries do not serve as hard limits. Channels indicate where a reversal is likely to occur but do not guarantee it will in fact occur there.

With prices so weak and the bears so strong, should we look into shorting GRMN? My late great friend Lou Taylor taught me a useful technique—instead of trying to solve every single puzzle that life presents to you, go back to the general principle and decide on that basis.

In principle, most trades can be divided into two broad groups—value trades and greater fool theory trades. In a value trade we short a stock near its upper channel line and cover near the moving average or near its lower channel line. Shorting below the lower channel line is a greater fool theory trade—you know you're shorting at a low price but hope to meet a greater fool who will take this trade off your hands at an even lower price, giving you a profit. There are very few fools in the financial markets—which is why this tactic usually fails.

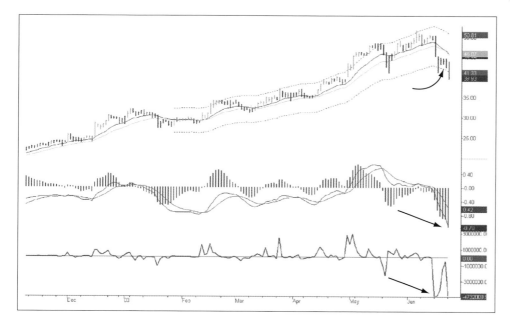

The new record lows of MACD-Histogram and Force Index at the right edge of the chart indicate yet again that the corresponding price low is unlikely to be final. They show that the bears are extremely strong, and even if there is a temporary rally, they are likely to push prices down to a lower low or at least retest the current one. How far back do we look before calling a low a record low or a high a record high? About half the computer screen.

Jesse Livermore, a great market speculator of the early twentieth century, once said, "There is a time to go long, a time to go short, and a time to go fishing." Looking at the right edge of GRMN, I would have reached for my fishing rod if I owned one.

# RETURN INTERVIEW

In September 2004 I returned to San Francisco and took a ferry to Sausalito. Sherri met me at the dock and we zoomed up the hill in her sports car. Not much had changed in the house with its intoxicating water view. Sherri's favorite cat had gotten thinner—Sherri had finally put her on a diet. The traders' group Sherri had been running since the previous year was still going strong. Just like the year before, Sherri was getting ready for another horseback trek in Europe:

> I was bored to tears in stocks and during this year have largely switched to trading futures. I had to change my style quite a bit in order to look for opportunities and confirm them. I am my own teacher and student; there are not many mentors in this department.
>
> The first month I traded futures I thought I was a genius. I had opened a $10,000 account and in three weeks it grew to $25,000. After that I no longer put stops on my positions because they could cause me to miss something. Then, one day, something happened to the U.S. dollar overnight, while I was holding metals futures. That's when I learned the hard way to use stops.
>
> Now my activity level is lower, my approach more deliberate and refined. I allow myself to hold only two futures positions—when I started I would be dealing with 10 positions at once. In futures that would be too treacherous because in some way all positions are related—you can have an avalanche come down on your head.

I used to want to trade as if that were my job. I wanted to be active, but now I want trades to come to me. I still do not have as much patience as is required. There are setups that are perfect, but you have to wait for them to come together. You must observe every day but not trade every day. Such deliberate trading makes more money. The more active you are, the more things can go wrong.

I love candlestick charts because they really tell you a story. I use fewer indicators and keep each on a separate tab so that my screen is not cluttered. I prefer MACD to everything else and have it on my screen at all times, but I occasionally check other indicators. I draw trendlines all the time—I am a very visual person and see patterns better than most traders. Before making a move, I always draw the trendlines.

Every evening I do my commodities homework—I am constantly changing and refining my methods. I recently started sending a nightly e-mail to a few friends—it helps keep me on my toes. I only review those markets that offer possible trades for the next day, plus the U.S. dollar—I think it is central to all futures. To review each and every market would be too distracting. I can do my entire list in an hour, sometimes even half an hour, depending on my schedule.

I prefer commodities but will trade a stock if I see what looks like a perfect setup. In recent months I have traded just a handful of stocks. My stock account is now only 50% invested, while a year ago it would have been 100% or even on margin. To trust this market again I would need to see a sustained rally on high volume.

---

**ON SHERRI'S MONITOR**

I took a picture of Sherri's monitor, festooned with dozens of cards and notes. She waved me off—"I do not want people to see my account numbers and passwords!" but let me copy one of the notes she has taped to her monitor. It listed questions Sherri asks herself before every trade:

Does a trade meet ALL of these criteria?

- Trade less
- Hold longer
- Be committed—deliberate
- Move fast in/out (don't hesitate)
- Cut losses at the earliest possible moment

*—AE*

---

After working for several hours, Sherri announced she was hungry and we drove to a sushi restaurant on a quiet Sausalito street. I asked about a photo I had seen pinned to a bulletin board in her trading room—a slender man with a strong angular face in an open-cockpit airplane. It was of Sherri's father:

He was a successful doctor but made much more investing and trading. He started charting by hand when he was 50, I was 20 then. He was very academic, always studying, reading, going to seminars, and he took me along. At seminars he had this very humble persona. But he was brilliant, always exploring; he developed systems, had software written for him.

He was an intellectual but he was also a wheeler-dealer who took risks and lived big. He invested in other things—diamonds, inventions. He made a couple million investing in this electrical invention that made light bulbs last longer. He took chances, took risks. When he bought himself a big boat 10 or 15 years before he died, he named it *The Speculator*. I like people like him—people who can step out of the box.

He passed away leaving a substantial estate even though he'd grown up poor. His own father had been killed in an accident when my father was an eight-year-old boy and there was no insurance. His mother did not speak English.

He used to be very tuned into world events—this or that happening is going to end up this way or that. He had a feel for macroeconomics—I would like to be more like that. I used to sit with him in his office—he tried to teach me and wanted me to trade with him full time. But I needed a steady income and he never offered to support me for, say, six months while I was getting the hang of trading.

I wish he were around now and I could show him what I do. When I look at markets, I often ask myself, "What would he say?" He had a very logical way of looking at things, not making wild choices.

We sat on the restaurant terrace in the soft light of an early evening. Everyone knew Sherri; the owner came up to say hello and several passersby waved to her. She talked about her tango lessons and mentioned she was buying a truck to tow her horse trailer.

"Wait a second," I said. "Isn't the horse supposed to tow you around?" Sherri laughed—"Not anymore. You should see some of those new trailers. They have padding, windows, mirrors, running lights, and air conditioning."

We drove back, and just as we finished our work, Sherri said that I was running late for the last ferry. We hopped into her Lexus. She backed out of the driveway and sped down the narrow mountainside street, going backwards faster than most people go forward. "Neighbors hate when I do that," she grinned.

# ONE YEAR LATER

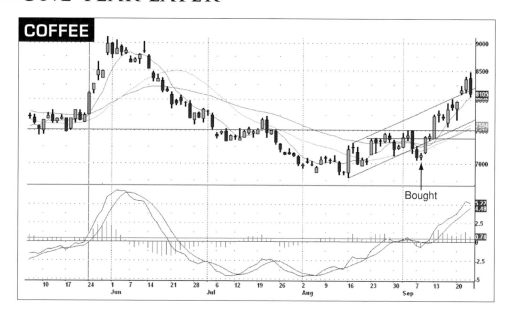

Sherri showed me two recent trades, one which she had closed that morning and another that was still running. "I bought coffee on a pullback on September 8 and I just got out today [September 23] because I saw this bearish engulfing pattern on candlestick charts."

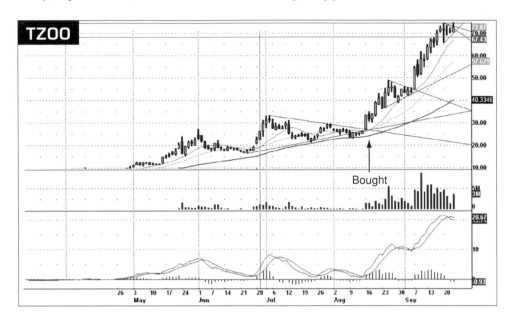

Sherri also showed me a still open trade in TZOO, one of the hottest stocks of the year. "I see pictures more clearly than most people—support and resistance, trendlines, channels. As long as the downtrend lines stay broken and the uptrend lines keep going up, it is okay to stay in. Also, this stock is still within its channel, making it okay to hold."

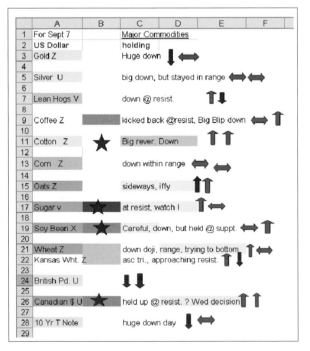

Sherri showed me a spreadsheet with a summary of her analysis of commodities, which she sends to a few friends every night. I noticed a Weekly trend column next to the Daily. While last year she looked only at the daily charts, this year she also analyzed the weeklies. I wondered whether in another year's time Sherri would put weekly analysis ahead of the daily, focusing on longer-term trends.

I noticed three important changes in Sherri's work during the year that had elapsed between our interviews: Her charts grew simpler and less cluttered; she became much more selective in her trading, not running so many trades at once; and she started paying attention to weekly charts and not just daily ones.

*An e-mail from Sherri:*

## THE BEST TRADING SYSTEM FOR ME

Have you ever walked up to a crowded craps table when people were screaming, the dice flying, and every imaginable expression seen around the table? If you didn't know the game, it probably looked like utter chaos. I've always thought of the stock market as a kind of global craps table. Instead of dozens of simultaneous games, there are thousands, with every conceivable kind of player, many different systems, odds and odds-makers (pundits). In addition, you must factor into the game potential influences: economic, political, and psychological. It's so daunting—until you determine *your game.*

In my early years I read everything, went to innumerable seminars and workshops, tried every guru's system. I started out like most people, looking for the Holy Grail. We think there must exist the best system and the best guru, and so we jump from game to game and end up frustrated.

Somewhere along the way I understood that I needed to determine my game and that the right system had to be my *own* system.

I spent some time thinking about my personal strengths, the way my mind and emotions operate, and the aspects of trading I enjoy the most. Where did I seem to do well consistently? I extracted bits and pieces from everything I had studied; the things that worked for me, made sense to me, and fit my own personal style. I customized that information along with personal formulations and discoveries, and created *my own system.* That was my epiphany.

The difficult part for me is the discipline. Not just the discipline of maintaining vigilance and not deviating from my system, but the discipline of not being influenced by others. I learned over time not to listen to financial programs on TV, to reduce the number of publications I receive, and to be very careful conversing with others about the market.

The market requires you to check some of your instincts while exploiting others. It's a psychological balancing act that I keep perfecting, but that takes time and conviction. The right emotional temperament helps, and so does a strong constitution. If you can start from a reasonable capital base, just like in any other business, as well as endure expensive early mistakes, the rewards can be fantastic!

A few suggestions:

- Learn candlestick interpretations. They bring the chart's story to life.
- Keep a diary and review it periodically. Write down the thoughts, emotions, and incidents at the time of each trade. You'll be surprised at the valuable information you'll find, particularly about your own behavior patterns.
- Be patient. Be deliberate. Wait for the perfect setup. When you see it, don't hesitate. If it's not happening, don't take action.
- Try not to make too many decisions during the trading day. Have your strategies mostly thought out during non-trading hours.
- Read *Reminiscences of a Stock Operator* about Jesse Livermore.
- Listen to the chart. What is it telling you? If you're not sure at once, step back. View the longer-term picture. What is it saying to you? If you're not certain, do nothing. I always let the chart speak to me, and I listen to the chart!
- Don't ignore your instincts. If you are successful at trading, your instincts have played a role!

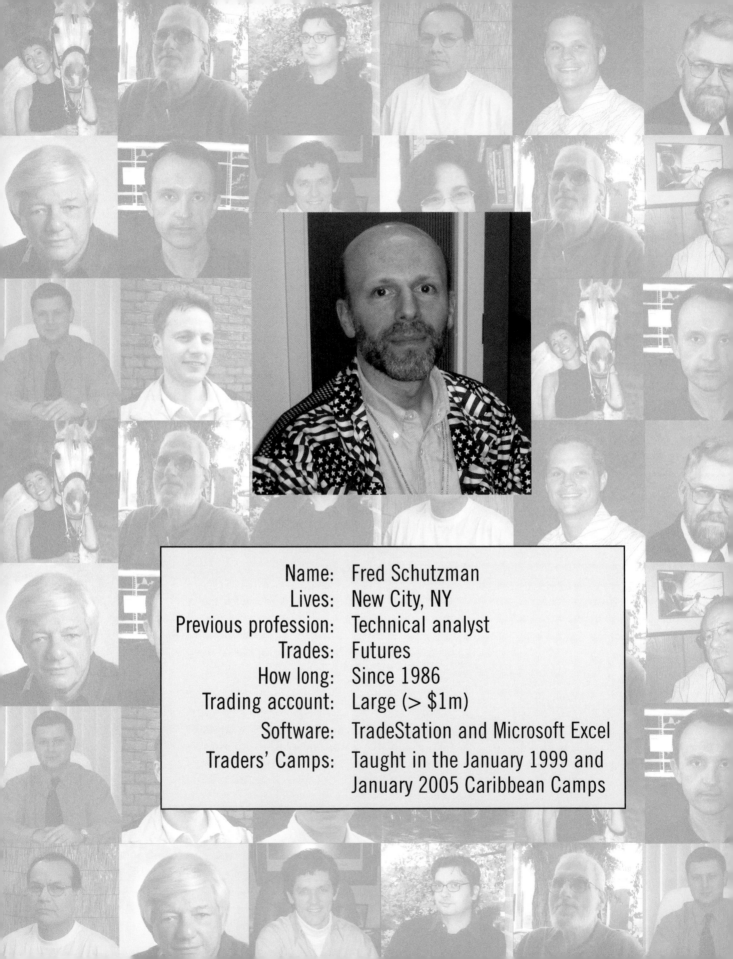

| | |
|---:|:---|
| Name: | Fred Schutzman |
| Lives: | New City, NY |
| Previous profession: | Technical analyst |
| Trades: | Futures |
| How long: | Since 1986 |
| Trading account: | Large (> $1m) |
| Software: | TradeStation and Microsoft Excel |
| Traders' Camps: | Taught in the January 1999 and January 2005 Caribbean Camps |

# CHAPTER 2

# FRED SCHUTZMAN

## MY COMPUTER CAN DO
## THE TRADING FOR ME

I met with Fred in an office above the trading floor of a commodity exchange, just a few blocks away from Ground Zero. The room in which we talked was named after Dennis Foo, a floor trader killed on 9/11. Bucky, Fred's partner in their hedge fund, joined us, listening, monitoring quotes on the terminal, and throwing in an occasional remark.

Fred used to work for me part-time in the late 1980s, helping produce a daily advisory service for currency traders. He left to become a partner in a money management firm, but only after he trained his own replacement. We have remained friends, and I have asked Fred to review the manuscripts of all my previous trading books, ferreting out technical errors. Fred has taught in two of my Camps; his dedication and friendliness made him very popular with campers.

> In the early 1980s I was studying to be an actuary, a statistician who measures risks for insurance companies. While in school, I became fascinated by the markets, discovered technical analysis, and subscribed to a Zweig newsletter. One of my college professors suggested I look for an internship on Wall Street. I could never get through to Zweig, so I got the membership list of the MTA (Market Technicians' Association) and started calling. An analyst named Gail Dudak took me in as an intern and I worked for her every Thursday.
>
> Six months later she sent me to John Murphy who was working at the CRB (Commodity Research Bureau). Few people knew of John then, before his first book had come out.[1] John was teaching a course on technical analysis at the New York Institute of Finance, and after a while he asked me to assist him. Then he became an on-air analyst for CNBC. The TV studio was in New Jersey and for the following semester he was unable to come back into Manhattan in time for his class. He told me to teach the first half of each class, and he would arrive for the second half. At the end of the semester he told me to take over his class.

---

[1] *Technical Analysis of the Futures Markets*, 1986, at that time considered the definitive book on technical analysis.

In 1990 I taught my first course and there were two floor traders from the Coffee, Sugar and Cocoa Exchange—Freddy and Bucky. They were successful on the floor, but wanted to prepare themselves for electronic trading. At the end of that semester they said, "We want to hire you as our private technical analyst."

We set up a money management partnership, with Freddy and Bucky on the floor and me working in an upstairs office with the charts and doing compliance. Then two things happened at once—coffee got very busy and our biggest client had personal problems and pulled out his assets. I went to work for various firms as a technical analyst and learned programming. In 1996 Bucky and I got funded and reopened the business. Today we're trading the methods we first applied in the early '90s, only then we did it subjectively. Now we're fully computerized and have improved our exit strategies and money management. Briarwood Capital has had a positive performance every year, and in 2001 we started to attract client money. Today we are managing $19 million.

System trading works for us because it takes the emotion out of trading. I am not good at making live decisions. I am more of a researcher, a scientist. I can talk to the computer and it can do the trading for me. Before we had computers, I was a researcher and could not trade without Bucky or Freddy on the floor. Now, if we can program concepts, I can continue as an analyst and the computer will trade unemotionally. I am doing the analysis, and the computer trades off my inputs. It pulls the trigger if the conditions exist.

System trading is not for everyone—a lot of people do not like handing the power over to a computer. They want to retain responsibility for the decisions. Sometimes the system gives you a trade I would not take as a discretionary trader—and that is usually a winner. If I am writing code, I see a lot of trades that look like stupid trades and I wish I could override them, but then my real performance would not equal the system performance.

To test a system, we apply it to 50 markets across 20 years of data and come up with roughly 4,000 trades using the same parameters in all markets. Pork bellies, coffee, currencies—the same in all markets. The beauty of back-

---

**WE COME UP WITH CONCEPTS FIRST**

*Fred commented:* Most people test a lot of systems, much like throwing 100 darts at a board. They find a system that has worked in the past and optimize it. They end up with a system that looks good on paper but never delivers the same performance going into the future—what they have is a past statistical fluke.

I would say 99% of people who backtest systems get it wrong and come up with results that cannot be replicated in real life. We come up with concepts first. If our system works, it is because it is well grounded in market behavior. Our systems are doing what they are supposed to do—replicating their test results in live trading. There haven't been any surprises so far. That is our greatest strength—we did the backtesting and know what to expect in the future. We are not going to tell people we will have 12% drawdowns and have 40% the next month.

testing on thousands of trades is that we know when we are likely to make money. You can never be totally certain but with our methods we are as certain as anyone can be. Our systems are often based on systems that we've been trading successfully on a discretionary basis for years.

I cannot repeat it enough—my job as a system trader is to follow the system. The only way I can realize hypothetical results on a go-forward basis is by following the system. I am a clerk, I am a monkey. My job is to think after hours but not when the markets are open.

Discipline and consistency are the two keys to success. The computer is consistent—it never misses a day or overrides a signal. A computer applies our methods objectively; it has no bullish or bearish bias. When I get pigheaded and get a bias, I think I can outperform the computer. While I might do that on one or two trades, I cannot outperform the computer on consistency and discipline. There is nothing like diversification: To succeed in the long run you need to take many trades, and the law of probability is in the computer's favor. If we want the best outcome possible, trading mechanically cannot be beaten. We operate like a casino, and the law of large numbers works for us.

We look for trades with a good risk/reward ratio and a decent payoff. We aren't looking for a runaway bull market with no place for close stops. We evaluate every trade, and our system attempts to get the best payoff per dollar of risk. Risking $5 to make $7 is not good for us. The trades I like best on the chart often have too large a risk and you are not being compensated appropriately for it.

---

**SOME GOOD TRADING IDEAS ARE AS OLD AS THE HILLS**

*Fred said:* A few of our ideas came from the booklet *Speculation as a Fine Art* by Dickson G. Watts. He was the president of the New York Cotton Exchange more than one hundred years ago, from 1878 to 1880. He wrote about psychology, discipline, and risk management.

Take a look at his "Laws Absolute," just as relevant today as they were 100 years ago:

1. Never overtrade. To take an interest larger than justified by the capital is to invite disaster.
2. Never double up. Never completely and at once reverse a position.
3. Run quickly or not at all. Run promptly at the first sign of danger, but if you fail to do this, hold on or close out part of a position.
4. *When doubtful, reduce the amount of interest.* Sell down to a sleeping point.

---

Without risk management, you cannot hang on to the money. We do not care about being right on every trade. Money management is even more important to us than the trading system. Someone could give us the best system in the world but if its risk/reward ratio wasn't good, we wouldn't take it. Our percentage of winning trades is about 40%, and so we shoot for at least a 2:1 return, but ideally we'd like 3:1. We are trying to get the best risk-adjusted returns—it is more game theory than technical analysis. We want to beat our competitors on a risk-adjusted basis.

Being a CTA (commodity trading advisor—a hedge fund manager) makes you trade differently than a private trader. We need to make our track record as attractive as possible, better than our competitors'. In recent years we have improved our exit strategies and risk management, reduced our drawdowns. Less risk means more return. As a subjective technical analyst I may like a market, but as a CTA I may pass it up because you risk giving back too much and a drawdown would be bad for our track record.

The attraction of being a CTA is the money. Typical compensation for CTAs is 2/20. If someone gives us a million, we'll get 2% of that money as a management fee, plus an incentive fee of 20% of the profit. Most people, if they had 10 million of their own money, would not want the headache of being a CTA—dealing with a lot of administration, compliance, and accounting. The way we trade, I would not be comfortable with an account smaller than 10 million.

When I first invited Fred to participate in this project, he wondered whether I would feel comfortable publishing an interview with a system trader, since he knew I was a discretionary trader. I told him that was precisely my point—I wanted to introduce my readers to all types of traders. Fred warned me that he wouldn't be able to show me the main system he was trading. It took him and his partner Bucky over 10 years to develop that system, it was their bread and butter, and they would not disclose it. What Fred could show me was one of several systems he had recently developed, tested, and traded. I told him that was a fair solution.

We keep looking for long-term trend-following systems based on our ideas. When we develop a system, we first backtest it using a computer, then test it with our own money in our R&D (research and development) account; only then will we use it to trade clients' money. Once a system is in place, we absolutely follow its signals, but while we test it, we allow ourselves to override its signals and experiment with its parameters.

## TRADE 1 | FRED'S ENTRY

These are the three entry rules in this system:

1. Define the major trend and trade only in its direction. Here we use an 89-day SMA (simple moving average). We also like exponential MAs but initially simpler is better.
2. Place Bollinger bands one standard deviation above and one standard deviation below the MA; watch for a breakout in the direction of the MA (a green line on the chart).
3. Place lines extending forward from each 34-day high and a 34-day low; watch for a breakout in the direction of the MA (a red line on the chart).

To enter a trade, all three signals have to occur, but not necessarily at the same time: The moving average has to turn in the direction of the trade and prices have to penetrate both the Bollinger band and the 34-day line, in the same direction. For #2 and #3 the latest signal simply has to be in our favor and not against us.

This chart uses cash data because the trade spans several contract rollovers. At the right edge of the chart we see all three signals in place: The MA has turned up and prices broke out of both channels—we go long.

**Upper pane:** Daily bar chart. Blue line—89-day SMA. Green lines—Bollinger bands, one standard deviation above and below the MA. Red lines extend forward from each 34-day high and 34-day low.

**Lower pane:** MACD Lines and MACD-Histogram, both 12-26-9.

## EURO

This is a channel breakout system—it identifies a trend and enters a trade when the volatility increases in the direction of that trend. Most people do not like this type of system because drawdowns tend to be large. We found that by using two channels we can tighten the parameters for both. By using both a Bollinger band and a Donchian channel, we try to tame the volatility beast. A Donchian channel is built by pushing horizontal lines forward from the highest high and the lowest low of a set number of days. Here we use a 34-day Donchian channel. Note that the upper and the lower boundaries of this channel can change independently from each other.

will this
trade make
or lose money?

## TRADE 1 | FRED'S EXIT

This system has two exit rules—either an MACD divergence (we prefer to identify them visually, even though we have written code to recognize them) or when prices move against the trend and close on the opposite side of their 89-day MA.

This system backtested well; it was profitable but the drawdowns were too high. We rejected it because we could not reduce the risk. If we could have cut the risk, I would not be showing you this system today.

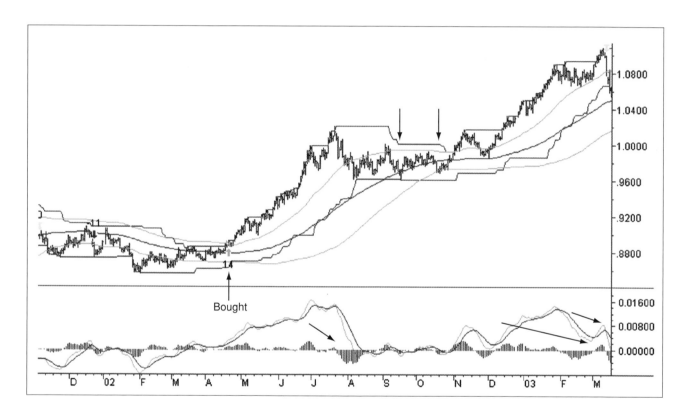

In July 2002 MACD-Histogram showed a divergence, but MACD lines did not diverge.

In September prices did not close below their MA. They did violate the MA in October, and much as we hate to override signals, we were testing the system. All of our other systems said hold. We said the market was closing below the MA not because it was going down, but because it was going flat. We put our stop below the September low—and it ended up holding.

January to March shows a great divergence. Both MACD Lines and MACD-Histogram divergences took longer to develop, which makes them more meaningful.

When the euro closed below its MA we sold it.

## ▲ TRADE SUMMARY

4/19/2002 buy Euro @ $89.12

3/13/2003 sell Euro @ $107.88

Profit per contract $18.76

# TRADE 1—ENTRY COMMENT

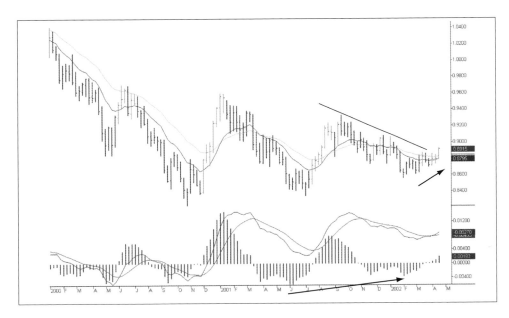

Trendlines are notoriously tricky because people can draw them a little higher or a little lower on the same chart, depending on their bias. Still, at the right edge of the chart, prices are coming up against the downtrend line at a time when both EMAs are turning up—a sign that an upside breakout is likely.

Buy low, sell high. The euro was definitely low in April 2002. The new European currency, recently launched on par with the U.S. dollar, promptly sank below 85 cents. This weekly chart shows that amidst mass pessimism the euro found support in the mid-80 cent range. The 2003 bottom of MACD-Histogram was shallower than in 2002, indicating that bears were becoming weaker. At the right edge of the weekly chart both the 26-week and the 13-week EMAs are turning up, along with MACD-Histogram, showing that bulls are in control—the Impulse system is flashing a buy signal. The red line (13-week EMA) is still below the yellow line (26-week EMA) and ready to cross above it; such crossovers tend to occur during the most dynamic stages of rallies.

**YOUR TRADING STYLE**

We make some of the most important choices in our lives for partly rational and partly irrational reasons. Few of us decide to become a systematic or a discretionary trader purely on the basis of numbers. We choose what allows us to avoid what we fear most. A systematic trader, such as Fred, is bothered by the incessant noise of the markets; he uses a computer to perform analysis and to execute trades without having to bother with constant attention to the markets and endless decision-making. A discretionary trader, such as myself, likes being in charge and dreads going into a trade that he dislikes merely on the command of the system. Both approaches have their merits and demerits; you have to choose your pleasure and your poison.        —AE

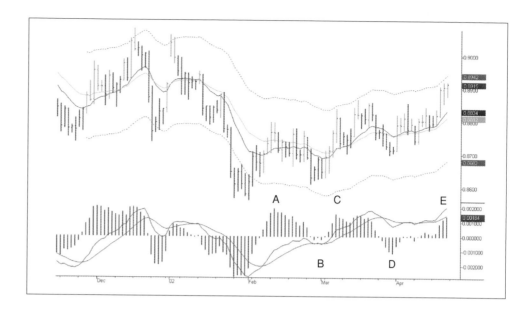

Prices "breathe" on the way up, inhaling and exhaling. Since the uptrend began in February, powerful peaks A, C, and E (not yet completed) show that healthy bulls are getting a full chest of air. Weak bottoms B and D show that when the market "exhales" bears have hardly any power. Vigorous peaks and shallow bottoms of MACD-Histogram confirm the health of the uptrend.

A system trader often finds himself on the opposite side of the market from the discretionary trader. At the right edge of the daily chart, all the key indicators are up—both EMAs, MACD-Lines, and MACD-Histogram. Still, while Fred was buying his upside breakout, I would have stood aside. Buying so high above value—so far from the EMA—would not sit well with me. After seeing a buy signal, I would be inclined to place a buy order in the vicinity of the EMA, adjust it every day, and try to get long on a pullback to value.

The risk with this tactic is that you may miss a runaway uptrend which keeps rising, with no meaningful pullbacks. That is a risk I am willing to take. I am in no hurry to get into any individual trade. I feel that trades are like city buses—there is always another one just a few blocks away.

## Futures

When change of contract occurs, in many cases the new contract will gap up or down from the previous one. How do you use technical analysis in such cases?                    —*Trader*

In analyzing futures, I always look at two data series—weekly and daily. For my weekly charts, I use continuous contracts, which take the kinks out of contract rollover. For my daily studies I use the front month. When that month changes, I switch to the new month, but go back several months in my analysis to get the proper indicator flow.                    —*AE*

# TRADE 1—EXIT COMMENT

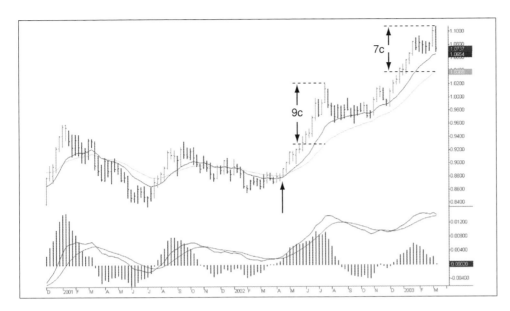

At the right edge of the chart, MACD-Lines are tracing a double top. This pattern shows that the market is seriously over-bought and warns you to take profits.

"Prices are connected to values with a mile-long rubber band," one of my clients once said. If we agree that a long-term MA is a reflection of value, we can measure the normal length of that rubber band by calculating the distance from the high of the highest bar to the EMA. On this weekly chart of the euro the "rubber band" could stretch to nine cents—that is how far prices got away from the 26-week EMA in July 2002. In March 2003 prices rose seven cents above value, almost the full length of the rubber band, before snapping back and taking out the previous week's low. Such sharp snapbacks rarely end before hitting the value zone.

Currencies are among the most trending markets. A well-designed system, while subject to whipsaws in trading ranges, should lock onto the long-term trends in currencies. Fred's system, which caught a breakout from a base and stayed long for almost a year, riding a major bull move, illustrates this point.

A factor that kills many amateurs in currencies, besides poor money management, is the fact that currencies trade almost 24 hours a day. They can move violently against you while you sleep. If you trade currency futures, you need to set up your account in such a way that a stop from futures is automatically executed in the cash markets if currencies move while futures are closed. A trader who gets into currency futures without this setup is like a man who decides to protect his property by putting up a fence on only one side.

**SUPERIOR RISK-ADJUSTED RETURNS**

*Fred remarked:*   Some CTAs have had large drawdowns—30, 40, or even 50%. Our largest drawdown thus far is 10.47%. We differentiate ourselves by superior risk-adjusted returns, compared to other systematic traders. If an advisor achieves 30% return with a 30% drawdown, then our 15% return with a 10% drawdown is 50% better.

When the markets are good, people say, "look at so and so returning 30%," but they forget that he just lost 30%! A CTA may have a higher return than we do annually but what risk are you taking to get that return? When everyone is earning 30 to 40%, we may get only 15%. Then in a drawdown, our competitors have 40 to 50% drawdowns, we get 10%. You have to give them $40 to make $40. You give us $10 to make $15.

# Moving Average Turns

Is it better to pick a stock whose weekly moving average has just ticked up or a stock whose weekly MA has been consistently moving higher for the past few months?        *—Trader*

The answer depends on your trading style. If you like to pick reversals, look for stocks whose EMA has just changed direction. If you like to trade swings within an established channel, look for stocks with an established trend.        *—AE*

**IT IS A PASSION FOR US**

*Bucky (Paul DeMarco, Jr.) is a floor trader on Coffee, Sugar, and Cocoa Exchange (CSCE) and Fred's partner in Briarwood Capital Management; he joined us during the interview and threw in a few comments:*

A mechanical system with good rules and proper risk management allows us to remain emotionally stable when placing bet after bet after bet. How many individuals can be wrong *x* times in a row and still place the next bet? Very, very few.

The most satisfying feeling I have is losing money for the right reasons. When you lose money for the right reasons, you will be a very successful trader in the long run because you will be taking smaller losses which will enable you to be around for the big trends. When the system says to get out—get out! I have never heard anyone say, "I blew out of the trading game by taking small losses." If we trade with proper risk management, we know we will make money in the long run.

Freddy and I have spent billions of hours on the phone. It is a passion for us—we want our equity curve to be as smooth as possible. You have to have a passion for this to be successful. Michael Jordan does not go to the gym to hang out and have a good time. No matter what Freddy and I are doing, at some point during the day we think of this—on the beach, in a store, anywhere. You have to do what you love because only then can you fail and get up and go forward again. There are people more talented than Michael Jordan, but they never made it. We make thousands of trades to improve, he makes thousands of shots. I have met many talented people who could run circles around me—and I make more money trading than they do.

# TRADE 2 | FRED'S ENTRY

## COTTON

It is hard to show a colorful losing trade when you are a system trader. With most losing trades we are out very quickly. We get in, lose 0.2%, and we're gone. Such trades do not damage our track record. I want to show you a loss that was one of the worst—prices moved so fast that our stop did not have time to catch up with them.

Our entry into this trade was delayed because first we got a signal from the Bollinger bands and the Donchian channel, but had to wait for the MA to turn up. When it finally did, we went long much higher above the MA than we normally like and bought fewer contracts.

A discretionary trader looking at this chart could say this is a sucky entry—the price is hitting overhead resistance and oscillators are overbought. He could say that the odds are against this trade because we got in so late. In our experience, those are the kinds of trades that really get going!

Will this trade make or lose money?

# TRADE 2   FRED'S EXIT

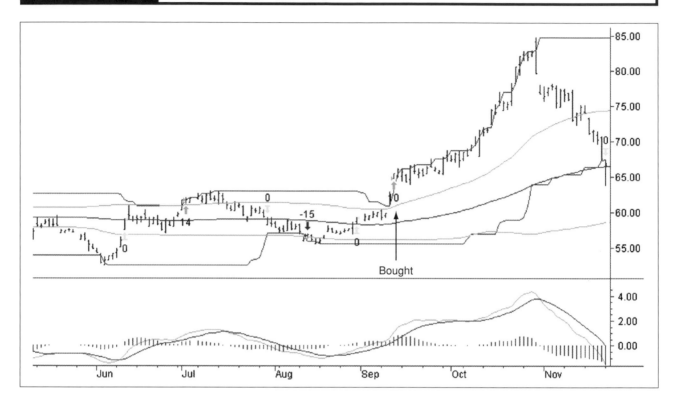

We have a long-term system designed to capture big profits. A trailing stop moves slowly and steadily, but this market moved so rapidly up and down that the stop did not have the time to catch up. A trade like this does not hurt our pocketbook—we lost little money—but it hurts our track record.

This trade is a system trader's worst nightmare. It included the end of the month: We booked paper profits in October, then showed a loss in November—it hurts to start a month with a drawdown. A small loss is okay, but a big run-up and a big run-down will hurt your track record by making it more volatile.

Our rule is to exit if the price closes across the MA against our position. We try to exit on close rather than wait until the next day's open. You have to be careful when you give an MOC (market on close) order. Some markets have 30-second closing periods, others even longer. A closing period in coffee is two minutes—place an MOC (market on close) order to get out early and the market will have another minute and 59 seconds to run against you. We try to finesse our exits. We have a computer algorithm to decide where the close has to be to give us a signal.

It is a good system, producing nice profits; it is a tradable system, but taming the drawdown is hard. We want to produce not just profits but the best risk-adjusted returns. We easily have 20 to 25 systems that do well on the profit line, but we look for systems to minimize risk and those are the ones we keep trading.

## ▼ TRADE SUMMARY

9/11/2003 buy Dec 03 Cotton @ 64.75 c/lb

11/25/2003 sell Dec 03 Cotton @ 63.87 c/lb

Loss per contract = 0.88 ¢/lb

# TRADE 2—ENTRY COMMENT

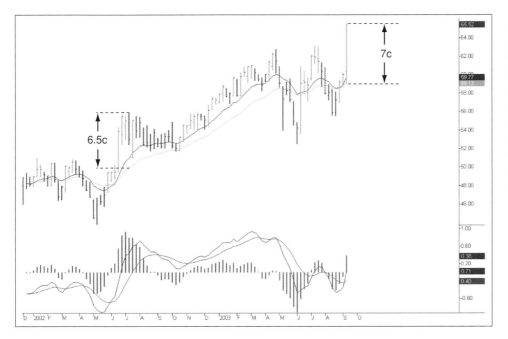

How long is the rubber band in cotton? In June 2002 it was 6.5 cents from the high to the EMA. Both in April and July 2003 it was 4.5 cents. At the right edge of the chart it is already seven cents—the overextended rubber band makes me want to stand aside.

At the right edge of the screen the buy signals are in. Both EMAs are rising, MACD-Histogram points up—but the excitement is way too much for me. I do not chase runaway trains and I do not chase runaway trends either. It is too late for me to jump in. I understand that a system trader does not have such latitude. When he gets a signal, he has to buy to remain faithful to his system.

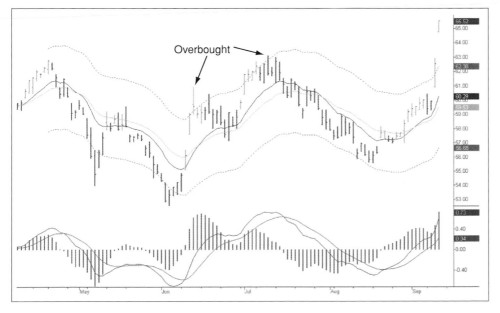

I like to buy near value, and cotton at the right edge of the daily chart is way above value. It is flying, blown up like the thin cotton dress in a famous photo of Marilyn Monroe. I may not short cotton here because all the indicators point up, but I would not buy it either because there is no place for a reasonably close stop. I appreciate Fred's discipline in taking all his system's signals and his fortitude in showing this trade—but this type of trade makes me glad to be a discretionary trader.

# TRADE 2—EXIT COMMENT

A key reversal occurs when prices gap above the high of the previous bar, reach a new high, then turn down and close sharply below the low of the previous bar. This shows a break in the predominant bullish sentiment. The peak is the last gasp of the bulls, after which the bears take over and push the market much lower.

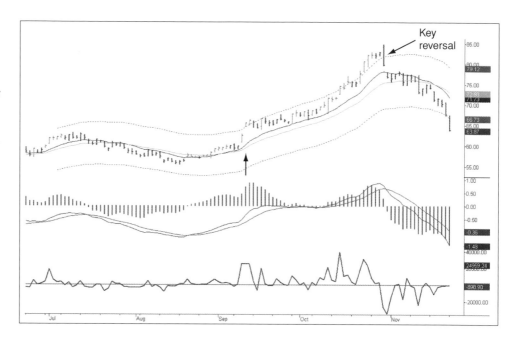

Trades that are difficult from the start tend to remain difficult to the finish. At first, cotton vindicated Fred's trend-following system. After he went long, cotton kept going higher and higher, with occasional shallow pullbacks to the red line, the 13-day EMA.

This looks like a fundamentally driven market. A sudden disruption in supply must have goosed up cotton. Some disruptions develop slowly, allowing a technical trader to recognize emerging bullish patterns. Other disruptions strike suddenly, and the market gaps up and keeps on running. A mirror image of this occurs in downtrends. New supplies may come in slow waves, creating a distribution pattern, so that a technician can recognize bearish divergences and prepare for a downtrend ahead. At other times there is a sudden surge of supply or a collapse of demand. The market appears to hit its head on the ceiling, reverse, and go into a freefall. That is exactly what happened to cotton during this trade.

It is a credit to Fred's system that it handles such a difficult market with so little damage to the account. After being forced to get long high above value and getting caught in a major downside reversal, his system escaped with minimal financial damage. If a system loses so little in such a difficult, highly volatile market, its owner should survive and succeed in the long run.

# SYSTEMATIC OR DISCRETIONARY

Trading is a vast field. There are so many markets and methods that it's impossible to know everything. Just like a doctor cannot be an expert in surgery, psychiatry, and obstetrics at the same time, a trader cannot be an expert in fundamental analysis, technical analysis, insiders' reports, and day-trading. Successful people in any field usually specialize in a fairly narrow area, while having a good general grasp of the rest of the field. You must know where your knowledge is weak and be humble enough to stay out of those areas.

How people choose their fields is often a mystery. We had a trader in one of our Camps who was a proctologist by training. Before early-onset arthritis put an end to his surgical career and drove him to the markets, he spent his working days with his hands in you know what. Go figure.

System traders like Fred and discretionary traders like myself often seem to be at opposite ends of the field. Fred spends hours each day testing systems. He trades over 20 futures markets using his favorite mechanical system, but has little interest in the outcome of any individual trade. He keeps meticulous records on system testing but no trader's diary. A discretionary trader pores over his charts, then makes his decision and watches the screen in order to squeeze the trigger for an entry or exit.

When you look closer, you see that the two fields overlap in some important ways. A sophisticated system trader begins his research with ideas that come from discretionary trading. As Fred pointed out, it is silly to use a computer to massage the data, looking for repeating patterns; that would mean trading the past. Fred's systems are derived from what works on the floor. Bucky, a second-generation floor trader with vast experience in intuitive trading, serves as the main idea generator. However, good discretionary trading is more systematic than it seems upon first glance. I have a visual set of well-established patterns; in scanning charts and indicators I filter market data through those systematic snippets.

The decision to get into systematic or discretionary trading depends more on an individual's temperament than on any objective numbers.[2] My impression is that system traders do better as a group, while the best traders overall tend to be discretionary. Whatever path you choose, you must learn as much as possible and grow into an expert in that area. At the same time you need to have a reasonably good working knowledge of the other side of the field. Much of this book deals with discretionary trading that should also be useful for system traders.

# CAPITAL MANAGEMENT

Fred's interview raises the issue of managing money for other people. The rewards of even a moderately successful capital management business can be staggeringly high. For example, if a hedge fund manager raises $100 million, he will earn $2 million a year just for

---

[2] A discretionary trader may anticipate the signals of his trading system. Occasionally I hear comments from the readers of *Come into My Trading Room* that some of the trading examples in the last chapter do not strictly follow the Triple Screen system. I should have put more beginner-type examples into that book; some of my actual trades were advanced ones, in which I slightly anticipated the signals, something that discretionary traders tend to do.

being a nice guy and putting someone else's money into play. Then, if he manages to generate, say, 15% annual profit, or $15 million, he will get 20% of that as his incentive fee, earning another $3 million. $100 million is a middling size for a fund; at the time of our interview Fred and Bucky had about $20 million in their fund and growing. Fred and I have a mutual friend with $2 billion under management, earning more in a year than most successful people earn in a lifetime.

At the same time, the headache quotient in this field is pretty high, as Fred pointed out. Dealing with clients and regulators is a major job. Very early in my trading career I stumbled onto a lesson that turned me off money management. I had a very close friend—Phil who is mentioned on the first page of *Trading for a Living*. Impressed by my early trades and being a bit of a gambler, he opened a small account and gave me power of attorney. Within a few months I generated a high double-digit return for him (I did not keep good records in those days so I can't say for sure how much it was). At the end of that exercise I was no longer on speaking terms with Phil; it took us a year to reestablish our friendship. What happened was that Phil, excited about that venture, took to calling me almost daily, second-guessing my trades and occasionally putting on a trade himself. I felt stressed enough without his meddling and got angry at him. If successful trading led to such results, I wondered what losses would have done. I learned to keep my trading strictly private; the only accounts I run today are my own plus small accounts for my kids who know better than to stress Daddy.

If you love markets and are committed to research and trading, how can you trade for a living with only a tiny account? Profits from a $20,000 or $50,000 bankroll are not enough to live on. People with small accounts are tempted to take wild risks, and it is only a question of time before an undercapitalized trader who takes big risks blows himself out. Relax, shift gears, take a deep breath. Instead of shooting for the stars, choose a different target—start trading for a track record. You will need it to get into capital management and make money that way.

There are huge pools of capital sloshing through the financial system, looking for competent managers. Start growing your small capital and keep meticulous records. It may take you two years to start getting money to manage, but you are in this race for the long run, aren't you? What most capital owners want is steady returns with shallow drawdowns. If you follow this path, in a few years you may be joining the likes of Fred, Bucky, and their peers in the trading community.

*An e-mail from Fred:*

# I Do the R&D, the Computer Pulls the Trigger

I've never been a very good discretionary trader. I'd usually start off by making money, but then make way too many mistakes and end up with mediocre results. My personality is much better suited for mechanical trading systems where I do the R&D, but the computer pulls the trigger. Mechanical means objective: If 10 people follow the same rules, they should achieve the same results. A 100% mechanical approach increases the odds that past performance can be replicated in the future. It offers us three main benefits:

- We can backtest ideas before trading them. A computer allows us to test ideas on historical data rather than on real cash. Seeing how a system would have performed in the past allows us to make better decisions when it really counts—in the present.
- We can be more objective and less emotional. Analysis, where we have no money at risk, is easy; trading is stressful. Why not let the computer pull the trigger for us? It is free of human emotion and will do exactly what we instructed it to do when we developed our system.
- We can cover more markets, trade more systems, and analyze more timeframes each day. A computer can work faster and longer without losing its concentration.

Whenever I develop a system, I have a five-step plan:

1. Start with a concept.
2. Turn it into a set of objective rules.
3. Visually check out the signals on the charts.
4. Formally test the system with a computer.
5. Evaluate the results.

Developing a trading system is part art, part science, and part common sense. My goal is not to develop a system that achieves the highest returns using historical data, but to formulate a sound concept that has performed reasonably well in the past and can be expected to continue reasonably well in the future.

Our money management firm follows most futures markets worldwide and we currently trade 19 of them: foreign currencies, interest rates, energies, precious metals, grains, oilseeds, softs, industrials, and equities. We simultaneously use between two and eight trend-following trading systems, designed to catch intermediate and long-term moves. Each is based on a logical concept and tested in real time with our own money. In determining the suitability of a system we look first at its impact on our overall equity curve and its risk-adjusted returns.

Trading systems have helped me improve my performance and made me a successful trader. They forced me to do my homework before making a trade, provided a disciplined framework, and enabled me to increase my level of diversification.

With lots of hard work and dedication, anyone can build a successful trading system. It is not easy, but it is certainly within reach. As with most things in life, what you get out of this effort will be directly related to what you put into it.

Name: Andrea Perolo
Lives: Zeminiana di Massanzago, Italy
Previous profession: Asia manager for a tour operator
Trades: U.S. futures
How long: Since 2001
Trading account: Small (< $250k)
Software: www.tfc-charts.w2d.com and www.futuresource.com

# CHAPTER 3

# ANDREA PEROLO

## SIMPLE CHARTS, CLEAR AND UNCLUTTERED

I n October 2004 I flew to Sicily, about as far south as one could go in Europe, to extend my summer by an extra week. I was based in Central Europe that month; it was gray, cold, and rainy, with people already bundled up against the coming winter. Under the sunny Sicilian sky, you could still swim and drive to the vineyards in a convertible, and buy the freshest local produce and cheese from friendly locals.

We stayed in a place with a reasonably fast phone line, and my friend, a computer expert, rigged a wireless network for our computers. The U.S. stock market was starting to reverse its almost two-year-old uptrend, and we were busy closing out long positions and putting out shorts. We worked all day, and at night across the valley, we could see an angry red gash on the slope of Mt. Etna, where an eruption was going on and the lava was flowing.

Andrea—a man's name in Italy—was a trader who lived near Venice. Several months earlier he had e-mailed some very sensible questions to me about commodities. I had replied and asked him to send me a few screenshots of his recent trades and explain why he had decided to buy and sell. I liked his approach and, knowing I would be in Sicily, invited Andrea to fly down for a couple of days to talk about trading and be interviewed for this book. Andrea wrote back:

> Are you really sure to include me in your book? Please, consider that I am a full time trader for just three and half years, that I have discovered absolutely nothing, that I just studied many books and took what I considered the best of many well known techniques. As you have seen, my method is very simple: Check the weekly, discover a trend, analyze the daily to discover a good risk/reward ratio, manage it with solid money management. Nothing else!
>
> Last but not least, if you saw my "trading room" you would laugh. I have just one computer and one monitor, with no real-time quotes (I don't need them for my trading). I use only internet-based charts, totally free. If you still think I am worthy to be included in your book after you read this last reply, I will be honoured to reach you in Sicily and to talk with you about trading, and about my trader's life. But if you change your idea, certainly I will understand.

We had to schedule our meeting so that Andrea, who is divorced, would not miss a Tuesday, which he always spends with his six-year-old son. On Wednesday evening I met him on a street corner in the village where we were staying. Andrea was tall and deliberate; he spoke very good English but apologized for not being perfect. We zoomed through hairpin turns up to Taormina, walked through the medieval fortified town, and settled on the terrace of a restaurant for dinner.

At university I got a degree in economics, then did my civil service. In Italy back then, you had to serve a year in the army or give a year to the civil service. I preferred that to the army and worked with retarded children. Afterwards, because I loved to travel, I went to work for a large travel firm and in less than four years became their Asia manager. I got married, had a child, bought a big house, and worked hard to make payments.

There was a huge bull market in Italy in the 1990s, and everyone got involved. My father talked to me about stocks, and even my grandfather, who always bought bonds, invested in a stock fund for the first time in his life. There was a stock called Tiscali: It went from 6 to 120. There was a trading championship in Italy, and the eventual winner took a 15,000 euro account up above €400,000 in just a few months. I bought a call-covered warrant for Telecom Italia, held it to the expiration without a stop, and it went out worthless—I ended up losing €4,000 on my first trade. That's when I began to study.

I trade commodities in the United States because the liquidity is so much better. There is one bank in Italy that takes U. S. futures orders. I do not want to have an electronic order entry—the mouse is too fast; it is easy to become impulsive. If you trade daily charts, you do not need live data; having it is dangerous because it can easily prompt you to jump.

When the futures markets start opening after 8 AM Eastern time in the United States, it is already 2 PM in Italy. I analyze the markets from 9:30 to noon, then call my broker at lunchtime to place orders for the day ahead. In the afternoons I read, swim, do other sports—I do not look at the markets while they are open. My six-year-old son comes to stay with me on Tuesdays and Thursdays after school ends at 3:30 PM. We have dinner together and then I take him back to his mother at nine.

Failing for me is not an option—I must succeed in trading or die. I do not need very much money—life in Europe is cheaper than in the United States. €2,500 a month is enough for me. I have an €80,000 account, so I have to generate €30,000 a year return. I want to be free; I can never go back to having a job, and I want to travel around the world. I try to go to Asia twice a year. Also, trading for me is about more than money. There is no other task that is so difficult—it is a challenge I have within myself.

I start my analysis with the weekly charts, drawing trendlines, support and resistance, looking for major trends and consolidation patterns. I also check the COT—Commitments of Traders Index (see box, page 56). I will not trade against an extremely bullish or bearish position of commercial hedgers, and I especially like those trades where I go in the same direction as the commercials. I get these numbers from Steve Briese at *www.bullishreview.net* and I like how he always explains the COT concepts.

I start reading the *Bullish Review* from the last page, where he gives the positions of the commercials—in my opinion he should have called that index a COT oscillator. It shows the bullishness or bearishness of the commercials relative to their historical norm. At 100 percent, the commercials are totally bullish, they have huge net long positions, and a strong upside reversal can happen quite quickly. When COT is below 10, or, even better, 5, hedgers are totally short. In searching for a short entry I become more aggressive if COT is below 5. I like trading with the commercials and will not take a position or will be especially careful trading against an extreme net position of the commercials. Wheat is currently at 100—please do not try to short it, look for an entry to buy. Corn is now 87, very near a major buy signal.

I also rely on seasonals which I get from Moore Research Center, *www.mrci.com.* They analyze the last 15 years or more of every single contract of every commodity and come up with the roadmap of what it is likely to do in the month ahead, based on historical seasonal patterns. For example, I am long sugar now and I can see, looking at their charts, what sugar is likely to do this month, based on its 15- and 5-year pattern history. I see the COT index and seasonals as a kind of fundamental rather than technical analysis—they provide a completely different perspective on commodities.

Each of my trades starts with a weekly analysis, then I check the COT index and the net positions of the commercials, and then seasonals. When the weekly trend and the seasonal trend point in the same direction, you have wonderfully strong uptrends or downtrends with very shallow retracements. To have weeklies, COT, and seasonals all pointing in the same direction, which happens perhaps two or three times per market per year, means you have bingo.

I track grains, the soy complex, tropicals, and several meats, such as live cattle and especially lean hogs. Hogs have perfect patterns, their retracements always end at the previous rally highs—their charts belong in a chart book. I also always analyze the U.S. dollar; when it goes down, it has a bullish impact on all commodities, but especially gold and silver.

You know, these are very simple charts, clear and uncluttered. My best tools are trendlines, a very simple concept. I draw diagonal trendlines and also horizontal support and resistance lines. And I use Fibonacci numbers for measuring retracements of price and time. When there is a trend, I anticipate where the retracements could stop by using the three main numbers—38.2%, 50% and 62.8% of the previous rally or decline. My two additional numbers are 23.6% for shallow retracements in very strong trends and 78.6%—that is the last line of defense, and if the market violates it I begin to think it is no longer a retracement, but a reversal.

Another way I use Fibonacci is to validate breakouts from trading ranges. To filter out false breakouts you can use 23.6% of the height of the range. If the market goes beyond that level, you have a real breakout.

I asked Andrea why he thought Fibonacci numbers worked, and his only answer was that he could see those levels on the charts all the time. We met to look at his trades the next morning, and in the evening had our last dinner in a little "osteria," a local tavern Andrea had chosen. The owner sent glass after glass of grappa to our table; I smoked a cigar and Andrea rolled his own cigarettes, tamping their ends with the earpiece of his glasses. After we finished our grappa, he drove me back to the villa on the back of his scooter. We stood at the front gate talking about travel books, then shook hands, and Andrea left.

# TRADE 1   ANDREA'S ENTRY

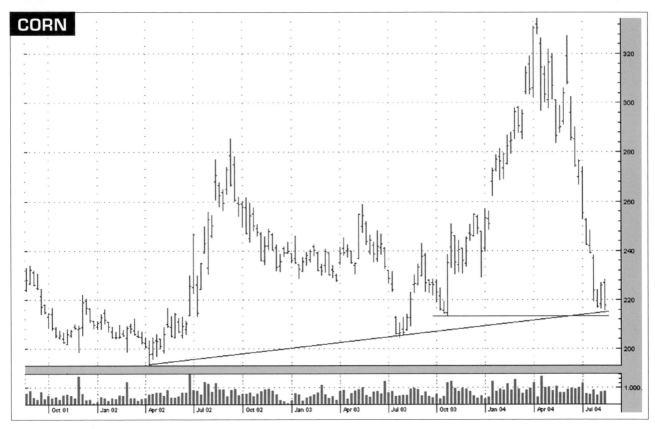

**Upper pane:** Bar chart (weekly)
**Lower pane:** Volume

### CORN

I do not look at the monthlies often, but I do keep them in mind, especially when I see a chart like this one, with a four-year uptrend. The uptrend started in the middle of 2000 and corn had touched it five times, quite a good number.

This weekly chart ends in the second week of August 2004. After the great rally of 2003, corn came down to a major support, both at its trendline and at the horizontal support line. You can also see the double bottom of October 2003–August 2004. I use bar charts on the weekly and candlesticks on the daily charts.

Andrea asked me about some famous U.S. market personalities whose books he had read. In talking to foreign traders, it never ceases to amaze me how slowly bad news travels overseas. Market characters generally known to be frauds in the United States still maintain their high status among foreigners. The heavy-duty marketers and the so-called winners of rigged contests who paid their penalties long ago to settle up with the U.S. authorities are still viewed with awe from across the ocean. Andrea appeared pained whenever he asked me about yet another of his U.S. heroes, and I gave him "the true skinny" on him or her. I felt sorry and apologized for ripping his icons off the walls.  —*AE*

**GURUS**

**Upper pane:**  Candlestick chart (daily)
**Middle pane:**  MACD-Oscillator (12,26)
**Lower pane:**  Volume

On the daily charts, there had been a major MACD divergence building up for months. RSI, which is not shown here, had an even greater divergence. I used a simple technique that Victor Sperandeo taught in his *Trader Vic*—a simple trendline, then a break, followed by a pullback into a double bottom. After a double bottom was established, I went long at the swing high of 224.25.

will this trade make or lose money?

# TRADE 1 | ANDREA'S EXIT

Even though there was a breakout, my target of 50% distance to the stop was never reached. I was stopped out of the whole position, on a gap down. After a long trading range, breakouts often come with a gap.

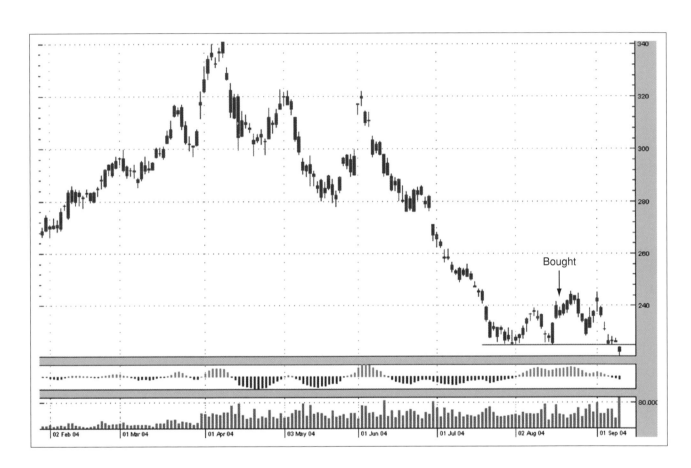

### An Entry Technique for Reducing Risk

I search for a position that I can hold, and may have to attempt entry many times before finding the right one. One bad consequence is that you can have two or three stop-losses in a row. How can you minimize that? My solution is to take profits on half of my position at a point between half and two-thirds of the distance to the stop-loss. Ideally it would have been equal to stop-loss, but even at a half you cut risk by 75%. I found this technique at the end of *Trading in the Zone* by Mark Douglas.

Say you enter four contracts, and your stop-loss is $600 each, so that the total risk is $2,400. Once you have $300 gain, if you take that profit on two of your contracts, you'll have only $600 of risk left on the remaining two. You cut 50% of your position, but your risk is now only 25%—this is fantastic. And the best result for me is the improvement in the state of mind—I feel *tranquillo*.

▼ **TRADE SUMMARY**

December 2004 Corn
Long 8/17/04 $2.4025
Stopped out 9/10/04 $2.2375
Loss = 16.5¢ per contract

I think I have found a wonderful technique to enter positions because you may need several attempts to get them right and your stops will be hit several times. If you use breakout techniques, 9 times out of 10 you'll have this work for you, but not always. The secret is that afterwards you do not have to trail the remaining position to break even too soon. You have more discretion. You can leave the remaining position in place and not trail the stop very fast.

# TRADE 1—ENTRY COMMENT

The most striking feature of this chart is the severe bear market near its right edge. Corn has crashed by more than a third from its March 2004 peak. The decline was so vicious that it left several gaps between weekly bars—an unusual occurrence. Corn prices slid in response to perfect growing weather in the Midwest and one of the best crops in U.S. history. Markets are driven by supply and demand—and here the supply clearly overwhelmed the demand.

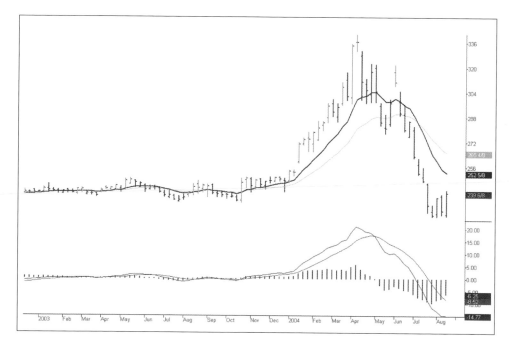

*Price bars reflect crowd behavior. Notice the very short weekly bar, the fourth from the right edge. It is still red, showing that bears are in charge. Still, its extreme shortness compared to the previous bars indicates that the dominant group has run out of steam. Whenever you see a major market move followed by a short bar, it is a pretty good sign that the dominant trend is ending.*

The Impulse system had locked onto the trend and traced out the bulk of the bear market in a series of red bars. Three weeks ago the Impulse had turned from red to blue, permitting traders to go long. Still, I do not feel any hurry to jump into corn. When prices fall by such a huge percentage from their peak, they act like a man who falls from a great height. He is not likely to get up and run anytime soon; he is going to lie on the ground for a while, just trying to breathe. At the right edge of the chart, corn is historically cheap, and it is not going to stay that cheap forever. Still, it is likely to take a while before it gets ready to rally again.

The daily chart confirms that it is a bit early to be a buyer of corn. On the one hand, it does look like a bottom is being formed, with the rate of the decline tapering off. The fact that in August corn fell lower than in July, then reversed and closed above the breakout level is bullish. The 2-day Force Index is tracing a bullish divergence and making a new multi-month high at the right edge of the chart. Still, those features alone are pretty thin reeds on which to hang a long trade after a vicious bear market.

*A serious warning to stand aside and wait comes from MACD-Histogram. It had traced a broad bottom from June to August and then rallied above zero. To give a strong buy signal, it needs to return below zero and bottom out at a more shallow level, creating a full-fledged bullish divergence. Its height at the right edge of the chart is more indicative of a top than of a bottom.*

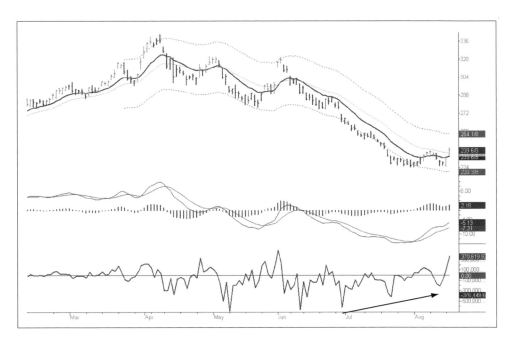

## COMMITMENTS OF TRADERS

The Commodity Futures Trading Commission collects reports from brokers on the positions of traders and releases their summaries to the public, revealing the positions of three groups—hedgers, big traders, and small traders. Hedgers identify themselves to brokers because that entitles them to several advantages, such as lower margin rates. Big traders are identified by holding a number of contracts above "reporting requirements" set by the government. Whoever is not a hedger or a big trader is a small trader.

In the old days, big traders used to be the smart money. Today, the markets are bigger, the reporting requirements much higher, and big traders are likely to be commodity funds, most of them not much smarter than the run-of-the-mill trader. The smart money today is in hedgers, such as agribusinesses, mining and oil companies, and food producers.

Understanding the positions of hedgers isn't as easy as it seems. For example, a COT report may show that in a certain market hedgers hold 70% of shorts. A beginner who thinks this is bearish may be completely off the mark without knowing that normally hedgers hold 90% of shorts in that market, making the 70% stance wildly bullish. Savvy COT analysts compare current positions to historical norms and look for situations where hedgers, or the smart money, and small traders, many of whom are gamblers and losers, are dead set against each other. If one group is heavily short while the other heavily long, which one would you like to join? If you find that in a certain market the smart money is overwhelmingly on one side, while the small specs are mobbing the other, it is time to use technical analysis to look for entries on the side of the hedgers.

*Abridged from Come into My Trading Room*

# TRADE 1—EXIT COMMENT

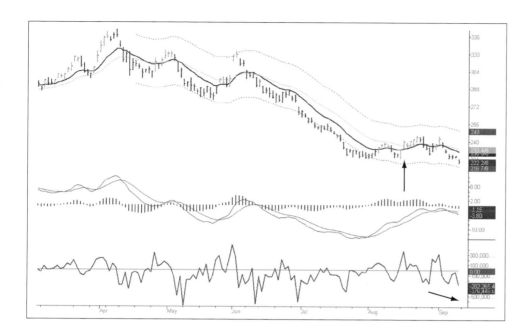

The decline that triggered Andrea's stop took corn to a new low. A new low of the Force Index shows that bears are strong and prices are likely to dip even lower. At the same time, several potentially bullish signs are developing. MACD-Histogram, though declining, is now at a much more shallow level than in June—an uptick from here would complete a bullish divergence. MACD Lines are declining, but their upturn is even more likely to create a bullish divergence. Corn seems to be engaged in what I used to call the "Austrian national sport" (in reference to Arnold the Terminator's campaign for governor of California)—it is groping for a bottom.

Andrea's use of stops puts him into the comfortable position of watching corn from the sidelines. Earlier he had mentioned that he often attempts several entries before establishing a position in a major trend. This is a much better stance than that of many amateurs who continue to sit on their losses. As the losses grow, their confidence diminishes until they eventually sell at the lows. Andrea, on the contrary, admitted his mistake early and preserved both his capital and his peace of mind, ready to trade again when a better signal comes in.

# TRADE 2 | ANDREA'S ENTRY

**SILVER**

### SILVER

Looking at the weekly chart, I think that the downmove in April indicated a trend reversal. A new trend is beginning, and I want to trade the downmove in the direction of the new major trend. Oscillators confirmed my view as MACD showed a new multi-year low. At the right edge, the retracement up is typical—it is exactly 50% of the preceding downmove. I think silver is in a bear market, and only if it goes above 8.31 will I be proven wrong.

*Andrea commented:*  People say divergences are among the best trading tools. I definitely do not accept that as a general rule: One needs to be more specific. I found that if the main trend is up and you look to enter on a retracement, bullish divergences are good. But divergences against the main trend do not work.

**DIVERGENCES**

　　Every day I see strong trends with major divergences that last for months, but the trend continues and runs away. I identify major reversals using double or triple tops and bottoms. There is a kind of myth about divergences. They work in ranges and in retracements, but not against the main trend.

The daily chart confirmed the weekly downtrend, with a sharp break and a slow pullback. We can see a triangle on this chart, bordered by an uptrend and a downtrend. I shorted silver after it broke its uptrend and then pulled back up to the downtrend that defined its long-term triangle.

Will this trade make or lose money?

## TRADE 2 | ANDREA'S EXIT

As soon as I am in a trade, I start using trailing stops, based on the weekly highs. I place my stop at the high of the previous week. Even if I like the trend, I'll cover my short at the previous week's high. This is why I got out of this trade. Looking forward, if silver had broken the low of its congestion at the right edge, I would have shorted it again.

## ▲ TRADE SUMMARY

Short December 2004 Silver 9/03/04 @ $6.575
Covered half 9/07/04 @ $6.30
Profit = 0.275 = $1,375 per contract
Covered second half 9/21/04 @ $6.38
Profit = 0.195 = $975 per contract

# TRADE 2—ENTRY COMMENT

This weekly chart of silver shows a parabolic rise into the April 2004 top. That unsustainable rise was followed by a crash. Observe the sequence of five red weekly bars, the last of them quite short: It is similar to what we discussed when we looked at Andrea's corn trade. A very short bar following a massive move often indicates that a reversal is coming. I have not tried to quantify the exact ratio of tall to short bars—this is something I have learned to recognize after years of looking at charts and trading.

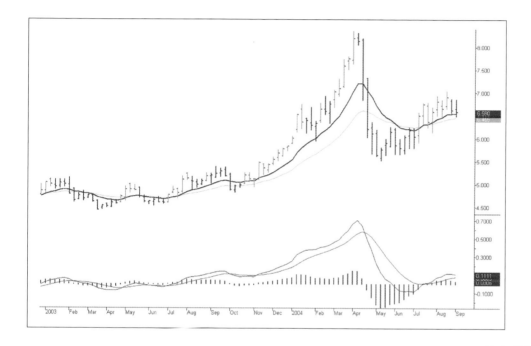

When the Impulse had changed from red to blue, after the crash, it removed the prohibition against buying. An uptrend began and went on for several months, picking up enough steam to turn the Impulse green. That uptrend ran out of green paint in the two rightmost bars. When the Impulse stops being green, it removes a prohibition against shorting. At the right edge of the chart the weekly MACD-Histogram is declining, the fast EMA is visibly slowing down its rise—bulls are becoming weaker, bears are coming in. Silver has been rising without a reaction for several months and is overdue for a spill—this chart suggests shorting.

The daily chart shows that the rally that emerged from the May bottom was very strong. As silver rallied, its MACD-Histogram reached a new record peak in May and remained above zero through July, a sign of strength. The reaction in mid-July took this indicator below zero. When silver rallied to a new recovery high in August, MACD-Histogram petered out at a much lower level than in July, completing a bearish divergence. The weekly Impulse was still green at that time, allowing no shorting.

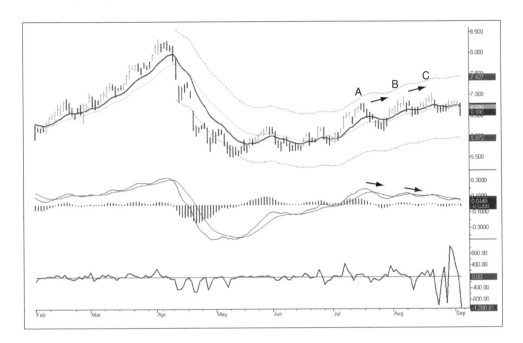

There was a second rally in August, reaching a new recovery high, but MACD-Histogram rose to a puny high. It completed a triple bearish divergence, showing that there was very little power behind the rally. That second rally in August took silver above the psychologically important "round number" of $7/oz. It could stay in that elevated territory for only one day. Silver's decline below the level of the first August rally had exposed the second August rally as a false breakout to a new high. Remember—buy new lows and sell new highs. A new high of MACD-Histogram in May helped identify a strong breakout that started a new uptrend; a divergence in August helped identify a false breakout and a readiness for a reversal.

# TRADE 2—EXIT COMMENT

It is emotionally hard to take profits when prices are flying in your favor. "More, more, more" seems to be the cry of the day. It is to Andrea's credit that he had the discipline to follow his plan and take profits on half of his position just one trading day after shorting silver.

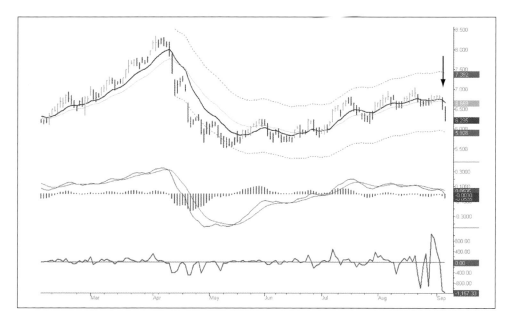

Covering one-half of the position one day after shorting had worked out better than exiting on a stop. Planned exits almost always work out better than exits on stops. The new low in MACD-Histogram in September shows that bears are becoming stronger and suggests that silver is likely to fall even lower. But Andrea is disciplined: He would not allow a short to take out the previous week's high and gets out on that stop. This strict discipline—the setting of an absolute level beyond which one will not hold a trade—is the hallmark of a professional trader.

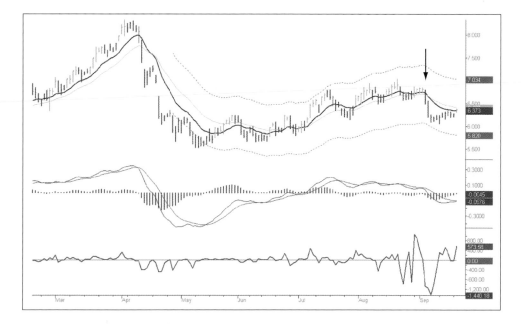

This daily chart shows a nice progression of the Impulse system. As Andrea went short, there were two wide red bars, confirming the ease of the downmove, followed by three narrow red bars, showing that the downmove hit support. The red Impulse changed to blue and finally, at the right edge, to green, which is where Andrea covered his short.

# CLASSICAL CHARTING VERSUS COMPUTERIZED ANALYSIS

Charts reflect crowd behavior. The high of each bar marks the point of the bulls' maximum power while the low reflects the bears' maximum power. Series of bars coalesce into patterns whose highs and lows look like a scarred battlefield in the never-ending struggle between buyers and sellers.

Human beings change very slowly, if at all, which is why similar behavior patterns recur year after year. Crowds are more crude and primitive than the individuals who comprise them, and their behavior patterns are easier to identify. Whenever a chart pattern appears confusing, ask yourself what it tells you about the crowd of traders whose behavior it reflects.

Andrea relies mostly on classical charting for his trading. He is not a pure chartist—he also uses Commitments of Traders and seasonals, and an occasional indicator—but the bulk of his technical research can be done with a pencil and a ruler. This works for him in part because of his personality. Andrea is very cool, calm, and deliberate as he lays his ruler on a chart.

There are so many ways to fudge a chart. Do you draw a trendline through the extreme points or through the edges of congestion areas? Do you consider intraday penetrations or only the breaks on a closing basis? If the two bottoms are at somewhat different levels, do you draw your support line across the lower or the higher bottom? I occasionally joke with friends, saying that classical charting does not work for me because I have a terrible tremor in my fingers. When I put a ruler on a chart, my fingers tremble up when I feel bullish and down when I am bearish.

This is why I prefer to put the ruler and pencil aside and turn to computerized indicators. The Impulse system on the weekly and daily charts helps me identify the dominant market group; new peaks and bottoms of MACD-Histogram identify strengths or weaknesses; their divergences call attention to likely reversal points; envelopes provide objective profit targets.

There is no right way or wrong way—both classical charting and computerized analysis are valid methods of market analysts. You need to choose what makes sense and works for you. This decision is going to be based on your temperament. Andrea feels drawn to the simplicity and clarity of bar charts and trendlines; I prefer to operate within the benign censorship of the Impulse system and the objectivity of the indicators. You have to choose what appeals to you.

Successful traders maintain an open mind, without becoming fanatics or extremists about their methods. Andrea is primarily a chartist, but he values such data as COT indexes and has no problem throwing a MACD-Oscillator on his chart. I am a computerized analyst but use such classical methods as drawing support and resistance lines in my search for false breakouts.

Your charts reflect the behavior of bulls and bears. You can profit by catching even a portion of their moves—or you can get trampled by them. It matters little what specific methods you use to detect their approach. You need to identify the beast, place your bet, and take it off in time.

*An e-mail from Andrea:*

# THE PROMISE OF INDEPENDENT LIVING

My story is similar to that of many others. I had chosen a job because of my interest in travel and was totally committed to the firm. I worked hard and learned a lot, and felt that the firm's interests were my own, but as time went on it started to feel like jail. After four years I gave up and decided to start something by myself.

Trading attracted me with its promise of independent living and complete personal freedom. I started with a small sum of money and underestimated or did not seriously consider three aspects of this business: learning takes a long time, experience plays a large role, and both cost tons of money.

At first I became interested in covered warrants but soon dropped them after realizing they were manipulated by market makers. Then I tried futures on the Italian stock index, but realized they were too heavy both for my bank account and my level of experience; in addition, their volume was very thin.

My gains kept turning into losses, while at the same time my family life was coming apart. I was getting divorced and had to provide for myself, my wife, and my son. I was feeling insecure about my trading and kept searching for advisors, trading systems, Elliott waves, and so on. I kept looking for a system, but the results were always the same—losses larger than profits.

Finally, I learned my lesson: I had to become autonomous and independent and rely on myself and my own analysis. The high cost of experience was my "entry fee" into the minority that succeeds in earning a living from trading. I realized that one of my mistakes was trading stock futures with five-minute charts. I used to think that the stop-loss could be minimal and that high volatility would offer hundreds of entry points. I came to see that this might work for someone else but not for me. Few activities are as electrifying and emotionally demanding as day-trading. This realization was another turning point on the road to my own way of trading.

I trade commodities using weekly and daily charts. I go over my charts in the morning, examining them over and over. It helps a lot to close the charts and take a break, reopening them later. I always look for opportunities, but sometimes they seem to jump at me from the screen. I do not try to catch turning points; I let the trend establish itself and feel satisfied with a piece of it.

Simple tools work best for me, and trade management and money management are essential. A plain technical system brings good results if combined with strict rules of trade and money management. If you like using oscillators, choose one or two after studying and testing them on paper for a rather long time. Keep your eyes first on the bar and then on the oscillator because its movement gets fuel from the price. Draw a few trendlines to define the trend and its strength and longevity. If I were allowed to choose only one tool of technical analysis, I would choose the trendline. Price patterns and trendlines are enough to grasp the exact points where one should enter and exit a trade.

When your account starts to increase, keep humble and fight the feeling of arrogance. Whenever you get a strong opinion about the market, shut down the computer and take a long walk. Your opinion is not helpful; it can influence your judgment when you look at the chart. Trade your chart, never your opinion.

To sum up my experience:

- Trade using a minimal part of your capital (money management).
- Follow your plan—you must have one, without any exceptions (trade management).
- Take only the trades that are in compliance with your technical signals.

| | |
|---:|:---|
| Name: | Sohail Rabbani |
| Lives: | Derbyshire, United Kingdom |
| Previous profession: | Medical researcher and business owner |
| Trades: | Mostly futures, some options and stocks |
| How long: | Since 1986 |
| Trading account: | Medium ($250k–$1m) |
| Software: | QCharts |
| Traders' Camps: | Costa Rica 2001, Advanced Camp in New York 2001 |

# CHAPTER 4

# SOHAIL RABBANI

## THE DISCIPLINE OF LOSS CONTROL

I like receiving e-mails from my campers telling me of their comings and goings. This message came in early 2004 from a repeat camper:

> ...I have put an end to short-term trading. As for longer-term investments, I've completely cashed out of my equity holdings and invested in tangibles, including gold and land. Moreover, it is an old pattern repeated. In September 1987, a month before Black Monday, through pure good luck, I cashed out of stocks and bought a retail business. After that I didn't place a single trade until 1991. Then in June 1998 I again cashed out, fully convinced that the market would crash. The next 18 months were sheer agony as I faded the market and kept getting knocked in the head. Fortunately the discipline of loss control has prevented my complete wipeout. Then 2000 to 2002 were quite rewarding as I was in sync with the trend. In fact, 2002 was my best year ever. My short-term trading accounts returned an unbelievable 163%...Then disaster struck.
>
> In early 2003 I had a heart attack and bypass surgery. Following that I went mad and proceeded to give back my winnings from the previous year before putting a moratorium on short-term trading.

The e-mail went on to describe in colorful detail all the things men do in a fully blown mid-life crisis and continued:

> I stopped keeping my trading journal. Stopped doing meticulous research, stopped reviewing records, and started playing options like a drunk plays darts in a bar. I was simply insane. I started doing ultra-short-term shoot-from-the-hip style trading and generated lots of commissions for my broker but my account equity curve steadily declined. By early fall I had exceeded my maximum loss limit, so I stopped cold turkey. By then my insanity was also getting tamed.
>
> I think a one-year sabbatical from stock trading is the minimum penance. Interestingly, I only messed up in my stock trading. In my futures trading I didn't do anything crazy. I do not trade futures short-term, but hold positions for long periods and roll over at expiration. All I had were some positions in gold and euro futures. Those were the life savers that prevented

my performance from looking like an absolute disaster. I've decided to stay away from the stock market and particularly from short-term trading for at least one year. Nonetheless, my study of the market continues, as do my subscriptions to various publications and data services.

I have read this e-mail to several groups of campers, and it has always generated a lively discussion on whether this trader was likely to succeed or fail in the long run. We kept in touch, and when Sohail heard that I would be spending a week in Sicily, he volunteered to fly down from London for a couple of days and bring his trading records. Several weeks later he arrived in a village in the foothills of Mt. Etna. We had dinner together and the following morning he came to the villa for an interview.

Sohail has a master's degree in epidemiology, and with his background in science he relaxes doing quadratic equations the way other people do playing solitaire.

In 1986 I was doing statistical research at the University of Alabama but started becoming fascinated with financial markets. I had two friends at Drexel Burnham (a major brokerage house that went out of business in the 1980s following financial scandals), and one of them invited me to join their training course.

I quickly realized that being a broker was the worst way to learn to be a trader; it was all about sales. My friend put me into the back office where I could track the flow of orders. I felt things were morally questionable—we were doing front running, even though at the time I did not know that term. We were placing our own orders ahead of discretionary accounts and funneling part of the profits into dummy accounts. I bowed out, made a few good trades, and on October 5, 1987, by pure chance completely cashed out and returned from Los Angeles to Alabama. On October 19 the market crashed, all hell broke loose, and my knees trembled when I realized that I had escaped. I got so scared that I did not do a single trade until 1991. I invested with a friend in a business and generated a small stream of income.

In 1991 I started dabbling a little, in 1994 I became a little more active, and from 1995 to 1998, as the market went rip-roaring, I made money. The more I read and understood economics, the more it seemed to me that it was an absolute bubble which could not go on. Cash burn rate was an insanity which I could not buy. I could not understand how companies that were making no money were worth more than industrial giants. In 1998 I started shorting, fading the uptrend, and getting burned, but I took small losses and survived. Occasionally I would catch a downleg and make some money, but most of the time I sat out.

In 2000 things started turning around, and I made money through 2002. The only way to stay in this game is not to take big losses. I have two articles of faith. One—no one can know the future, and so I am very skeptical of every tool. Technicals or fundamentals give us convictions or courage about making a move, but ultimately it may not work and we must be ready to get out of the way. Ultimately, the market is about the mind of the masses—and who can predict them? Two—most people in the market are wrong most of the time. The theory that the market knows everything and discounts everything is nonsense. The only time we make money is when we are right ahead of the market, and if the market was efficient, we would never make money. If the market was always right, was Amazon really worth $300, and how did Micro Strategy (MSTR) go from $16 to $333 and then back down to 42 cents?

I am really disillusioned with the stock market—it's a fool's game. The current values [in 2004] are unsustainable. Those who think they can retire on their buy-and-hold investments have a foolish dream. The retirement legislation sends a constant flow of funds into the markets, prices go up, but the value of money is deteriorating. That is why I got out of the U.S. dollar and moved to Europe. The reserve status of the U.S. dollar gives the economy a ridiculous edge, but it is not sustainable, and eventually the bottom will fall out. It may happen in a week, in a year, or more. The unfunded pension liabilities will come home to roost. The stock market slowly swings between high and low valuations, and today we are still near the high edge. In 1974 price/earnings ratios went down to single digits, dividend yields came up to 4–5%. The regression to the mean tells me that in the foreseeable future the trend will be down. Eventually there will be great values to benefit future generations, but now is not the time to put money into the stock market.

I have become much more interested in commodities. They offer a better arena because they are based on something tangible. Wheat can never go down to zero or run up to a thousand—there is a natural range and you can trade in it if you are not too leveraged. The thing about commodities, such as gold, currencies, and crude oil, is that big world trends impact them, maybe not day to day, but over several months. Commodities are more transparent over the long term—just take long-term positions and don't overleverage. My best trades in recent years were in the euro and gold, as the Fed keeps pumping liquidity into the system as if we were a Weimar republic.

That's how I got involved in the markets—by accident—and I love it. I've done high-pressure minute-by-minute trading, but realized that this activity is for a very robust person in his twenties who has someone guiding him. Now I want to spend 90% of my time thinking and studying and 10% in front of the monitor.

Rather than show his current commodity trades, Sohail presented several trades he had completed prior to his self-imposed moratorium on stock trading. Both trades had been done using options rather than underlying stocks, perhaps reflecting Sohail's increasingly hectic attitude just prior to his self-imposed moratorium. He arrived in Sicily with his brokerage statements but without a computer, and we used locally available MetaStock to reproduce the charts that he would have normally plotted in QCharts.

**LONG WAY FROM HOME**

*Sohail was born in Lahore, Pakistan, but his family moved to the United Kingdom when he was a very young man, and he earned his degree from an American university. He reminisces:* My father was a very educated man, a professor of medicine, an Anglophile. Where I grew up, people like him were called *bau* or *sahib*—their roots were local but their living was Western, the mentality was Western. I had no religious schooling, no indoctrination. I do not understand how the fundamentalists could take over that region. I remember being taken to Kabul in the 1970s, and there were bars, nightclubs, girls wore miniskirts. Our family left to move away from fundamentalism.

# TRADE 1 | SOHAIL'S ENTRY

### SPXET

No one can know the future, but a sharp decline gives a good indication that a bounce is coming—you push the spring and it is likely to recoil. On March 10, 2003, a very significant thing happened—the market went down, S&P lost 21 points, Dow 172 points, but the volume on the NYSE was relatively low, and fully 90% of that was downside volume.

At the same time, there was a spike in New Lows—there were 248 of them against only 70 New Highs. Also on that day the Nikkei reached its 23-year low, the European markets were down. When markets reach extremes, they tend to snap back. I had been waiting for a run-up and was ready to catch it.

The thing that prompted me to enter was that though it was a significant downside day, there was no energy in the downmove. It was a warning that there was to be a snap-back rally, a temporary bottom. I made the decision to go long after market hours. I usually get up at 4 AM to do my market work and plan trades for the day ahead.

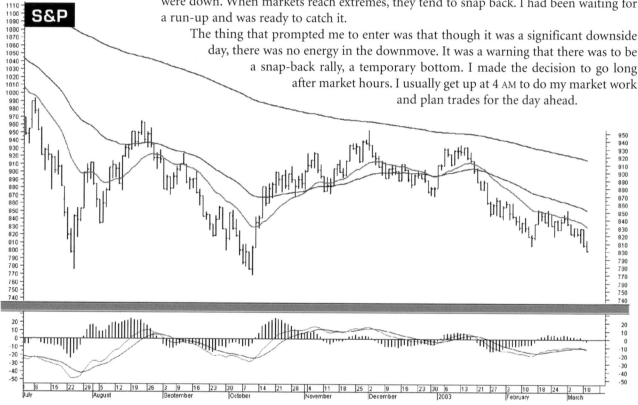

**Upper pane:** Daily bar chart with three exponential moving averages—20, 50, and 200 days
**Lower pane:** MACD Lines and MACD-Histogram (12-26-9)

| THREE TRADING RULES | *Sohail says:* I am sure you've heard the three main rules for buying real estate—location, location, and location. Well, there are also the three main rules of trading. They are—use stops, use stops, and use stops. You have to protect yourself if you want to survive in the markets. |
| --- | --- |

## Financial Entropy

I have noticed an interesting phenomenon which deserves the name "Financial Entropy." After twenty or thirty trades the cash I had available for trading was slowly diminishing because I ended up with an increasing number of trade positions which were neither bad enough nor good enough to sell. They hadn't reached my stop loss or my sell point for a modest 2 to 5% profit. They were just going sideways. It is clear that after a reasonable amount of time I will just have to get rid of this dead wood to allow me to continue to purchase shares which offer greater potential. A small group of friends who also use your techniques have also noticed the same problem. If you have any criteria to deal with this frustrating problem, we would be interested in hearing your views.                 —*Trader*

Seems to me that it makes sense to put a time stop on your trades and shoot lazy puppies after a reasonable interval. Set a date in advance when you're going to get rid of those which do not perform!                                          —*AE*

I decided to do this trade with options rather than S&P futures. For me, the biggest plus was that there was a fixed amount of money that could go to zero. The biggest negative with calls is that time runs against you. Also, spreads are greater in options, but that's the cost of doing business. I can afford to lose the option premium, but with futures I am afraid of another October '87, especially if I am not watching the market intraday.

The options should have two or three months of life left in them, afterwards the time decay becomes very severe. At the tail end of an option's life I want to sell it. I like to buy options that are in the money. The deeper in the money, the more movement you are likely to see in the option relative to the underlying—it will have a higher delta. Still, the S&P premiums are so high that I would have to allocate much more funds to get deeper into the money.

March 11 was another down day—and that's when I entered, buying slightly in-the-money calls with two months to go. I put in a limit order and it was filled—I almost always enter with limit orders. I also placed a stop-loss five points below my entry. You have to use stops because you could be wrong and it could be the start of a new downleg.

will this trade make or lose money?

# TRADE 1    SOHAIL'S EXIT

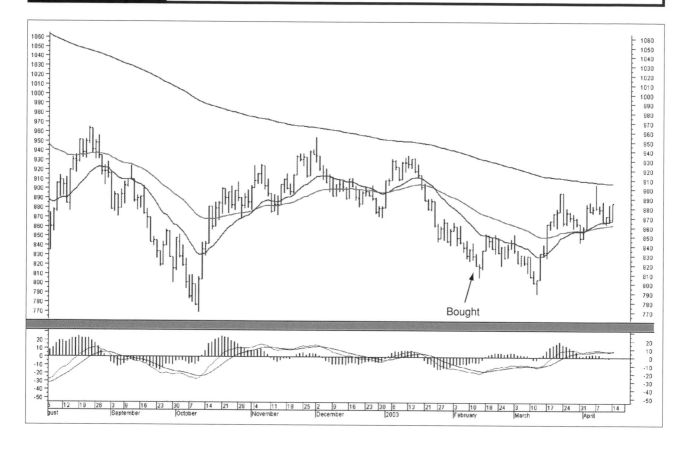

Bought

The stock market had a good run, more than a month had passed, and the option was entering a rapid deterioration phase. I knew I would have to get out soon. Another thing was beginning to happen—the dollar was showing weakness and I thought that would drag the stock market down.

On Friday, April 11, the stock market was down slightly—the S&P was down three points, the Dow 18 points. In doing my homework on the weekend, I noticed that the advance/decline line was negative, and the VIX was confusing; it was slightly down. With the option well into its deterioration phase, I could not afford to wait; in futures I would have rolled over. I decided to pull the trigger and I got out on Monday.

# TRADE SUMMARY

Long S&P May 800 calls (SPXET) 3/11/2003 @ $41
Sold 4/14/2003 @ $83.50
Profit = $42.50 = $4,250 per contract

# TRADE 1—ENTRY COMMENT

The stock market peaked out in 1999–2000 and entered a vicious bear market. This weekly chart shows S&P losing nearly half of its value within two years. The decline was punctuated by several sharp rallies. Bear market rallies tend to be explosive, fueled by short-covering rather than by slower and more deliberate buying in the bull markets.

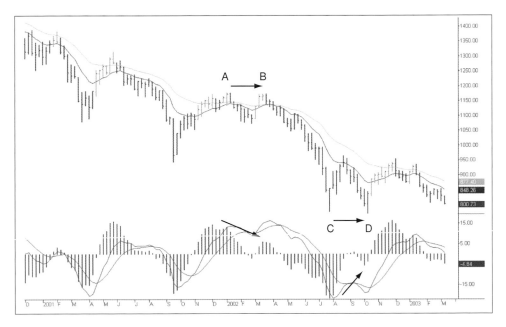

Divergences of MACD-Histogram and prices give perhaps the strongest signals in technical analysis. In September 2001 the S&P tried to turn up after penetrating the 1,000 level and then rallying. Compare the height of MACD-Histogram in November 2001 and March 2002—this bearish divergence gave a clear indication that the bulls were running out of steam and the downtrend was about to resume. Now compare the depths of the bottoms of MACD-Histogram in July and October 2002—that bullish divergence clearly showed that the bears were becoming weaker and a rally was coming. The fact that the October low was a few points lower put the icing on the cake. Buy new lows and short new highs when divergences are present!

The Christmas rally in November and December 2003 was accompanied by a record peak in MACD-Histogram—a sign of bullish strength. Compare the height of the weekly bars in July and October 2002 with the bars near the right edge. The recent bars are much shorter, which indicates that a decline no longer evokes such strong emotions: Weak holders have already been flushed out and strong holders are sitting tight. This behavior is indicative of a bottom, but unfortunately the Impulse system does not allow me to put on a long trade at the right edge. A red bar acts like a censor that says: "Go short or stand aside." It forbids buying, but it cannot forbid me from looking at this chart and waiting for the bars to turn from red to blue, allowing me to buy.

The daily chart (on the following page) confirms the message of the weekly. At the right edge prices are declining, hugging the lower channel. They seem unable to break out of it the way they did in February. Also notice the depth of the February MACD-Histogram bottom and compare it to the current indicator depth. There is no divergence yet because MACD is still declining, but should the histogram tick up from this level, it will complete a powerful bullish divergence.

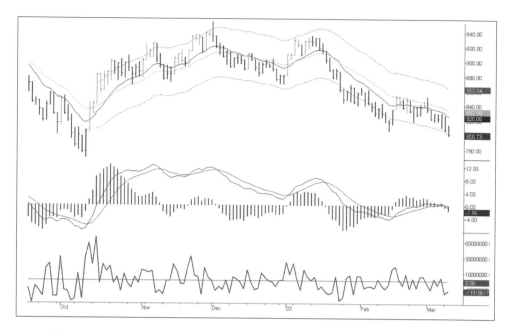

Still, at the right edge of the chart, both the EMA and MACD-Histogram are declining, and the Impulse system is red. It prohibits buying just now, but the picture is rapidly becoming more and more attractive for the bulls and demands close attention. While waiting, can you identify an earlier massive bearish divergence on this chart, topped off by a small kangaroo tail?

# TRADE 1—EXIT COMMENT

*Sohail had nailed the bottom of an explosive rally, with the Impulse system turning green and giving a buy signal one day later. That rally swung up from the bottom, penetrating the upper channel the following week. Gerald Appel (Chapter 7) teaches that when a rally is strong enough to blow out of a channel, it often gives us a second chance to buy, when prices pull back to the moving average after the breakout. That's what happened here in March, with the second rally to the upper channel line in April.*

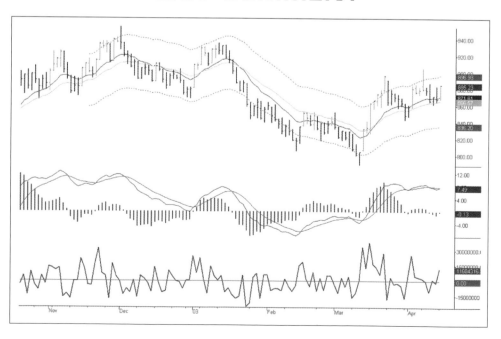

In April the picture became considerably more ragged. While the breakout in March was strong and convincing, with prices staying above the channel for several days, in April there was just a lone spike above the channel, looking suspiciously like a kangaroo tail. It was accompanied by a divergence of MACD-Histogram, warning of the weakness of the bulls.

At the right edge of the chart, the market is rallying again, but it feels very weak: MACD-Histogram is feeble and Force Index is tracing a massive bearish divergence. The Impulse system is green, prohibiting shorting, but it certainly does not forbid selling. It is a high time to sell, taking profits on long positions.

## TRADE 2 | SOHAIL'S ENTRY

### KLAC

This trade violates every trading principle known to man. No sane person would do this. I made this trade at the height of my personal crisis, and it shows what happens when a trader goes mad. When I sat at home doing homework, consulting a chart or two, I was mentally somewhere else. I had become sloppy, shooting from the hip to regain youth, vigor, and power, not being a professional anymore. It is not the money loss that rankles, it is the loss of discipline.

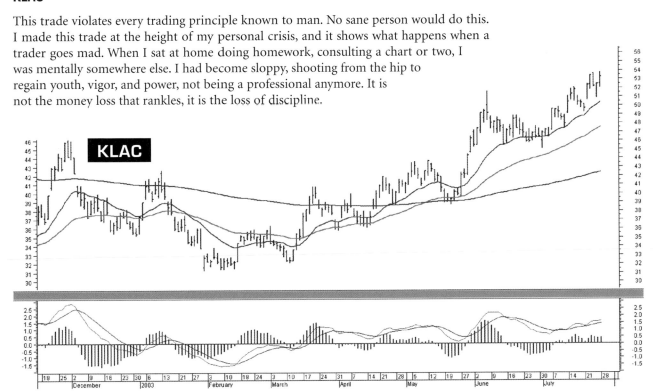

Normally, most of my options trades are multilayered. I buy calls and then sell puts to cover part of the premium paid for the call. Here I went in outright, selling a naked call because the premium seemed so hefty—I thought the stock was overpriced. Call prices were high, out of whack with puts, with high implied volatility. I thought there was a premium to be taken because some fool wanted to buy a call. I compounded my mistake by selling an in-the-money call—those are good for buying but when you sell, you are better off going out of the money—selling more time value and less intrinsic value.

Will this trade make or lose money?

# TRADE 2 | SOHAIL'S EXIT

As KLAC skyrocketed and my position lost more and more money, I froze like a deer in headlights. It was not professional behavior. Normally when I trade, I keep daily notes of what is happening—stock indexes, New High–New Low readings, my feelings. I stopped doing that and was just sitting there, wishing and hoping, and not getting the hell out: "I cannot be wrong; the market is wrong." Meanwhile the freight train was coming.

Every time there was a slight pullback, I'd go on a power trip: "I am not going to take a loss; I am going to get out at a plus." And then there was a moment of clearing. The real trader deep inside of me told me it was a total disaster and I exited.

September 3 was an upday and the volume increased; the Nasdaq was up on heavy volume. The market started surging again and I realized that if I did not get out, I could get hurt.

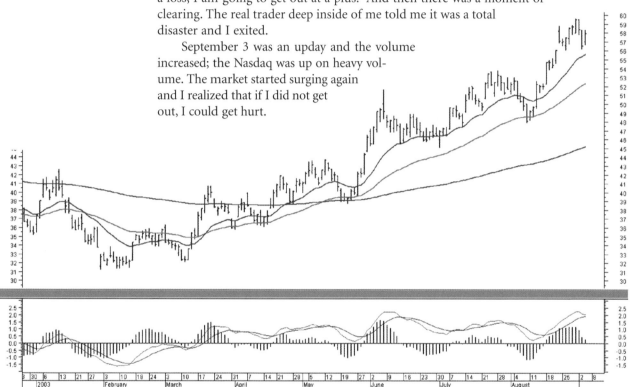

Monetarily it was not such a huge loss, but psychologically and professionally it was a very bad trade. It was a very humbling experience—something has taken you over, you violate your own guidelines, something you promised yourself you'd never do. A lesson in humility needs to be reinforced.

Later that year I decided I needed to take a year off and just clean out my system, be stress-free. Maybe do some charity work, hold a children's camp, whatever. My family and I left the United States and went to live in England.

## ▼ TRADE SUMMARY

**Short KLAC January 30 calls (KCKAF) 7/28/2003 @ $24.10**

**Covered 9/4/2003 @ $28.10**

**Loss = $400 per call**

# TRADE 2—ENTRY COMMENT

Sohail is shorting KLAC, or rather, its calls—doing what the Impulse system would prohibit us from doing. There is great emotional pleasure in drawing a line in the sand and saying, "This is it, the market will not rise any higher, I'll short right here." It is a very expensive pleasure that very few, if any, traders can afford.

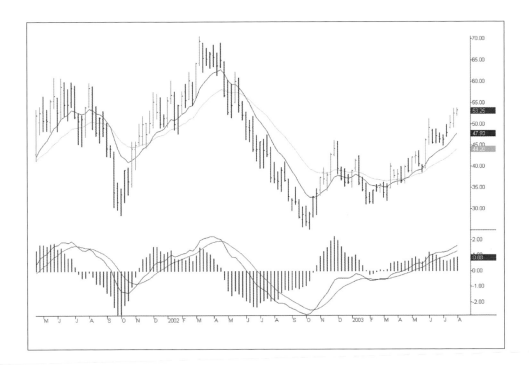

Mature traders have long ago learned not to forecast but to follow signals from the markets. This chart shows an uptrend—both moving averages are rising, MACD-Histogram is rising, the uptrend is in gear. The facts are right here, on this chart—the stock is going up, and no matter how bearish you feel, the Impulse system tells you that shorting is forbidden.

The daily Impulse on the chart on the following page is also green—no shorting is allowed. The chart shows a slow and steady uptrend. Prices touch their value zone between the two EMAs, rally to the upper channel line, decline into the value zone, rally to the upper channel line, decline to the value zone again . . . . Trading this pattern is like going to a cash machine where a bullish trader (you're allowed only to buy in an uptrend) can keep buying at the EMA and selling at the upper channel again and again.

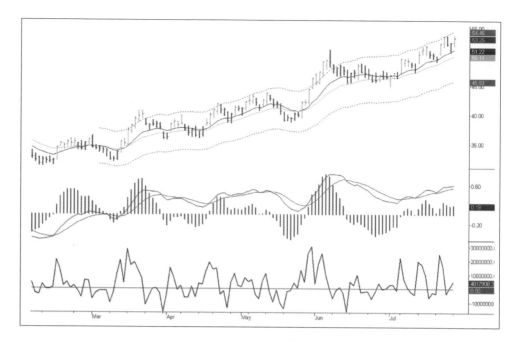

Notice how Force Index rises to approximately the same peak level during each rally—the bulls are maintaining their level of power in each rally without any divergence. Overall, this looks like a healthy uptrend. Only a trader looking for an adventure would try to pick a top here.

# TRADE 2—EXIT COMMENT

Following the dip in its uptrend, KLAC regained its strength and rallied higher. Notice a new peak in MACD-Histogram in mid-August—it indicated a great inflow of bulls, calling for higher prices ahead.

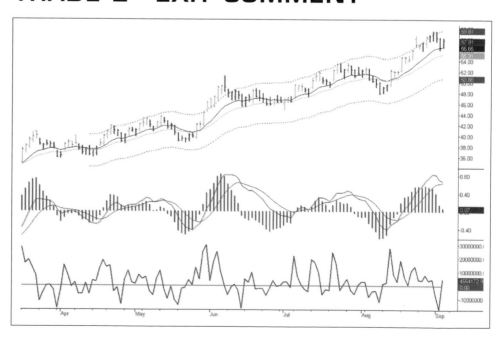

KLAC sank a little below value following Sohail's short—he had a chance to take a small profit but missed it. He is an experienced trader who correctly picked a short-term top—but then made the mistake of allowing his profit to turn into a loss. It is very important to move your stop to a break-even level once a trade starts moving in your favor. This is essential for capital preservation. Without it, you're not likely to become a long-term winner.

At the right edge of the chart KLAC is becoming a little ragged—Force Index is tracing a bearish divergence and MACD-Histogram is trending lower despite the fact that prices had made a new high only three days earlier. The painful result of not covering your shorts when the covering was good is that you end up throwing in the towel and covering at a level where you should be thinking of shorting! The mirror image of this occurs when early bulls do not sell in time—and then end up dumping their position out of sheer frustration and pain precisely when and where they should be thinking of buying!

# SETTING LIMITS

Markets are the least restrictive areas of society; no other area is as free. There are no dividers on the market highway: You can drive in any direction you like, bump others, observe no speed limits, and stop and go when you please. With more markets going both electronic and global, even time limits are removed. You may trade at any time, in any place, for any reason or lack thereof. Few people are consciously aware of this, but the feeling of freedom helps pull them into trading. If this freedom has a flip side, it is impulsivity and irresponsibility.

We all enter the markets with a practical goal—to make more money than we can get from bank deposits. Caught in the excitement of trading, most of us quickly lose track of this good goal and start looking for some private version of fun. The trouble is that you cannot "have fun" and make money at the same time. Good trading includes many boring aspects. You know what has to be done, you do it, and rate yourself on how faithfully you've done what had to be done—Michael Brenke in Chapter 8 offers an eloquent description of this algorithm.

The average private trader in the United States is a 50-year-old, married, college-educated male. In a great many cases he is not a happy man. He gets up in the morning, looks in the mirror, and thinks unhappy thoughts. He looks back at his youth and realizes that professionally he is not anywhere near what he dreamed about in college. The kids are grown and have their own lives; they talk to him only when they need money. He is tired of his wife but cannot afford a divorce. He knows that those beautiful models in *Playboy* will never be his. The man sighs, gets into his car, and drives to the office. There is not much joy or excitement there—until he logs into his brokerage account and gives an order to buy or sell. Suddenly the world is in living color.

The markets go up and down, flooding traders with adrenaline. Of course they would prefer winning to losing, but even losing provides plenty of kicks, making them feel excited, connected, and alive. We have to be grateful to Sohail for describing how, after establishing a track record as a serious successful trader, he threw caution to the wind and started shooting from the hip, trying to regain the sense of virility and vigor lost after having a heart attack. He shows us what happens to a good trader when he starts having a midlife crisis in the market.

The time to prepare a lifeboat is before you need it. If you are reading this book on a relatively non-stressful day, now is the time to draw up a list of rules. Make it short and pin it to the wall near your trading desk so that you can always see it. Let me offer you a few lines as a template, which you may edit and expand to fit your own circumstances. The purpose of this list is to draw danger lines, to keep you from stumbling into fire zones in a field that has no safety barriers.

Limits:

- I will strictly observe the 2% and the 6% money management rules.
- I will not add to losing positions (unless planned in advance as part of building a large position).
- I will not put on trades against my censorship rules, such as the Impulse system.
- I will not allow a profit of greater than (fill in the blank) to turn into a loss—use a hard stop to protect gains!
- I will use stops.

This last point is the hardest, since there are several types of stops:

- A beginning trader must use what I call "hard stops"—placing actual orders with his or her broker. The trouble with hard stops is that most people put them in obvious places—below the latest low or above the latest high, where professionals keep hitting them before the market reverses. If you use hard stops, do not place them at obvious levels but either closer to or farther away from the market.
- A more sophisticated trader may use SafeZone stops. This will allow you to place your stops outside the general level of market noise and at prices that are not commonly known.
- "Soft stops"—my favorite method—involves getting out of any trade whose weekly Impulse System goes against me 15 minutes before that market closes on Friday.

**HARD AND SOFT SIGNS**

Soft signs are early warnings of a trend change. Hard signs tell that a trend is definitely in force.

Soft signs include divergences of MACD-Histogram or breakouts to a new low or a new high with no follow-through. Hard signs include the trend of a moving average on a weekly chart and a follow-through of a breakout, as prices accelerate in its direction.

Experienced traders look for soft signs for entering trades, buying bullish divergences of MACD-Histogram or shorting apparently false upside breakouts. By the time the hard signs are in, it is often too late to enter a trade. On one hand, hard signs give a strong message to exit a trade. For example, if I go long after a soft sign, I may continue to hold even if that sign disappears, providing other signs remain. On the other hand, if a hard sign, such as a weekly moving average, is down by the end of the week, I will get out of a long trade before the weekend. —*AE*

Trading is a psychological game, as Sohail makes abundantly clear. He is an active trader who at his peak more than doubled his account in a year—not with a single lucky hit but by steady short-term trading. The following year he was in a drawdown. The market had not changed—he had! It is to Sohail's credit that he can say, "Fortunately the discipline of loss control had prevented my complete wipeout."

Discipline is essential if you want to survive and win in the markets. Setting some realistic limits on your trading is a key aspect of discipline; you must decide and spell out the basic rules of risk control before you plunge into trading. Most importantly, you need to define your maximum risk level for any single trade and your account as a whole.

*An e-mail from Sohail:*

# SMALL CANDLE IN A DARK CELLAR

Trading is completely different from investing. In the short term the markets can do anything—absolutely anything whatsoever, without any visible rhyme or reason. Short-term price action, for all intents and purposes, is arbitrary and capricious. Long-term investments must only be made on the basis of valuation, fundamental analysis, and due diligence. A long-term investor has to focus on economic facts. Such considerations have no place in the short-term trader's lexicon. Only by harmoniously synchronizing one's inner being to the mood of the market can one hope to trade well. Self-knowledge is critical to trading success.

To follow up on the three M's of successful trading, I thought of three psychological factors that can make or break a trader. I call them the three C's—concentration, clarity, and confidence. You must keep your head clear of emotional and intellectual clutter in order to trade at a sustainable pace. Most successful traders agree that this is not easy to do, even with years of experience. All of us face the challenge of controlling emotions and overcoming personal biases. It is difficult to prevent one area of life from influencing another. An upheaval in your personal life can create emotional clutter that plays havoc with your decision making and turns perfectly good market opportunities into trading fiascos.

You need to be rational and well-informed, but paradoxically, being rational and knowledgeable can also be a trader's downfall. If you become dogmatic about your rationality and knowledge and oblivious to the prevailing mass sentiments, the outcome can be disastrous. John Maynard Keynes warned that the markets can afford to remain irrational longer than any rational investor can remain solvent while fighting irrational markets. A cursory scan of the historical charts shows that the madness of crowds often trumps sound fundamental judgment.

Charts filter out a lot of clutter and prevent information overload. I like to study them to get a general feel for the mood of the crowds in the immediate past. Charts can help a trader concentrate, provide clarity of vision, and give him confidence in his action. Yet, unfortunately, charts alone have never worked for me.

The problem I have with my chartist friends is that many of them take chart reading way too seriously. They think it enables them to predict the future, but that goes against one of the two axioms I hold supreme.

The first is that no one can know the future. I believe that not only no one knows the future, but no one *can* know the future and reliably predict tomorrow's market action. This excludes illegal, insider, or privileged information. An unscrupulous Fed governor's mistress, for instance, could make a killing trading interest rate futures.

My second axiom is that most people are wrong most of the time. To learn from the multitudes, you have to see through their follies and position yourself on the other side of the trade. Someone asked Socrates where he got his wisdom, and he replied that he learned from the fools. This is the basis of the contrarian view. Going with the crowd, as one does in momentum day-trading, leads to mediocre results at best and more often to losses. Yet, there is a serious downside to the contrarian approach. Taking a contrary position too early, even against the most absurd folly—such as shorting a dot-com at a thousand times earnings—can get you trampled by the stampeding herd. It is said that the graveyards of Wall Street are filled with traders who were correct, but too early. The proverbial early bird may find the worm, but the late worm will get away from that bird.

The charts show us past market action. The chart reader takes a leap of faith and assumes that the recent action will continue into the near future. No matter how sophisticated your analysis, the fact remains that this is not a science. It is ultimately a leap of faith. No quantitative technique, mathematical model, wave theory, or technical analysis can reliably predict tomorrow's market action. Nor can one trade on fundamentals. Valuations and fundamentals do not have any bearing on the near-term price fluctuations of a stock or a commodity. With every price prediction technique comes the warning: caveat emptor.

Near-term price fluctuations reflect the cacophony of collective perceptions and emotions, such as greed, fear, hope, and faith. It is a live auction where the adrenaline rush is the currency of the moment. Each transaction represents a momentary consensus between a buyer and a seller. If one could know what all the other participants wanted, one could reliably predict price action. The market is a price discovery mechanism. A short-term trader is essentially playing a guessing game, trying to decipher what all the other guessers are guessing.

Is there any point in fundamental, technical, or sentiment analysis, or is trading like a random roll of the dice? A new trader is like someone who enters a dark cellar for the first time. Without any guidance, he will grope around in the dark and may stumble into what he is looking for. On the other hand, the trader who is armed with a good analytical tool enters that cellar with a small candle. He can discern the general layout of the room, even though the dim light does not reveal all the details. Some of what he sees may actually be illusions caused by the flickering candle and the long shadows. Despite these limitations, a trader is more likely to find his way through the cellar with a small candle than with nothing. However, if he places too much faith in the candlelight, the distortions caused by the flickering flame may lead him to misinterpret what he sees and lead to financial disaster.

A game of chance, such as roulette, is quite different from a game of blackjack, in which skill makes a difference. The outcome of the former is determined entirely by fate, while the outcome of the latter involves an element of choice. The essential difference between them is that the player can manage risk when skill is involved. Chance is inherent in trading the markets, but traders' choices make the difference.

Trading is perhaps the most difficult way to make a living. A trader's life is the life of a *ronin*: the independent warrior of feudal Japan who did not have the protection of a liege lord. Under a lord's protection, his comrade the *samurai* could practice his art carefree. The *ronin* had no such luxury and had to rely on his own resources. To be a successful trader, one needs a sufficient financial cushion to see one through the lean times. Without such a cushion, the individual whose sole livelihood is trading lives a very precarious life, like a barracuda in shark-infested waters. Each day the barracuda sets out not knowing whether it will get dinner or become dinner.

Most people who make a consistent living from the markets do so either under the umbrella of an institution or on the backs of other people's money. Fund managers, analysts, market gurus, and broker-dealers all fall into one of these two categories. They either sell something or charge commissions or fees for services to other market participants. Many of them are also traders in their own right, but their bread and butter does not depend exclusively on their trading.

Trading is not a science, and not a craft either. If anything, it is an art, and like any other art, trying to capture its essence will defy all attempts at programming or systematizing. There are people with an intuitive gift for the subtle art of trading, so nimble that they can gracefully dance their way through the snake pits of the market without getting bitten. Sadly, most mortals are not so gifted. Winning or losing over time, therefore, strictly depends on a disciplined approach to money management and loss control. Without it, if one lives by the sword, one dies by the sword.

An individual trader has one great advantage over the institutional one—he may sit back and do nothing. The ability to wait and take no action until market conditions are suitable for your trading style is perhaps the most important risk control measure. There are market conditions you can, and others you cannot, trade with confidence. You need to know your weaknesses as well as your strengths. Holding your fire and keeping your powder dry are critical disciplines that can make a life or death difference in a trader's career. This discipline, more than any other, has kept me alive in dangerous times. Dr. Elder quotes a mentor of his who used to say that the best trades went right from the very beginning. The trades that go underwater should be quickly abandoned. One should expect about half the trades taken to end up as losses, but as long as these losses remain small, they are tolerable.

In real estate they say that only three factors determine success: location, location, and location. Likewise, in trading there are also three factors that determine success: loss control, loss control, and loss control. To prevent a major loss, you must be willing to embrace minor losses and lots of them.

What is a little loss and how often can one take it? Old Nick, a manager at Drexel Burnham back in the 1980s, used to describe his traders as either elephant hunters or rabbit hunters. The elephant hunter, old Nick used to say, mostly returns empty-handed and his children often go hungry. The rabbit hunter, he said, feeds his family three square meals regularly. Occasionally, when the elephant hunter makes a kill, it is a feast for the entire village. But in the long run, it's the rabbit hunter who stands a better chance of success.

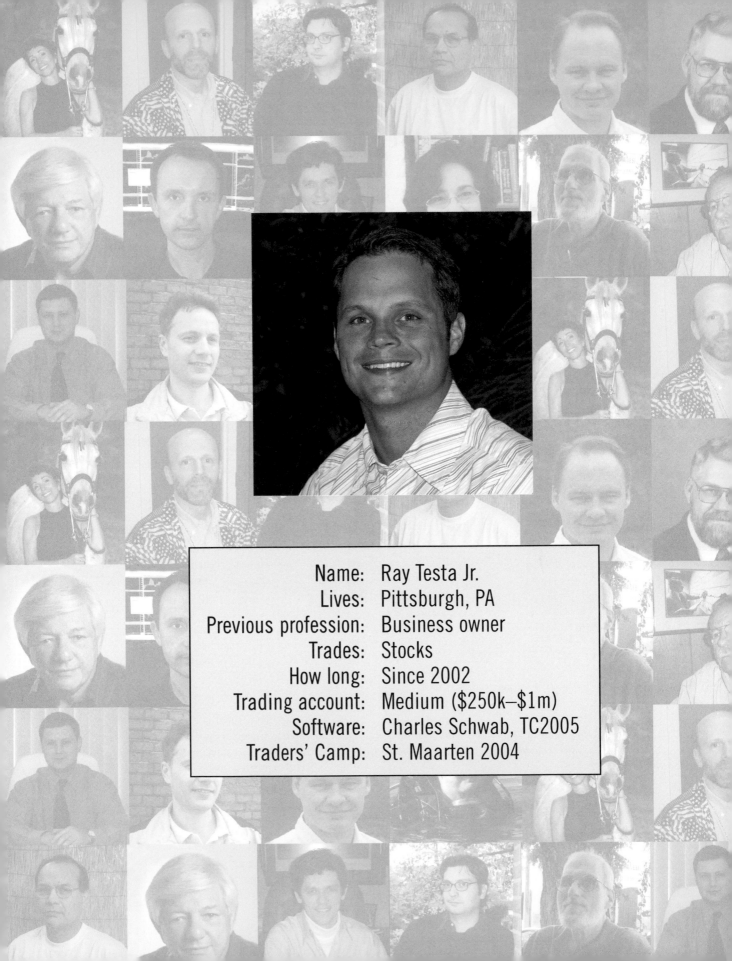

Name: Ray Testa Jr.
Lives: Pittsburgh, PA
Previous profession: Business owner
Trades: Stocks
How long: Since 2002
Trading account: Medium ($250k–$1m)
Software: Charles Schwab, TC2005
Traders' Camp: St. Maarten 2004

# CHAPTER 5

# RAY TESTA JR.

## DEVELOPING A CONSISTENT APPROACH

There were two brothers in our Caribbean Traders' Camp in February 2004. Ray and Bryan were in their early 30s, but both looked so much younger than their ages that I teased them and called them juvenile delinquents. In fact, both were mature beyond their years. They traded and worked in the family business; both were raising young kids.

Their wives wanted to come to St. Maarten with them—a Caribbean beach feels a lot more appealing in February than a suburb of Pittsburgh—but both brothers left their young wives at home. This was not a vacation, they said. They came to the Camp to study, and wanted no distractions. They called home several times each day, but spent all their free time with other traders. That set them apart from many older traders who were chauffeuring their wives while Ray and Bryan were doing their Camp homework.

Campers often bring up their favorite stocks in class, and Ray wanted us to evaluate GT. I declared it the most interesting stock pick of the Camp, and traded it after returning home. It became one of my most profitable trades of 2004. When I began to offer remote access to our monthly campers' meetings in Manhattan, Ray immediately signed up and I always paid attention to any stocks he brought up.

Ray flew to New York with his laptop and a stack of brokerage statements. I put him up in my guest bedroom, and he went out for a bit of sightseeing—he had never been in the city before. He made full use of my wireless Internet, repeatedly checking his stocks and sending e-mails regarding his business.

I am the youngest of four children; I have a sister and two brothers. We all work together; we have a family business that does contracting work for utility companies. We read, install, and maintain gas and electric meters. My father, who is now retired, began with a local utility company and left to start the business in 1984. Working closely with him was a wonderful experience; he was the ultimate mentor. We are all active in the markets, but I am the most interested in trading.

I graduated from Ohio University in 1995, went to work, and shortly afterwards opened a brokerage account. Making money in the market from 1995 to 2000 was pretty easy. We read *Value Line* and did some momentum investing—"the Dogs of the Dow," "the Foolish Four"—that sort of thing. We were buying names, never looked at charts, and didn't know anything about technical analysis. *Value Line* was giving us pretty good stocks—Qualcomm,

Texas Instruments. It was great until the market peaked and crashed. We got hurt like everyone else; after suffering through the bear market, I decided I was not going to give up. I was going to learn from my mistakes. Had I known then a fraction of what I know now, I could have done something as simple as selling my positions when the 50-day moving average crossed below the 200-day average and I would have been hugely better off.

We thought of using a full-service broker and spoke to a few of them. Most used mutual funds. Well, I can read *Morningstar* just as well as they and find the best performing funds without paying one percent of equity. The more I learned about the markets, the more I liked the idea of trading for myself. That's why I attended the Traders' Camp.

When you start studying, you see that it is not out of the realm of possibilities that the market could go sideways for the next 20 years. If I were a strictly buy-and-hold investor, that means by the time I reached my early fifties my savings would not have appreciated very much—unless I learned to trade and take advantage of swings.

My greatest advantages are my age and the fact that I continue to learn. Like that trader you quoted in *Trading for a Living*—"If I get half a percent smarter every year, I will be a genius by the time I die." The stock market fascinates me; I will never lose interest in trading. I love the opportunity to trade for a living, to set my own schedule, and take control of my future. Did you read *Rich Dad, Poor Dad*? There are a few ways to really get ahead—real estate, business, or paper assets. Kiyosaki says that in addition to your regular job, you need to educate yourself and pursue opportunities in one of those asset classes. I chose paper assets. I am not afraid of the extra work. I probably work harder at trading in my spare time than some people do at their regular full-time jobs. I do it so my family will be financially secure and I will be able to retire early.

The bull market crash left me with a bitter taste. When the market started to rise again last year, it was difficult to pull the trigger—basically out of inexperience. The most frustrating thing was that last year, in 2003, everyone made money. Still, people who haven't learned their lessons from the bear market will not hold onto their gains.

The hardest thing this past year was to develop a consistent approach. There are many different ways to trade—you can buy pullbacks or you can buy breakouts, when a stock takes out its previous high. Both methods make a lot of sense, but they are completely different. You have to settle on the one that works for you.

The most success I had this year was buying down and selling up. When I look at stocks that are making new highs, I do not know where to get into them. Instead I wait for prices to pull back to value on the weeklies—wait for the industry group to go blue on the Impulse System, then pick the stock with the most convincing bottom on the daily chart—a triple bottom or a divergence. The year 2004 was a very hard year to trade, with no sustainable trends and many false starts. If you did not enter in time, it was hard to get in later, but if you got in too early, you got whipsawed.

You have to choose not only the method, but also what stocks you're going to monitor. After the Camp, I started doing regular homework—I took stocks in Nasdaq 100 and began to track only those industry groups that contained at least one Nasdaq 100 stock.

The list came to 51 groups out of 239 in TC2005. Most of them are high-tech, and I sometimes wonder whether that is diverse enough. The goal is to track enough without tracking too many. The added advantage of my choice is that if you track Nasdaq 100, you can trade QQQQs.

# TRADE 1 | RAY'S ENTRY

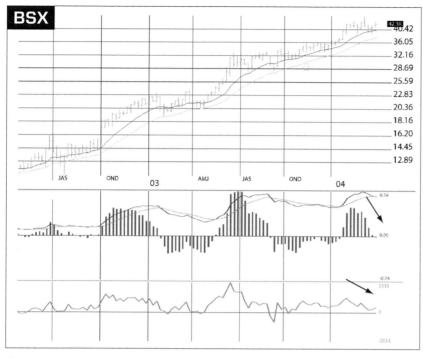

**Upper pane:** Weekly bar chart with two exponential moving averages—26 and 13 weeks
**Middle pane:** MACD Lines and MACD-Histogram (12-26-9)
**Lower pane:** TSV:13 (a near-equivalent of 13-day EMA of Force Index)

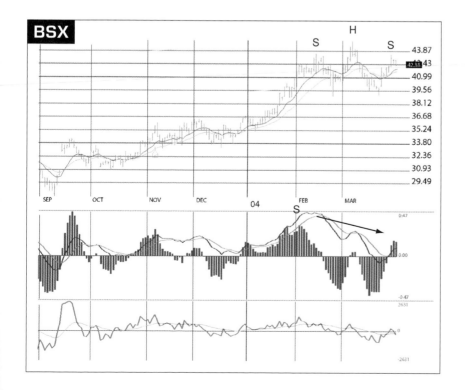

## BSX

At the right edge of the weekly chart, MACD-Histogram is falling while prices are starting to pull back a little bit. I found this trade on a daily chart and confirmed it on the weeklies. I shorted it. I would not go against the weekly Impulse system, but it was the daily that had me more intrigued. Here on the weekly, MACD lines are turning down. TSV has been making lower peaks on the way up, creating a bearish divergence.

On the daily chart I see a head-and-shoulders top with a massive bearish divergence a few days earlier. Prices are swinging up and down, unlike the steady uptrend that had lasted from October through early March. That was a nice uptrend, but now there is a lot of action in the stock—wider swings, but no progress. There is a tail at a peak in early March—another sign of a reversal. TSV is lower at the last peak than it had been at the previous one. Everything is geared to the downside.

will this trade make or lose money?

# TRADE 1   RAY'S EXIT

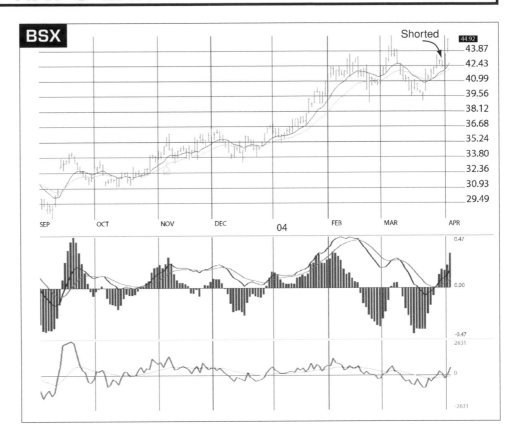

This was one of those great trades where it did not take too long to feel the pain—just one or two trading days. Two days after the entry, it was clear that the market did not confirm my opinion.

When I entered short, the weekly chart wasn't great, but the daily looked interesting. The main reason I took the trade was the divergence in March. I expected further weakness in the stock. I read things into the chart because of the divergence and the head-and-shoulders top. I had missed the opportunity to short in early March and then decided to create an opportunity when it was not really there.

## ▼ TRADE SUMMARY

Short BSX 3/31/2004 @ $42.59
Covered 4/02/2004 @ $44.20
Loss = $1.61 per share

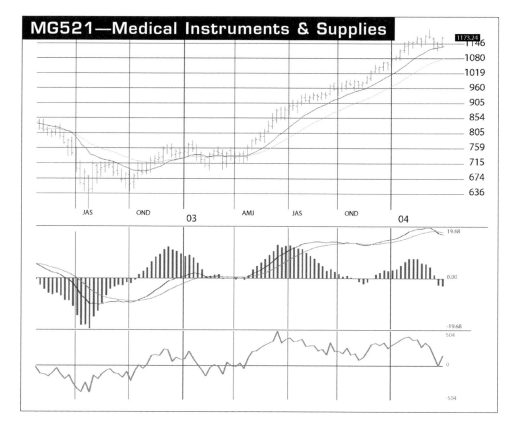

As I do a post-mortem on this trade, I see that my problem was that I did not trade in the direction of the industry group. I realize in hindsight that I did not check how the group had ticked up even though its Impulse system was still blue.

This is where I've had much success lately—watching industry groups and not individual stocks. I should not have traded against the group's momentum.

# TRADE 1—ENTRY COMMENT

The weekly chart shows a long and steady bull market that took BSX from below $10 to above $40. Both EMAs keep rising; prices keep returning to the value zone between the two lines every few months, then pull up again. The trend is up, and it is easier to trade in the direction of the rising tide. Still, the Impulse system had turned blue several weeks earlier, as weekly MACD-Histogram began to decline; this signal means that we are allowed to short.

*It looks like the sweet spot to short BSX came four weeks ago, when the rally to a new high failed and the stock turned from green to blue. That show of weakness was followed by a shallow pullback into the value zone. BSX had since rallied above its value zone. The stock is hard to read at the right edge; it could be either a broad top formation or a resumption of an uptrend.*

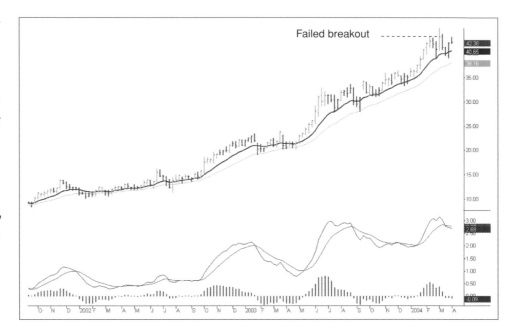

The daily chart shows a persistent rally that had come to an end in March. You can see a bearish divergence between the February and March tops in prices and MACD-Histogram—in early March BSX shot up to a new record high above $44, while MACD-Histogram had traced a much more shallow top than it did in February. The resulting decline drove BSX towards $39, over 10% below its peak. A new rally had emerged from there, taking the stock up toward $44 before it ran out of steam, with the Impulse system turning blue.

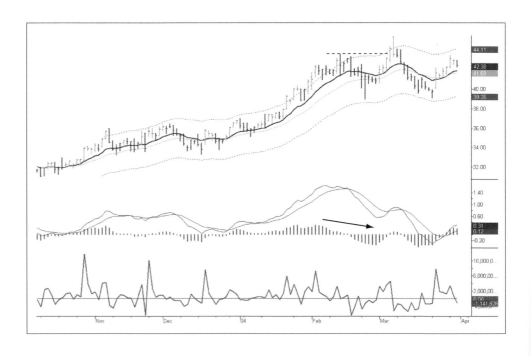

At the right edge of the chart, we see a legitimate short trade—but not an especially attractive one. The Impulse system is blue, permitting shorting, but there is no current bearish divergence of MACD-Histogram and prices are pretty far from the upper channel line where the best shorting is done. The trade feels like a bit of a stretch. The best trades jump at you from the chart, grab you by the face, and scream: "Here I am, take me!" That's certainly not the case with BSX. The market presents such a wealth of opportunities that you are better off waiting for the best ones rather than stretching for the questionable ones.

# TRADE 1—EXIT COMMENT

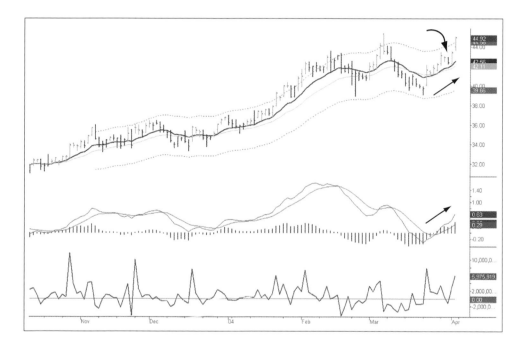

Ray deserves praise for his exit from this trade. The entry looked fairly typical for an eager young trader who reaches a bit too far to find a trade. At the exit, however, Ray acted with the speed and resolve of the pro he hopes to become—he did not waste any time before admitting his error and getting out. He reminded me of what Bucky had said during my interview with Fred Schutzman (Chapter 2): "The most satisfying feeling I have in trading is losing money for the right reasons. When you lose money for the right reasons, you will be a very successful trader in the long run, because you will be taking smaller losses which will enable you to be around for the big trends."

At the right edge of the chart, the Impulse system has turned green again, MACD-Histogram is rising to a new high for the move, and the rally in Force Index is canceling a bearish divergence. Everything is in gear to the upside, and there is no reason to hang around in a short position. Ray is correct in cutting his loss and preserving capital for another trade.

# TRADE 2 | RAY'S ENTRY

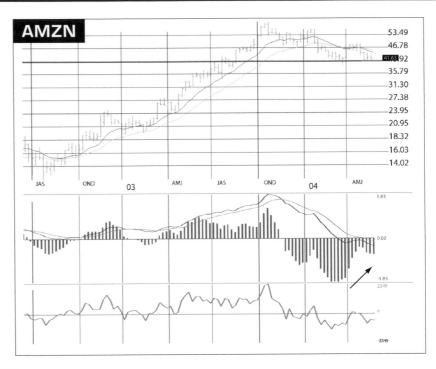

### AMZN

The weekly bars are coming down into an area of support. AMZN had pierced the support line earlier in 2004, then rallied, but now is coming back down. MACD is making a smaller bottom on the current decline, the last weekly bar has turned blue.

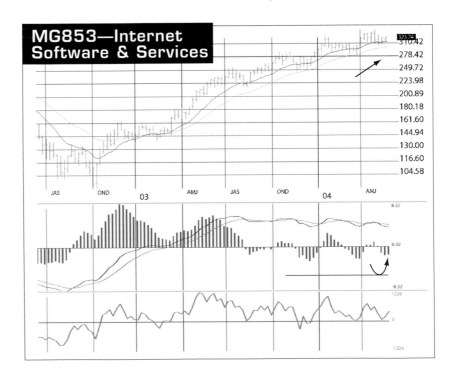

The industry group is in the same situation as AMZN. It is in an uptrend; prices on the weekly charts had pulled back into the sweet zone and ticked up. The Impulse System is the best tool for any beginner, for any trader—it keeps you out of so much trouble, especially if you're buying rebounds. Here it is go time!

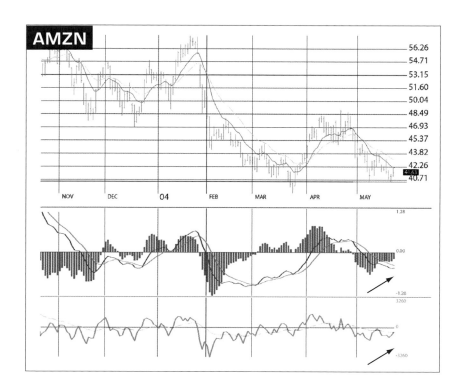

The daily chart is the most interesting to me, even though I follow Triple Screen and always start with the weekly. You have a lot more success if you do that. Back at the end of March I watched AMZN at support but did not trade it. This stock was not on my radar then—I just saw it flipping through charts. The market jumped in late March, and I missed the trade but continued to watch the stock. It came down in May and hit almost the same area, around $40. There was a big fat bottom of MACD, and because of that, I was not too interested. I kept it on my radar, and nine days later it came down to the same area and bounced off that support again. The dailies turned blue, the weeklies were blue, and the industry group was blue. The TSV had a little notch. I took this trade at the level of support—it did not want to go below 40.

will this trade make or lose money?

## TRADE 2 | RAY'S EXIT

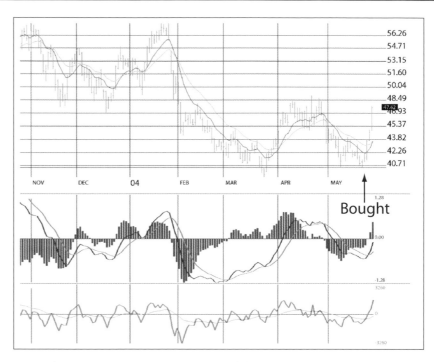

I set my original target at 47.50—it was the area of the top of the previous rally. I sold it at 47.64, near the high of the day because it had reached my target. In hindsight, it was not a great target—but a reasonable one.

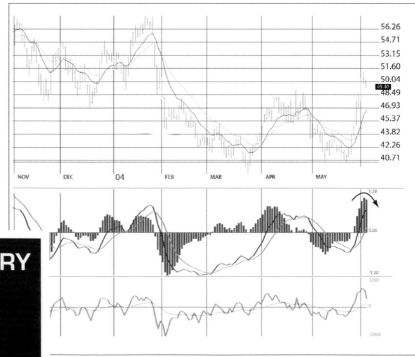

## TRADE SUMMARY

Long AMZN 5/24/2004 @ $41.70
Sold 5/27/2004 @ $47.64
Profit = $5.94 per share

It is not often that I pick a stock that makes 5.5 points in three trading days. If I were doing this trade today, I would not have sold while the daily MACD-Histogram was rising. I would have waited until it ticked down—simply following the daily Impulse System.

Lately, I have been looking for the charts that have sold down and have the most convincing bottoms in the area of support—a double bottom, a triple bottom, or a tiny bottom with MACD-Histogram making a bullish divergence.

This system was first described in *Trading for a Living*. Its key principle is to analyze any market or any stock in more than one timeframe. Whatever charts you like to trade, you may not look at them until you have first analyzed a chart one order of magnitude longer and made your strategic decision there. If, for example, you like to trade daily charts, you may not look at them until you have studied the weekly charts and used them to make a decision to go long or short. Once you have made a strategic decision on the weeklies, return to the daily charts to make a tactical decision—where to enter and where to set a stop-loss and a profit target.  *—AE*

**TRIPLE SCREEN TRADING SYSTEM**

# TRADE 2—ENTRY COMMENT

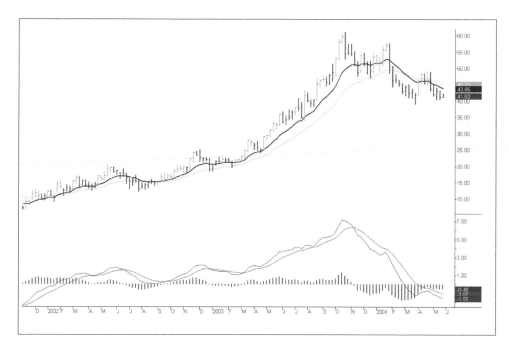

At the right edge of the weekly chart, the bars had shortened, indicating that lower prices are not attracting public participation and the decline is running out of steam. MACD-Histogram is bottoming out at a much higher level than in March. This is not a true divergence because the indicator never crossed above the centerline between the two bottoms. Such clear divergences are rarely seen on the weekly charts. Still, the current pattern tells us that bears are weaker today than they were in March 2004—an important factor to keep in mind when deciding whether to go long or short. At the right edge of the weekly chart, Impulse had turned from red to blue, removing a prohibition against buying.

The chart shows the long slow recovery of Amazon, one of the leaders of the 1990s bull market, from its bear market low. After crawling out of the doghouse below $10, it climbed up all the way to $60 before serious profit-taking drove it down to $40. Notice a kangaroo tail poking below $40 in March 2004; it was followed by a sharp short-covering rally and another slow grinding decline towards $40. Compare the speed of the rally with the slowness of the decline—this stock clearly does not want to go down.

The pattern of MACD-Histogram on the daily chart is similar to that on the weekly. There is no clear divergence, as MACD never crossed into positive territory between its bottoms in early and late May. At the same time, the second MACD bottom is more shallow, telling us that the bears are becoming weaker. The bars have turned from red to blue, no longer prohibiting buying.

*There is a very attractive bullish factor: The low on May 10 was at 40.57, while the low on May 21 reached down to 40.55—two ticks lower. You do not have to be an insider to know that all amateurs who went long between those two dates put their stops "a tick or two below the previous low." As so often happens, they were taken out at the second bottom—such false breakouts transfer stocks from weak holders into strong hands and clear the way for a rally.*

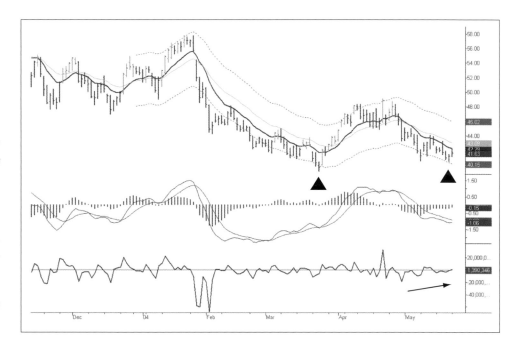

Notice a beautiful bullish divergence of Force Index. It shows that the bears are completely out of breath, and AMZN is falling only out of inertia. At the right edge this stock has a preponderance of bullish signals; the only fly in the ointment is the lack of a clear divergence of MACD-Histogram. Many trades look imperfect during an entry; the signals become crystal clear only in retrospect. An analyst can afford to wait for perfection; a trader must put his money on the line in an atmosphere of uncertainty, protecting himself with good money management.

# TRADE 2—EXIT COMMENT

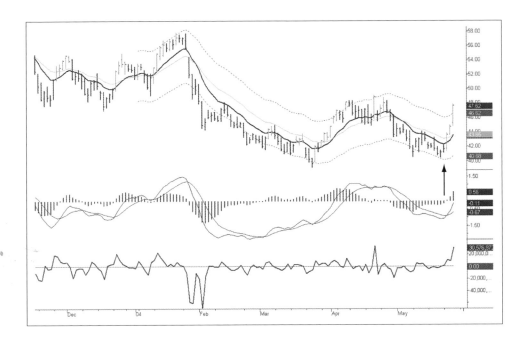

At the right edge of the chart AMZN closed above its upper channel line. I believe that envelopes provide the best short-term targets for profit taking. As Ray looks at his trade in retrospect, he regrets having left so much on the table—the stock went up several dollars after he sold. He is both right and wrong.

Hindsight is a 20/20 vision: If we could buy tomorrow's newspaper, we'd all get in at the absolute low and sell at the extreme high. Looking out into the uncertain future, it is impossible to tell for sure whether a stock will rise or fall the following day. This is why taking profits above a channel line is a perfectly reasonable thing.

Ray says he should have held until the daily MACD-Histogram had ticked down. Here it ticked down softly, but it also could have ticked down hard. A stock can reverse very sharply, wiping out the bulk of profit. If Ray wants to try a different exit technique, I would suggest exiting the bulk of the trade with a more conservative technique at the channel line and holding a small fraction of his position to test something more adventurous. If he traded 1,000 shares, he could take profit on 900 shares and hold 100 for a different type of exit.

All of this has to be properly documented in a Trader's Diary. Trying something new once or twice and then forgetting about those tries is not much different from gambling. Trying repeatedly, while keeping good records and comparing two methods side by side—now *that* will make you a better trader.

# TRADING CHANNELS

The two main types of channels are straight envelopes and standard deviation channels, often called Bollinger bands. A straight envelope runs parallel to a moving average, while standard deviation bands expand and contract in response to market volatility. They are useful primarily for options traders since volatility is a prime factor in option pricing. When the bands expand, it is a good time to write options, and when they contract, it is better to buy them. Traders of stocks and futures are better off with straight envelopes, which help identify overbought and oversold conditions.

A well-drawn envelope contains approximately 95% of prices on the screen. We want the envelope to contain the last four or five months of prices on the daily charts, so that only the most extreme prices penetrate above or below. The market is a manic-depressive beast: Normalcy is within the channel, mania is above the upper channel line, and depression below the lower line. Channels help us gauge the mood of the market crowd and trade against it.

The public tends to follow trends, becoming increasingly bullish as prices rise. Beginners love to buy upside breakouts, hoping for a runaway move. Occasionally they turn out to be right, but in the long run, most breakouts are false, which is why professionals tend to bet against them. When prices slide, the crowd becomes increasingly bearish. When people see a downside breakout, they tend to dump their holdings, and professionals buy from them at a discount, knowing that most downside breakouts are false. Envelopes help us identify the areas where the crowd becomes depressed or manic—and bet against it.

Neither envelopes nor any other single indicator can be used as an automatic trading tool. In a powerful uptrend, prices can cling to the upper channel line for a long time, and in a powerful downtrend, they can stay below the lower channel line. We need to combine envelopes with other tools to recognize the best trading signals—for example, an envelope breakout accompanied by an MACD divergence (see a bearish divergence in AMZN in mid-April 2004). These words of caution apply first and foremost to entries; taking profits at the channel line is almost always a good idea. Ray's exit from AMZN shows that he is on his way to becoming a pro, as he sells the upside breakout.

Channels are better tools for setting profit targets than support and resistance lines. Professional traders look for uncommon tools. Everyone knows about support and resistance, since marking them requires nothing more than a pencil and a ruler. Channels, on the other hand, require a degree of computer sophistication and an investment in time. They are less obvious on the charts.

Envelopes, like many other indicators, provide both positive and negative signals. When you buy inside an envelope and sell when prices hit the upper channel line, you know that you're ahead of the market crowd. You bought while the crowd was asleep and sold when it woke up—that is a positive signal. A negative signal is a warning not to buy above the upper channel line or to go short below the lower channel line. These messages help prevent the worst of the "greater fool theory" trades. Envelopes provide the best short-term targets for profit taking and very useful warnings—Ray would be well advised to add them to his charts.

*An e-mail from Ray:*

# MY TRADING PLAN CONTINUES TO EVOLVE

At the time of the interview I was focusing on short-term trading. This year, other business commitments and increased personal demands on my time started putting pressure on this approach. I decided to divide my capital into three baskets and add two new strategies—one that I could manage mechanically, and another that I could approach using a longer time frame.

My long-term strategy is simple: to get exposure to the strongest stocks in the strongest groups. As I write this in the middle of 2005, the stock market is basically flat for the year. At the same time, many industry groups are up 25 to 40 percent. As long as we are not in a bear market, I'm content to hold stocks in leading industries, using trailing stops to protect profits. Additionally, I use options or direct index shorts to hedge my portfolio when necessary. Industry groups perform well because their underlying fundamentals are slow to change. It is easy to identify the strongest groups. The key is to monitor them and wait for a proper buying opportunity: a pullback to value on a weekly chart.

Alex said during one of our monthly campers' meetings that if you woke up every morning and your account was positioned in the same direction as the 26-week moving average, you wouldn't do too badly. I decided to add a trend-following component to my trading, after studying several charts similar to this one of the S&P.

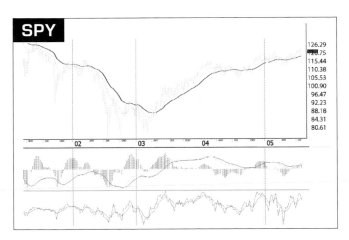

I backtested trend-following systems using different moving averages. The results varied, but the returns were far superior to the buy-and-hold approach touted by Wall Street. My system is simple. I use a crossover of fairly short-term exponential moving averages to generate trading signals, both long and short. Although this strategy does not catch tops or bottoms, it has you staying with the trend. Entering and exiting trades results in constant errors in judgment; you always think that you could have done better. It is nice to have a portion of your capital managed mechanically. When the EMA changes direction, it keeps you out of trouble and ahead of the market averages.

I still devote a substantial percentage of my capital to short-term trading. I have modified the methods I learned at the Trader's Camp and added a few of my own. Applying a top-down approach, I first study the markets, then industry groups, and finally individual stocks. Most of my trading picks come from completing my weekly Impulse system homework. I try to run my basket of stocks like a hedge fund, keeping a balance of long and short positions. My short-term trading performance has improved since I have expanded my trading plan. By utilizing these additional strategies, I have become a more patient trader. With plenty of capital already at risk, I find it much easier to wait for a perfect setup to enter a trade than to try to force things.

| | |
|---:|:---|
| Name: | James (Mike) McMahon |
| Lives: | Phoenix, AZ |
| Previous profession: | Engineering manager |
| Trades: | Stocks |
| How long: | Since 2000 |
| Trading account: | Small (<$250k) |
| Software: | TC2005, TradeStation, Trader's Governor |
| Traders' Camps: | New Zealand 2002, Dominican Republic 2003; Spike group member |

# CHAPTER 6

# JAMES (MIKE) McMahon

## A Successful Engineer Has a Disadvantage

I met Mike in 2002 at our Traders' Camp in New Zealand. He sat near the back of the room, taking notes on a laptop. I was waving my fingers in the air, explaining the 2% and 6% Rules of money management. He came up to me during a break: "You know, those concepts lend themselves very well to programming."

The next morning he brought a stack of floppies to our class—that was before USB devices became popular. Mike announced he had created an Excel spreadsheet to implement the 2% and 6% Rules for controlling risks and offered anyone in the class a free copy. The next day he stood up in class and asked for the floppies back. He had been working on the program the night before, upgraded it, and was offering the new file to all campers, but was running out of floppies. The group loved him.

At the end of our Camp I suggested to Mike that he write a commercial-quality program, complete with a manual. He wanted to do it in partnership with me and we shook hands on our deal. For the past three years he has been producing better and better versions of risk management software, moving forward in his quiet and dogged way. Our current Trader's Governor has over 20,000 lines of computer code and delivers an unheard-of level of control into the hands of private traders.

I enjoy working with Mike and appreciate his thoroughness, focus, and unflappable good humor. We run into each other several times each year and always share a meal, even though I like a glass or two of wine with dinner, while Mike, a devout Baptist, never touches the stuff. We usually talk about money management, but I became interested in his views on trading and sent him an invitation to participate in this project. Mike wrote back:

> I'm extremely honored to be considered for the book—although I'm not sure I qualify to be a member of the group. I do not consider myself to be trading professionally yet, although I am trading seriously.
>
> I think the benefits of my experience are not so much in the area of trading tips, tricks, and methods but rather in overcoming some of the obstacles to successful trading. I am convinced that having been a highly successful computer engineer has been a disadvantage to my trading rather than an advantage. It is a difficult task to quit thinking like an engineer after so many years of positive reinforcement.

We met at a Traders' Expo in Las Vegas where I taught a day-long class and Mike stepped into my room as a guest speaker to deliver a crisp PowerPoint presentation on risk control. Generous as ever, he offered to e-mail his entire presentation to the members of the class. Later that night we shared a meal, and continued our conversation the following day.

In my previous career as a computer engineer and manager for an oil company in the Middle East, I had built great confidence in my ability to do analysis and derive solutions that work. Then I approached the markets, did great analysis, but the solution often did not work. One cannot fix the chaos of the markets. Being right is everything in an engineering job, but in the market you need a method that works more often than not in producing winning trades.

In trading it is possible to have a process or a method that works maybe 3 out of 10 times, and with good money management you can make it profitable. Just let your winners run and cut your losers short. In almost every other endeavor in life, that would be an unthinkable proposition. One thing I did in my previous career was process control—computers take measurements from the field and send out signals to control temperature, flow, and pressure at an oil refinery. If I approached my boss and said, "We'll control the plant so that three times out of ten it will work very well, but seven times it won't work," he would not have been happy. But in trading that might work very well.

A beginner trying to find the right method goes to seminars, starts trading, but when you look at his trades, is he winning or losing as a result of the method? He may apply the rules and trade correctly sometimes, but not at other times. If that is the case, looking at the results of a trade is inconclusive. The results are meaningful only if you apply your methods rigorously. If you stretch because you're hot to trade, you taint the quality of your results. The less experienced a trader, the less defined his method.

To define a method takes a good number of trades—10 is not meaningful, 100 is good. A trader often jumps to another method before he gets numbers where they should be. A private trader without good education or discipline and poor record-keeping does not know whether his method is good. "I am making money, so I know what's right." In the nineties people were making profitable trades for the wrong reasons. All stocks went up, but if a stock went down, they did not worry about stops because the stocks always returned and roared up. They were winning even though the quality of their trading was poor. Then the year 2000 rolled along.

All my life I've been confident I could do complex analysis and develop working solutions. If a solution worked, it was correct. In the market it is different. Some trades are winners but not because analysis is correct. Other trades fit the entry criteria very well but turn out to be losers. Winning or losing in any single trade has nothing to do with the quality or viability of the strategy. Looking at my diary entries reinforced this for me. There were some winning trades where I deviated from my criteria and which did not deserve to be winners. There were losing trades where I did everything right, but the market moved against me. Trading is not about "Am I right or am I wrong?" but about "Did I apply my methods correctly?"

I have met a lot of people who are in a similar situation—very strong technical people, programmers, great analytical persons who enter the chaos of the markets and are unable to produce answers. Casual investors got badly burned in 2001–2002. You've got to have some kind of strategy for the downside; you cannot be holding in the midst of a bear market. If you followed the simple strategy of getting out when a complete bar moved below its 200-day moving average, then around September 2000 you would have sold out and stayed in cash until April 2003.

When I left Saudi Arabia in July 2000, I had my 401k and an IRA; I had invested only in mutual funds before. People kept saying that the stock market was going crazy and it was the time to get involved. The idea of not having to work 9 to 5 felt attractive; I thought I could trade part-time and make a lot of money—sounds familiar, right? A friend was involved with Wade Cook, and I went to his conference but started getting disillusioned with his thing right away. There was that feeling of forced joy and the purpose was to show you how little you knew. They'd teach you 30 strategies in three days until you said, "Wow, this is really complex, I need to sign up for three more workshops." One of the instructors handed out a reading list, and I picked up *Trading for a Living*. I said, this guy makes a lot of sense and he is opposed to everything Wade Cook says.

And that's how I came to my first Traders' Camp. In my first career I developed the mindset that I was going to be right always or almost always, but when I got into trading, I knew I had to change that. I still have not completely made the breakthrough to reach that way of thinking, but I am applying good money management until I get there. That fellow in your class yesterday brought up a question about being confident and you said you could never be confident. This is a psychological change that is hard to achieve for most people who come from other fields.

When you propose to people at a conference or on a message board, "Let's talk about our 'trading demons,'" not one person responds, no one wants to handle that. They'd rather talk of gold prices, or divergences, or brokers. I have often thought that I could be a more successful trader if I had a robot entering and executing for me. You know, like in Isaac Asimov's book *I, Robot*. The first law is that a robot cannot harm a human by its action or inaction. I could see myself getting emotional during the trading day and giving the robot instructions to place or cancel an order and he'd say, "No, I cannot allow you to come to harm; I have to execute the plan."

---

**CONFIDENCE AND UNCERTAINTY**

A fellow raised his hand in my class where Mike had appeared as a guest speaker. He wanted to know how to reach the degree of expertise at which he could approach trading with a great feeling of confidence. "That is not likely to ever happen," I said. "There is always a feeling of uncertainty in working on the edge. If you feel certain about a project or a trade that you're getting into, it is probably going to be a loser."                                                                —AE

---

It is a very different thing looking at the game from the outside or with the experience of having been in it. Like that joke—two fellows go fishing in a canoe and one of them throws a stick of dynamite overboard—boom!—all kinds of stunned fish float to the surface. His friend says, "Are you crazy? This is so illegal." And the first guy takes another stick of dynamite, lights it up, hands it to his friend, and says, "You gonna talk or you gonna fish?"

In trolling for trades, I start with TC2005 where I have two EasyScans. First, I look for stocks that have reached a new 52-week high during the past 30 trading days. They have to be priced over $10 and have volume in the top 25% of all stocks. Today, for example, we have 613 stocks on this new high list, and I sort them from the highest price down. I take a quick look at every weekly chart and, if they're interesting, glance at the daily. Most of them are up, stretching the rubber band. I am looking for shorting opportunities— for those that are overstretched and starting to roll over—and flag the ones I like for deeper study.

I tend to find more candidates mid-list, rather than at the top or the bottom of the list. I create and date a new text file and copy flagged symbols into it. Then I do the same for new lows—looking for buys, looking at the lowest prices. I export their symbols to a text file, such as "shorts for 11/22"and put it into my TradeStation folder. Once I get the stocks into TradeStation, I go through my regular screens—weekly, daily, and intraday. Here I start seriously looking for trades. Sometimes I find crossovers—potential longs on shorts lists and vice versa. I work with each list for a week or two, and after that, I start throwing old files out.

# TRADE 1 │ MIKE'S ENTRY

At the right edge of the chart, the Impulse system has stopped being red and turned blue, permitting buying. Stochastics are oversold and crossing up. MACD-Histogram has stopped declining and ticked up.

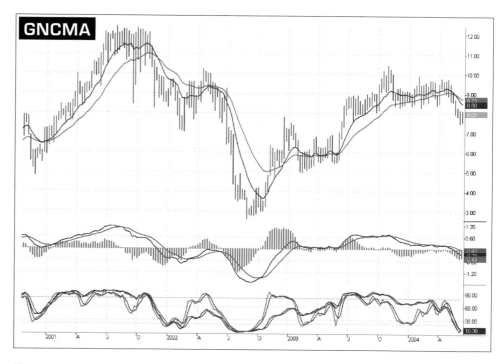

| | |
|---|---|
| **Upper pane:** | Weekly bar chart with two exponential moving averages—25 and 11 weeks and Impulse system |
| **Middle pane:** | MACD Lines and MACD-Histogram (11-25-5) |
| **Lower pane:** | Stochastic (10-3-3 and 40-3-3); overbought and oversold lines at 80 and 20 |

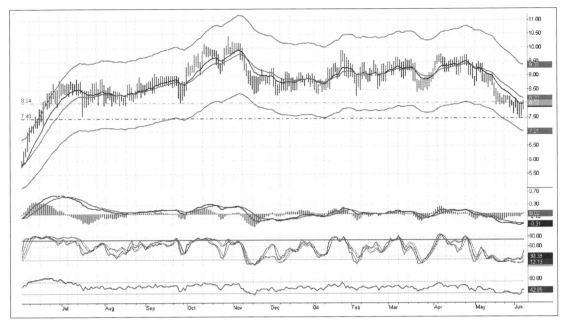

Same parameters in the first three panes as weekly, only referring to the number of days. Fourth pane 11-day RSI.

## GNCMA

The Impulse system has changed from red to blue to green. MACD-Histogram is rising and has just crossed above zero. Stochastics are rising and have just crossed above their oversold line. The stock fell to its 52-week low, but instead of following through on that decline, it reversed and started to rise. Prices are in the sweet zone between the two moving averages.

The second day of a bullish trend in prices confirms the buy signal of the weekly and daily charts.

**Upper pane:**  15-minute candlestick chart
**Lower pane:**  MACD Lines and MACD-Histogram (12-26-9 bars)

will this trade make or lose money?

# TRADE 1 | MIKE'S EXIT

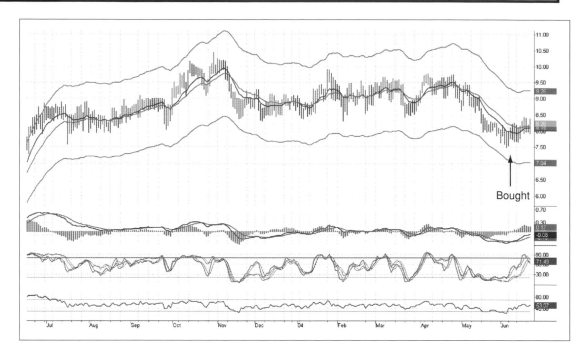

Bought

After 11 trading days, it didn't look like this stock was going anywhere. MACD began to fall and Stochastic crossed below its oversold line.

**THE BOSS WANTS TO SEE THE NUMBERS**

*Mike says:* Yesterday a fellow asked you in class what was a common psychological trait among winning traders, and you answered: "eccentricity." I figure I've got all the head knowledge I need to have—now I need to make a psychological change from a conservative, straightforward engineer to an eccentric, logical trader. I have a passion for trading. In every endeavor of my career I've been successful in overcoming obstacles and meeting challenges—there is great satisfaction in this. I like the flexibility of the lifestyle, being able to trade from anywhere in the world, any hour, but at times I miss the sociability of the office. Trading by yourself—there is some loneliness there.

Working on Trader's Governor has given me a tremendous appreciation for the value of record-keeping. Private traders can feel they are doing OK and not face up to their real performance. Having the Governor forces me to do that no matter how painful. I started a process of brutally punishing my ego by reporting to my wife. Now it is like work—good or bad, the boss wants to see the numbers.

## ▼ TRADE SUMMARY

Long GNCMA 6/8/2004 @ $8.10

Sold 6/23/2004 @ $8.04

Loss = $(0.06) per share

Channel 9.38–7.01

Lost 8.7% of the channel for a D trade

*Mike wrote:*   I'm sending you a booklet called *The Unwritten Laws of Engineering*. When I first   **PSYCHOLOGY**
began to read it, I thought this was really great stuff that every entry-level engineer should know.
I was astounded to learn it had been published in 1944! I see a close correlation between the
mentality of young engineers and that of beginning traders who are fixated on getting all the
technical tools, charts, indicators, system backtesting, stock-picking software, and so on. They
do not seem at all concerned with the unwritten laws of trading and how psychologically and
emotionally unprepared they are for the markets.

# TRADE 1—ENTRY COMMENT

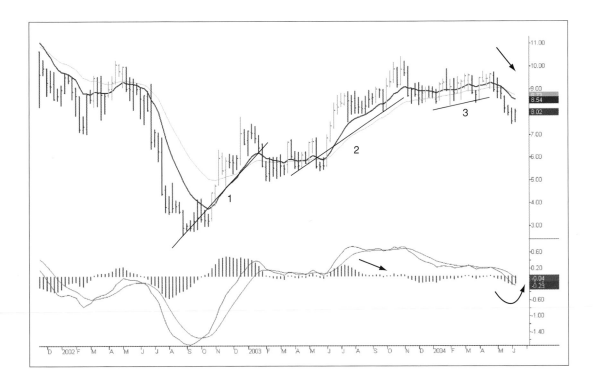

The weekly chart reveals three distinct stages in the bull move that took GNCMA from
under $3 to above $10. The first upleg, in 2002, was powerfully vertical. The second upleg,
in 2003, went up at a much more shallow angle and ended with a bearish divergence of
MACD-Histogram. The third upleg, in 2004, was nearly flat, did not reach a new high, and
ended with both moving averages rolling over to the downside. Clearly, the early bird
caught this worm in the stock market.

At the right edge of the chart the decline had reached deep below the EMA, over-
extending the rubber band. MACD-Histogram had ticked up, turning the Impulse system
blue and removing a prohibition against buying.

**DO NOT SQUINT AT A CHART**

Traders looking for bullish and bearish signals tend to squint at the charts. Squint long enough, and you'll recognize bullish or bearish signals—whichever you prefer. A much better thing to do, when in doubt, is to push back and look at the charts of a greater timeframe. If you feel confused by the dailies, look at the weeklies to make a strategic decision. Use them to decide whether you're a bull or a bear before returning to the daily chart and deciding what to do with your trade.

—AE

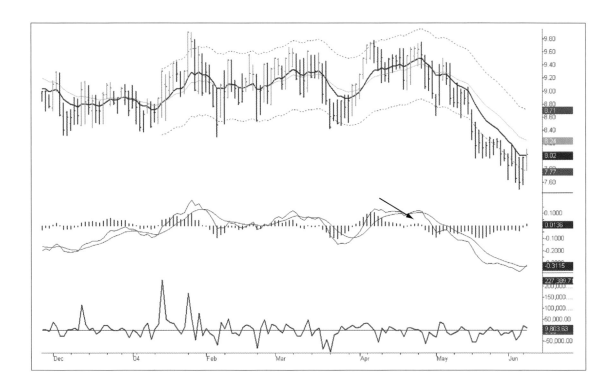

The decline on the daily chart appears a little steep for buying just now. There was a bearish divergence in April, and from there the stock lost nearly 25% in less than two months, going down in a nearly straight line. At the right edge of the chart the Impulse has turned green, permitting buying, but there is no bullish divergence of MACD-Histogram, of MACD Lines, or even of Force Index. There is only an uptick of the histogram and a crossing of prices above the fast EMA. That would not be enough to get me from the sidelines and into a long position.

Furthermore, it seems a little late to be entering this long trade. Mike's purchase price of $8.10 is near the top tick of the day and closer to the center of the channel than to its bottom. If I was going bottom-fishing, I would try to buy below value, in the vicinity of the lower channel line. At this point I would give a pass to this trade.

# TRADE 1—EXIT COMMENT

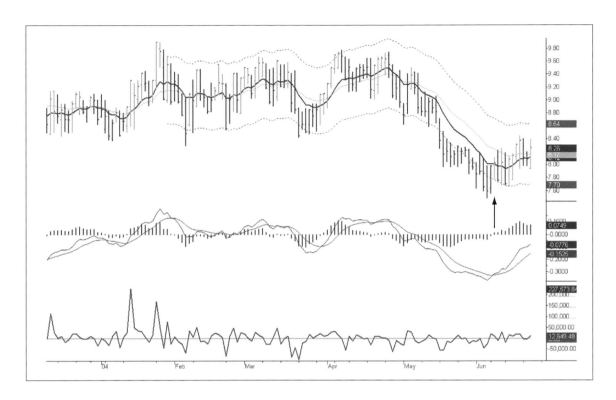

The rally had stalled, and Mike was quite right to exit his trade. I think it is important to have a stop for your trades not only in terms of price but also in terms of time. It can be a mental stop, but you should know that if a stock does not do what you expected it to do within a reasonable time, you'll be out of it.

You buy a stock expecting it to go up. If you thought you could get it cheaper tomorrow, you would not have bought it today. A day goes by, then two and three, but the rally you expected does not materialize. Even if that stock does not fall and go against you, it is giving you a subtle message that your analysis was wrong. This is like trying to pull your car into a tight parking spot: If you realize that you're not making it, get out of that spot and decide whether to get in again at a better angle or drive around and look for another spot.

This trade also brings up the importance of measuring where in the daily range you bought or sold a stock. The idea is to try to buy in the lower 50% of the daily bar and sell within the top 50% of that day's bar. This is harder than it seems because we do not know until the close what the day's range is going to be. Buying in the bottom half and selling in the top half is a skill that comes with experience, and even then, it is never flawless. In this trade Mike bought near the top tick of the daily bar and sold near the bottom tick of the exit bar. Had he been able to reverse this pattern, the trade would have been a big winner, instead of a small loser. Mike has access to live intraday data. His skills in analyzing weekly and daily charts can be transferred to intraday charts—not to daytrade, but to finesse his entries and exits.

# TRADE 2 | MIKE'S ENTRY

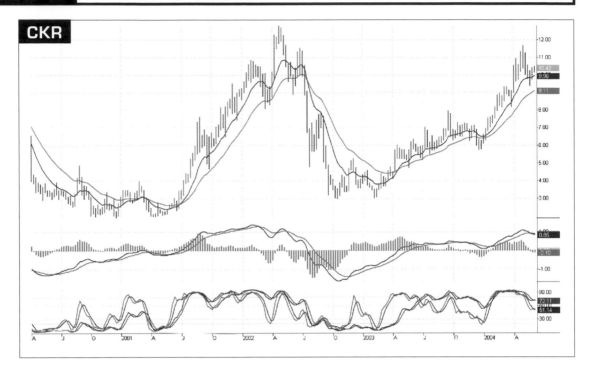

## CKR

The Impulse system is blue, allowing us to buy. Both Stochastics are starting to turn up—bullish. MACD has not yet ticked up.

## Non-Impulse Exit

**Q** In a webinar yesterday you said that due to the lack of follow-through in corn, now would be a good time to sell. Did you actually mean selling even though the Impulse System is green? *—Trader*

**A** The Impulse system is a censorship system that gives me permission to enter. When a market blows out of its channel, it shows an overheated condition and signals me to exit, without any input from the Impulse system. In other words, I may enter only when this system allows me to enter, but I may exit before it tells me to do so. *—AE*

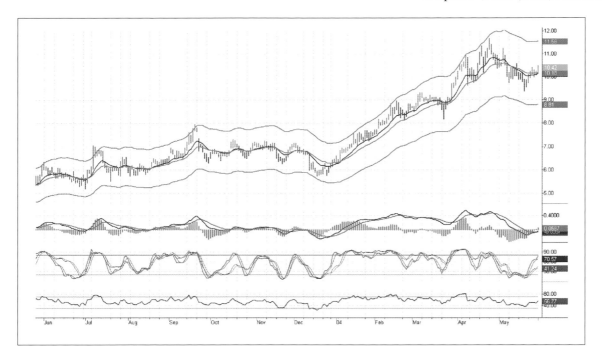

MACD-Histogram is rising, crossing its zero line MACD Lines are giving a buy signal. The price is in the "sweet zone" between two EMAs. RSI and both Stochastics are rising.

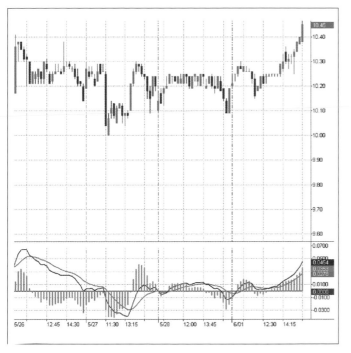

The fact that prices have closed up for the day is a positive sign.

Will this trade make or lose money?

# TRADE 2 | MIKE'S EXIT

The price looks like it is moving, but momentum and MACD are starting to diverge from the price a bit. Both Stochastic and RSI are starting to turn down.

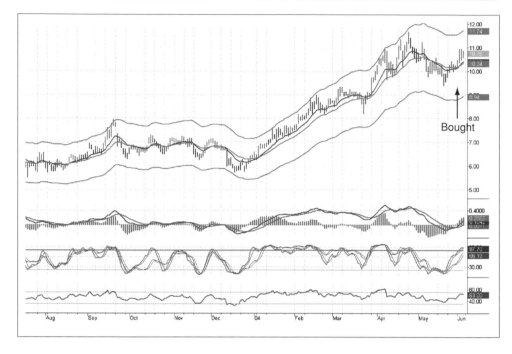

It looks like prices are going nowhere. There is a possible triangle formation.

## ▲ TRADE SUMMARY

Long CKR 06/01/2004 @ $10.38

Sold 06/04/2004 @ $10.717

Profit = $0.337 per share

Channel 10.85–9.51

Gained 25% of the channel for a B trade

# TRADE 2—ENTRY COMMENT

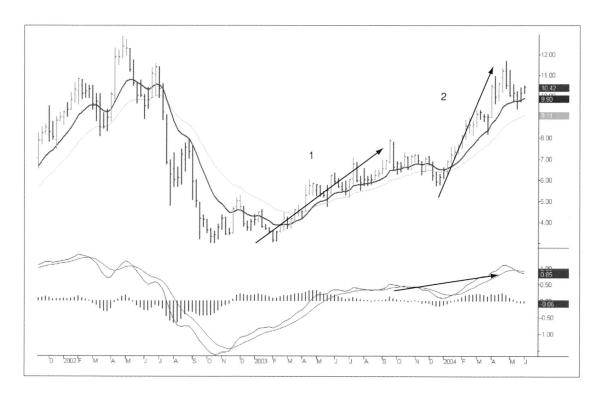

CKR is becoming stronger and stronger, in contrast to GNCMA whose rise on the weekly chart kept getting weaker and weaker. CKR's first upleg, from $3 to $8 in 2003, lasted over 30 weeks; the second upleg, in 2004, from under $6 to nearly $12, took only half of that time, as the stock went up faster. When bulls become stronger as the stock rallies, it is a sign that the stock wants to go higher.

The bull move is being neatly traced by rising moving averages; every few months a bout of profit-taking drives prices down into the value zone between the two EMAs or even lower. These episodes of panic among the weakest holders allow patient, conservative traders to add to their longs near value. The latest decline had just run its course a week ago, with MACD-Histogram declining below zero. Its oversold reading provides extra support to the bullish cause. The chart looked better the week before, but even here prices are not yet too far from value.

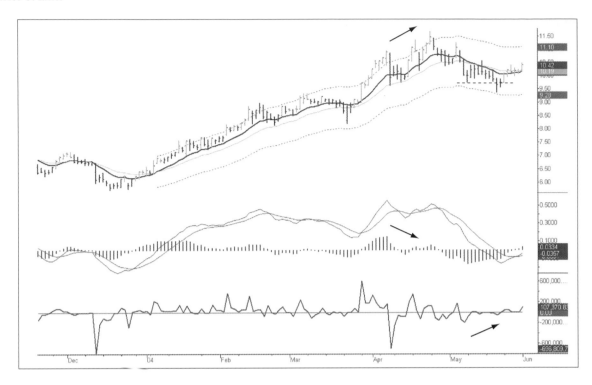

A bullish divergence of Force Index lends support to the bullish cause. Notice a relatively deep FI bottom during the first stab to the lower channel and a nearly flat Force Index during the second bottom. This showed us that the bears were out of steam. The markets run on a two-party system—bulls and bears. When the bears become weak, you know which party is likely to win the next election.

The daily chart confirms the message of the weekly—the stock is in gear to the upside. Notice the bearish divergence that had pushed the stock down in April, followed by two stabs to the lower channel line in May. The second bottom was below the first, but prices stayed below that level for only two days; when they rallied above it six days ago, the trap was shut on the bears. That sixth bar from the right edge, with the daily Impulse turning green and the weekly still blue, would have made a perfect entry into this long trade; Mike is on top of the game with trend direction but a bit behind on his timing.

## Targets in Flat Markets

**Q**

It seems to me that stocks in choppy markets, like the one we are in, often do not move to the percentage envelope like they have in the past. Do you use another price objective?

—*Trader*

**A**

I still try to take profits at the channel lines, but they have to be recalibrated to track the last two or three months of trading.

—*AE*

# TRADE 2—EXIT COMMENT

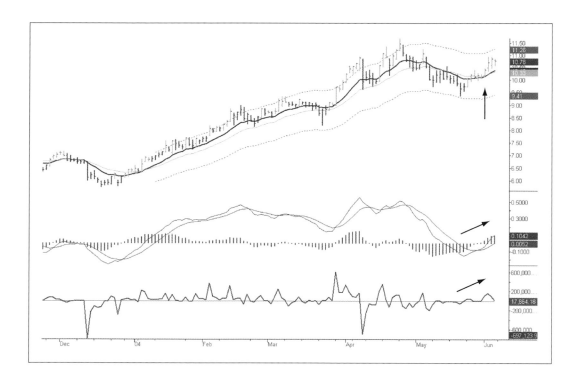

This is a very cautious exit—but then Mike is a very cautious man; and nobody has ever gone broke taking profits. There are both bullish and bearish signs at the right edge. The biggest negative is that prices had not advanced for the past two days, drawing a shorter bar each day. This could mean running into resistance and the end of a short-term uptrend. Of course it could also mean a tight triangle—a continuation pattern within an uptrend. Another warning to the bulls comes from the fact that prices are approaching their upper channel line. They are also starting to plough into the area of resistance, established during the April top.

At the same time, several indicators give bullish signals. A recent peak of MACD-Histogram marks the bulls' return to the market. A new peak of Force Index, higher than the previous one, shows that the bulls are becoming stronger.

Mike is cautiously moving forward through treacherous terrain. As he perceptively noted in his interview, his career as an engineer had trained him to look for certainty. While learning to function in this new field, he is cutting his losses short and nailing profits before they get away from him.

# RISK CONTROL

There are few if any young geniuses in trading. If you stay in this game long enough, acquiring experience and maturity, you will develop an edge. It is perfectly okay to make mistakes, but not okay to repeat them. If you follow this rule, you'll keep finding new mistakes to make, but eventually you're going to start running out of mistakes and making money.

Experience confers a big advantage in trading, but to benefit from it you need to survive the period of early inexperience. There is only one way to survive—by using strict money management. Many traders in this book speak about the vital importance of risk control. Mike McMahon's unique achievement is his creation of a money management tool—a Trader's Governor.[1]

Every trader faces two primary dangers in the market. First, his account could be ruined by a single disastrous loss; a massive loss can push a trader so deep into the hole that he can never crawl out. I call such a single ruinous loss a shark bite. Second, an account can be irreparably damaged by a series of piranha bites—a long string of losses, none of which is disastrous but which together bleed the account dry.

I have developed two money management rules to prevent such disasters. The 2% Rule limits the risk on any given trade to the maximum of 2% of the account value. For example, if a trader with a $100,000 account buys a $10 stock and puts a stop at $9, he is risking $1 a share. Since the 2% Rule limits his maximum risk to $2,000, he is allowed to buy no more than 2,000 shares of that stock, and preferably fewer.

The 6% Rule limits the total risk for the account as a whole. It states that the total risk on all open positions, plus any losses taken during the current month, may not exceed 6% of your account equity. Say you put on three trades identical to the one above. Your risk on each of them may be limited to 2%, but if all your trades turn against you at once, you can lose 6% of your equity. If you wanted to put on a fourth trade, the 6% Rule would have said "no" because you'd already reached the maximum risk limit for your account as a whole.

The intricacies of both rules are spelled out in *Come into My Trading Room*. If you trade a single account with just a few trades, you can probably do risk management in a simple spreadsheet. Mike McMahon's achievement is that his Trader's Governor allows you to track and control risks for multiple accounts, multiple positions, and different risk levels. He links all accounts to a single control panel, allowing you to monitor risks, play various "what if" scenarios, and even measure your risk in nearly real-time, using free 20-minute delayed data. By programming his Trader's Governor, Mike has performed a massive favor for the trading community.

---

[1]In the interest of full disclosure, I have to say that I am partners with Mike in this software. You can see the Governor manual on my Web site: *www.elder.com*.

## An e-mail from Mike:

# LIKE BALANCING YOUR CHECKBOOK

I developed a passion for trading soon after I started. Initially there was the attraction of quick and easy profits, although I knew from experience that if something sounded too good to be true, it usually wasn't that good. Still, I was confident that, based on my successful career in engineering and with sufficient effort on my part, I could master trading.

The markets quickly taught me that they were not bound by clear-cut laws and mathematical certainties—not only did they not follow the rules, but they constantly changed them. After completing two Traders' Camps, I became convinced that the key to success was teaching myself the three M's of trading—Mind, Method, and Money. I set a goal for myself to learn as much as possible in the shortest amount of time, balancing my understanding of all three. Like the legs of a camera tripod, I wanted each to be the same length rather than a combination of long and short legs that wouldn't stand up.

Since Dr. Elder placed great emphasis on record-keeping, I became deeply involved in developing the Trader's Organizer and Trader's Governor programs. Record-keeping felt like the least exciting part of trading for me. It did not begin to compare to the thrill of watching a live trade or playing with some new indicator that would unlock the secrets of technical analysis. It was like comparing the excitement of shopping with balancing your checkbook.

My greatest breakthrough in trading came when I realized that record-keeping, added to the three M's, completed the formula for successful trading. If the three M's defined what I needed to learn, then record-keeping defined how I could do it. It was the key to fully extending all three legs of the tripod.

The last thing I wanted to do at the end of the trading day was to create a diary entry for each of my trades. But when I reviewed my Trader's Diary, I was amazed at how clearly it portrayed "the good, the bad, and the ugly" of my psychology. Impulsive trades during market hours stuck out next to other trades that were well planned after the market close.

It became easy to determine how closely I was following my trading method. With the diary I could spot those times when I nervously and prematurely exited a trade without an exit signal or received a poor fill out of impatience instead of waiting for my planned entry price.

My advice to new traders is to learn all you can about the three M's and do it by diligently keeping good records. Thanks to that I am a better trader today than I was last year, and next year I will be a better trader than I am today!

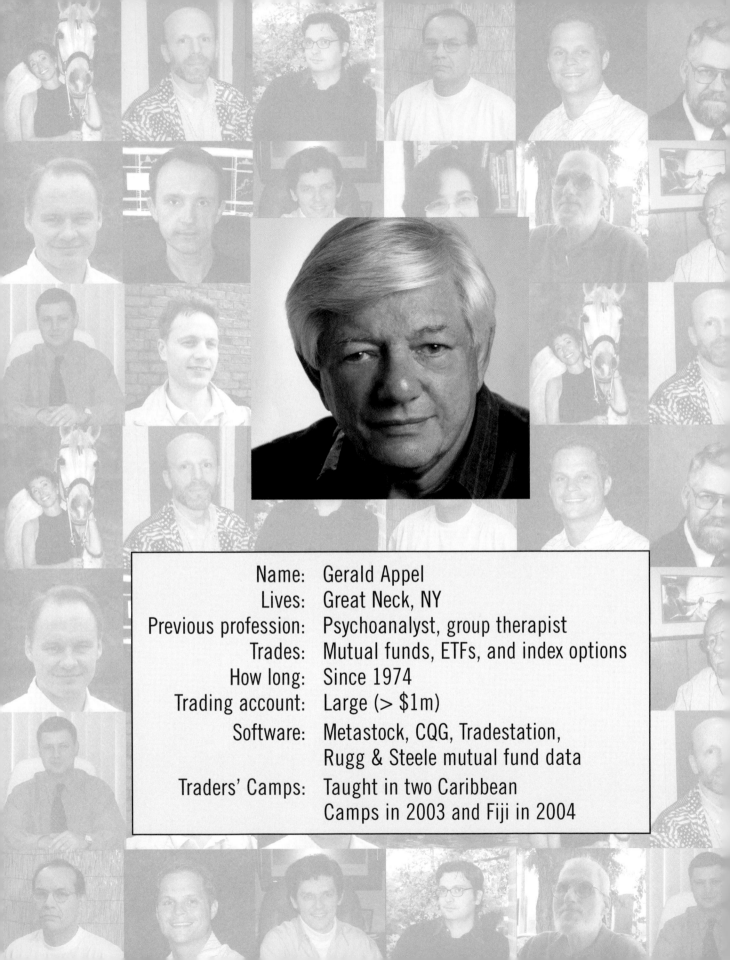

| | |
|---:|:---|
| Name: | Gerald Appel |
| Lives: | Great Neck, NY |
| Previous profession: | Psychoanalyst, group therapist |
| Trades: | Mutual funds, ETFs, and index options |
| How long: | Since 1974 |
| Trading account: | Large (> $1m) |
| Software: | Metastock, CQG, Tradestation, Rugg & Steele mutual fund data |
| Traders' Camps: | Taught in two Caribbean Camps in 2003 and Fiji in 2004 |

# CHAPTER 7

# GERALD APPEL

## LOOKING FOR FAVORABLE PROBABILITIES

When I entered the markets more than two decades ago, Gerald Appel was already an iconic figure in the field. An important money manager, the editor and publisher of *Systems and Forecasts* newsletter, and the author of several books, he became famous in the era of computerized technical analysis as the inventor of MACD. His Moving Average Convergence-Divergence indicator is now included in most software packages.

In 1989, when my company began producing some of the first videotapes for traders, I invited Appel to create a video on day-trading. We met in his private office, dominated by a partner's desk behind which he and his head trader, a very decisive woman, were trading stock indexes throughout our meeting. I returned with a video crew on a weekend, and what I learned on that day had a lasting impact on my own trading.

In 2002 I invited Appel to our Caribbean Camp as a guest instructor. He prepared for it obsessively, produced a handout the size of a book, but still appeared tense during his first session. Judy, his wife of over 40 years, his greatest cheerleader and an in-house critic, sat in the back of the room at every presentation and gave him feedback on audience reactions. As the week went on and Jerry realized how well he was being received, he began to enjoy himself more. He returned to another Caribbean Camp and in 2004 flew to our Pacific Camp in Fiji where he received star treatment from the group of Australians, New Zealanders, and Americans.

After Jerry agreed to be interviewed for this book, I took a train from Manhattan to Great Neck, an upscale suburb at the edge of the city where Jerry has his money management office. About 20 staff members worked in a large comfortable space. There were framed articles by and about Appel as well as photos taken by him—Jerry is an internationally recognized photographer. His private office had live screens on the desk, but the room was filled with African art, autographs of prominent people, and artifacts from his many travels.

> My father was a card player and he was addicted to the racetrack—he died broke, with me paying his rent. He worked as a cab driver until he was 78, but blew everything on horses. I will have no part in gambling, casinos, horses— the odds are against you. In the stock market I find probabilities that are favorable, but the casino and the racetrack have the odds stacked against you.
>
> My mother put four kids through college—and after the youngest of us graduated, she went to college herself, at the age of 65. She was an expert typ-

ist, a legal secretary, but she loved studying. After getting her college degree, she went to graduate school and kept going until the day she died at 73. She would come home from work, get on a bus, and go to college; she never complained. She was a terrific dancer. Judy and I take dancing lessons, but there is a big difference between taking lessons and being a dancer.

I am the oldest boy in the family, and I have an older sister. Both my brothers now work for me—one used to be a programmer for IBM, the other a middle manager for Lever Bros. I went to Brooklyn College, a free city school. To this day I very much appreciate that this country lets a poor kid like me become what he can be. I earned a state scholarship to graduate school, earned a degree in social work, trained in psychoanalysis, practiced for around 36 years. I taught, wrote articles, published, and supervised. All the while I operated this business, but kept the two pretty separate. About eight years ago, I phased out my practice completely.

In the mid-1960s I became interested in stock trading and got into the usual course of events. First you trust your stockbroker, then you realize he doesn't know what's up, then you look for advisory services, then you find they don't know what's up, and all the while you do a lot of reading and educate yourself in technical analysis. There was a magazine back in those days called *The Capitalist Reporter*—a tabloid, very schlocky, but with big circulation. One day they had an article on Malcolm Forbes, and I thought it was a character assassination. I wrote them that their article was the financial equivalent of *Screw* magazine, and if they wanted to see how to write articles, to tell me how much they were paying. They wrote back and asked me to write for them. Later I asked them, "How would you like to get a financial editor?" and they appointed me. For a while I was writing five articles under five names for every issue. They paid me and published my first book. I also wrote for other publications, but really enjoyed writing for those guys—they never changed a word. They did not mind me plugging a newsletter—so I started one—and then someone asked whether I would manage money. I started writing in '71 and got my first client in '73. He was with me until he passed away last year, and his daughter is still with me.

We started at the worst time, in the midst of the '73–'74 bear market, but we made money. I used to do a lot of convertible arbitrage in those years. I would go long a convertible bond and sell short shares in proportion to it, and whichever way they moved, we made money. We would pick up the interest and play the swings. Nowadays you do not see too many stock market derivatives getting out of whack. Before computers became available, there were more imbalances in the market. The game now is not what it used to be.

When options came out in 1973, premiums were much higher than today, and you could sell very safe options positions. Gradually the advantage disappeared as the market became much more efficient than it was in those days. In the beginning you could have 70–80% return if the stock stood still, but now you are lucky if you get 14–18%. Historically, when options are first introduced, they're overpriced.

Right now there is no special advantage to buyers or sellers of options. and there are two opposing views. One—let's buy them because they are cheap and the risk is small. The other—most options aren't exercised, so let's sell them and get the income. I think neither side is right or wrong. Buyers will make a lot of money a few times, sellers a little money many times, but in the end both will lose money to brokerage houses because of expenses. The markets are very efficient these days, and if there is an advantage, all the big houses have computers to look for it. Everybody deals against the handicap of the expense. In a rising market you can make a consistent profit by selling options but at a cost of lost opportunity. Options are good for flat or slowly falling markets.

I was one of the earliest people to begin timing mutual funds, starting in 1975. I had done a lot of research into timing models and concluded it was not difficult to create a system to outperform the market and keep risks low—if you could avoid getting hit by trading expenses. Trading costs and bid-ask spreads were higher in 1975. Say you did 20 trades a year with 1% average profit—this would compound to over 20% per year, but trading expenses would outweigh the advantages. If the costs were 0.5% per trade, they would eat up 10% per year.

**WHY WRITE A BOOK?**

Jerry mentioned that he occasionally finds useful ideas in other peoples' books, and I asked what motivated him to write. "I enjoy seeing my picture on book jackets," he laughed. "It's a good way to enhance your reputation. Sometimes you make money on a book. Get your ideas out into the world, leave a little of your imprint around. I have never lost anything by giving ideas away. If people find it useful, it makes me feel good." —*AE*

In the mid-'70s the funds introduced free telephone switching. They wanted to keep client money in-house when they went from stocks to cash, but they created a vehicle for my market timing models. FundPack was the first to allow phone switching—and I was one of their early investors, applying my timing models with no expense.

The funds had expenses, of course, but you just got a small share. I found that the instruments that reflected the entire market were more predictable than a single stock. I was timing market funds, basically trading without expenses. Gradually this became more popular, and by the mid-'90s funds became burdened by the amount of activity and started putting up restrictions.

The key strategy of my firm today is the selection of mutual funds, investing in the best, and timing our investments using models that are not as active as in earlier years but still active. An investor who only wants to buy and hold could do well with any number of mutual fund newsletters, such as *Morningstar*. What we add when he comes to us is the active management part in order to protect his capital when the market declines.

In developing systems I begin with a mental picture of how the market moves, based on my trading experience of almost 40 years. Most of the time the market moves sideways, but occasionally it breaks out and you can make money on such events once or twice a year. The idea is to create a timing model that automatically shifts from operating in a flat market to operating in a trending market.

We use a database of about 35 years—it is important to use as long a data stream as you can. Many beginners look at three years, but that is not enough. Ideally, you create a model on the first 10 years and go forward for the next 10 years to test it, then make adjustments and test on the next 10 years. You inevitably begin by making rules to fit the past—now you've got to test them going forward. You do it in segments, you play around with it.

Ninety-five percent of my own money is with the clients—what they get is what I get. I trade relatively little for my own account because I do not want to conflict with them, to be in a position where I am trading against my clients' holdings. By and large we do the same thing for all clients at the same time. My own accounts simply go where the clients go. We trade mutual funds on the close, ETFs and options usually towards the close.

It is one thing to create a timing model, another to live with it. Traders have to think of what is propelling them. The closer you sit to the screen, the more the issues of emotion and psychology come into the game. Watching the screen creates an urge to do something and a sense of constantly missed opportunities. Actually, you want to be much more selective—find a way to back off until the conditions you look for are there.

What is the direction of the significant trend? Is the minor trend in gear with it or are you trading against the tide? What are the triggers for entry? Are they in place? Are they confirmed by other signals?

A person should have a trading plan—almost any plan would be better than none. One should not trade because he feels scared today, or feels brave today, or missed a move yesterday. Take small losses. People hate to be wrong and want to be right, so they cash out too quickly. You need a plan of operation: This is what an entry is, this is what an exit is, this is what tells me I am wrong and need to get out quickly. You're not going to be right much more than 50% of the time, but if you keep your losses smaller than your wins, you'll come out ahead of the game.

After Jerry showed me two recent trades, I started getting ready to leave. His wife was not in the office that day. Jerry told me she normally dealt with all the personnel business, lawyers, and company finances. "She runs my life," he grinned. "But on Wednesdays she goes by train into the city to take a foreign policy course at New York University. She'll have lunch with our daughter, then go to a museum, I will come out later for dinner and theater and we'll come home together. Judy is a fantastic wife, I have been very fortunate." He walked me over to his son's office to say hello. Marvin had earned an MD and a PhD, becoming board-certified in anesthesiology, but he left medicine to work with his father. He has become one of the leading experts on exchange-traded funds and is writing a book on ETFs.

It began to rain, and Jerry insisted on giving me a ride to the station. We got into his high-performance BMW, and I was surprised that it had an automatic transmission. "I have a Porsche at home and it's also automatic—I always had stickshift cars but can't be bothered with them anymore. Also, I feel that a stickshift would be a liability in an emergency—it would slow down my response." He invited me to join him on an outing to a club, we shook hands, and I ran in the rain from the car to the station.

# TRADE 1 · JERRY'S ENTRY

**Upper pane:** Daily bar chart with a 21-day simple moving average and ± 4% trading bands
**Lower pane:** 12/25 MACD Lines

In March 2004 there was a good confluence of entry signals. The NASDAQ had moved below its 4% band—that was an extremely oversold condition. Even in a downtrend, you can make money buying below this band, but here we had several additional signals. Prices stopped accelerating down and entered back into the band. MACD had been oversold and turned up. A nice clean downtrend line across MACD peaks was being broken. Prices were tracing a downward wedge, with lines converging, which was a bullish sign. I bought the day MACD turned up and the wedge was being broken to the upside—everything was coming together to support the buy signal.

will this trade make or lose money?

# TRADE 1    JERRY'S EXIT

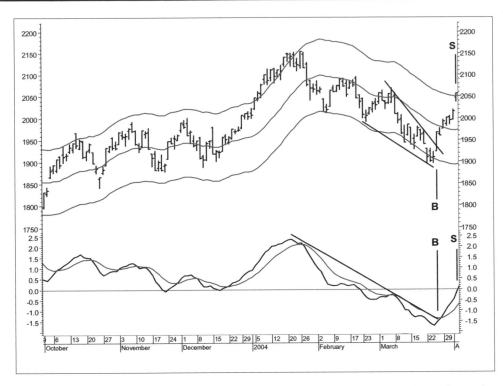

The rally was strong enough to carry to the upper channel. Since my view of the market at the time was basically neutral, I was not playing this for a major move but for a swing from the bottom band to the top band. I put in my sell order as the market approached the top band.

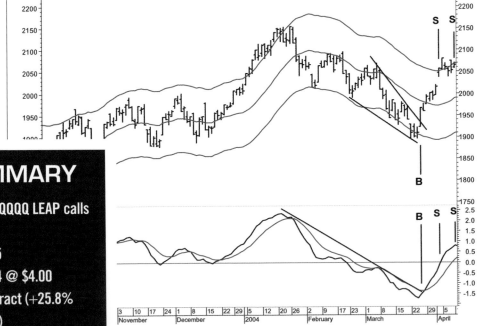

## TRADE SUMMARY

Long Jan 2005 strike 36 QQQQ LEAP calls

Bought 3/25/04 @ $3.16

Sold half 4/2/04 @ $3.95

Sold second half 4/12/04 @ $4.00

Profit = $0.815 per contract (+25.8%
   on the whole position)

I sold one half on the first move above the band and held the other half in case the rally kept going. The market turned up again but MACD began to weaken, its fast line turned down, and that's when I sold the second half. As it turned out, I got the best entry and the best exit for that little cycle.

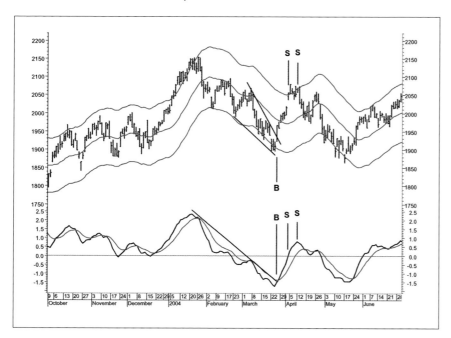

There was an interesting signal for a short sale in April as MACD was turning down, but I did not take it. Generally, the odds are not in favor of short sellers because the market has a long-term upward bias, except in a bear market. Being neutral overall made me less enthusiastic about shorting at this time.

## Study Time

I am an ophthalmologist, head of the department, and I have a question—what is the length of time I would need to master your knowledge?          —*Trader*

Some people catch on in a couple of years, other people never do. It takes more time, dedication, or humility than some possess. Your tuition, mostly in terms of losses, is likely to be as high as a medical school education. In the beginning, trading is a tremendous time-eater. Today you may be able to come to your office for a few hours and do competent work. Remember when you were a resident and the crazy hours you kept? How much you needed to learn then? That's what you'll need to replicate in your quest to become a competent trader.   —*AE*

# TRADE 1—ENTRY COMMENT

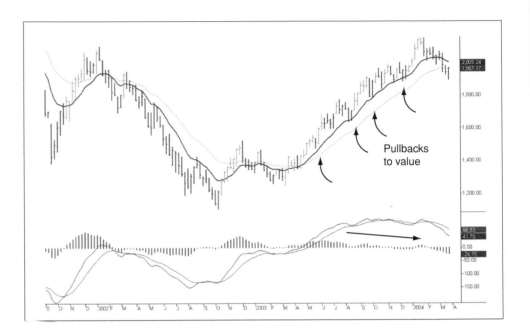

Stocks had a great year in 2003. The vicious bear market that drove prices down from their 1999–2000 peaks had overshot all reasonable targets and drove many stocks to ridiculously low levels. In 2003 they started popping up, like so many empty bottles pushed under water and released. The NASDAQ kept trending higher, with each shallow dip to its 13-week EMA presenting a buying opportunity.

The first deep reaction against this uptrend began in January 2004, driving prices below value, below their 26-week EMA. At the right edge of the chart there are signs that the decline is coming to an end: The latest weekly bar had closed near the top, leaving what looks like a tail pointing down; the decline of MACD-Histogram is flattening out. Still, the rightmost bar is red, meaning the Impulse system does not allow us to buy—not yet. Just as Jerry said, each trader needs a plan. He has his and I have mine; some days he is going to be ahead, and other days I will. You can work on improving your plan, but you should never change it in the middle of the game.

We can see on the daily chart that the decline from the January peak is losing steam; the bears are becoming weaker. Look at the deep bottom of MACD-Histogram in February and compare it with the much more shallow bottom in March. The rally in early March had lifted this indicator above its centerline, breaking the back of the bear; the latest decline is going on out of inertia, with no power behind it. Prices have been hugging the lower channel line, an undervalued area.

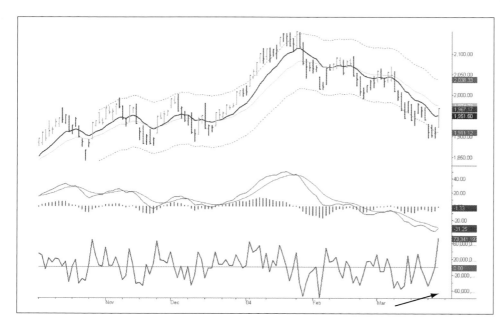

The sharp rally on the last day of the chart shows that the character of the market has changed. We see the tallest bar in several weeks, which shows a great level of conviction in this rally. The Force Index has shot up to its highest level for the year, showing that the bulls are extremely strong. It is very tempting to jump right in and buy, but my system tells me to wait until the weekly Impulse stops being red before I may go long.

# TRADE 1—EXIT COMMENT

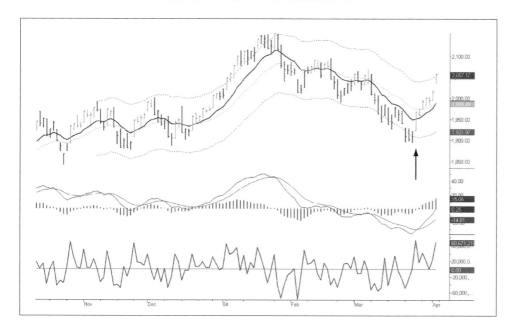

Jerry followed a very good entry with a brilliant exit, nailing profits on long positions at the upper channel line. His performance is a pleasure to watch, and reminds me once again of the impact his methods had on me a decade and a half ago.

At the right edge of the chart, MACD-Histogram is about as high as it ever gets in this market, with the Force Index also at its peak level. When prices penetrate the upper channel line, everything looks perfect to amateurs: "We have an upside breakout; let's buy!" That is precisely where a professional goes the other way and sells his longs to some optimistic late-comer.

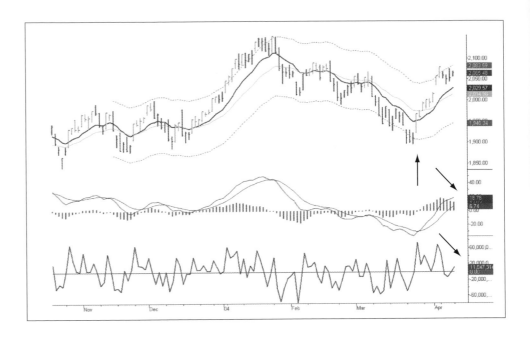

NASDAQ had risen to a new high the day after Jerry sold the first half of his position. There it stalled, unable to rise above the channel again, going nowhere fast. The Impulse system has turned from green to blue, telling us that the most dynamic part of the rally is over. At the right edge of the chart, the Force Index is tracing out a bearish divergence, warning us that the bulls are losing strength.

When Jerry sold the first half of his position, both prices and indicators seemed perfectly aligned to the upside; as a true professional, he saw trouble while prices were still on the way up. He sold the second half of his position after the market acted sloppy for a few days. This is where a semiprofessional trader should have recognized the rally was in trouble. The beginners are probably still asleep—they will sell their positions which were bought near the top only after prices fall to the bottom.

One of the key differences between professionals and amateurs is the speed with which they recognize market signals and react to them. A beginner usually waits for a clear signal to emerge, for a breakout to fail, for an indicator to turn around. By the time a turnaround is clearly confirmed, the new trend is already underway. A professional sees his patterns and indicators starting to come together and acts without waiting for total clarity. This ability to act in an atmosphere of uncertainty is a hallmark of a professional trader.

*Jerry shared his views:* Historically, speculative bubbles take a decade or more to resolve. In Japan the bubble ended in 1989, and the country just started to climb out from under the rubble in 2004. It took the United States two decades after the 1929 bubble. Gold had its bubble in the 1980s and it still has not recovered. What tends to happen after a bubble is that you get a decade of relatively quiet, below-average performance. But keep in mind that five years have already passed since the peak of 2000, during which the stock market had a net decline. Once the market hits a bottom, it will have an upward slant, like the one that followed the bottom in 1932. We have already paid a lot of dues for the excesses of the 1990s. I see stocks being about fairly valued today, neither overvalued nor undervalued. The S&P price/earnings ratio was 40 at the top; 16 is the historical norm, and now it is 19. There is room for the market to go up somewhat and down somewhat, nothing dramatic, but it can finish this decade much better than it started. I do not see a runaway market, nor do I see a collapse. The Bush administration is doing everything to support the market—all those changes in the tax code, reduction of taxes on dividends, and other business incentives, from chopping down forests to everything else—it is a very pro-business administration. Even the movement to privatize Social Security—you can imagine the extra demand for stocks built into that, a predictable and forced demand. People will have to put money into balanced mutual funds.

**WHERE ARE WE TODAY?**

# TRADE 2 | JERRY'S ENTRY

This is a bleak trade; I am not proud of it. I decided to short the market because it had recently broken below its support level. It had rallied from below the bottom band, above the moving average, and into the area that used to offer support but has now turned into resistance. At the first sign that the market was turning down from its resistance, I bought puts—partly to hedge the fund portfolio and partly as a trade in its own right.

Will this trade make or lose money?

# TRADE 2 | JERRY'S EXIT

At the opening the next day, my trade showed profit and I closed out half of my position. I often do that, since it takes the pressure off the rest of the position (see also Chapter 3).

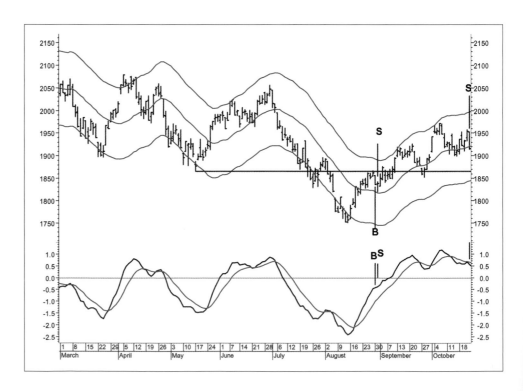

I had a big problem—no exit plan in case the trade went wrong. This position would normally be stopped out as soon as prices made a new recovery high. Lots of things were not in gear, unlike the other trade. MACD was actually rising—by shorting I was fighting a rising MACD even though it looked as though it was weakening—the lines were narrowing—at the moment of the trade. The other trade had several factors in its favor, this one only two—its chart pattern and the resistance. As soon as that resistance was penetrated, this short should have been immediately covered. Why didn't I do it? I was still committed to a bearish outlook and instead of seeing what was happening, I was thinking about what should happen. The most you can ever say about the future is the probability of what may happen. The best timing models rarely exceed a 55% success rate. You have to respond quickly to contain your losses. You have to ask yourself: "What's going to prove me wrong and how will I respond?"

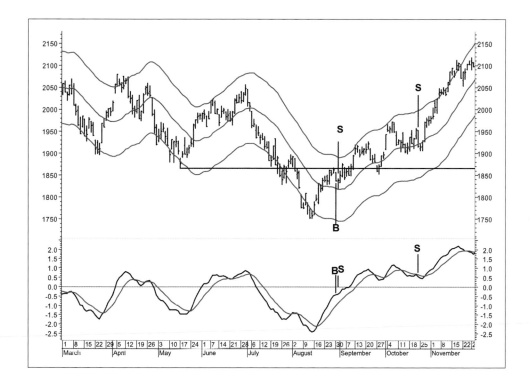

I had another chance to cover, missed that, sat through another rally, and finally called it a day—not at the worst place but hardly the best. What I had here was a trade based primarily on a support/resistance line. Once that line was broken and stopped being an operative factor, I should have responded much faster.

**TRADE SUMMARY**

Long January 2006 strike 32 QQQQ LEAP puts
Bought 8/30/04 @ $2.90
Sold half 8/31/04 @ $3.05
Sold second half 10/22/04 @ $1.70
Loss = $0.525 per contract
    –18.2% on whole position

# TRADE 2—ENTRY COMMENT

At the right edge of the weekly chart, both moving averages are declining, confirming the downtrend. MACD-Histogram hangs heavily below its centerline but is attempting to rally, turning the Impulse system blue. This color does not prohibit us from either buying or selling.

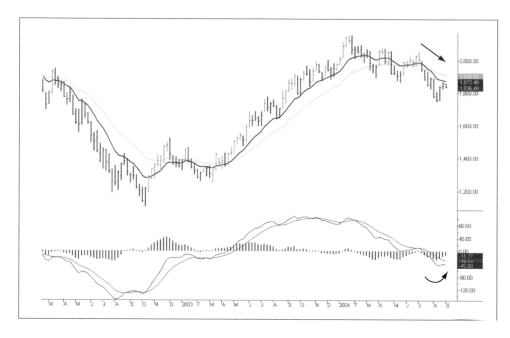

If 2003 was a sweet year for stock traders, 2004 was a bitter one. There were many sharp reversals throughout the year, with few sustainable trends. The stock market fell to a new low prior to the presidential election, making it reasonable to expect that the brief bull market of 2003 was over and a bear market had begun. When prices rallied back towards May lows in September, we could interpret that as the first pullback within a bear market prior to the next downleg.

The daily chart of Nasdaq is sending mixed messages. There is a strong bullish divergence between the August and September bottoms. During the August rally, the histogram rose to its highest level in months, signaling strength. On the other hand, the August rally was accompanied by a broad bearish divergence of the Force Index, a definite sign of weakness. The Impulse system has switched from green to blue at the right edge and therefore no longer prohibits shorting. Still, with the weekly chart neutral, I find myself squinting at the daily chart: "on the one hand, on the other hand..." With the weekly chart unhelpful in making a strategic decision, I would be inclined to stand aside.

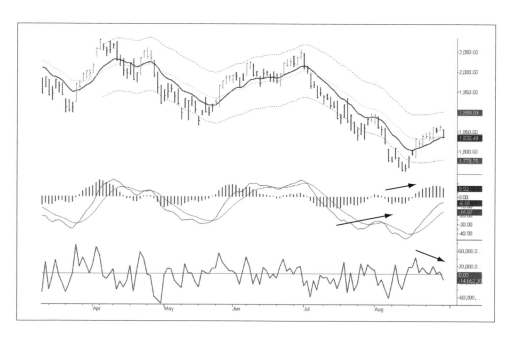

# TRADE 2—EXIT COMMENT

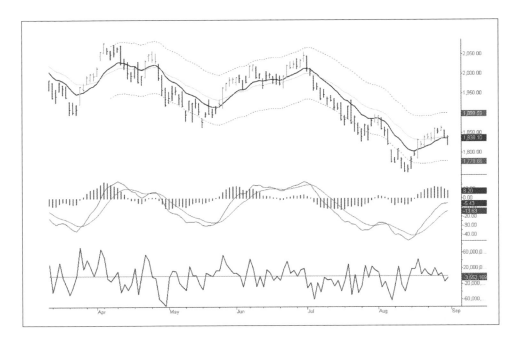

Here, as in the previous trade, Jerry takes advantage of a price spurt in his favor and grabs a quick profit on one-half of his position. Much of what professionals do deals with limiting risks—and taking a chunk of profit early in the game certainly helps set a trade on the right track.

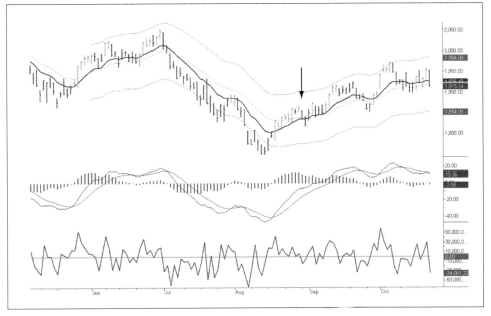

*This short should have been closed out after the market rallied above its July low, leaving behind a false downside breakout. The Impulse system told us to cover after the weekly turned green soon after the short entry, on Friday, September 10, 2004. Jerry missed an opportunity to cover with a minimal loss in September, but when he finally bit the bullet, he did it masterly, covering during a decline rather than throwing in the towel near the highs.*

Traders often beat themselves over the head for their mistakes. They may find it reassuring to know that even a top pro occasionally makes fairly basic errors. Jerry's bearish prejudice led him to stay with his short trade way too long before he cut his losses.

# ACT EARLY OR LATE?

The market does not try to ambush or surprise you—it usually gives plenty of warning before it moves, but its signals tend to be quiet and subtle. Think of the signals a baseball catcher makes to his pitcher. He does not wave his fingers in the air to get attention, but makes signs visible only to a trained eye. The signals are definitely there amidst the noise and the shouting in the grandstands, and you have to learn to recognize them.

Jerry follows chart patterns and indicator signals but also has a tremendous intuitive feel for the markets. Before you rush to imitate him, keep in mind that he started out like most of us, listening to brokers and advisors, taking bad advice and losing money. Jerry survived the stage of initial ignorance by quickly cutting his losses. One of the key lessons he teaches us is that you must survive in order to succeed. Paradoxically, Jerry's abhorrence of losses stems from the sad example of his father. Rejecting that path was at the root of his success.

Jerry has acquired one of the best track records in the money management business but still occasionally makes mistakes and finds himself in losing trades. Whenever he has an open loss on his hands, he knows how to dance his way out of trouble with minimal damage. If you have no plan for getting out of trouble, you have no business being in a trade.

The simplest way to keep out of major trouble is to use stops. You may place a "hard stop" order at a specific level with your broker. Alternatively, you may use a "soft stop" and rely on indicator signals or personal judgment of the market. A beginner needs hard stops—only remember not to place them at the obvious levels. An experienced trader like Jerry is more likely to use soft stops. He knows that his trade is in trouble, and it is time to cut and run without setting a specific escape level.

What both hard and soft stops have in common is a cold determination to cut and run if a trade goes against you. You must be absolutely ready to cut your losses before they cut your account—shove a pistol into the ear of a bad trade and pull the trigger.

While Jerry and other highly experienced traders function on a somewhat intuitive level, a beginning trader has no right to intuition. When a beginner gets the feeling that a market is going to move a certain way, it is usually not an intuition but merely an itch, an attack of gas, or an urge to act. The best thing that a beginner with "an intuition" can do is lie down and wait until the feeling passes. A beginner needs to have a list of clearly defined signals and a matching list of strictly defined actions. I sometimes say to my students: A beginner has no right to intuition until he or she has traded successfully for 18 months.

*An e-mail from Jerry:*

## CALM, RELAXED, AND REASONABLY CONFIDENT

I've just finished reading—maybe for the fifth or sixth time—Alex's summary of our meeting. It was a little strange, actually, to see myself described in print that way. He certainly did get it right. By then, my thoughts began to wander to what makes me trade well when I am trading well, and to what makes me trade badly when I'm trading badly—which does, unfortunately, happen from time to time.

It is similar to playing golf or tennis. When I play well and trade well, I'm playing and trading with a certain confidence—not grandiosity—just quiet confidence. It is nice when

I succeed, but OK if I don't. I think I'm going to be right, but the stock market is often not that predictable, and I could be right in my technique and planning and still have a losing trade. The same way I can sometimes hit a tennis or golf ball just a little long, with just a little slice. The trick is to stay calm, relaxed—being relaxed is very big in tennis and golf—and reasonably confident, while maintaining realistic goals (I definitely do not drive 300 yards, and the harder I try, the worse it gets).

My athletic ability, such as it is, sometimes drops rapidly—usually when I become too confident, or try too hard, or set unrealistic goals, losing my relaxed rhythm. If as a result of this drop I lose my confidence and try a series of corrections to fix things, they further interfere with my swing, and I end up becoming tense and pessimistic. Matters do not get fixed until I find the sense and time to back off, go back to basics, and concentrate more on my attitude and feelings than anything else.

Trading is similar to that. A number of winners in a row, which usually takes place in a nicely trending or cyclical market, can feed greed, and perhaps even worse, those illusions of control, omniscience, and magic that often drive traders as much as the wish to support themselves financially through trading. Trying to trade every minor swing is like trying to serve an ace in tennis every time, often with the same poor result.

Similarly, a few losses, whatever caused them, can lead to self-doubt, fear of further loss, stiffness, and, at times, almost paralysis. At such times I can feel myself entering into trading positions late and too ready to close them prematurely. Sometimes on a bad trading day, I may duck out of making any decisions at all.

The solution is the same as in sports. I have to back off, return to the basics, think more about myself and less about the market, try to get back into a relaxed frame of mind and back into the game. This is easier said than done but definitely possible.

As I write this in early May 2005, the stock market has just completed a string of about ten days in which the direction of prices reversed each and every day—up, down, up, down, sometimes by a lot, sometimes by a little. The bull market that started in the fall of 2002 seems barely alive.

Patterns of price movement in the stock market have clearly changed since the onset of the great bear market in March 2000. For example, day-to-day trendiness—the tendency of the stock market to do tomorrow what it does today—has vanished. The Nasdaq Composite, the most trendy of market indices, has become more likely to reverse direction from day to day than to continue in the same direction.

These changes have had a significant impact on many stock market timing models. Time horizons for active stock traders have shortened. With price trends vacillating daily, online short-term trading has come to dominate price movement on many days. With so many traders watching the same screens, often the same indicators, and using computers to enter orders, the pace of the stock market has quickened. The short-term trading game has become both more crowded and more difficult.

Contrary to that, longer-term technical patterns appear to have retained their significance. Time cycles, measures of market momentum, moving average trading channels, MACD, RSI, interest rates, earnings, and other influences and reflections of the stock market remain influential. I have learned to place greater emphasis on the relative strength of market sectors, portfolio diversification and balance, mutual fund and ETF selection—which is, I trust, a more sophisticated approach to what to buy as well as when to buy and sell.

The times change, the stock market changes, and investment strategies are likely to have to change as a result. Traders should remain relaxed, balanced, and as objective as possible. They should also remain flexible, able to recognize changes in the investment markets, and to respond to them. This can be quite demanding, but it is also very stimulating. I think this keeps me young.

My best wishes to all for good trading.

| | |
|---|---|
| Name: | Michael Brenke |
| Lives: | Charlotte, NC |
| Previous profession: | Business owner |
| Trades: | Stocks |
| How long: | Since 1995 |
| Trading account: | Small (< $250k) |
| Software: | MetaStock, eSignal, Quicken |
| Traders' Camp: | Caribbean Camp in 1998 |

# CHAPTER 8

# MICHAEL BRENKE

## TO KEEP REPEATING WHAT I DID RIGHT

I met Michael in one of our first Caribbean Camps, in 1998 in the Dominican Republic. We lost contact for several years, but in early 2004 a recent camper looking for help with trading software connected with him, and a few months later both men flew to a campers' meeting in New York. I was pleased to hear that Michael had become a full-time trader and invited him for an interview. He timed his return to New York to attend another campers' meeting, and the next morning we sat down to talk about trading.

I was born in Greenville, Tennessee, but had my parents waited a few months I would have been born in Germany. I visit there often and like it there, but moving is out of the question—Kimberly wants us to live close to her parents.

My original career choice was photography—I took pictures for the yearbooks in high school, but then decided to do something else. I thought most photographers were starving artists; I wanted to get rich quicker and enjoy photography as a hobby. That and travel are the most fun things for me.

I never went to college—that was my choice. I read about the Hunts of Texas, how they had minimal education but were great in business. I had all these ideas on how to make money. My first plan was to get into high-end house painting—I could see myself hiring a bigger crew, getting into real estate—but painting was too hard. I moved from Asheville, a small sleepy town, to Charlotte—it had a big skyline, big clubs. I bartended—it's a great job when you're 21, they play music you like, and everyone is happy.

Then I tried to import car polishing cloth from Germany. It is very popular there, you see it at every gas station, but here it was a tough sell. I enjoyed the creative part of business—taking pictures, designing the label—but did not know marketing. I was doing business with a few mom-and-pop stores, but did not have connections to get into big stores. To get a product out you have to go to the major retailers, such as Sears, but big buyers do not buy just one item from a supplier. I recently calculated that I still have a 1,200-year supply for my car in a mini-warehouse.

I learned a valuable lesson—don't get into a business unless you know the industry. In house painting I did my research and was profitable from day one, but here I broke all the rules. Then, after hearing about the damage to new cars from acid rain and a new paint sealant to protect them, I started EuroShine. I thought it was a big million-dollar idea and committed every last penny to it. I ran the company for 11 years and graduated from distributing others' products to making my own, having my own line of chemicals.

I first heard about trading from a former girlfriend. She was studying accounting and asked, "Why don't you do something with your savings?" I bought LTV at 10, a few weeks later sold it for 12, and was hooked. In the mid-90s I was running my business but wanted to be in control of my financial future. You do not get that from business because you have 30 to 40 bosses at once—your big customers, suppliers, employees—they all have fingers in your future, you depend on them. I wanted to become my sole boss and get paid exactly what I was worth. One day I spoke about trading with Kimberly, then went to take out the trash, and on the way back checked the mailbox—there was a postcard for *Trading for a Living*. It all came together within the same 10 minutes—I realized the business was not going to give me what I wanted, and suddenly there was this postcard. A couple of days later I ordered the book, and when it arrived, it was signed. I never had a signed book before and called a couple of friends.

I made the same mistakes as everybody else who gets into trading with big dollar signs in front of my eyes. I had about $20,000 saved and thought I would turn that into a million in two years—take 20 good stocks and wait for the right patterns, like printing money with my computer. And I fell into another beginner trap—thinking the more information I had, the better trader I'd become. I subscribed to several expensive fundamental data services, a chat room, and was running around with a Quotrek FM receiver with a little antenna. I spent too much on the information—almost $3,500 a year, as if more tools would make me a better trader.

The market has a very quick way of letting you know how good or bad you are. I had this big realization that took a long time to get—if I got paid for paper-trading, I'd be a multimillionaire. But with real money, it was a different story. It was easy on paper, but in the markets there was this fear of losing money, pulling the trigger, and greed. My big fear was losing money. Money I saved from my chemical business created a window of opportunity. I hated that business by then, but with every loss my window closed a little.

This fear of losing money held me back for a long time. You paper-trade five or six times, have good trades, then stretch the rules and get in—and that trade turns out a loser. You go back to paper-trading and have five or six winners, then back to trading real money and losing. It was an emotional roller-coaster—you feel brilliant, then make a bad trade and feel like such an idiot. Your mind plays tricks, and you do not see the warning signs.

Had I stuck to my own trading rules, I would have made money, but instead I struggled for several years, unable to break out of the rut I was in, like in that movie *Groundhog Day*. I was slowly becoming more organized, started keeping a log. What saved me during that time was sticking to the 2% Rule— I actually reduced it to 1%, and after a few losses to 0.5%. I was losing less than 10% a year. I would not have survived without that rule.

I did not think much about psychology, did not believe it mattered. I thought that you see a good chart pattern and go. Trading did not begin making sense to me until I started noticing my own patterns. You can know what to do—be an expert on patterns, on designing systems—but be unable to do what needs to be done when it comes to real money. I would never have believed it. Take chemicals—there is a way to blend them, and that's how you do it—day in, day out. Or carpentry—you would not say, "I know how to build it, but let me build it differently." If you do the same with trading, the results are automatic. Some of the guys who write books cannot do it, cannot handle risks with their own money. If you do not have the psychological strength to stand the risk, you cannot trade.

I was like a hamster in a wheel and did not begin to change until I started printing every chart and marking it. At the end of the month I'd go back and make notes on my mistakes. After a while, I'd see a pattern—the same mistake over and over. I nailed a big piece of foam matting to the wall and put the examples of perfect trades there. I would see a pattern on the screen, then look at my board—is it a clean pattern, not too many long tails? I made a list of the most common mistakes and put that checklist next to the monitor, all these little rules based on past mistakes. If everything lined up visually as well as on the checklist, I would place my trade and that started to help.

Your advice on the 2% saved me. You also talked of creating a journal. I started looking at trading more like a business—wrote a mission statement and a business plan. In the beginning, if I could not find a pattern for a while, I'd look for another pattern, very disorganized. I started writing notes at the end of each day on the trades I made or missed. At the end of each week, I would write "What I learned this week." It was a huge help to see patterns in my trading—what I was doing right and wrong—especially after losing on a day when I should have been making money. I started looking at past trades, putting all the charts together to see what trades I had made and which ones I should have made. I always print charts of the S&P in all timeframes. I really credit my turnaround to looking at past trades, making notes, and reviewing them to come up with rules for future trades. Before that, I could be going long on the dailies without knowing that a weekly was having a huge bearish divergence.

Everything just slowly evolved. Last year I created my own trading manual. I got the idea after hearing Kimberly talk about her job. In her bank they have documents outlining different procedures for her department. Fred, with whom I came to the campers' meeting, is an airline pilot; he told me they use printed checklists in the cockpit.

I condensed my manual to 10 pages. I start the day by looking at the S&P. If the market is at a turning point, which is where I like to trade, I start scanning stocks—first weekly, then daily charts. I have 200 stocks to review and I look to see whether they are in sync, turning in the same direction. If I find something, I go to the page where I have my rules for swing trading. I have four or five patterns and several rules, such as "Do not hold a swing trade over an earnings announcement." I go to Yahoo to check earnings dates, and if it is within one week, I stay away. Occasionally this rule bites me and I miss a good trade, but the risk of a huge downward gap is not worth it. If everything passes my second sheet, I go to the third.

At the next page I set up money management. The better I'm doing, the closer to the 2% risk I raise my size. If I am on a roll, I'll raise it to 1 or 1.5%, but after three losing trades in a row, I go back to 0.5%. I never hit the 6% monthly limit. At the next page I set up my alerts in MetaStock. I prefer to enter orders after the open to avoid gaps. Also, if the hourly charts show a huge divergence against my planned trade, that's a no-go.

The other part of my manual is for day-trading. I always stay in sync with the S&P. Everything is written out step by step—how to track hourly, 25-minute, and 5-minute charts. All the rules are spelled out—what patterns to look for when the hourly is oversold or overbought, same for the 25-minute and even the 5-minute chart.

---

**MONEY NEVER SLEEPS**

*Michael says:* During the day, the house feels quiet and isolated. It is easy to become distracted or bored, especially when there hasn't been a trade for two or three days. You can start watching TV or go grab a bite to eat and suddenly you've missed a perfect pattern—your sandwich cost you $400. I find all these little weaknesses, attention deficit maybe, so I plug them up to avoid missing a perfectly good trade. To deal with the distractions on slow days, I created an alert in MetaStock to remind me when it is time to scan for setups.

I got this audio.wav file from the movie *Wall Street*: The phone rings and Gordon Gekko says, "Money never sleeps, pal; this is your wakeup call, go to work." I attached it to my five-minute S&P chart, and it goes off at the start of every bar. If the S&P is at a turning point, I go to work, otherwise I ignore it until it goes off again five minutes later.

---

Even with day-trading, I quickly go through the sheets in my manual—first, the list of patterns, then the second page with the rules, such as "Always use limit orders to get in and market orders to get out." These are all based on past trades that went wrong. My goal is to continuously repeat what I did right, and follow my manual leads to more consistent trading.

No rule can make you place the trade; you've got to have the nerve to pull the trigger. If a stock looks almost perfect but something is missing, walk away and do not beat yourself up if it turns out to have been a good trade.

The last sheet in my manual is on how to close the day: Enter the trade into Quicken, put it in a notebook, and write a little note to finish the process. Once you get into the habit, it is not much work, taking five minutes a day. I kick myself that I did not start doing this five or six years earlier; I would have done much better, discovered mistakes earlier.

Right now the big thing for me is to be consistent. My manual is now complete after a year. The goal is to be as robotic as possible, follow the manual day by day, manage the risk, and be very consistent. Not missing anything is hard—when the market stays choppy for a few days, your attention lapses. Then the market traces a clear pattern, but if you miss one day in swing trading, the entire month can be shot. The market turns and now you have to chase the trend—I never do that, it is too risky.

In the morning I get my coffee, turn on my monitor, get the manual, and go through the steps. I treat it like a business—arrive in the morning, turn on the lights, call the customers. It can be a very boring routine, especially when volatility is very low, and I can spend days without finding any setups to trade. Doing both swing-trading and day-trading keeps me more alert, even though that .wav file sometimes drives me crazy.

In day-trading you have to stay on your toes; if you're not there within seconds, you'll miss it. I'm trading for 20-cent moves and risking 10 cents. If I am 5 cents late, that trade is not worth taking: It is not worth risking 15 cents to make 15. Some days are very boring, others exciting. When it gets too exciting, when the heart starts pumping, something is wrong; do not take that trade, step outside for a bit of fresh air. I only trade well when I do not feel excited, elated, or fearful—Mark Douglas calls it being "in the zone." Becoming excited is usually a bad sign.

You've seen *Star Trek* and know how Vulcans are—logical, no fear, no excitement, stay very cool, very calm. I once joined a day-trading room at a brokerage firm. The manager pointed out a guy and said, "He is our best trader and the dullest personality." Of course you want to make money, but you have to treat it like playing a video game for points. To be successful in trading, you have to reprogram yourself—get rid of greed and fear, become as close to a robot as possible. For me this has been the hardest part of trading; it's very hard to detach yourself from the money and think of it as points in a game.

There is a non-glamorous side to trading—isolation, no coworkers, being cut off from people. You do not meet new people like everybody else, through school or work. People who go to work, pay for dry cleaning their business clothes, and sit in traffic may envy you, but you have to make a much bigger effort to get out and about. The way you look at money really changes. You think of spending $25,000 to buy a car, but then ask, "How much income will I lose? Is that car worth the loss of income?"

I am in the house all week; all I do is trade, sleep, and exercise. I need to get out. I want to get into fencing—meet people and do a sport that's fast and aggressive and may help with trading to some degree. I may take photography classes. My next step is to get my life back on track, to have a life; otherwise you burn out no matter how much you enjoy trading. On Fridays I wonder, "Bummer, what am I going to do for the next two days?" But on Sunday nights I feel excited. If I start dreading Mondays, I'm in trouble.

Kimberly is waiting quietly but nervously; she is not comfortable with the risk but trusts me and is very supportive. If your wife is not supportive, forget it. You have your own demons, and if your wife adds to that, you definitely need to make some adjustments—stop trading or the other way. The pressure against you sabotages trading. Having another source of income helps while you're learning to trade. The less pressure you have, the more likely you are to do well.

# TRADE 1 | MICHAEL'S ENTRY

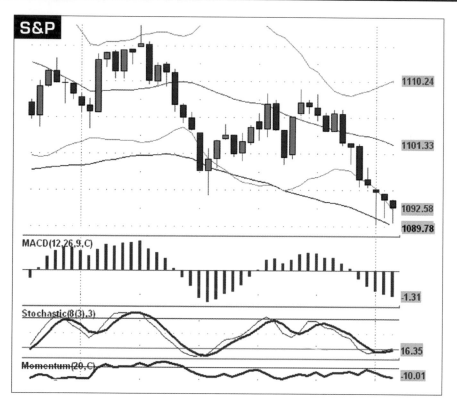

**Upper pane:** Hourly candlestick chart with two sets of Bollinger bands using default settings (20-MA with 2.0 standard deviation). Light grey hourly, dark grey daily bands. Red line—20-bar simple moving average. All my MAs are simple—after missing several trades with EMAs, I experimented with simple MAs and stayed with them.
**Second pane:** MACD-Histogram, 12-26-9
**Third pane:** Stochastic, 8-3-3
**Fourth pane:** Momentum, 20 bars

## YHOO

I look for day-trades by tracking the S&P—first the hourly, then the five-minute chart. If they give me a signal, I toggle through my list of 26 day-trading stocks to find the one whose pattern is the closest to the S&P to put on a trade.

The hourly S&P looks like it is at a turning point. It is oversold, with a double bottom at the lower Bollinger band. Stochastic is oversold, MACD-Histogram does not have a perfect positive divergence but is still diverging a bit. Conclusion—S&P may be at a turning point.

The five-minute chart shows a double bottom into the lower Bollinger band. It is not a perfect bottom—the closings on the two lows are not exactly the same. If the second low is the same or lower than the first, that divergence is good. If it is higher, that could be bad—the win/loss ratio is not so good on those trades. I am overlooking that and letting it slide because the hourly looks so good.

Stochastic is also oversold and making a higher low than at the previous low. MACD-Histogram looks like what I want to see in a divergence. When the amount by which it drops below the zero line is less than the amount by which it went above that line, I consider that a strong divergence. Momentum confirms this divergence—you do not have to squint to see it. After seeing these two charts, I decided that the market was at a turning point.

My day-trading list has 26 stocks, arranged alphabetically. I toggle through them to find the one whose pattern is the same as the S&P. I trade stocks rather than ETFs, SPY, or DIA because they are too expensive and do not run as far as stocks with the same patterns.

That day the last stock on the list was YHOO, and it almost identically matched the market, bar by bar. On the five-minute chart prices were hitting the lower Bollinger band, Stochastic was oversold, MACD had a nice divergence. It came up high and did not even drop below its zero line. The momentum confirmed the bottom, and I entered a limit order one cent above the high of the last bar, at 34.70. My stop was at 34.58.

Will this trade make or lose money?

# TRADE 1   MICHAEL'S EXIT

My target was at 35.20, near the old high; the hourly MA was just above that level, a potential resistance area. The stock fluctuated after I entered and my heart started beating, but the stock took off. After it made my normal 20-cent run, I deviated from the plan and sold half. I did this even though double bottoms on hourly charts tend to produce better runs than just five-minute double bottoms.

I wanted to hold the other half until it hit my target of 35.20. At 35.10 it started stalling, the next bar could not go above the previous bar, and that's where my emotions got in.

*Michael explains:*   I have two accounts—about three-quarters of my money is in swing-trading, the rest in a day-trading account. I keep comparing their profitability—weekly P/L, fees, net P/L. I also grade both accounts. Say there were five double tops in my universe of trades, but I saw and traded only three—I compare the number of setups that the market presented and the number I traded. Maybe I didn't trade because I got to the computer late or was a little nervous, a little squirrelly. Each pattern has a name, and I want to see whether I'm doing the best job by catching every pattern. Some months are terrible; I catch only a half or a third of patterns. If there are 12 patterns per month, then my traded score should be 12, with the same win/loss ratio. Some things could not be helped—a dental appointment or the DSL was down, but that's what I'd consider a perfect month. The fact that I made a decent profit is not enough—I've got to have a perfect score.

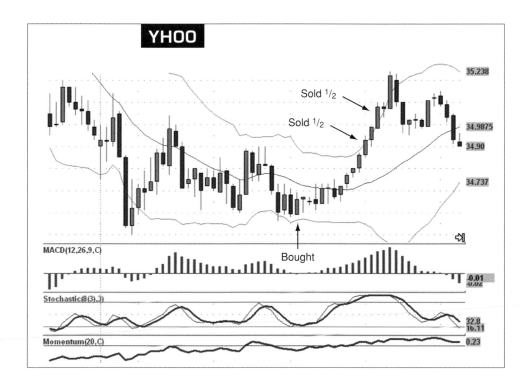

I was kicking myself for not holding the entire position which would have made it my best trade in months. I felt nervous about a reversal, chickened out, and got out of the trade early at 35.05. It felt almost like a conspiracy of other traders who waited for me to get out—as soon as I sold, they hit my target. Had I held, it would have been a $1,000 day in less than an hour. It was a bittersweet trade.

## TRADE SUMMARY

Long YHOO
Bought 10/25/2004 @ $34.72
Sold first half @ $34.92—profit $0.20 per share
Sold second half @ $35.05—profit $0.33 per share
Position profit = $0.265 per share

# TRADE 1—ENTRY COMMENT

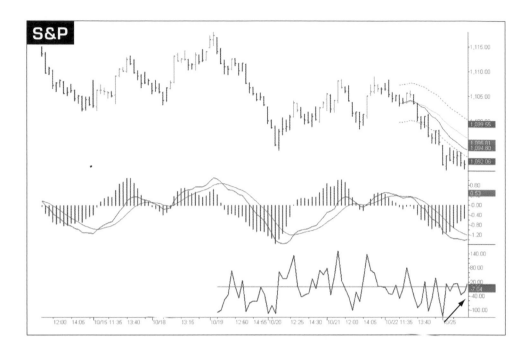

Michael makes his decisions to enter trades on the index charts and implements them in individual stocks. I prefer to take each instrument individually—if the indexes give me a signal, I'll trade index futures, and if a stock gives me a signal, I will trade that stock. Clearly, the markets are interrelated, and I have to keep an eye on one while trading the other, but ultimately each decision is separate. I am not suggesting that my approach is right and Michael's is wrong—far be it from me to criticize the method of a successful trader! Markets are huge and complex, and serious people can approach them from different angles.

I will follow in Michael's footsteps as I review this trade, looking at the indexes before turning to individual stocks. I will use the 25-minute and 5-minute charts because the Rule of Five, first articulated in *Trading for a Living*, states that charts in multiple timeframes should be related to each other by a factor of five. I think that 60-minute and 5-minute charts are a little too far apart.

On the 25-minute chart the Impulse system is blue, allowing us to go either long or short. On the plus side, prices are in the undervalued zone below the lower channel line. They have broken below the low that occurred three days earlier, and their decline appears to have stalled, reminding us to "buy new lows and sell new highs." There is a bit of a bullish divergence in the Force Index. On the minus side, both moving averages are still trending down. Overall, this 25-minute chart of the S&P does not look terribly exciting, but it is more of a buy than a sell.

The 5-minute of the S&P shows that the previous day was a "trend day," with prices declining all day long in an orderly step-like pattern. Today prices opened sharply below the previous day's low, shaking out weak holders. Bears could not follow through on their gains, and prices had stalled. There is a clear bullish divergence not only of MACD-Histogram but also of MACD lines, which we see less often. The 5-minute chart confirms the message of

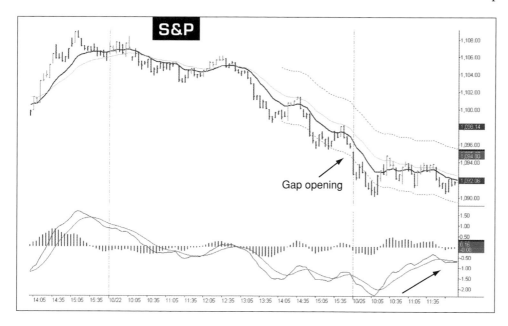

the 25-minute chart—the bears are exhausted, and in a two-party system this means that the bulls are ready to grab control. The likelihood of a rally is much greater than the risk of a downside move. If one is to trade this market, one has to look at the long side.

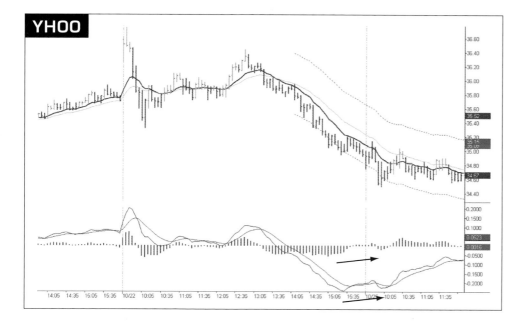

Michael is quite right in saying that the pattern of this 5-minute chart of YHOO almost perfectly tracks the pattern of the S&P. The stalled decline and the bullish divergences point out that a rally is much more likely than a decline. At the right edge, the Impulse system has just shifted from red to blue, removing its prohibition against buying and allowing us to go long. This final signal tells us there is nothing else to wait for—if you're bullish, now is the time to put on a trade!

# TRADE 1—EXIT COMMENT

Michael is a very cautious trader, steadily grinding out small profits from his day-trades. Someone who likes to trade larger swings might have wanted to hold his position a little longer. At the right edge of the chart prices are starting to accelerate to the upside, with bars becoming longer and rising at a steeper angle. MACD-Histogram is also rising, confirming the rally, without a single downtick, and it has not yet become extreme. MACD lines have just crossed above zero, still at a relatively low level, indicating plenty of room overhead. Prices are nowhere near the overvalued zone at the upper channel line. There is nothing wrong with taking profits on half the position, just as Michael did, nor would there have been anything wrong with holding a little longer.

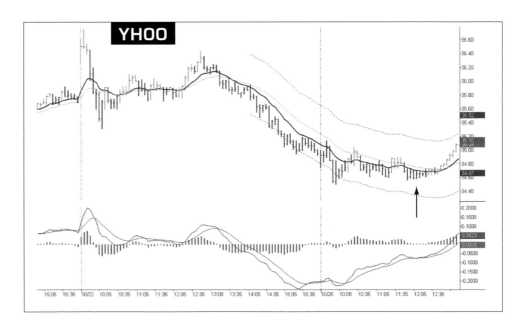

Michael takes profits on the second half of his position in anticipation of future weakness, rather than any current signs. The rally is clearly accelerating, supported by the indicators. In the longer run, this rate of ascent cannot be sustained, but as long as each new bar is making a new high, MACD-Histogram rising, and the upper channel line still a distance away, it is tempting to hold.

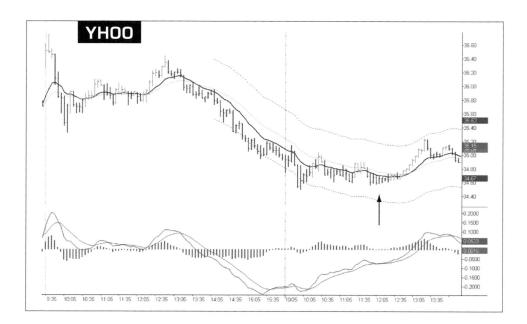

Michael did what every professional likes to do—he took a big chunk out of the middle of an uptrend. He did not try to nail its bottom or its top. This chart confirms the value of channels for setting targets—prices almost reached the upper channel line during the rally. Near the right edge of the chart, the Impulse system has gone red again, following a broad top in MACD-Lines. When the market closes, Michael will do his homework and prepare his shopping list for the next day.

**CHOOSING SOFTWARE**

*Michael says:*  In eSignal you can build a quote window, put different stocks there, and just toggle through them. I hit the down-arrow key and the chart comes up instantly—I can review 20 stocks in less than a minute, great for day-trading. MetaStock is much better for doing explorations, looking for stocks following your own criteria, and they have great technical support. The explorations feature in eSignal costs an extra $50 per month. In my opinion, a position trader is better off with MetaStock and a day-trader with eSignal. I use both programs.

# TRADE 2 | MICHAEL'S ENTRY

This daily chart of the S&P has an additional blue line—a 100-period moving average. It is a 20-period moving average for the next higher timeframe multiplied by five—a 20-week MA brought over to the daily chart. The S&P is oversold and pulling down. The weekly trend is up, and daily prices are at the lower Bollinger band, which is good. Other good signs are that there are no bearish divergences and Stochastic is oversold.

## RSH

I look for turning points in position trading as well as in day-trading. I like going long after the market had a pretty nasty decline. When the weekly and daily charts form a base, you get longer runs.

I prefer catching the market at extremes. These turns tend to produce good runs which are not too choppy. There are fewer pullbacks because the market has just completed a large pullback and stops are easier to manage. That's the only time I use the Fibonacci retracements. Once the market runs a little way, I'll see where the 50% retracement is going to be and hold until there or until the daily starts becoming a little toppy.

The daily chart of RSH seems perfect, looks like it bottomed out. It has a double bottom into the lower Bollinger band and Stochastic is oversold, making a slightly higher low than at the previous bottom. MACD-Histogram has a very nice divergence. It shows a higher high at the latest top and a higher low at the latest bottom. Another sign of strength is that MACD-Histogram rallied higher above zero than it went below the zero line on the latest decline.

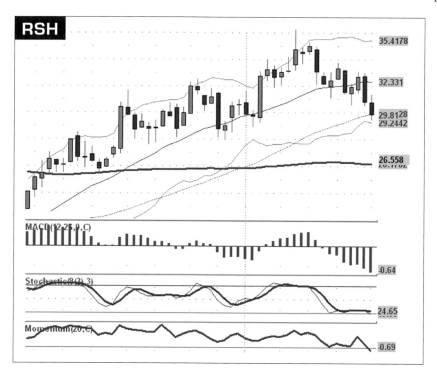

The weekly chart of RSH shows an uptrend, the decline has stopped at the 50-period MA (orange), Stochastic is oversold. Both S&P and RSH show weekly uptrends, with RSH being oversold. Price had touched the lower Bollinger band that week, but the reaction ended and the bar closed above its 50-period MA. There are two slight negatives—the latest price top is not accompanied by a higher MACD top—this is slightly bearish. Also, it is not a very good signal when MACD-Histogram is so far below zero.

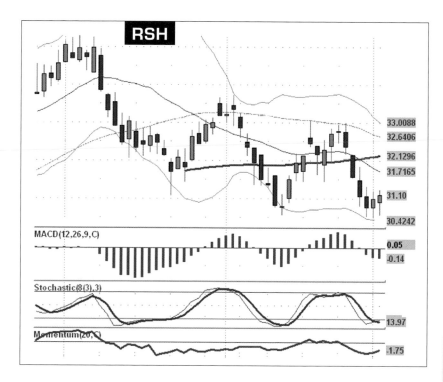

Momentum does not confirm a divergence but Stochastic does. Normally, I like MACD and Momentum to be in gear; Stochastic is my second choice. When neither confirms, that means no trade. I do not pay attention to fundamentals in swing-trading because my time-frame is too short. I only stay away if the stock was very recently downgraded or the earnings report is due. I placed an order to enter one tick above the high of the last daily bar. My stop was just below the low made one day earlier.

Will this trade make or lose money?

## TRADE 2 | MICHAEL'S EXIT

I exited the day after I entered. The S&P gapped down that day, and even though RSH did not gap, it got dragged down—it opened lower and kept going. I was extremely disappointed because it had a weekly and a daily pullback on Bollinger bands, which is normally a pretty good setup. I had no apprehensions and was almost 100% sure it would turn out to be a good trade.

What I learned was that the broad market definitely has to be behind you. No matter how good the stock looks on weekly and daily charts, when the market turns it will take your stock with it most of the time. That's why you always have to make sure that the S&P has the same basic pattern and is at a turning point.

## ▼ TRADE SUMMARY

Long RSH
Bought 5/5/2004 @ $31.28
Sold 5/6/2004 @ $30.51
Loss = $0.77 per share

# TRADE 2—ENTRY COMMENT

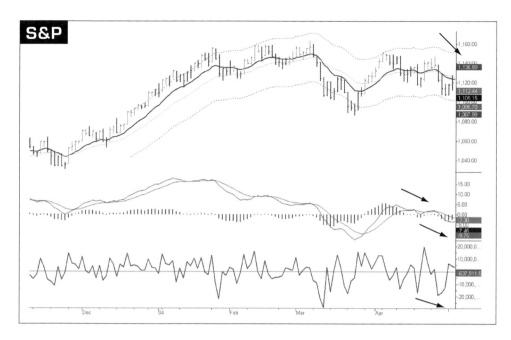

It feels awkward to look at the daily chart of the S&P without having studied the weekly. The rightmost bar is blue, permitting us to go either long or short. Prices had shot up a day before, but the bulk of signals leans to the bearish side. There was a double top in April with a bearish divergence of MACD-Histogram; this indicator fell to a new low a few days earlier, confirming the strength of bears and warning of further trouble ahead. Both moving averages are pointing down, confirming a short-term downtrend. Force Index has been drawing lower bottoms at every minor decline in recent weeks, showing that bears are getting stronger.

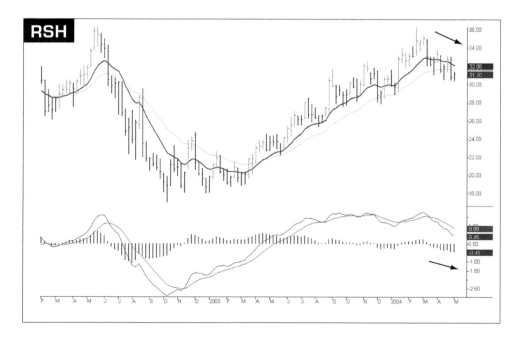

The Impulse system gives an unequivocal "no" to buying RSH. The rightmost weekly bar is red, meaning that both the fast EMA and the MACD-Histogram are declining; the downtrend is in gear. This censorship system does not allow us to trade long against the downtrend—only to go short or stand aside.

With the weekly Impulse being red, there is not much point in studying the daily charts. If I want to buy a stock, but its Impulse turns red on the weekly chart, I usually do not even bother looking at the daily. When the weekly says no to going long, it is time to look at some other stock.

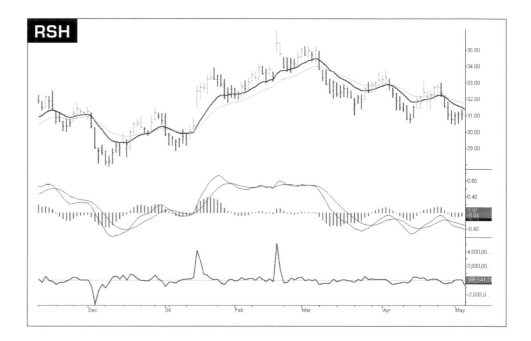

The daily chart of RSH shows several bullish signs: The downthrusts have become weaker since March, MACD-Histogram shows a bullish divergence, and the last bar has turned blue. Still, with the weekly Impulse being red, these are no more than early warning signs; I am not allowed to buy until the weekly goes off red.

# TRADE 2—EXIT COMMENT

Michael deserves high praise for running very fast from a losing trade. As a professional, he does not stick around waiting to see what happens next; he cuts the loss and moves on. A beginner concocts a bullish scenario and winds up believing in it as if it were a fact. An experienced trader tests every scenario against reality, and when the two diverge, he drops the scenario and goes with reality.

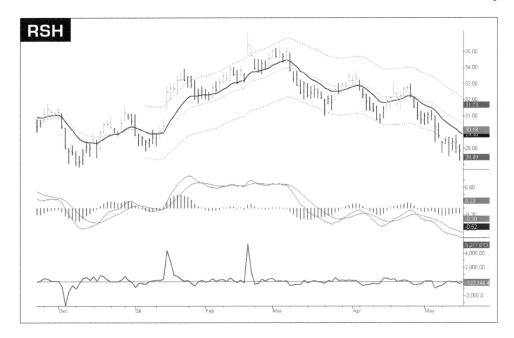

# "THE 2% RULE SAVED ME"

You can come to trading as a wide-eyed amateur and grow into a serious professional. This game can be won—but you must survive the inevitable setbacks. You can learn several valuable lessons from Michael's journey.

Trading education is expensive. The $3,500 per year Michael used to spend on services, including useless subscriptions, was small change compared with the tuition he paid in terms of trading losses. He realized early on that his capital was his window of escape and that every loss pushed on that window, closing it a little tighter.

Michael says that what saved him during his period of groping in the dark was the discipline of the 2% Rule. This Rule, first described in *Trading for a Living* and elaborated in *Come into My Trading Room,* states that a trader may not risk more than 2% of his capital on any given trade. Of course, you do not have to risk 2% on every trade—you're welcome to risk less. Michael, cautious and conservative, risks no more than 0.5% of his capital for many of his trades.

Suppose you have a $100,000 account. Two percent of that comes to $2,000. Say you want to buy a stock for $15, with a target at $20 and a stop at $13.50. This stop puts $1.50 at risk for every stock that you buy. Since your maximum permitted risk is $2,000, it is easy to calculate what maximum number of shares you may buy. Your actual size should be less than the theoretical maximum, since you'll have to cover commissions and perhaps even slippage.

Following the 2% Rule protects you from disastrous losses, the shark bites that destroy most trading accounts. Greedy traders want to buy a large position and make a killing. The 2% Rule saves the trader from getting killed.

Another valuable lesson we can learn from Michael is that he started becoming a successful trader only after he began keeping good records and rigorously analyzing them. The 2% Rule ensured his survival, but his equity continued bouncing up and down until he started keeping a Trader's Diary and learning from his mistakes.

Back in the days when I was actively practicing psychiatry, a new patient would occasionally come in with a serious drinking problem. If the patient disagreed with that diagnosis, I would not argue but make a simple suggestion—keep drinking as you did before but write down every drink that you take and come back a week later. No active alcoholic could ever keep notes because it took too much fun out of drinking. A few people came back a week later with notes, saying that I was right and they were ready to work on their problem. Good notes allow people to learn from their experiences and start turning their lives around.

In trading, most people rush forward without reviewing what they've done, not learning from their experiences and repeating their mistakes. I always say to my students, "It is perfectly fine to make mistakes; it is part and parcel of trying new things: It is definitely not okay to repeat them." Michael's trading diary and other records allowed him to break out of the vicious cycle in which many traders are trapped.

When I first called Michael to schedule our interview, he told me he doubted we would get enough material—he was a man of few words who spent most of his time alone in front of the screen. I chuckled while editing his chapter, one of the longest in the book— during his years of solitude he had accumulated a torrent of ideas. And of course, Michael's level of sheer mental toughness makes him stand out. When I think of that .wav file going off every five minutes, I'd probably put a hammer through my computer. You have to find a style that works for you—as Michael has.

## An e-mail from Michael:

# THE TOUGHEST CHALLENGE I'VE EVER TAKEN

The journey from making your first trade, knowing nothing about the markets, to the point where you're finally making consistent profits is long and hard. You go from feeling like a genius one day to a complete moron the next. Each time you think you've finally got it and the money is about to roll in, the market lets you know you still have a long way to go.

To imagine that you can start out knowing little or nothing, buy a few books, attend a seminar, and then a year or two later trade for a living is like thinking you can buy a set of golf clubs (when you've never played in your life), take a few lessons, and compete with Tiger Woods in a year.

Looking back over the last 10 years, I wish I had kept detailed records from the beginning and taken the concept of trading psychology more seriously. Then I probably would not have experienced so many aggravating and difficult years. Here's what I found to be most helpful:

First, don't quit your day job unless you have another means of support. However long you think it is going to take until trading for a living, triple that time. If you are under pressure to turn a profit to pay the bills, you can kiss that trading account good-bye.

Keep good records; don't wait for five years like I did. Print a chart of each trade; mark the entry and exit points. Also print a chart of what the S&P did while you held that stock. It cost me dearly to learn that most stocks follow the market, and going long in a down market is a hard and risky way to make money. At the end of each week or month, take a close look at all your trades. Search for any recurrent mistakes—are your trades in sync with the market? Were there any divergences working against you?

You need a coherent trading system with rules on when to enter, where to place stops, when to move them to protect profits, and when to exit. Buying XYZ because it bounced off this level last month, and ZYX because someone on TV said it was a buy, is not a system. When you make different trades for different reasons, it is hard to figure out what you're doing wrong with your losers.

A lot of people think that paper trading is a waste of time, but they're missing its most important point. Paper trading helps you learn to spot the pattern you plan to trade as it develops. It helps you gain confidence in your system so that you can pull the trigger on your setup. Finally, it helps you see how your system will perform in different market conditions. If your win/loss ratio for paper trades is 70%, and real trades only 40%, then the problem is not your system, it is your execution.

With no emotions getting in the way, paper trading is a great way to monitor a system. Once you know how it works, you can start with real money, which will make you learn about the psychology of trading. You need a system that produces more profits than losses and the psychological control to implement it. You need both—there is no way to consistently make money with one and not the other.

Start trading small positions. When I was in a rush to make money and traded too large, I could make or lose in three hours what took me two weeks of working to save. That was very intimidating. Smaller positions will reduce the inevitable burn rate on your account while you're learning. It is a lot easier to hang onto a position and watch it play itself out when your stop limits the potential loss to only $150 and not $1,000. After winning a trade or two, increase the size by a small amount.

Market volatility is constantly increasing or decreasing. Different trading systems work better under different market conditions. If your system no longer gives you good setups, don't throw it out; wait for conditions to change back. I've never found a pattern or method that gave me the same number of setups every month—some months are always busier than others.

Learning to trade for a living is pretty similar to starting your own business. If you know enough about a business and have enough capital to get through the first years when you're not making a profit, you stand a chance of making it. There are only two big differences. The first is that in a business your emotions do not play such a big part because the money is not made or lost so quickly. The other is that when business takes a turn for the worse, you have to get in there and work harder, more hours, make more sales calls to bring the revenue back up. In trading, there are times when the best thing you can do is sit on your hands and do nothing. This was hard for me to accept at first. What seems like doing nothing is actually doing something—preserving capital.

Learning how to trade was by far the toughest challenge I've ever taken on, but I couldn't imagine being happy doing anything else.

Name: Kerry Lovvorn
Lives: Scottsboro, AL
Previous profession: CEO/business owner
Trades: Stocks and futures
How long: Since 1995
Trading account: Medium ($250k–$1m)
Software: TradeStation for trading,
TC2005 for scanning stocks
Traders' Camps: Caribbean Camp in 2004; Advanced
Camp in 2005; Spike group member

# CHAPTER 9

# KERRY LOVVORN

## A SQUEEZE PLAY

I met Kerry in the chatroom for traders that my firm maintains on the Internet. I liked several of his comments, e-mailed him, and the following year we met face to face when he came to our Traders' Camp in the Caribbean. Kerry seemed attentive but shy—until one night, during a party at a local restaurant, he let it slip that he liked singing. We took the microphone away from the band leader and gave it to him, the musicians hit the chords—and Kerry forgot his lyrics. I teased him afterwards that since there seemed to be no future for him in professional singing, he had no alternative but to learn how to trade.

We continued to e-mail each other after the Camp, and when I started working on this book, I invited Kerry to New York for an interview. He came with his wife and stayed for several days in a nice hotel near Central Park. Manhattan is a great city for walking, but many out-of-towners feel intimidated by its size and pace. Kerry and Karen, coming for the first time from a small town in Alabama, walked everywhere. On the first evening Kerry took the subway to my apartment for a campers' meeting and returned the following morning for an interview.

Ever since I was a kid I was fascinated with numbers, business, big cities, Wall Street. I was born in Gary, Indiana; my dad worked in the steel plants. When I was six, a new plant started up back home in Alabama, and the family returned south. After working at that plant for a while, my dad started his own steel fabrication business. We all grew up around the steel industry and worked for my dad.

In 1986 my dad sold his business. My ambition was to be a business owner—I wanted to be independent and so in 1988 I started TELKO. We fabricate structural steel for buildings, primarily restaurants and retail chains. We have grown over the years and have 35 employees—working with them is probably the best part of the business.

All I knew was the steel business, but I had always dreamed that one of these years I'd figure out how to invest. I thought you bought a stock, held it for 50 years, and accumulated massive wealth—buy-and-hold was all I knew about. My dreams were big, my expectations fairly extreme. In the 1990s I started a retirement account and turned to advisors and brokers who had me buy mutual funds. The first two funds I bought no longer exist—and they keep telling you mutual funds are safe. I put a little money in but got even less back—and that was in the early '90s bull market!

When 401k came out, we created a factory plan, and in 1997 I bought my first individual stock, in a company that was our largest client at the time. The stock had already quadrupled, and I bought near the top, then watched it slide from 43 to 9. When it fell to 9, I said, "It's cheap, let's double up." I actually tripled up and watched it go from 9 to 25. I had no clue what I was doing. Even though I eventually made a little money on it, I waited from 1997 to 2000 to make about 31% on this investment. After selling at 25, I watched it go up to 40, and made a commitment to learn this market game.

During this time, in 1999, the market was going sky-high, and everyone you came in contact with was buying stocks. Luckily I did not start in 1999—I was still too strapped to the daily business, working 15 to 16 hours a day. The year 1999 was probably my most stressful year—we went through a total management change, a large client went bankrupt, I was going through a massive burnout. If at that time anyone had offered me one dollar for that business, I would have taken it—but I would not just get up and walk away. I have a plaque in my office about quitting—I would not quit, would not stop, unless it was on my own terms.

It was the worst time in my business life. I wanted out and started questioning what I really wanted to do. That led me to the markets, reading books, and one of the first was *Trading for a Living*, in 2000. As I kept reading, my passion grew—I felt as if the markets were made for me. I loved the idea that the markets were what you made of them; there was no one else on whom to depend. I decided to rebuild the business, create a management team, and manage that team and company finances, while diversifying into other ventures.

As the markets started selling off in 2000, I started monitoring stocks, expecting to find some good buys. In August 2000, I opened my first online brokerage account, without realizing that the educational journey was just about to begin. The markets will teach you many things about yourself. I had read a few books but did not know anything. I started with a small account, $25,000, which in the first nine months simply bobbed up and down between slightly negative and break-even. I started feeling more comfortable with trades—but all I knew was trading long. There we were in one of the fiercest bear markets ever, and I was trying to learn trading on the long side! Shorting seemed mean and evil, as if you were against something. After 9/11, my account was down to about $7,000. I did not turn on the screen anymore—just waited it out. The market bounced back after 9/11, and as 2001 came to an end, I closed all my positions and wiped the slate clean, to start anew. I thought a fresh start would be good for the mind.

In 2002 the bear market continued, and I was still trying to make long trades, struggling to break even, running my account down 15 to 30% and then trying to make it back. I started going to some of the trade shows, got into your class in Vegas. I was starting to establish a method for myself—using Force Index, moving averages. I tried everything, read a bit of everything, gave my share of money to Mr. Market. I would read about a new indicator, apply it, mess with the settings, look for the golden secret. Now I laugh when I think I used to believe there was a secret to this. You look at a chart, think of a dozen different strategies, and they all contradict one another; you do not know what to do. By that time I was learning to short a little bit—a good time to do it, just as the bear market was coming to an end!

In 2002 I came closer to break-even, and in the latter part of that year, started formulating a regular method. At that time I felt I was coming along with my own ideas on what to do, not just copying someone else. You are not going to read a book, open an account, and be successful. That's what everyone wants—pay $50 for a book, program it into a computer, and have it spit out dollar bills while you sleep. In 2003 I started concentrating on my own system, and that's when my trading turned around. I still enjoy reading other people's ideas, going to trade shows and conferences, and listening to what others have to say. Now if I hear someone and it does not make logical sense in the first few minutes, I am not interested.

I read and heard a lot—from fakes to legitimate people, then put together what made sense to me. One of my favorite trades is when a stock is acting very quiet, boring, in a tight range, with little activity—I try to position myself in it because it will often explode. The trick is to figure out which way it will go. Riding it for a few days is very gratifying—you take what the market offers and then go elsewhere to look for a similar setup. The question is not what indicator to use, what lines to draw. The question is within myself: "What do I want to do?" It is like going to college: "What do I want to do when I grow up?"

What kinds of trades are you going to make? When you look at the charts and do not know what you like, how will you recognize the trade when it is there? And worst of all—when there is no trade, you'll find one. People want to make money but do not know what they want from the markets. If I am making a trade, what am I expecting of it? You take a job—you know what your wages and benefits are going to be, what you're going to be paid for that job. Having a profit target works better for me, although sometimes it leads to selling too soon.

I now put a signature on the bottom of my e-mails: "It is hard enough to figure what the market is going to do. If you do not know what you are going to do, the game is lost." How many times do you put on a position trade, then an intraday signal comes in, and you sell? I had to figure out what I wanted to do, what my personality was. Matching your trading to your personality is the critical part of success. I like quick trades, and find it difficult to ride trades for a long period of time; I do not have the patience. If I get in at 10 and the stock runs to 15, I do not like to ride it down to 12, even though the big trend might still be up.

People talk of being unemotional, but the market is a sea of emotion—it is all about how you control those emotions. I thought successful traders had good trades all the time—but in truth the main feature of a good trader is how he bounces back from his mistakes. Just look at a great athlete like Michael Jordan—how many shots did he miss? How did he bounce back from his errors, failures, and mistakes?

Karen is very supportive of my trading as well as my business. She has always shown 100 percent faith in what I do. She is also my biggest critic—she does not go along just to be supportive. When you're fixing to do something that is not good for you, a true friend will tell you. When I am at my worst, she is at her best. She has never complained about my trading. She has always told me, "Set your mind and go for it, you can do it."

# TRADE 1 | KERRY'S ENTRY

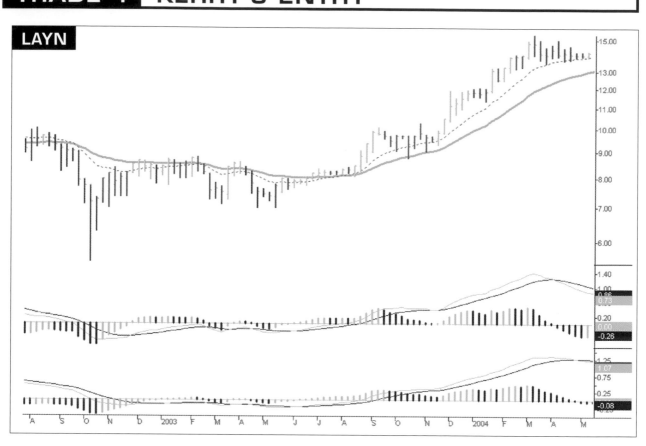

**LAYN**

| | |
|---|---|
| **Upper pane:** | Impulse system (11-25-8 with 12-EMA). Dotted line—12-week EMA, solid line—26-week EMA. |
| **Second and third panes:** | Use dual MACD on weekly charts—two panes with different settings: mid-pane 11-25-8, bottom 19-39-8. Green if MACD ticks up, red if it ticks down. |

### LAYN

I call this a "squeeze play." We've got a stock in an uptrend. I look for a pullback to the fast EMA, accompanied by shrinkage—smaller and smaller ranges during the pullback, while the Impulse system does not turn red, stays blue during the pullback. I look for an entry when the ranges are the smallest since the pullback began. If the ranges expand, I become less interested because the risk becomes higher. This is a very low-risk entry—you have to get in before the stock moves—you must anticipate but the risk is minimal.

The setup involves a reduction in range and price resting on support—I learned this from David Weis in your Camp. What is the support level during this pullback? The lowest low was 13.53—if that gets broken, I definitely want to be out of this trade. A break would tell me that this pullback could develop into a turn, and I do not want those lows violated.

The pattern at the right edge is like a coiled spring—the stock is in a tight coil ready to explode and strike. I check to see that there are no major divergences of MACD and then go to the daily charts to look for an entry. What I want out of this setup is a very low-risk trade with less than a dollar stop. It does not always work; half of breakouts fail.

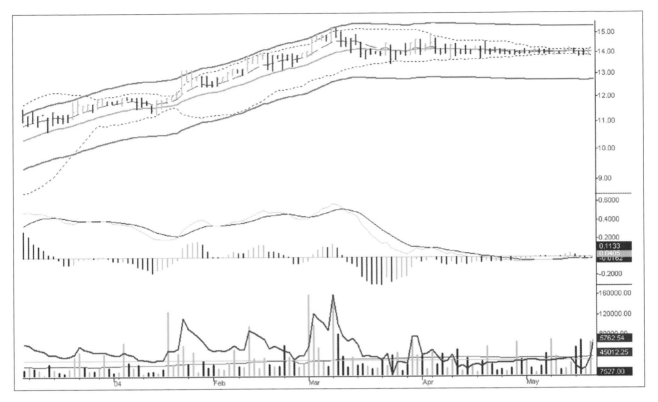

| | |
|---|---|
| **Upper pane:** | Impulse system (11-25-8 with 11-day EMA). Dotted line—9-day EMA, solid line—22-day EMA. Grey envelope is a 2.7 standard deviation channel based on a 22-day EMA. I turn Bollinger bands on and off to see how tight the coiling is—how wide are Bollinger bands in comparison to price bars. |
| **Middle pane:** | MACD Lines and Histogram 11-25-8 |
| **Lower pane:** | Volume bars and Force Index. Volume bars are green if the stock closed up for the day, red if closed down, blue if unchanged. Force Index with 11-day EMA and a zero line. Purple line—63-day EMA of volume because there are 63 trading days in a quarter, and big funds and brokerages deal on a quarterly basis. |

I have been waiting for an entry, and the pickup in volume alerts me. At the right edge volume is above its 63-day average—it has started picking up in the past few days. The price barely moves out of the Bollinger band range. With all this volume, prices do not move, and so even with the day closing down, it appears it was not sellers who were in charge, but buyers, who were accumulating. The next day I put in my buy order. I like to buy at the bottom of the range—I do not like buying breakouts, when the move is already on. 13.85 and 13.88 were the latest daily lows. I want to buy close to that range, but you never know whether you will get that entry. It is important to get on the train before it leaves the station.

I enter on May 20 at 14.06, placing a stop using the daily chart. The lowest low during this consolidation period was 13.53—and I like to put my stop about 11 cents lower. I use this number to keep me out of the noise range. I do not like even numbers—dollar, 50 cents, 10 cents. I like to put my stop a dime below the low, and so I add a penny, make it 11 cents. If that low breaks, it will be a sign of trouble. I try to avoid placing a stop where everyone else's stops are going to be.

I look for a squeeze on Bollinger bands, and then take them out and go to a regular channel. The target for this trade is at the top of the channel. When the bands squeeze, this baby is ready to explode. Which way? We established that on the weekly chart where we saw an orderly pullback within an uptrend. Meanwhile most traders lost interest in this stock—it is lying flat.

will this trade make or lose money?

# TRADE 1 | KERRY'S EXIT

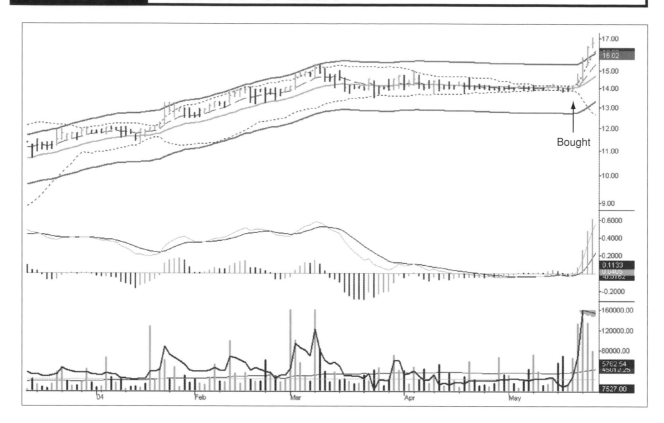

Bought

We're in—an explosive volume comes in the next day, on May 21. I decide to hold it over the weekend. The next trading day, May 24, we see a continuation of enormous volume, prices close near the high of the day, hitting the top of their channel. That is my target, but I do not want to automatically sell, only raise my stop at this point at least to break even. With such an explosive move, a stop below this day's low would protect a small profit. The trade is a free ride from here. This type of move can last for several days.

The next day, May 25, we exceed the top of the channel, and on the 26th the entire bar is out of the channel, but prices stall on lower volume—and that's when I sell. A narrow range out of a channel is a typical sign of weakness. There is a saying: "Sell when you can, not when you have to." I decide to close and see how the pullback acts. And that's the beauty of the EMAs—often you see a breakout, then a pullback to the EMA, and then the move continues.

I had a setup, managed the trade, aimed at the top of the channel, and got a little extra. I risked 50 cents and got two dollars out of it. That was a 4:1 reward-to-risk ratio. I can be wrong three times with a trade like this, win once, and still maintain a small profit. This was not the home run that many beginners look for—but you can hit a lot more singles and doubles. I used to fall into the trap of thinking, "Let me see how far this can go." That's where you start turning winners into losers. A few days later this stock was back down at 13 dollars.

## ▲ TRADE SUMMARY

Long LAYN
Bought 5/20/2004 @ $14.06
Sold 5/26/2004 @ $16.29
Profit = $2.23 per share

# TRADE 1—ENTRY COMMENT

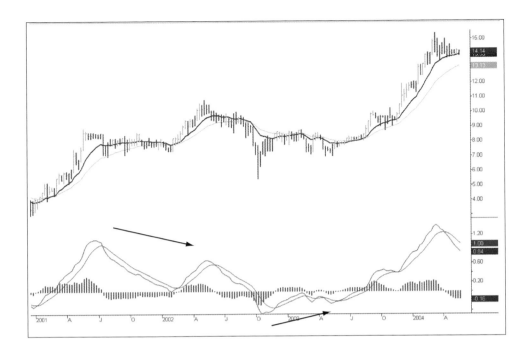

There are many ways to analyze the markets and to trade them. Only a beginner can be arrogant enough to say that his method is good and others' methods are bad. A seasoned pro surely has lived through enough times when his opinion was proven wrong. This is why experienced traders are broad-minded and respectful of others' opinions.

I would fall asleep watching a tight trading range but have no arguments against Kerry's approach. His logic is elegant and consistent, and his method works for him. On my weekly chart, the Impulse system offers no objections to buying here. The weekly bars are blue, allowing us to go long or short. Prices are in an uptrend but had pulled back to value in recent weeks. MACD-Histogram is at a low level, consistent with price bottoms.

## What Is a "Tick"?

You suggested placing an order one tick above or below the recent extreme price. What does "one tick" mean?  —*Trader*

A tick is the smallest price change allowed in any given market. When you trade U.S. stocks, a tick is usually 1 cent. When you trade grains, it is ⅛ of a cent because those markets still trade in eighths, and so on for any market.  —*AE*

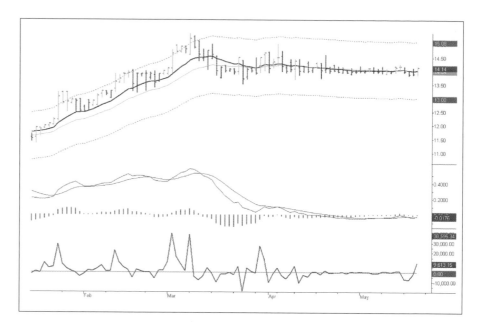

"Like watching paint dry"—for almost two months the average height of a daily bar remained under 20 cents, with the total range for the entire period under a dollar. It takes a highly disciplined and focused individual to follow this pattern day in and day out, scanning for signs of an upcoming reversal.

The Impulse system is fairly non-contributory during such tight ranges—up one day, down the next. MACD-Histogram is snaking around its zero line and is not really useful here because it tends to give better messages when it is far away from its centerline. Only Force Index has started to show some signs of life in recent days. At the right edge of the chart the Impulse system is green, permitting us to buy.

# TRADE 1—EXIT COMMENT

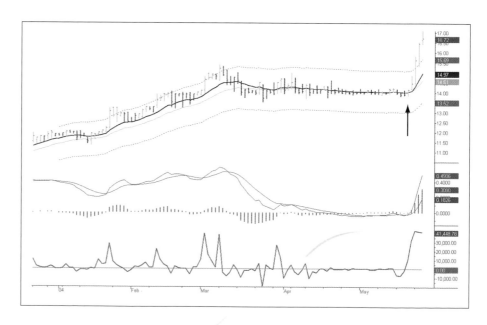

Kerry's patience has paid off. The stock has exploded from its channel, covering a greater distance in three days than it had in the previous three months. Kerry's system obviously works for him. At the right edge of the chart, all indicators are in gear, the Impulse is green, the rubber-band overextended to the upside. You could wait to see how far the move will carry before taking profits or you could say that the picture looks just perfect. If it cannot be improved, the stock should be sold, which is what Kerry did.

Notice Kerry's calm tone as he gets out of this trade. There is no gloating or beating his chest. Nor is there any complaining about the money left on the table because of selling too soon. The man has his system, follows it, and calmly accepts the consequences of his actions.

## Part-time

**Q** I lost about $25K out of $50K capital in day-trading back in 1999. The trading house insisted we all actively trade, and I think I was a victim of overtrading without having a plan or system. I now earn a good living, but eventually want to get back into trading. Do you feel there is any case for part-time trading smaller amounts while having a flexible career?    —*Trader*

**A** I think part-time trading is a very viable option—if you swing-trade rather than day-trade. Choose a few stocks that swing well and track them day in and day out, trying to profit from moves that last several days. You can do that without sitting in front of the screen all day.    —*AE*

## A Tiny Account

**Q** I am a college student, planning to invest my saved money in the stock market. At this point I have saved $8,000. Could you tell me what is an adequate amount of money with which to start trading?    —*Trader*

**A** First of all, congratulations on being a very frugal student! $8,000 is a good amount to invest, but not enough to trade. The reason is transaction costs. Let's say you pay $20 commission to buy or sell. A single roundtrip will cost you $40, or ½% of your account. If you trade once a week, by the end of the year commissions will eat up 25% of your account, creating an insurmountable barrier to winning. Invest your money for the longer term and continue to accumulate capital and study the markets. Also, at your age, you may want to look for a trader trainee position and learn on someone else's dime.    —*AE*

## TRADE 2 | KERRY'S ENTRY

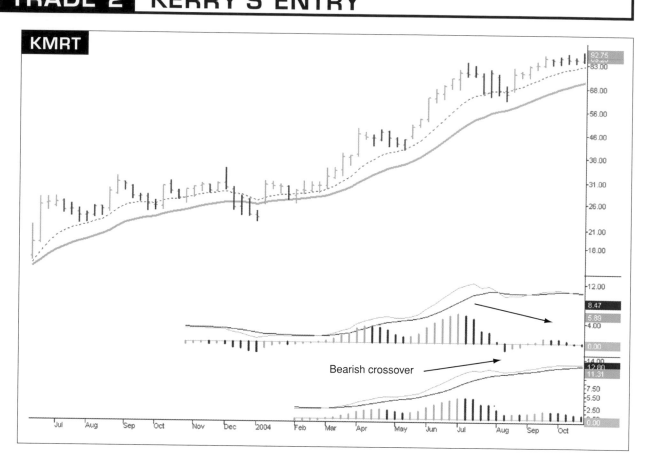

### KMRT

Too many people look at a divergence and think automatically that it will reverse the trend—but it often does not. Here on the weekly chart you see that the back of the bull was broken in August. KMRT has been in a strong uptrend, and after that break, during the week of September 17, it reached a new high, with very little strength in MACD. It was a massive bearish divergence. The Impulse system remained green, so no shorting was allowed the following week, but the stock caught my attention. During the week of September 24 the Impulse turned blue as MACD-Histogram ticked down. Even MACD Lines showed a little negative divergence—I felt this stock was getting ready to roll over.

Give me this setup a hundred times, and I will take it a hundred times. That is one major difference between mature traders and beginners—we take our setups every time. As I've heard Alex say, "If you do not take this trade, what are you going to take?"

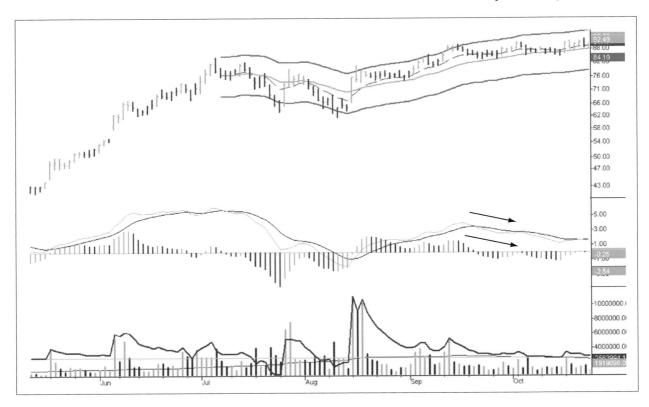

Not only is there a weekly divergence, there is also a daily divergence, and not only MACD-Histogram but also MACD Lines! Look at the Force Index divergence—all that volume in August could not make KMRT go up—it just went flat after that. A stock that cannot go up is just waiting to jump off a tall building. I had steam coming out of my ears on this trade, and am glad I did not bet the farm on this one.

*Kerry says:*   I use the same parameters on my weekly and daily charts. I've stopped trying to change them—every time I try to do it, I get myself in trouble. Everybody is so into settings, asking you what yours are. The question is not what they are but what they are telling you. EMA-13 and EMA-11 are not going to tell you very different things. I use parameters I've become comfortable with, and changing them has never done me any good. All those changes in parameters simply give you faster or slower signals. Faster settings give you more false signals. Slower settings make you give up more time because of slower signals.

**INDICATOR PARAMETERS**

# TRADE 2  KERRY'S EXIT

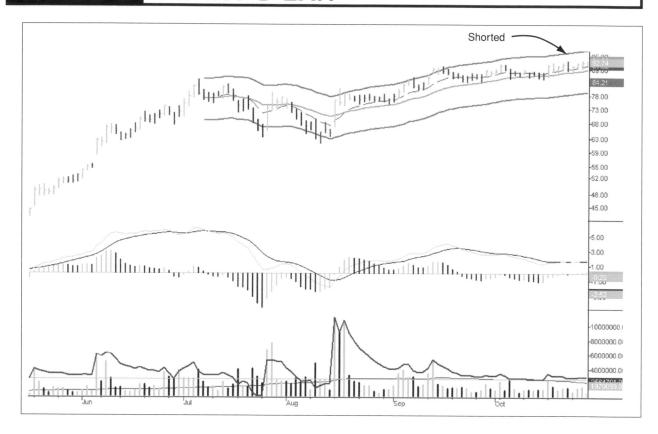

Shorted

Even the best setups sometimes fail. I want to protect myself if my short breaks above its highs. On the day I entered, KMRT reached a new high of 92.80. I shorted because it closed down and failed to hold its new high. The next day it closed up a bit—it made a new daily low but closed near the top of its range, MACD ticked back up, turning the daily Impulse system back to green. It had not violated the stop, and I was still in the trade, but I did not like that action. That stock should have gone down! The next day it closed up again—two days of higher closes, and the Impulse system stayed green. The next day, October 27, it hit the high of 93.18. I covered intraday, sooner than planned because of the price action.

My point is: You have a setup, and if a trade is not acting as you had expected, you're better off on the sidelines. It's like driving—someone gives you directions to get somewhere, and as you drive, you realize something seems wrong; the signposts in the directions are not there. Then it is time to stop and ask directions again, rather than just blindly follow something that's not working. This trade might have been my best trade of the year in terms of risk management. I lost money, but I avoided being impaled on a spike which ran all the way up to 117.

I printed out these charts—they went into my record-book as a reminder why it is so important to follow your plan and know what you are going to do.

## ▼ TRADE SUMMARY

**Short KMRT**

Short 10/22/2004 @ $89.79

Covered 10/27/2004 @ $91.59

Loss = $1.80 per share

# TRADE 2—ENTRY COMMENT

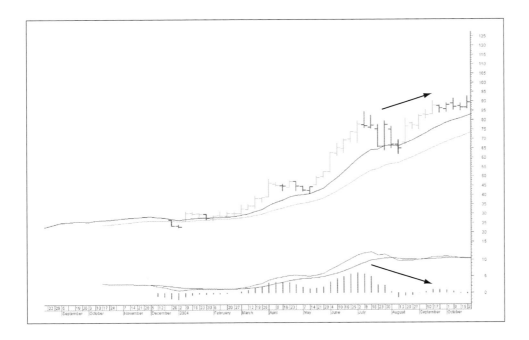

Several months had elapsed after my interview with Kerry before I wrote this review of his trade. When I tried to plot KMRT in my TradeStation, I got nothing, and TC2005 also gave me a blank. In the months since our interview, Kmart had been taken over by Sears. Fortunately, a friend had downloaded a database from MetaStock before the takeover, and he plotted these charts for me in his program. This is why they look slightly different from my other charts. This slight visual difference confirms the point I've already made—the specific brand of software makes little difference for traders, as long as you use a serious toolbox.

The weekly chart shows a major bearish divergence between prices and MACD-Histogram. The October top is higher than the one in July, but the indicator is tracing a lower second top. Even more ominously, MACD Lines are tracing a rarely seen double top with a bearish divergence. The right-most bar tried breaking out to a new high but failed. The Impulse system is blue, allowing us to short.

Trades based on bearish divergences tend to offer good reward-to-risk ratios. Set the profit target on the weekly chart—it is reasonable to expect that prices will fall back into their value zone on the weeklies. Set the stop on the daily chart—prices are not supposed to rise to a new high after a bearish divergence. With KMRT trading near 90, a profit target near 80, and a stop near 93, we have a better than 3:1 reward-to-risk ratio.

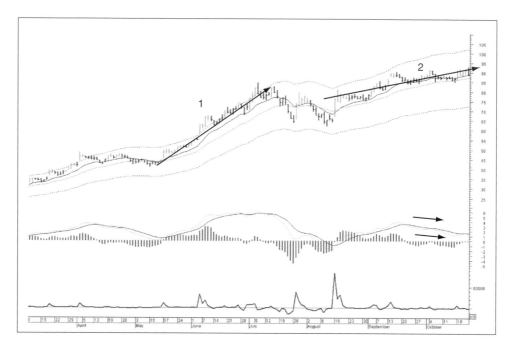

The daily chart fully confirms the message of the weekly. The uptrend is becoming less and less acute, while MACD-Histogram exhibits great weakness; its latest rally, peaking just one day before the right-most bar, barely poked its head above zero. MACD Lines are clearly diverging from the uptrend and headed lower. The Force Index has not shown any serious bullish action in more than a month. The uptrend appears weak, rising only out of inertia. The right-most bar has turned blue; the Impulse System permits shorting.

# TRADE 2—EXIT COMMENT

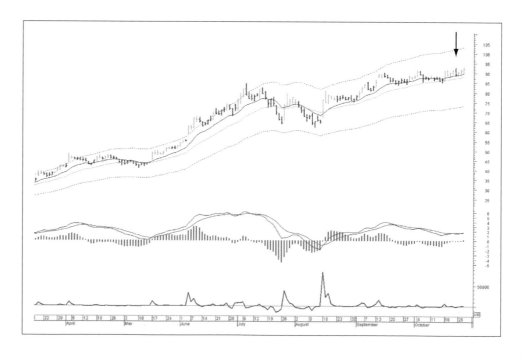

Cold discipline is a hallmark of a successful pro. Kerry had shorted what looked like an ideal setup—but as soon as the trade started going against him, he banged out with no regrets. As he points out, the stock eventually went up to $117, and had he hung around like an amateur, he would have ended up in heaps of trouble. Kerry is quick to say that he continues to like this setup and will trade it again when he sees it in the future.

A highly important quality of the stock market is that most processes in it are probabilistic rather than deterministic. In a deterministic process, a specific action leads to a specific consequence: Push on the door, it will open. In a probabilistic process, an outcome that you seek is likely but not guaranteed: Stick your hand in a drawer with three white socks and seven black socks—you are more likely to pull out a black sock, but this outcome is by no means certain.

At the right edge of the chart, the daily Impulse has turned green. It looks like we're dealing with "The Hound of the Baskervilles" signal described in *Trading for a Living*: When a powerful divergence refuses to work, it tells you that something is fundamentally changing below the surface of the market. In the famous story by Sir Arthur Conan Doyle, the clue to solving a murder came from the fact that the family dog did not bark while the crime was being committed. That was a sign that the criminal was a family member, known to the dog—the absence of a signal gave the detective his signal. When the market does not do what strong technical signals say it is going to do, it is a warning that there is likely to be a strong move in the contrary direction.

# SELF-IMPOSED LIMITATIONS

Many serious traders have a handful of patterns they like to trade. The market is too huge and flashes too many signals to trade every move. Success is a matter of accepting discipline and limitations. You may not feel like running in the morning, but still put on your jogging shoes and head out into the drizzle. You may see a nice piece of cake but decide to pass it up because of your earlier decision regarding weight control. A trader looks at a market where thousands of stocks rise and fall, sucking amateurs into their trendless chop and false breakouts. Amateurs jump in, dreaming of fat profits. A professional does not chase every piece of cake; he knows that only a few patterns offer him an edge, and he does not trade unless he sees them.

What patterns to trade is the personal choice of every trader. You may buy and sell on the basis of fundamental developments, technical signals, or news, but in any situation you need to stick to your method. Amateurs are easily influenced by other people—they hear good stories and jump into trades for which they are totally unprepared. Professionals, even if they hear an interesting tip, test it and use their own system to make a "go/no-go" decision.

Kerry showed us two of his favorite patterns—a squeeze play and a divergence. He probably has a few more, but the total number of patterns used by serious traders tends to be small. There are thousands of stocks and dozens of futures—this huge number of market instruments provides plenty of opportunities even if you trade only a few patterns.

Notice that each pattern reflects Kerry's understanding of the market. He did not come by his ideas through computerized testing of past market behavior. Instead, he has certain concepts of how the market moves and how to take advantage of that.

Kerry readily acknowledges that he got his idea for trading a squeeze play from David Weis, his instructor in several Traders' Camps. What goes without saying is that Kerry used David's idea only as a starting point. For example, David rarely uses computerized indicators (see Chapter 11), while Kerry relies heavily on them. He starts with another person's concept, but develops it and implements his favorite tools to make it his own.

Kerry said in his interview, "I started concentrating on my own system, and that's when my trading turned around. I still enjoy reading other people's ideas, going to trade shows and conferences, and listening to what others have to say. Now if I hear someone and it does not make logical sense in the first few minutes, I am not interested."

To develop your own method, it helps to keep good working notes. Write down what you're trying to do. Write down how you plan to reach those goals. Write down what behaviors of the market you'll be trying to catch. Write down what tools you'll use and how you'll interpret their signals. Seriousness, accountability, and self-imposed limitations will get you far ahead of the herd of disorganized, greedy, and fearful traders.

*An e-mail from Kerry:*

# ADAPT YOUR TRADING STYLE TO YOUR PERSONALITY

When I set out to pursue the profession of trading, I read a few market books, studied a few indicators, and it looked simple enough to me. Little did I know I was embarking on a journey of self-discovery. In reviewing my trades I find that the more profitable ones are those in which I knew what I was pursuing. Even when such trades do not work out, the losses are held to a minimum because I quickly realize that what I was looking for is not there and exit to preserve precious capital. On the flip side, all trades in which losses are far greater than they should have been have one thing in common. They all have the ingredient of confusion and not knowing exactly what I was looking for in that trade.

When you do not know what you're doing, you let small losses turn into larger losses and then capitulate into selling just to get rid of the pain. I believe that at some point all traders have had such experiences; what you learn about yourself from them can propel you forward in the trading profession. Finding a trading style that matches your personality is the most important factor in your success or failure. I remind myself every day to continue to observe myself.

I have been fortunate to learn from several successful traders, and the most important lesson I've learned is the importance of finding exactly what game I want to play. Saying you want to trade the markets is like saying you want to be an athlete and play sports and then running out and playing the first game into which you happen to stumble. There are many games, and I do not think it would be advisable for a horse jockey to take up competitive weight-lifting, but then again, it is not the job of a power lifter to race a thoroughbred horse.

I have found that knowing and understanding your personal tendencies will do more for your success than any indicator or trading method. You must discover what works and does not work for you. For example, Michael Jordan is one of the greatest basketball players in the history of the game, but he underperformed as a baseball player and was just above par as a golfer. Did that make him a poor athlete? Absolutely not! His game is basketball, and that does not translate into success in baseball. There are many games in the marketplace, and you need to find the one you can play well. You also need the dedication and perseverance to perform to the best of your ability.

For example, I found that I do not have the patience for riding long-term trends. They simply wear me out, and I get tired and restless. I cannot stand to watch a position go against me and give profits back, waiting for the long-term trend to move in my favor. By understanding that, I can look for other methods and use other tools. I came to use what I call "an inventory method"—building a position up and reducing it, trading in and out, again and again, as I attempt to ride the trend. There is no great revelation in this but a simple understanding of what makes the difference between winning and losing for me. I am a perfectionist by nature, which is very stressful if you want to make a single entry and exit—I always feel I should have done better. Once I understood this, scaling in and out of positions started working better for me. Perfection does not exist in the markets, but with the "inventory method" some of my entries and exits are likely to be nearly perfect.

I could go on and on about my deficiencies as a trader, but the most important thing is to understand how your personality works and adapt your trading style to it. In the beginning, most of us follow the crowd and doubt ourselves, looking for someone else to guide us. It is hard enough to figure out what the markets will do; if you don't know what you are going to do, the game is lost. To succeed you must know your unique abilities, strengths, and weaknesses.

| | |
|---:|:---|
| Name: | Diane Buffalin, PhD |
| Lives: | Lathrup Village, MI |
| Previous profession: | Clinical psychologist |
| Trades: | Stocks and options |
| How long: | Since 1996 |
| Trading account: | Small (< $250k) |
| Software: | QCharts |
| Traders' Camp: | Florida in 1999 |

# CHAPTER 10

# Dr. Diane Buffalin

## Dancing Like Fred Astaire, Only Going Backwards and in High Heels

I met Diane on Sanibel Island in Florida in 1999, at the only Traders' Camp we have held in the United States. Back in those days it felt a little unusual to see a woman in class while her husband played golf, although more such couples came later. Diane had made enough money writing options to pay for George's early retirement. Some men tried to tease him, but he brushed them off; after almost 30 years of marriage, he and Diane still held hands.

Diane had a PhD in psychology, and in talking we discovered that she did her internship at the same time and in the same hospital where I had done my residency training in psychiatry. We must have eaten in the same dining hall a hundred times but never met until this Camp. Diane and I hit it off, and whenever she visited New York, we had dinner together. One summer she came with George, and I suggested an outdoor restaurant, but he told me that after returning home from Vietnam he had made two resolutions—never again to fly in a helicopter or eat under an open sky.

When I invited Diane for an interview, it took quite a bit of juggling to coordinate our schedules. I was spending much of the winter at a villa in the Caribbean, while Diane kept going on cruises with George. She eventually flew to New York, timing her visit to attend a campers' meeting.

> There was this one week in 1996 during which three different people told me I should be trading options on the stocks I owned. I had no idea what they were talking about, but when two brokers and a girlfriend who was an engineer all suggested the same thing, I thought I should listen. My girlfriend, a real-life rocket scientist, wanted to subscribe to a service that for $5,000 would tell you exactly what to do. I was not going to do what some man told me to do; I do not even do everything George tells me to do. I said to her, "Let's each get a book and figure it out for ourselves." I bought the thinnest book I could find (James Bittman's *Options for the Stock Investor*, 1996), and at first could not understand how you could sell something you don't own. The language and technical concepts continued to baffle me no matter how much chocolate I ate, and after struggling for hours, I gave up by page 12 (later, I found the book to be lucid, helpful, and easy).
>
> Finally, I drew a square and divided it in four quarters—buy/sell, call/put. In filling out the possible scenarios of what the stock would have to do to make

a profit, I realized that for the money to come in, you had to sell options. I called my broker: "Let me explain options to you because if I cannot explain them I should not trade them." He tried to talk me out of it, but I said, "If most options buyers lose money, who gets it?" Sellers! If all the boys are buying options, I'm going to do the opposite. You know how Ginger Rogers danced? Just as well as Fred Astaire, only going backwards and in high heels!

The day I made my first trade, George came home at night—I was in a purple flannel nightgown, had not taken a shower, and dinner, certainly not made. He said, "You didn't do much today." And I said, "I made $475, let me take you out for dinner!" After a few weeks of this, George said, "Why don't you trade more than one contract?" I had to admit I was trading five contracts and the profits were $1,500 a week, but I thought it was unbelievable. I had an old computer, dial-up AOL, it took two minutes to load a five-minute chart—and the data was delayed 20 minutes. The bull market was going on, and I was writing stock symbols and option prices on yellow lined paper and looking to see which moved the most, gathering data for my financial experiments. My goal was to earn enough for my husband to retire.

**LOOKING FOR TRADES**

*Diane laughs:* Most traders are men, and they approach markets the way men look for women—go into a bar, scan for characteristics like curviness or hair color, then hit on a woman, and if they have no luck, hit on another one. Men always ask, "Where do you get your picks?" All those scans—the right form, the right shape, they think it is going to work. By contrast, when you introduce a man to a woman, her first question is going to be, "What does he do for a living?" Men care more about looks, women about fundamentals.

Men are looking for a tip and a score, and I tell them that you can score with any stock, as long as you have the right moves. Does she like wine, dancing, or flowers? If she has asthma, do not send flowers. Get to know your stocks and under what circumstances they are likely to go up or down. I have a list of stocks that move with the market and another list of those that often move against it.

I always check the earnings calendar. Normally stocks go up before earnings and down afterwards, no matter how good the earnings, because the good news is already out. I keep an earnings calendar for all my stocks the way younger women keep menstrual calendars. Women are more attuned to planning around certain dates, but men are just hot—"I want it now, let's do it." Do you pay attention to your stocks' signals or do you have a single model and hope to score with it?

It is not picking the stock, it is managing the position. I look at the news and the date the earnings are released, then dance to the music that's on, not to the music I wish were on. What I like about options is the game is never over. There is always the fifth quarter—you can roll and roll.

Nothing in my life prepared me for trading options. I knew nothing and had no aspirations. I never took a class in economics. My father had told me to "buy low, sell high," but he never sold because stocks meant security to him. Then I realized everything in my life had in fact prepared me to be an options trader. I teach stress management for a living. I love to think, to have fun, to be right, and to test hypotheses. I did not know I was a risk taker, but found out that I was. I am a chess player, and my father taught me that in chess, when under attack, you have three options—move, attack the threatening piece, or attack another piece. Options allow you to play against the market, covering your positions and cashing in when the market moves. When the market moves against your position, you can sell a call, short the stock, or buy a put to offset your potential loss.

I was selling puts in the bull market and making money. But when the market turned, I was able to use options to make profits from rapidly falling stocks. For example, by aggressively selling at-the-money calls, I was able to earn $120,000 when Yahoo! dropped from 180 to 90, even though I no longer owned the stock.

*Diane remembers:*   My father was the smartest man I ever met, and he knew how to live well. He had 21 patents; he taught me to think, to make decisions. The more options you have, the smarter choices you'll make. If you think you have only two options, you will not make a smart decision. Your job is to create more options. He learned early the importance of having your own business, not working for someone else. He made money selling his ideas. He taught me the value of learning—anything you learn cannot be taken away from you. That was the lesson from Europe—possessions can be confiscated, but skills cannot. He taught me to play chess. He had a successful business and used to say, "I am responsible for 62 mortgage payments," because he had that many employees. He remained physically and mentally active until his death at 83. I know he would have enjoyed watching me make 5% a month selling options on his beloved Bell stocks.

**MY FATHER'S LESSONS**

Most option players are like roulette players on cruise ships—they wear gold jewelry and drop cash. They are flashy, but do not have the money to buy 1,000 shares of Microsoft, only a few dollars for calls. The croupier spins the wheel, none of their numbers comes up, and the dealer scoops off the money. I was selling time and keeping the cash. Every time I told anyone I was selling puts, they'd say it was too risky. But if a stock is at 50, and I sell a 45 put for 5, how is it more risky than buying a stock—as long as I do not freeze if it goes against me? And if it does, I have three choices: sell the call, short the stock, or buy the put and get out of the position.

One Saturday night at 2 AM, while searching CBOE data for the put with the biggest open interest, I met this guy Vinny in a chatroom on America Online. He knew everything about options but had a tiny account. I'd been trading options for more than a year, had made between $40,000 and $50,000, but never heard of support or resistance. When Vinny had me click on the screen and Bollinger bands came up, I gasped on the phone. I had been blind; now I had vision. He taught me to use Stochastic, MACD, and introduced me to your book. He taught me to use long-term charts and daily charts for screening, and 5-minute charts for entries and exits. I was still using a free data service with a 20-minute delay; he had real-time, and it was as if he had a periscope. Vinny certainly brought me up to a professional level of trading.

We were trading my account, and splitting the profits from the trades we did together. We had different styles, but at first worked remarkably well together. One night, at 2 AM, Vinny saw on Reuters that someone had died in a clinical trial of a stock we were trading. He said, "The bottom will fall out." And I said, "The worst thing that could happen has already happened, so when it gaps down at the open, let's sell puts. And when the stock rebounds, let's sell calls—because the volatility is high, but the stock can't rebound much." We made $9,000 on each of those positions. We were very successful for a year, but eventually split because of a divergence in styles. I was very happy selling three-month options and holding on to a 100% profit. He was more of a short-term trader. We remained friends, and I am forever grateful to him.

I found a class at CBOE—they talked of collars and butterflies, but how do you make money with that? I was keeping score—testing the hypotheses and keeping good notes. On DELL alone I used to make $4,000 per month, without owning the stock. I bought the Yahoo! IPO—both brokers said it was junk, sell it quick, but I have a thing of not always listening to male voices. I held, made $400,000, and bought a condo in the Virgin Islands, so George could play golf year round.

My spreadsheet for the year 2000 shows 80 trades, 8 of them losses. My profit for the year was $286,000, and I thought I had figured out how the world worked. My system was to sell puts when the stock was low, calls when it was high. The only thing better than making money is making the same money twice. Sell the puts, take profits, then sell puts again. A stock does not have to soar—you can do the same trade over and over again. When Vinny first showed me the charts, I said to him, "I have seen this before. This is like my weight chart—it goes up and down, with a slight upward bias." If I can see the tops, I can sell calls, and if I can recognize bottoms, I can sell puts.

The market started getting more ragged in 2001. I was selling puts on XTND—and one day lost $35,000 on the way to the airport, 20 minutes after the market closed. We were going to fly Spirit to save $100, and I had lost $35,000! There was another loss in INTC when I held into the earnings announcement. I decided never to be in that position again. The 14 days prior to earnings can be very volatile.

In 2001, I had 31 wins and 8 losses, made $120,000 and lost $64,000. That was no good—I was losing 50% of the money I was making. I began analyzing my losses and experimenting with stops. I set up a paper account with an electronic broker who religiously used stops—and I automatically bought everything he got stopped out of. I made money on all those trades—he lost 50% of his account, I made 20%. My data says that stops create a guaranteed loss. I do not have an answer to that. That's what I am working on now.

In 2003 I had 29 wins and 3 losses, made $78,000 and lost $15,000. That showed me that I was improving as a trader, but my losses were still too large. In 2004 I turned 60 and changed my money management strategy. At 40 you have 20 years to build a retirement account, at 60—this is your retirement account. I had reached my goal in 1998 and paid for my husband's early retirement. I put the bulk of money into safe paper earning 7.5%, and started trading a small $100,000 account. That year I produced an expo for my women's group, and the second half of 2004 turned out to be the least active since the start of my trading life. Then I got a call from you for the interview, and started becoming more active. By the end of 2004 I had 35 wins and 9 losses, made $35,000 and lost $19,000. A yield of 16% was definitely not a pro level of trading, but at the same time I am not addicted to this thing.

Today options premiums are not anywhere near as high as they were during the bull market. That's why, more and more often, I trade stocks. The most you can make on writing a call or a put is its price, if it goes down to zero. If a put is selling for 50 cents, while the stock looks good for a $2 move, I am better off doing that trade in a stock. That's why both recent trades I'll show you are stock trades.

# TRADE 1 | DIANE'S ENTRY

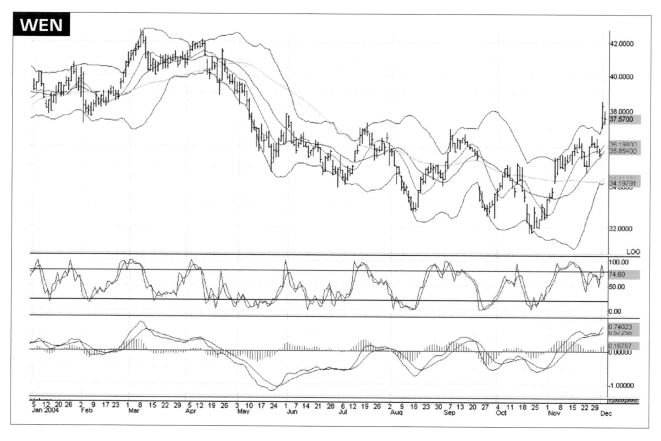

**WEN**

| | |
|---|---|
| **Upper pane:** | 10-, 20-, and 50-day SMA; Bollinger bands |
| **Mid-pane:** | Stochastic 14-1-3 (defaults in QCharts) |
| **Bottom pane:** | MACD 12-26-9 |

## WEN

This trade was triggered by the news—that is one thing I haven't seen in any system in trading literature. News is like gravity out there, pulling or pushing stocks. I read in the news that Wendy's was having a meeting where they expected to announce that their new Southwest menu was going to be tremendously profitable. The stock soared on 12/1, but the 12/2 meeting delivered bad news—that the menu was a disaster, they were going to discontinue it, sell some of the restaurants, and take a one-time huge loss.

I pulled up the chart, and it showed that the day before there had been a gap to the upside, piercing the Bollinger band in the expectation of this fabulous profit. Then on 12/2, Wendy's failed to reach its previous day's high and slid back down to its upper Bollinger band. The Stochastic turned down and MACD-Histogram, while continuing to climb, was not making a new high. The chart confirmed the high expectations of 12/1, but on 12/2 at the right edge, it showed that investors were not getting what they thought they were going to get—and I shorted before the close.

Will this trade make or lose money?

# TRADE 1   DIANE'S EXIT

I covered for the simplest reason—this stock stopped going down. The bar at the right edge of the chart had jumped up; Stochastic stopped going down. The trade did what I expected it to do, and then it stopped. That was a nice trade—clean, not a lot of emotion, no gut-wrenching.

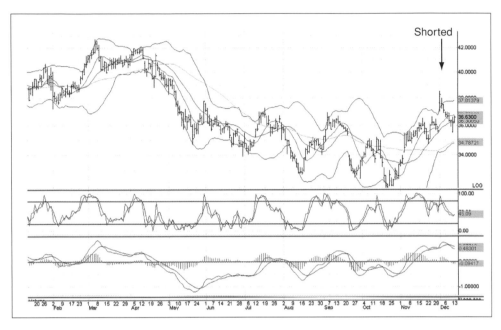

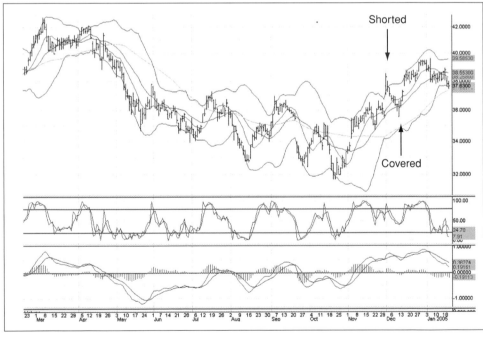

## TRADE SUMMARY

Shorted 12/02/2004 @ $37.56

Covered 12/13/2004 @ $36.47

Profit = $1.09 per share

The action of WEN since I covered confirms that my decision was correct—the price went up from where I got out. The lesson of the trade is that when a stock gaps up outside the envelope on good news and then stalls as the bad news comes out, it is crying out to be shorted.

# TRADE 1—ENTRY COMMENT

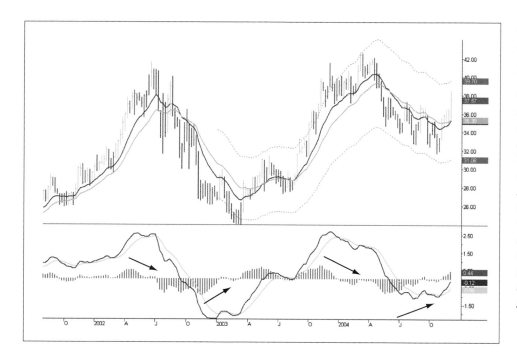

At the right edge of the chart WEN is rising from its latest bullish divergence. The last five weekly bars have been green, confirming the uptrend and permitting us only to buy or stand aside, not to short. The latest bar is approaching the upper channel line, showing that the stock is becoming overextended to the upside. Prices are high above the sweet zone between the EMAs; it is too late to buy, but my system does not permit me to short.

The weekly chart shows that WEN has been in a trading range between $42 and $26 for the past two years. The tops and bottoms of MACD Lines help trace the tops and bottoms of the trading range, while the bullish and bearish divergences of weekly MACD-Histogram keep nailing stock reversals. The bearish divergences of April–June 2002 and November 2003–March 2004 have signaled important tops. The bullish divergences of November 2002–March 2003 and May–October 2004 identified significant bottoms.

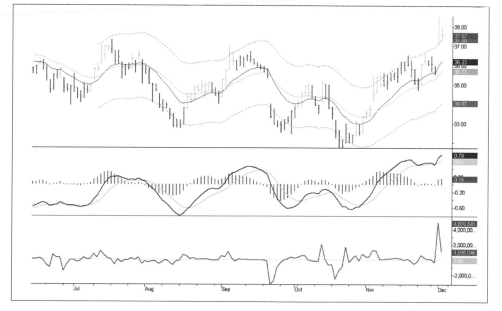

The daily channel has contained the highs and lows very nicely in recent months. Whenever prices flirted with the lower channel line, it was a good time to buy, and whenever they scratched the upper channel line, it was a good time to short.

The last two daily bars look very tempting to short. Prices have rocketed above the channel—and stalled there. A rocket that stalls is slated to fall. MACD-Histogram is still rising out of inertia, but the slightest downtick will turn it down, creating a massive bearish divergence and confirming the shorting signal.

I can see how a chart-reading trader, looking at a failing upside breakout, could be tempted to fade it and go short. I would not argue with Diane's logic, but if I am to follow the discipline of my system, I must pass up this short. When the Impulse system is green on the weekly and the daily charts, I am not allowed to short. The system allows me to buy—but I certainly have zero interest in buying at this level and will stand aside.

# TRADE 1—EXIT COMMENT

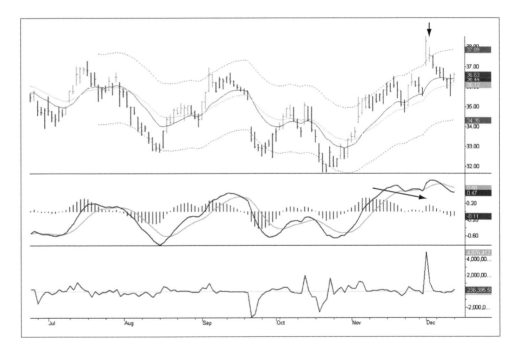

Diane has completed a very professional trade. She shorted a false breakout above the channel and covered when an overvalued stock fell below value, under its moving average.

The bearish divergence on the daily chart says that prices may go even lower, but Diane had accomplished what she wanted and is off looking for her next trade. A divergence may well push prices lower; however, a spike below the EMA indicates a rejection of lower prices and a possible end of this downmove.

If we squint at a chart long enough, we may find the signs telling us to go both long and short. A professional does not squint—she sees a pattern she likes, trades it, and closes her trade as soon as that pattern, in this case a false upside breakout, plays itself out and disappears. This is not a trade I would have taken—but I appreciate the quality of Diane's entry and exit.

# TRADE 2 | DIANE'S ENTRY

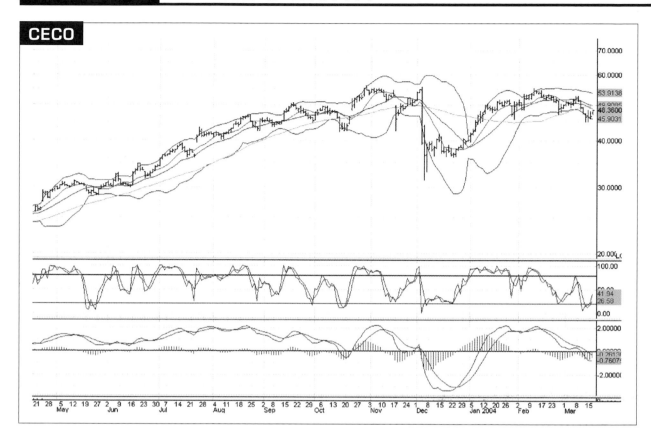

## CECO

This is one of my most vexing recent trades. I bought CECO following the news—not about the company, but about the administration in Washington. President Bush was talking about the importance of education; the unemployment figures came out on the high side, and he was saying, "We need to retrain these workers."

Retraining—that's what this company does. I heard the news, put up my chart, and said this looks like a good entry point. The stock is moving up from its Bollinger band, the Stochastic is moving up, the MACD is moving up. The stock is below its 50-day moving average—I think of that line as the spine of the stock, and if the price is below that line, it has so much more space to go up. So I bought and sat back happily.

Will this trade make or lose money?

# TRADE 2    DIANE'S EXIT

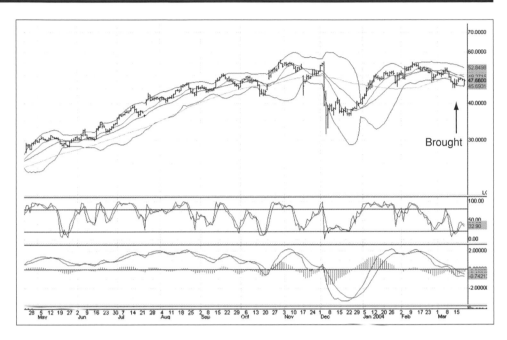

I always try to limit my losses in stocks to one point. CECO was no longer doing what it was supposed to do. The uptrend of the previous few days was broken, Stochastic turned down. I do not like watching losses—I lose a point, and I am out.

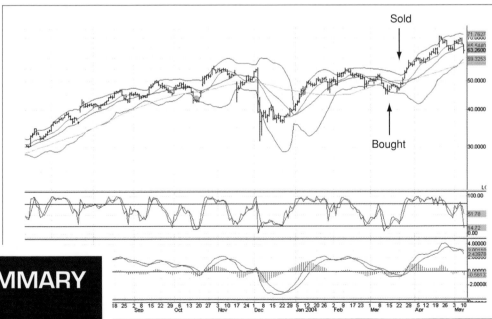

## ▼ TRADE SUMMARY

Long CECO
Bought 3/16/2004 @ $47.99
Sold 3/19/2004 @ $46.86
Loss = $1.13 per share

This stock went to 67—I missed a $20 move which lasted 21 days. I am still asking myself, "What was my mistake? What did I not see there?"

## TRADE 2 | ENTRY COMMENT

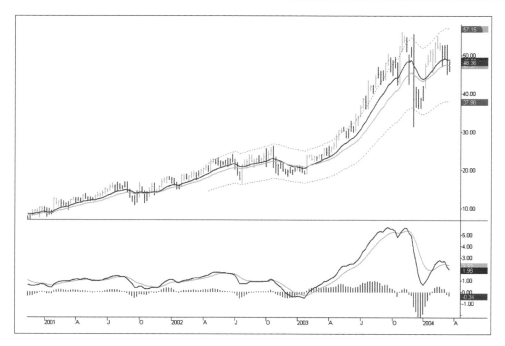

I stay away from stocks that have suffered large violent moves. They badly hurt investors and traders, who tend to remain skittish about that stock for several years to come. Their prices tend to become very jumpy, like a highly traumatized person is likely to remain nervous for a long time after an accident. Such stocks tend to have few sustainable trends, making them difficult to trade.

The weekly chart, covering the past three years of trading, shows a rise from below $10 to nearly $60. That rise culminated in a double top. The severe drop in 2003, precipitated by rumors of a scandal, left a huge tall bar that swung from above the upper channel line to below the lower line in one week.

At the right edge of the chart, the red line of the fast EMA is declining, along with MACD-Histogram. The Impulse system is red, prohibiting buying. If I had to trade this stock, I'd feel tempted to buy because the long bull market had not been cancelled; prices had just stabbed below value and recoiled. In any event, squint at any chart long enough and you'll find some trade—not necessarily the correct one. Here, a recent traumatic move turns me off from this stock, and the Impulse system only permits shorting, which does not look especially attractive for the same reason—the trauma is too fresh.

The daily chart shows that the move that cut the stock price from $55 to $30—nearly in half—took only two days. Think of the crowd of hurt and angry investors and traders it left behind. Following that drop, prices slowly and grudgingly pulled back up towards $55, creating a massive bearish divergence, and then turned down again. The bottom of MACD-Histogram in February is deeper than the one in January, indicating that the bears are becoming stronger and lower prices are likely ahead.

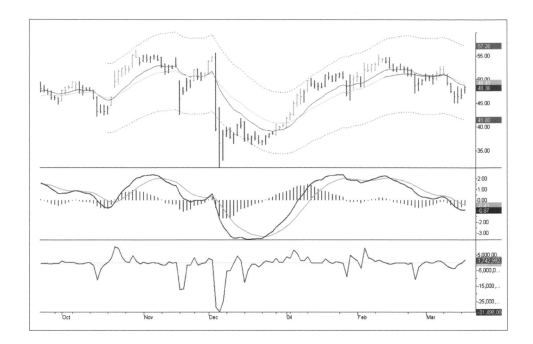

At the right edge of the daily chart the Impulse system is blue. Bulls are trying to find traction at the $45 level and the indicators are bottoming out. Still, with the weekly Impulse flashing a red signal, no buying is permitted.

# TRADE 2—EXIT COMMENT

While I am not thrilled with Diane's entry into this trade, I like her exit. She was out with a tiny loss as soon as the stock started sagging. She did not hang around, hoping and waiting. When her stock did not perform as expected, she cut it without delay. Some pros use stops based on time as well as price: They give their picks not only a price cushion to perform but also a time cushion. If a stock does not move their way, they cut it fast.

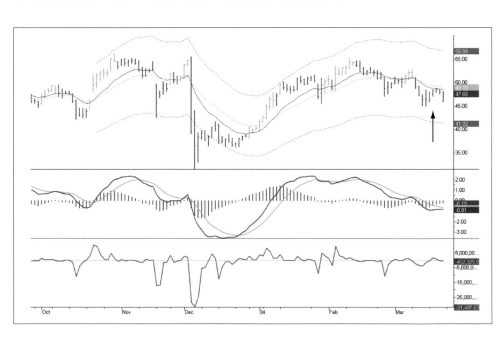

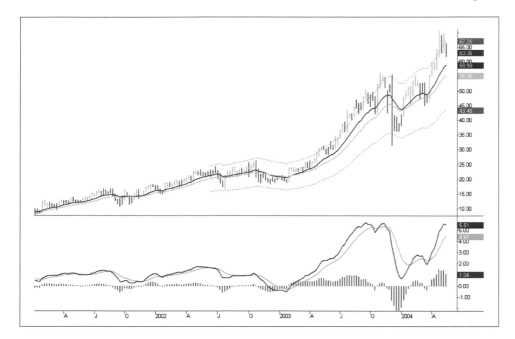

When Diane asks how to identify major moves, I turn to the Impulse system. It measures the inertia of the market with a moving average as well as the push of the bulls or bears with MACD-Histogram. The Impulse turns green for every major rally and red for every major decline. This change of color identifies every major price move.

The system is not magic—no system is—but as long as the weekly Impulse stays green, the uptrend is on; as long as it stays red, it confirms the downtrend. Here we see that the weekly Impulse turned green a few days after Diane got out of her trade; it remained green until weekly prices blew out of their channel to the upside. Had she wanted to reposition long in CECO, the Impulse system would have encouraged her to do so.

# OPTIONS: GET POOR QUICK

Even though Diane showed us two recent stock trades, she had earned the bulk of her profits writing options. In comparing options buyers to gamblers on a cruise ship, she highlighted an important point—buyers as a group lose money, while sellers as a group make money. In my experience, the situation is even harsher. In talking to hundreds of options buyers over the years, I have never met one who made money in the long run. Of course, each one had some successful trades or even series of trades—but I have not met a single person who built up equity buying options. A few told me they managed to do it, but none showed any evidence, leaving me to conclude that buying options is the deadliest game in the financial markets.

Poor beginners keep telling me they trade options because their capital is small; they cannot make enough money trading stocks. They think of options as a proxy for stocks—and I keep telling them that that is a dangerous delusion. Options move differently from stocks; a successful stock trader would lose money in the long run if he bought calls and puts instead of buying and shorting stocks.

The main reason that options are so deadly is that they are wasting assets. You can buy a stock, and if it rises slower than expected, you can hold it a little longer, giving it time to work out. You have no such luxury in options. As the expiration date approaches, their value drops towards zero. You can be right on the market, right on the sector, right on the stock—and still lose money on the option.

Trading is extremely competitive, with most winners bunched up in a tight pack. Winners are just a tiny bit better than the losers—their margin of victory is very narrow. The slightest deterioration of performance can push a winner down into the pack of losers. The fact that options are wasting assets is a powerful negative factor that cannot be overcome in the long run, only in a rare trade.

You may have heard the saying, "There is money in poverty." There is money in being a slumlord or selling overpriced goods in a depressed part of town. Similarly, there is money to be made in promoting options to small customers. Commissions add up rapidly, and even though most turkeys have their throats cut, enough new birds come in to keep the game going. As long as the poor dream of getting rich quickly, sales of lottery tickets will continue.

While buying options all but guarantees losses in the long run, writing options is not such an easy game either. Not all the money lost by options buyers goes to options writers. There are two brokers between them, one for the buyer and another for the seller, each taking his cut. Options writers tend to be more profitable when there are lots of beginners in the market. When new options are introduced, they tend to be mispriced in the sellers' favor, with options selling for more than they should according to theoretical valuation models. When listed stock options were introduced in the United States in the 1970s, most were overpriced and writers made easy money (see Chapter 7). It is no surprise that Diane made the bulk of her money writing options in a crazy bull market with its irrational exuberance. Remember this if you live in a country whose financial markets are just starting to add options—early options sellers do the best!

A beginner has no business trading options. For those who insist on buying calls, I have one bit of advice—take your money to Las Vegas or Atlantic City instead. The outcome will be the same, but at least you'll have free drinks while achieving it.

*An e-mail from Diane:*

## OPTIONS AND CHESS

I love options. They are flexible, exciting, and enable me to be creative in anticipating and reacting to the market. Strategies and positions can be as varied as your thinking and creativity. The intricacies of complicated spreads stand in stark contrast to the dramatic beauty of the naked put, boldly daring the market to "put it to me" to make me buy a stock.

When I first struggled to understand the complexities of options, I developed a simple chart to help me keep the moves straight. It very quickly became evident that buying options was a risky proposition. To begin with, my money would be leaving the account, which was the opposite of my goal. I could profit only if the stock moved by more than the price of the option in less than the time allowed. No wonder most buyers wash out—buying options is a

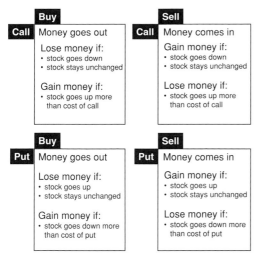

| **Buy** | |
|---|---|
| **Call** | Money goes out |

Lose money if:
• stock goes down
• stock stays unchanged

Gain money if:
• stock goes up more
  than cost of call

| **Sell** | |
|---|---|
| **Call** | Money comes in |

Gain money if:
• stock goes down
• stock stays unchanged

Lose money if:
• stock goes up more
  than cost of call

| **Buy** | |
|---|---|
| **Put** | Money goes out |

Lose money if:
• stock goes up
• stock stays unchanged

Gain money if:
• stock goes down more
  than cost of put

| **Sell** | |
|---|---|
| **Put** | Money comes in |

Gain money if:
• stock goes up
• stock stays unchanged

Lose money if:
• stock goes down more
  than cost of put

very efficient way to lose money. "Who do they lose it to?" I wondered. "They might as well lose it to me!" And so I started taking the opposite side of the trade. When I sell options, money comes into my account, a much more comfortable proposition. And I always have a choice—I can close the position, hedge it, or let it expire at 100 percent profit.

I developed a very simple strategy: Sell at-the-money puts when the stock is low and sell at-the-money calls when the stock is high. The odds were in my favor because I was selling time. Even if the stock remained at the same price, the time decay gave me a profit. Thus I began naively taking money from the market, before ever learning about Bollinger bands, Stochastics, MACD, etc.

I was often asked, "If this is so simple, why don't more people do it?" My response: Options are like chess. Why don't more people play chess? Beginning players are interested in the "pieces"—puts and calls—and the "moves"—buying and selling. Few have the concentration and fascination to learn strategy: When to make an offensive move (open a position) or a defensive move (close a position). Few understand that their opponent is the market, and to win we must anticipate the opponent's move up or its move down. It is better to anticipate and close a profitable position after the market has moved than to be reactive and open a position after a move has taken place. Successful chess players often use the tactic of sacrifice, offering a major piece to gain a tactical advantage on the board. Selling a naked put is like a daring queen sacrifice (in chess), when a trader offers to be forced to buy stock on a downturn, but also at a prepaid discount. In both chess and options, success depends on a combination of strategy, courage, and discipline; the idea is to anticipate the next move and not to fold a position at a loss.

Most new traders invest too much time in searching and screening for the "right" stock, and too little time thinking out a successful strategy for managing the position. With options, a trader can profit from more ambiguous positions, and use the fourth dimension—time—to enhance profits.

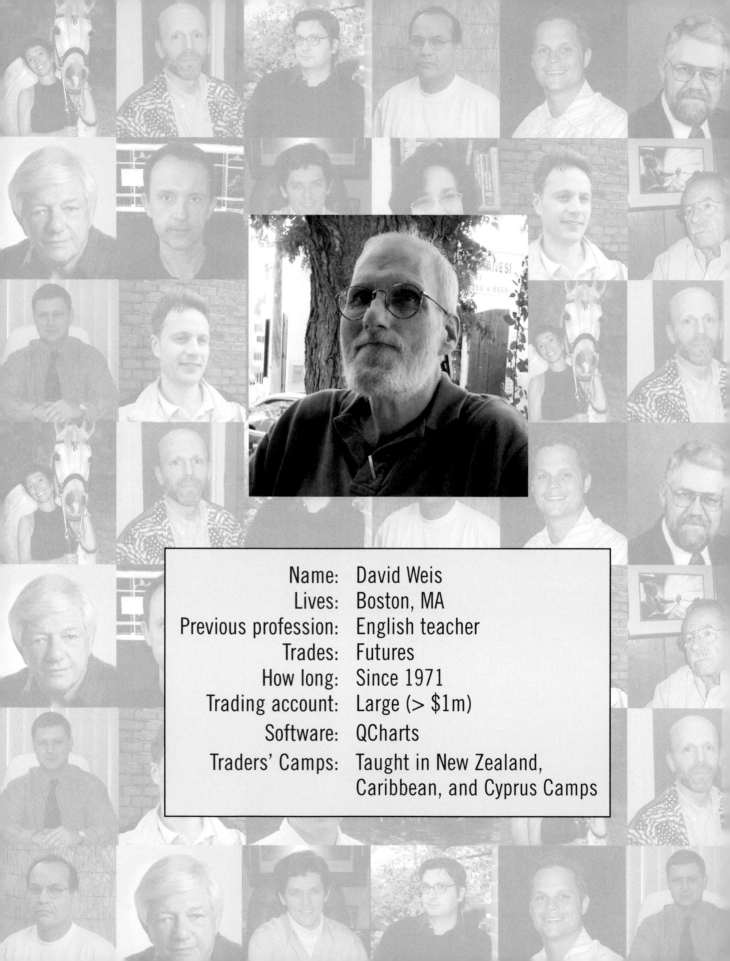

Name: David Weis
Lives: Boston, MA
Previous profession: English teacher
Trades: Futures
How long: Since 1971
Trading account: Large (> $1m)
Software: QCharts
Traders' Camps: Taught in New Zealand, Caribbean, and Cyprus Camps

# CHAPTER 11

# DAVID WEIS

## PRICE-VOLUME BEHAVIOR IS STEEPED IN REALITY

In the early '90s I read David's book on the Elliott Wave and called to congratulate him. I was not a fan of the Elliott theory, but felt that his book explained it better than any other. He came to teach a seminar for my firm, and we enjoyed each other's company. I invited David to teach at my Traders' Camps, but he did not want to be away from the screen, and I stopped calling. Years later he called me out of the blue: "I see you have a Camp coming up in New Zealand; Karen wants to go to New Zealand; who will be teaching there with you?" "You," I said immediately. Once David taught at that Camp, he wanted to come to more, and in recent years he has become one of our most popular instructors.

David pulled away from Elliott, calling it "an attempt to impose a static form on the dynamic structure of the market," and focused instead on the price-volume relationship. Every intelligent person who takes a class with David is influenced by his superb chart-reading techniques. When I look at charts with my friends, we often say to each other, "David would draw a line here!" David is writing a new book, moving forward at a glacial pace. All my attempts to speed him up, including an offer of a free ticket to Europe if he finished in time for Christmas, have proven fruitless. Still, when I invited David for an interview, he hopped on a train from Boston and came to New York to talk and have lunch.

In the 1960s, while studying for a graduate degree in English literature, I got a teaching job and received my first lesson in supply and demand—that English teachers were a dime a dozen. I left and joined a friend working in the research department of a commodities firm in Memphis, my hometown. I spent days doing charts by hand for technical analysts, while reading Edwards and Magee and R.N. Elliott. In 1971 the markets were heating up, the firm made me a technical analyst, and I also qualified as a broker. One of my accounts was making a fortune trading large positions, going up to the size limit in some markets. The man whose account it was told us about the Wyckoff course offered by the Stock Market Institute, which was then in Chicago. Wyckoff was one of the early giants of technical analysis and the course he wrote is still being taught today. It led to a great improvement in our ability to forecast for the company—and ultimately this man hired us away. He traveled the world, and he would contact us regarding his positions, calling from the Great Wall of China or Machu Picchu, knowing we spoke the same language. Deficit spending was coming home to roost, and the inflationary spiral was lifting commodities from their long bases and creating long-term capital gains.

I worked for this client for three years. Then he got involved in other things, and I went back to the commodity brokerage house and became their director of technical research. After the firm was bought out, I worked for Bob Prechter, writing *The Elliott Wave Commodity Letter*, and shortly after the crash of 1987, started *Technical Forces*—my own newsletter, much more oriented to Wyckoff. I contributed several articles to *Technical Analysis of Stocks and Commodities*, which were later incorporated into a book. I also wrote a handbook, *Trading with the Elliott Wave Principle: A Practical Guide*, but it is out of print now. I stopped my newsletter in 1992. Now I just run a few accounts on a discretionary basis without holding myself out as any kind of advisor. I consult, occasionally write reports, and speak at conferences. I keep trying to write my book on Wyckoff which has been brewing inside of me for many years.

My approach to trading has evolved over the years. Like everyone else, I went from pillar to post, looking for a secret automatic method for making money. I played with indicators—they did not work for me, although they work for other people. I thought they provided intermittent reinforcement, just enough for you to come back—"Will the real divergence please stand up?" You have to concentrate on what's right for you, and for me it was price-volume behavior. I focus on that and am trying to rid myself of the Elliott Wave. As elegant as the Elliott Wave is, with all its mathematical qualities, it is trying to impose a static pattern on the dynamic entity that is price movement. Price-volume behavior is steeped in reality, and appeals to me more than the mathematical approach.

In his famous book *Studies in Tape Reading,* Wyckoff wrote "Successful tape reading is a study of force. It requires an ability to judge which side has the greatest pulling power and one must have the courage to go with that side. There are critical points which occur in each swing just as in the life of a business or an individual. At these junctures it seems as though a feather's weight on either side would determine the immediate trend. Anyone who can spot these points has much to win and little to lose."

I apply the principles of tape reading to daily charts, but I do not like cookie-cutter rules. I accept only grayness in the world, and rarely see black or white. The only certainty is uncertainty, and I love living with it. I study price and volume, pay a great deal of attention to the height of every price bar, whether daily or intraday, and the position of the close. You have to be aware of the ease of movement either up or down.

Finding a trade is like finding fish in a lake. You do not go to the middle of the lake and drop anchor. You work where the fish feed and build nests—around the edges. You look for trading ranges, whether on weekly, daily, or intraday charts. If there is a breakout and no follow-through, you wait to see how it acts on a pullback.

If you get a legitimate breakout, and later the market pulls back into that area and the ranges become narrow while the closes gravitate to the high of the bar, it is a sign of strength. Conversely, if after a breakdown the market pulls up in narrow ranges and closes low, it is a sign of weakness. When the market breaks out on high volume but there is no follow-through, it shows that a strong effort brings no reward, and it may be gearing up for an upthrust—a false upside breakout. Or it can do that on the way down, setting up a potential spring, a false downside breakout.

I try to buy where the reward is high and the risk is low. I do not like chasing breakouts. I like fading them after they start to fail. Another thing I watch for is what Wyckoff called absorption. The market is coming up to resistance—old longs sell, new shorts come in to establish positions. You can often tell when the market undergoes absorption—there is a great deal of volume, but not enough reward as the market gets ready to reverse.

## Inconsistent Trading

What book or author would you recommend for working through trading problems? I'm too optimistic about losing trades, and hoping for them to come back. Initially, I set stop-losses, then loosened them during the trade. By my calculations, I'd be making at least twice as much if I didn't do this. I continue my behavior, possibly because it works sometimes. About one-third of the time, when I give a trade more room, it comes back and becomes a break-even or winning trade. When it fails, it wipes out the profits from several winning trades. Of course, I've read the complete works of Dr. Alex Elder already. And Mark Douglas. And several others. Are there other books that might benefit me?          —*Trader*

Instead of recommending a book, I suggest a little competition. Open a small account in addition to your main one. Continue to play games in your main account (selective reinforcement is a great motivator), but do trades according to your rules in the little account—again, an account so small that it almost does not matter. See which account outperforms the other. Give free enterprise and competition a chance on the home front.          —*AE*

# TRADE 1 | DAVID'S ENTRY

### Sugar

In 2004 I had a long-term bullish perspective on sugar, based on the yearly cash chart going back to 1932. It showed an enormous multiyear apex, and on long-term charts I especially look for price tightness. It means that forces of supply and demand are coming to the point of equilibrium, which eventually is going to be shattered. The long-term study is really mouth-watering, but it requires enormous patience.

Sugar made a low in 1999, rallied briskly in 2000, and then for four years held within the range of 2000. Toby Crabel made a study of narrow bar ranges—if you see three or four bars in a row that are the narrowest of the last 20 bars, it shows a tightening of forces, and there is going to be an eruption one way or the other. He did not apply this to yearly charts, but I think it is appropriate to do so.

There was also some cyclical evidence of a bottom. There is a 17.5-year cycle in sugar, as well as in many other markets. Sugar had major lows in 1932, 1949, 1967, 1985, and either 2003 or 2004. So I've got cyclical evidence in addition to the tightening of the ranges. Sugar is a cheap market—a penny here, a penny there, but if you pile up contracts, it adds up.

Sugar was in an uptrend coming into June 2004. On June 18 there was a sharp selloff which threatened to derail the trend, but the market rallied immediately. It became tightly congested in area *B*. I thought it represented absorption because the closes in area *B* were near the highs. The buyers kept coming in intraday, and by the end of the day the bears

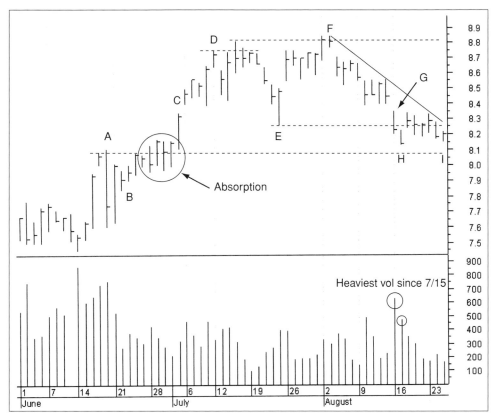

**Upper pane:**  Daily bar chart
**Lower pane:**  Volume

In July and August of 2004 I was trading March 2005 sugar to gain more time. You need that when you trade long-term. I am not worried about the rollover cost—I want to give the market more time to develop. I may reduce or expand my position, but I like to sit with the basic core position—get in at a good level and be ready to give back some profit. I learned this from my mentor, who took large long positions and traveled the world—I guess his training left an imprint on me. This is not how I conduct the bulk of my trading, but when it happens, it provides the greatest potential for profit as long as you have the discipline to leave the market alone. It is difficult to hold long-term when you sit in front of the screen.

would capitulate. At point *C*, demand overcame supply, and sugar continued upward to point *D*. There on July 15, we had only a slight new high above the previous high—it represented the shortening of the upthrust. On that day sugar closed well off its high, making it logical to expect a pullback and then a retest of the breakout.

At point *E*, there was a test of the previous highs on heavy volume—that support held, and a trading range formed between levels *D* and *E*. Sugar went back to the top of the range at *F*, but on August 3, you can see that the daily range narrowed. There was no ease of upward movement, which raised the possibility that the breakout was going to fail. Sugar broke down on a gap and started to decline.

At point *G* on August 16, we had the heaviest volume since the high of July 15, and the market went through the low it had established at point *E*. The next day at point *H*, sugar moved lower but with a smaller range, while the volume was still heavy—there was not much reward for all that effort. In that area, demand overcame supply, and the next day the market jumped back into its range. That's when I was watching closely where to reenter the sugar market. At point *I*, the day's range was very narrow, the volume low, the bar closed higher and near the top of that day's range. This retest of point *H* told me to go long. I got in at 8.19 and put a stop at 8.10, as if telling the market: "Prove me wrong, sucker!"

# TRADE 1 | DAVID'S EXIT

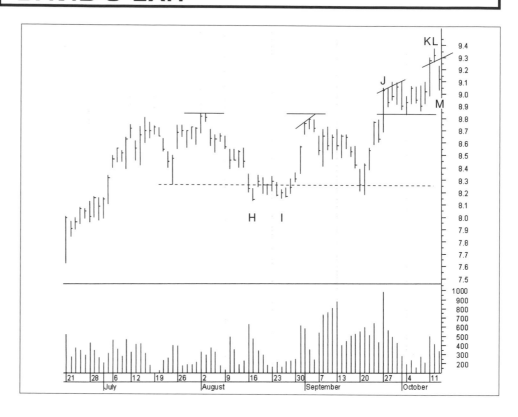

I went long on August 25 at 8.19, at point *I*. There was no instant gratification the next day, but I kept the position and the stop, and then the uptrend resumed. It unfolded in a series of higher highs and higher supports. On September 27 at point *J*, sugar broke through its July high on very heavy volume—a wide price move with a strong close, as demand overcame supply. This was followed by nine days of lateral movement as the market absorbed profit-taking, long liquidation, and new short selling. On October 11 at point *K*, the uptrend resumed, but the volume was quite a bit lower than at point *J*. The next day, October 12, the market moved up with a very short high-low range, closing at midrange. The volume was almost as heavy as the day before. That was troubling behavior which warranted raising stops, but not getting out. I raised my stop to just below the low of bar *K*. The next day, October 13, the last day on this chart, the market gapped lower, and I got out, closed out my position.

The reason I got out of this trade was that in his tape-reading course Wyckoff said you can identify turning points. You can tell when the trend is ending by watching the length of the bars and the volume during buying and selling waves. The day before I exited the price narrowed, but on the last day it jumped to the widest level in months. As sugar went up, its daily ranges narrowed, and then it went down on the biggest downday since June 18. That's what told me to get out of my long position. This was one of several trades I made in sugar in 2004, applying tape-reading methods to reading bar charts.

## ▲ TRADE SUMMARY

Long March 2005 Sugar
Bought 8/25/04 @ 8.19¢
Sold 10/13/04 @ 9.15¢
Profit = 0.96¢ per pound

# TRADE 1—ENTRY COMMENT

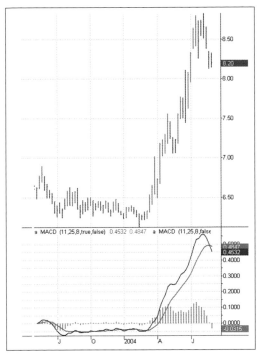

The left side of the weekly chart shows the start of a bull move in sugar. Look at the bottom of MACD-Histogram in July 2003, when bears still had some power. A few months later, in the early part of 2004, they drove sugar to a new low, but this indicator registered a much more shallow bottom. David would probably call the chart pattern a false bearish breakout and a spring. A bullish divergence of a technical indicator gives the same message—bears are exhausted, bulls are ready to take control. When different analytic methods give the same message, they reinforce one another.

The new high of MACD-Histogram in July 2004 indicated that bulls were extremely strong. The new peak of the indicator suggested that sugar was likely to rise even higher after its current pause. While we can expect higher prices ahead, at the right edge of the chart the Impulse system prohibits buying. As long as it stays red, bears are in charge, and buyers must sit on their hands and wait.

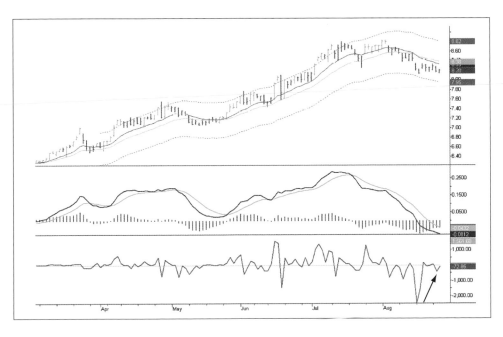

*Still, daily MACD-Histogram is pretty heavy, with a recent new low pointing to the short-term strength of the bears and no sign of a bullish divergence. The Impulse system is blue, allowing us to go either long or short. Sugar has the look and feel of a bull market nearing the tail-end of its correction—but still no clear sign that the correction has ended. The weekly Impulse tells buyers to wait until it goes off red.*

This daily chart suggests that sugar is getting close to the bottom of its pullback. The Force Index shows bullish divergence, and MACD Lines that have been declining for several weeks are starting to turn in the area previously associated with bottoms.

# TRADE 1—EXIT COMMENT

At the right edge of the chart, sugar is above its upper channel line, a severely overbought area, while MACD-Histogram is much lower than it was in September. The slightest downtick would create a bearish divergence. The next day prices opened lower, and David sold his position.

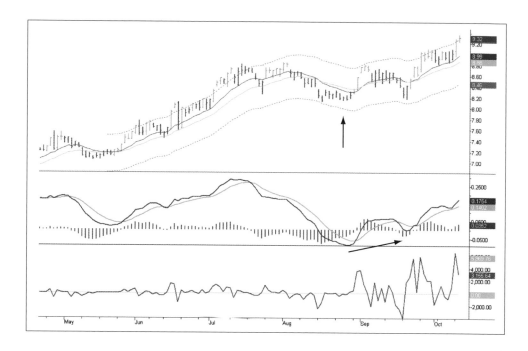

The rally that began after David bought sugar quickly ran into resistance near the upper channel line. Prices turned down again and kept grinding out buyers for two more weeks. In mid-September sugar futures stabbed below value, towards the lower channel line. The next day prices rallied, leaving behind a beautiful bullish divergence. From there on, sugar went straight up, hitting the upper channel line on convincing new peaks of MACD-Histogram and the Force Index. These new highs indicated strength and called for even higher prices ahead.

In looking at David's sugar trade, it looks like he entered a little too early. I would have waited until the weekly Impulse released me to go long. David's exit, though, is a thing of beauty—he sold into an upside breakout when the market was boiling, and latecomers were falling over each other trying to buy sugar from him. "Buy low and sell high" is much harder to implement than it may sound!

**AVOID THINGS THAT GIVE YOU COMFORT**

*David noted:* If I could recommend one specific piece of writing to struggling or would-be traders, it is Jack Schwager's interview with William Eckhardt in *The New Market Wizards*. His systems approach is contrary to my intuitive style. Yet, one finds so much reality and common sense in Eckhardt's words. Here are some samples:

"I'm not sure that I made any money from my ideas about the market."

"Too fine an eye for pattern will find it anywhere."

"We don't look at data neutrally."

On buying retracements: "Avoid those things that give you comfort; it's usually false comfort."

"If you bring normal human habits and tendencies to trading, you'll gravitate toward the majority and inevitably lose."

# TRADE 2 | DAVID'S ENTRY

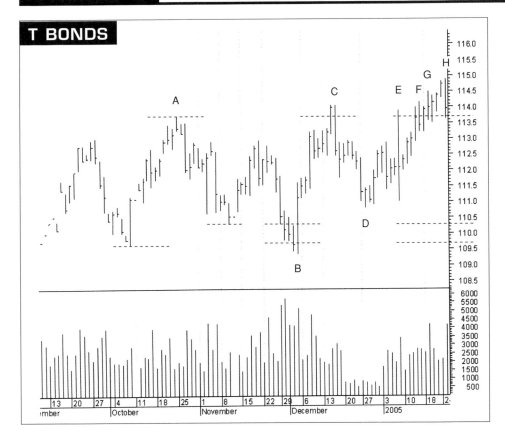

**T BONDS**

In approaching a market, I always begin by framing its trading range. I take the ruler to the paper, trying to see where the fish feed, so to speak. March 2005 bonds were in a volatile 3.5-point trading range from September 2004 to January 2005. At point *A* they hit resistance, went down, and in December washed out the bottom at point *B* before rallying back. An upthrust occurred on December 16 at point *C*, and then the market came down to a low at point *D* on December 28.

## T Bonds

I tried to figure out which way the bond market was going to go based on its trading range. I was leaning more towards the bearish side, as the reversal in area *C* weighed heavily on my mind. Bonds ran up to a new high on the Employment Report on January 7 and then fell sharply. I thought the evidence was mounting in areas *C* and *E* that sellers were becoming dominant. The market stabilized from its January 7 low and slowly began to rise.

I've been watching bonds very intensely since 1981, and such a creeping rise usually means that buyers are strong. Bonds broke out above the trading range, but then on January 14 at point *F*, reversed down. That made me think that sellers were flexing their muscles and were about to gain the upper hand. On January 19 at point *G*, there was a big effort to push the market up on big volume—bonds moved higher, but closed well off the high. The very next day, the market held like a rock, but I was still suspicious following the downside reversals *C*, *E*, and *F*. The rally looked like it was struggling—bonds were at a new high ground, but not moving with alacrity; it could be their last gasp. On the last day of this chart, at point *H*, bonds broke on big volume, and I thought it was a downside reversal on big supply. Bonds did not fall back into their trading range, but I thought they were going to. I decided that even if I was a little early, I would short a minimal amount of June bonds.

I have been charting the March 2005 future but sold June at 113.01. I also sold a minimal amount of the 10-year note. I used no stop—I felt certain we were very near a major extremity. With every fiber in my body I knew I was right.

will this trade make or lose money?

# TRADE 2    DAVID'S EXIT

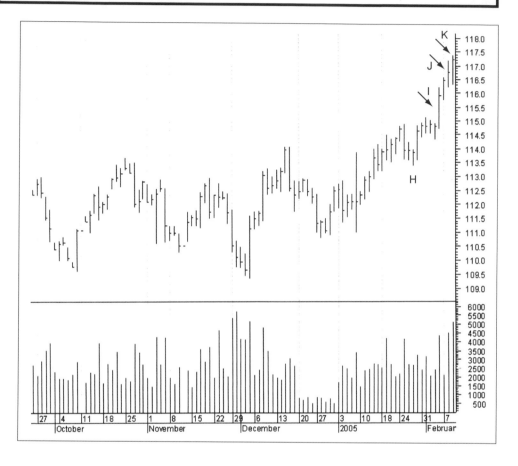

I went short at point *H*, thinking I was going to get eight points on the way down. The bonds started going up, and at point *I*, they accelerated to the upside. They moved even higher and with great force at point *J*. The volume at *J* was higher, but the range was lower and the close off the high—so I figured they were selling again.

At the right edge, at point *K*, I decided to make my position bigger. I knew we were at the top because, for all their high volume, bonds were making little progress. This time I put in a stop because by now bonds had become a burr in my side—every day I thought of my open loss. So I figured I'd put in a stop because bonds could not go any higher. I put in a stop at 116-20 basis June and was stopped out one tick below the high.

By then what had started as a very minor position had gotten to me. Intellectually I knew we were at a top, but because I had dragged it out for so long now, I felt forced to put in a stop. And then, after I got stopped out, I did not have the emotional flexibility to go back and short again. This was a good lesson to be patient and limit your risk from the outset—because if you don't, it becomes big and messes with your mind.

## ▼ TRADE SUMMARY

**Short June 2005 Treasury Bonds**
Shorted 1/25/05 @ $113.01
Covered 2/9/2005 @ $116.20
Loss = 3 19/32 points

## TRADE 2 | ENTRY COMMENT

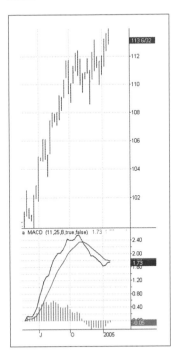

This chart reminds me that the main value of the Impulse system is its censorship role, flashing a "go" or "no go" signal for every trade. Whether you base your trade on technical or fundamental factors, it pays to glance at the weekly Impulse system before you put on your trade.

The last bar on this weekly chart is green, telling us that both the EMA and MACD-Histogram are rising. The inertia and push of the market are in tune with each other, lifting prices. The green bar on the weekly chart tells even rabid bears to stand aside and wait to short. At some point in the future, the bulls will stumble and MACD-Histogram will tick down, turn the Impulse blue, and permit us to short. This system will not catch the top tick of the upmove, but then no system would do that with any degree of consistency.

Near the right edge of the chart, MACD-Histogram is rising from below zero. This tends to indicate the most dynamic part of an upmove. Once MACD-Histogram crosses its zero line and starts rising above it, the rally is likely to become more ragged. While this sign is bullish, there is a very important bearish sign at a very early stage of development: Considering the age of the rally and the level of MACD-Histogram, there is little chance it will reach its 2004 peak. Prices are already at a new high, which means that when MACD does turn down, it will create a massive bearish divergence, giving a strong shorting signal. Bonds appear to be building a major top, but it is not completed and the uptrend is not ready to reverse.

The bonds are moving up nicely within an orderly channel. Near the right edge of the daily chart, they have rallied above their December peak. A question immediately arises: Is this a new rally within a healthy uptrend or a false upside breakout from which prices are likely to collapse? Let us review the evidence.

The Force Index keeps reaching a new high on every upleg of the rally since December. It confirms that bulls in bonds are becoming more forceful as the rally progresses. With everything in gear to the upside, it seems too early to sell bonds short.

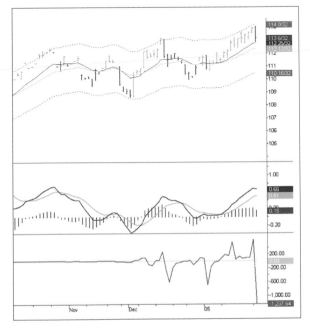

When bonds rallied to a new high in January, above the level of their December peak, MACD-Histogram also traced a peak, more massive than the one it hit in December. The January peak is not higher, but it is broad and reasonably high—its total area is probably greater than the peak in December. It appears that bulls were marginally stronger in January than they were in December—there is no divergence, the uptrend is confirmed.

# TRADE 2—EXIT COMMENT

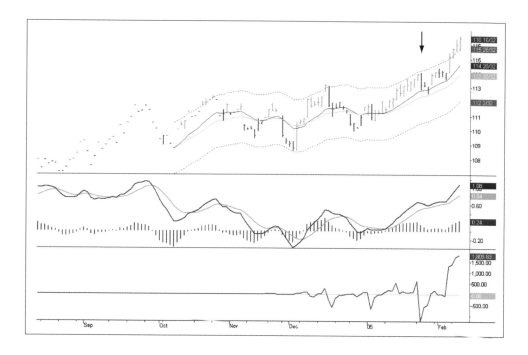

David, along with others in this book, has done readers a favor by allowing them into his trading room on a bad day as well as on a good one. His bond trade reveals that even an expert of his caliber occasionally makes mistakes. Beginners who make errors beat themselves over the head and become even more anxious, which does not help their trading. David calmly accepts his oversight, makes a mental note of it, and moves on to the next trade.

A trading loss is seldom caused by a single error. A trader usually makes a series of mistakes, which add up to create a loss, and that's what we see here. David shorted an uptrend, did not use a stop, then remained short even after prices broke out to a new high. He tried to explain away each new upside breakout, rationalizing his trade.

There is an old market saying: "Run quickly or not at all." A trader who does not run fast enough hangs on to a loss and finally runs in disgust at the worst possible time. Ask yourself whether you would buy bonds at the right edge of the chart. Of course not—they are completely overbought, way above their upper channel line. But that's what a person with a losing trade usually does—buys to cover his shorts and stop the pain. It pays to remember: "Run quickly or not at all!"

I normally avoid second-guessing traders, but could not resist showing this weekly chart of bonds.

It turned out David was right about the coming top and downside reversal in bonds. His timing was a bit off—he was too early, a typical error of smart people. Right after David was stopped out, bonds ticked down, creating a massive bearish divergence. The Impulse system turned blue, permitting shorting—and it was all the way downhill from there for bonds, with bears raking in profits. Had David waited to short or exited a losing trade early, he'd have been fresh enough to jump back into a short trade.

## A Money Test

I've kept meticulous records of my trades over the past 3 years and have earned a return of just over 30% per year. Recently, I subscribed to TradeStation for one month to see what would happen if I was able to trade in shorter timeframes. What would be the result if I watched 13-day EMA for the trend and used hourly MACD-Histogram (my modification of your system) to find good entry and exit points?

My backtesting seemed too good to be true. I wonder if, in your experience, these results show a fatal flaw somewhere in the strategy? Trading 10 stocks, there were 36 positions that I could have taken. Following the 2% and 6% Rules, it would not have been possible to trade all 36. My system generated winners 72.22% of the time, and losers 27.78% of the time. My average win was 1.71% of a hypothetical trading account. My average loss was 1.33%. My trades lasted an average 5.25 days, and the potential results seem astronomical . . . a return of at least 0.5% per trading day!

In your experience, is this too good to be true? I am intensely interested because I would love to find a way to trade full-time for a living. But with limited means I must seek out trading capital to work with.          —*Trader*

This is a fairly typical example of a letter that comes in about once a month. It differs from others only in that the author says he has been trading real money for three years. A typical letter presents great results from paper-trading. I usually write back—"The only test worth doing is a test with real money. I wonder why you do not trust your data enough to lay even a bit of your own money on it?" My advice is to start trading a small account and see whether you can generate your 0.5% per day with real money.          —*AE*

# THE TRACKS OF BULLS AND BEARS

There are three groups of traders in every financial market. Bulls want to buy as cheaply as possible and profit when prices rise. Bears want to sell as expensively as possible and profit when prices fall. Undecided traders may join either group, strengthening it and pushing prices in its favor. Each tick reflects a transaction between a bull and a bear, surrounded by a crowd of undecided traders. A tick is a momentary consensus of value, and as ticks coalesce into bars, they create chart patterns. David interprets those patterns in order to make trading decisions.

For example, David pays a great deal of attention to the height of every bar. A tall bar indicates a relative ease of movement, but if it is followed by a short and stunted bar, it means that the trend is running into resistance. He is very attentive to the placement of the closing tick within each bar, reflecting the outcome of the battle between bulls and bears. He relies on these and other observations, trying to decide whether the current trend is likely to continue or to reverse.

David also pays a great deal of attention to volume, which he links with price changes. For example, he may refer to a narrow-range day with high volume as "a lot of effort for a minimal gain." He sees that as a sign of resistance and expects a reversal of the preceding trend. While I value David's approach to charts and have learned a lot from him, I think that the Force Index provides a clearer view of market activity than volume bars.

I eagerly await David's new book, in which he may lay out his entire approach to the market. I am especially interested in what he calls "springs and upthrusts"—false downside and upside breakouts. One of the key differences between pros and amateurs is their handling of breakouts. Amateurs tend to buy upside breakouts and short downside breakouts, expecting a new trend to make them a lot of money in a hurry. Professionals tend to take the opposite view—they expect most breakouts to fizzle out. Pros are more likely to fade breakouts—trade against them.

I often say to my students, only partly tongue-in-cheek: "Buy new lows and short new highs." You cannot do this automatically without thinking, but when you see an upside breakout, it pays to look for evidence of weakness and a shorting opportunity. When you see a downside breakout, it is important not to overlook the evidence of strength, a buying opportunity.

Most trading books repeat the same advice—when long, put a stop below an important low, and when short, above an important high. When David draws support lines below the lows and resistance lines above the highs, it is nothing short of amazing how often the market will violate those lines by a tiny margin, only to reverse and come roaring back. One of the lessons I've learned from David after sitting in his classes in several Traders' Camps is to watch support and resistance lines. If a support line is violated and then prices come back and close above it, they give one of the strongest buy signals, with limited risk. If prices break above resistance by a small margin and then return to close below that line, they offer a low-risk shorting opportunity. I also rely on my indicators, but David's method lies at the root of my approach to trading reversals. In reading this book you should take from it what makes sense to you and blend it with your other methods.

*An e-mail from David:*

# A BATTLE MAP, A TREASURE MAP

It's odd how things evolve. When I landed a job with the technical research department of a commodity brokerage house, I plotted (and updated) charts manually. They became works of art: smooth paper covered with straight, black lines drawn with a fine-point pen. You could close your eyes, rub your hand across a newly made chart, and feel the imprint of the trend. It became a battle map, a treasure map, a pictograph telling a story from the past.

First, I studied Elliott Wave and was thrilled by its mystical implications. Anyone who would listen heard my discourse on the predictive powers of Fibonacci numbers, ratios, and reciprocals. Then through the beneficence of a client, I enrolled in the Wyckoff course. The idea of large interests manipulating the markets from behind the scenes added to the mystery of the charts. Supposedly, all one had to do was read the footprints of these large operators and follow along like a remora attached to a shark. These footprints told a story of accumulation and distribution which unfolded according to specific forms of behavior.

For about 20 years, I used the Elliott Wave to identify markets that were at or near extremities of varying degrees, and I studied price/volume behavior for signs of ending action that confirmed the wave count. Yet, I saw more and more that many trading opportunities arose without fitting into a neatly constructed wave count. So I drifted further and further away from the Wave Principle. Similarly, ending action rarely had the classic characteristics of accumulation and distribution. Instead, it was a matter of subtle changes of behavior that tipped the scale in favor of one side or the other.

I have distilled the study of price/volume behavior into the simple elements of price range, position of the close, effort versus reward, ease of movement, follow-through or lack of follow-through, and the interaction of various lines. The market is a kaleidoscope, a wheel of appearances, in which the only certainty is uncertainty. Nothing is black or white; it is gray. Every situation can be interpreted in two ways, creating a constant duality between bullishness and bearishness. It is my job to make a case for the more logical story. Mine is an approach—an art—without rules, without indicators, without cookie cutters. It can be summed up by the words of D.T. Suzuki: "If one really wishes to be a master of an art, technical knowledge of it is not enough. One has to transcend technique so that the art becomes an 'artless art' growing out of the unconscious."

In the beginning, an unmarked chart...

Name: William Doane
Lives: Lexington, MA
Previous profession: Technical analyst
Trades: Stocks
How long: Since 1999
Trading account: Large (> $1m)
Software: TC2005

# CHAPTER 12

# WILLIAM DOANE

## THE BIGGER THE FOUNDATION, THE TALLER THE BUILDING

I drove to Boston to see Bill at his home. He met me at a highway exit, and as he pulled his Lincoln into a two-car garage, I saw that the second space was filled with neat rows of carefully labeled boxes with market materials. Long shelves held stacks of charts, arranged by year.

Several rooms upstairs held more materials; large, well-oiled filing cabinets opened to reveal rows of alphabetized and color-coded folders. "Aluminum," followed by "Astrology," was next to "Bermuda Triangle" in one drawer. Another began with "New Highs—New Lows" and proceeded through "Mexico," "Municipals," "Numismatics," and down to "Oats." Still another filing cabinet held folders of newsletter clippings, some by current writers, others by long-dead analysts.

"I am a collector, a junk collector," joked Bill, but his collection was neatly organized, and he could easily find anything he wanted. He had been the head technician of the Fidelity organization in Boston, where he created a massive chart room, covering 12-foot-high walls with graphs of every technical and fundamental indicator under the sun. Bill seemed a little wistful when I pointed out there was no longer the need for such a room. A slender laptop in my travel bag held a complete database, and a trader could produce any chart by pushing a few keys.

Bill uses computers, with four sleek screens on his desk, but he still subscribes to a chart service. While we were talking on a Saturday morning, a fat package of charts arrived by priority mail, and Bill grinned: "An old habit; I like to have a hard copy in front of me."

After earning his master's degree in finance from the University of Denver, Bill got a part-time job with an accounting firm. The firm was underwriting a stock issue, and paid him with shares instead of cash. Those shares were floated at $1.50, Bill quickly sold at $3, and never looked back. In the days when technical analysts worked with India ink and pens, Bill, the son of a draftsman, felt right at home in a chart room.

> The average guy looks at a daily chart, scarcely at a weekly. I look at monthlies—and I remember those pictures. When stocks come out of their bases, they sprint. I look for long bases and trade breakouts. I am not smart enough to buy bottoms; I buy strength. This approach is dull and uninteresting, but there is potential there.

Look at this stock—it has just cleared its 1984 top. No one looks that far back, but if it's cleared its 1984 top, it means business. I use monthly, weekly, and daily charts. I tried different indicators and volume, but in the end it all came down to price. I was conditioned by Fidelity: They do not want a stock that'll break out tomorrow; they need several months to accumulate a full position.

After I left Fidelity, I started an advisory service and sent my top 15 picks each month to a handful of clients and friends. I would watch price levels and wait for breakouts. My best pick was WorldCom; it had a different name then, when it started up from that beautiful base. It was called LDDS Communications, Inc., and its sidewise movement extended from 1980 to mid-1990!

By 1998 and 1999 I ran out of bases and could not generate a list of 15 buys per month. So the service ended in 1999. Unbeknownst to me, we were at the top of the bull market. Now, in 2005, I see plenty of bases, as the cycle repeats.

I think that there is order to the market, and you can make money buying stocks that peaked at a certain time. We had major peaks in the market, and afterwards it just takes so many years to recycle those stocks. After the reaccumulation process, they are ready to run again. Some stocks peaked in 1996 or 1998, others in 1999, then of course, many peaked in 2000—and that's the order in which they are likely to come out of their bases once they've been reaccumulated and are ready to go. There will be some late starters and overlapping moves to confuse the picture, but the tendency does exist.

A stock erupting from a long base is like a rocket getting off a launch pad—it needs a powerful initial thrust to get going. Some people say it is overbought, but I say it is just the beginning. If a stock pulls back into its base, however, 9 times out of 10 it will not be a winner—something is wrong with it. If a stock dies on me, I won't look at it again.

Whenever they build a skyscraper in a city, they dig a deep hole in the ground and then put pilings even further down in order to build a solid foundation upon which this skyscraper is going to sit. The deeper the foundation, the more floors they can put up. It is the same way in the stock market—if a stock is going to take off, the bigger the base, the higher it can go. My game is big bases—that's what I would like to be known for.

I prefer lower priced stocks, though this principle of bases applies to all price levels and supply/demand situations. A small price move in a low-priced stock translates into a large percentage gain. A $2 stock going to $4 has a 100% gain. You have more stocks, more choices at the cheaper end of the bell curve. Many analysts say it is difficult to make money in stocks below $5 a share; they abort more often, decline, and disappear. This is true to an extent, but when they cross above $5, they get discovered by institutions which have the buying power to push them up substantially higher.

Commodities—copper, sugar, silver—often build long bases. Take a look at sugar in '65–'71, copper in '75–'79, and, of course, look what emerged from the bases of silver and gold in 1980. There is always a profit opportunity somewhere if you're smart enough to recognize it. Here we sit day after day worrying about a flat stock market while commodities are taking off. The problem with most commodity traders is that money burns holes in their pockets; they feel they've

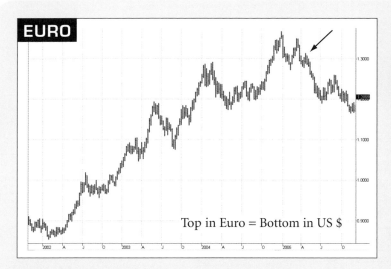

Top in Euro = Bottom in US $

## A CONTRARY OPINION CALL

Bill left his trading room, went out into the hallway, and returned with the latest issue of *U.S. News and World Report*. "The Incredible Shrinking Dollar" screamed the cover of the magazine. "We've got to be pretty close to the bottom," Bill grinned. "The only time they run such stories is when the market is at an extreme point."

The euro stood at 1.30 on the day of our interview in April 2005, and it has been going down ever since, while the U.S. dollar has gained strength. It takes an uncommonly long and steady trend for a chief editor of a major magazine to overcome his usual caution and put a financial opinion on the cover. By the time he slaps his stamp of approval on a trend, it is ready to reverse. Such striking covers come out only once every few years. It takes a person of great experience and self-assurance to recognize such signs.

*—AE*

got to be in something. Another group with the same problem is day-traders. I do not see what they see. It takes a certain personality to do what they do.

When shorting stocks, I look for sideways configurations and breakdowns. Currently my shorts are concentrated in real estate. I know people have been calling for the top in real estate for the past year or two, but I think the stocks are extended and vulnerable and fast approaching the point at which they should be shorted. Their decline will precede the decline in the actual properties.

After I stopped sending out my advisory service, the Brimberg brokerage firm in New York set up a hedge fund for me. I have been running Brimberg Trend Fund since 1999. In 2000 and 2001 many funds got clobbered. Typically, to collect a performance fee, a fund manager has to exceed his previous equity peak. Many advisors incurred substantial losses, closed their funds, and started new ones in order to collect new fees without having to recoup the losses. We got hurt, but never closed. I just couldn't do that to the limited partners.

Bill led me on a guided tour of his office. The windowsills and tops of filing cabinets supported his collection of bull figurines—the substantial herd, with just a few bears among bulls, has spread into several rooms. He pulled out a folder of charts showing long periods of flat prices abruptly coming to life with huge volume surges. "I am going to go back and evaluate them to see whether or not those spikes have meaning." He opened more folders. "This is the stuff I was working on over the winter in Florida. I am thinking of writing a book, something along the lines of *Skyscraper Profits in the Stock Market*. It will describe big bases in detail and contain numerous before-and-after examples to illustrate market moves." He then showed me some of his hedge fund data. "I can go out of the country with my laptop and run the fund while the New York people do my back-office paperwork. My wife and I love going to the Greek islands. Also, two of our granddaughters are on a world-class synchronized ice skating team, and you could say we're their groupies, following them to European competitions."

## TRADE 1 | BILL'S ENTRY

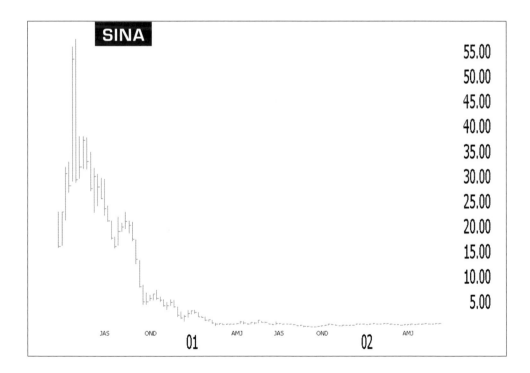

### SINA

Here's a stock that's down from a very high level, over $55 a share, trading in low single digits. It is out of favor and its price is depressed, but two years have passed since its run-up in the year 2000. I like stocks that are depressed, especially when they have a long sideways movement, building a base. SINA is trading in the lower part of its base, and the risk at this level is limited.

## Risk/Reward

**Q**

What is widely regarded as the minimum risk/reward ratio for entering a trade? How do you establish this ratio for stocks whose prices have broken into historically new price levels?

—*Trader*

**A**

There is no set number—it depends on your level of conviction about the outcome of the trade. Measuring risk/reward is not as simple as comparing the distances from the entry price to the profit target and the stop-loss level. You need to multiply each of those figures by the likelihood of that event—and hopefully your system gives you more than a 50/50 chance of winning. Still, if the expected profit is less than double the potential loss, I would pass up the trade.　　　　*—AE*

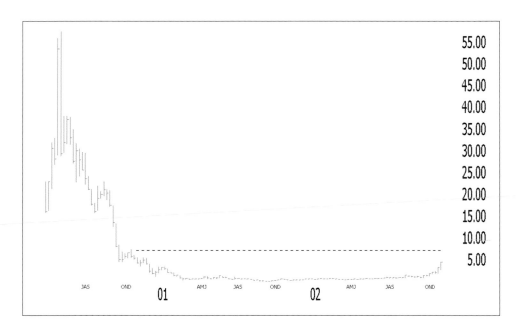

I drew a horizontal line on my chart at 10.60, and once that level was broken on the upside, I assumed another upleg would begin.

I would normally take a partial position in a stock like this and add to it as prices begin to improve. SINA, however, came to life rather abruptly.

In October–November of that year, SINA moved up to five dollars per share. I hesitated to add on such strength, which in hindsight was a mistake. The stock continued its rise to 10.50 in January of the following year. They say that the first correction is the most important, and if you can ride it out, then you're probably home free.

Will this trade make or lose money?

# TRADE 1 | BILL'S EXIT

I found out later it was a Chinese internet stock. Being a technician, I pay no attention to what the company does, and I was not aware it was Chinese until, all of a sudden, every-one wanted Chinese stocks. It was a perfect example of a low-priced stock being discovered, and I went along for the ride. It turned out to be one of the best per-centage gainers I have ever experienced.

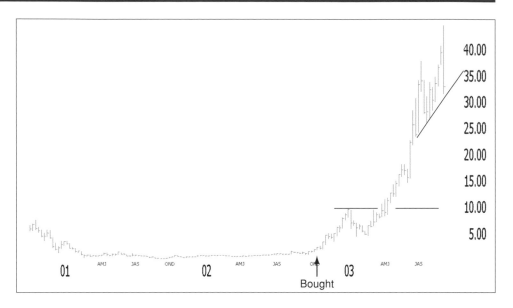

I did some selling in September 2003. I did not know whether the recent peak was the end of the upmove, but I could see an "outside reversal" on the bar chart, and it scared me enough to sell. I am a great believer in outside reversal bars. They can occur on daily, weekly, or monthly charts, taking out both the high and the low of the previous bar and closing in the direction opposite to the preceding trend. This pattern works at bottoms and at tops, often marking the extreme points of the moves.

I am also a great believer in trendlines and like to do some selling when impor-tant trendlines are broken. Here we see another beau-tiful technical situation— an outside key reversal to downside, a throwback rally into the top pattern, and the breaking of a very well defined uptrendline. I had to take action based on that evidence and sold the balance of my position.

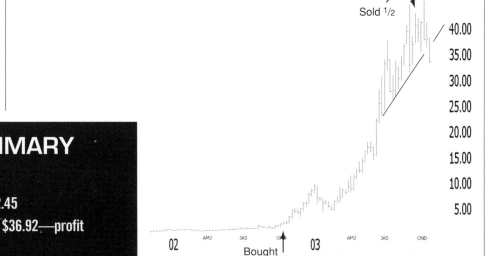

## TRADE SUMMARY

Long SINA
Bought 10/25/2002 @ $2.45
Sold first half 9/26/03 @ $36.92—profit
$34.47 per share
Sold second half 11/14/2003 @ $34.70—profit
$32.25 per share
Average profit = $33.36 per share

# TRADE 1—ENTRY COMMENT

This company's stock was sold to the U.S. public in the last heady months of the historic bull market. It went up from the start, more than tripling within six months. Back in May 2000, some poor soul paid more than $58 a share; he must have really needed the stock! From that lofty perch, SINA crashed and burned, touching the low of 1.02 a year later. Any stock that loses over 98% of its value earns the right to a quiet death, but SINA refused to die. It lay quietly on the bottom for almost two years, forming one of the big bases so favored by Bill.

I call any stock that falls more than 90% off its top and refuses to die "a fallen angel." Some of the most attractive long-term buys come from this group.

At the right side of the weekly chart, SINA is coming back to life, and its Impulse system is green. I take the readings of MACD-Histogram at a big discount when prices are so flat. This indicator shines by reflecting market psychology during price swings; when prices are flat, its messages are not that important. What is much more important to me here is that the weekly closing price is above both the 13-week and 26-week moving averages.

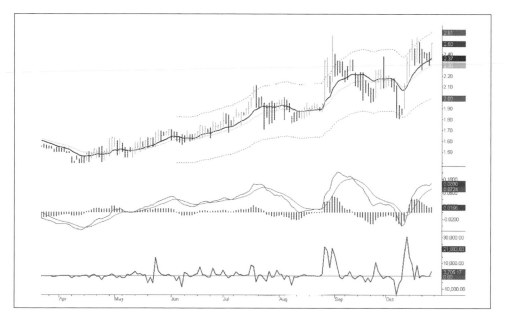

*Bill prefers to watch the monthly and weekly charts and pays little attention to the dailies. Looking at this daily chart, it is easy to see that his method makes sense for a long-term trader. Someone looking at the daily chart might feel tempted to sell prematurely in response to short-term signals. That would be perfectly fine for an active trader, but that's not Bill's game. He is looking for a major breakout from a long-term base leading to a sustainable uptrend, so a daily chart is of little interest to him. Still, this chart is in gear with the weekly; its Impulse is green, encouraging us to buy.*

*Prices, the MACD-Histogram, and the Force Index keep reaching higher levels; everything is in an upswing.*

Compare the height of the bars at the left and right edges of the chart. They are becoming much taller, telling us that the public is rediscovering SINA after it lay half-dead on the floor for the better part of two years.

# TRADE 1   EXIT COMMENT

Bill sat through the first top in July—a kangaroo tail that sent prices down for a sizable break. At the right edge of the chart, there is a bit of a bearish divergence in MACD-Histogram. It is not a pure divergence because the indicator has never crossed below zero between its July and October peaks. It shows, nevertheless, that bulls are becoming weaker even as prices rise higher. Bill, a classic chartist, identifies the key reversal pattern during the last bar and sells half of his position well above value.

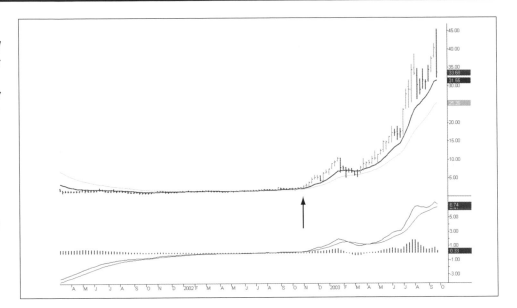

At the right edge of the weekly chart we see that the uptrend in SINA is starting to run into resistance. This is not surprising after its astronomic rise from $1.02 to over $45. Many bulls are sitting on massive profits and are prone to cash out at any sign of weakness, accelerating downdrafts.

At the right edge of the chart, prices have fallen below their fast EMA; the Impulse system is red. This is the first red bar in almost a year: A massive uptrend has ended, and the Impulse system allows us to sell short or stand aside, but not to go long. Bill, using classic charting methods, reaches the same verdict and exits his long position. It is not uncommon for serious technicians, using different methods, to arrive at similar conclusions.

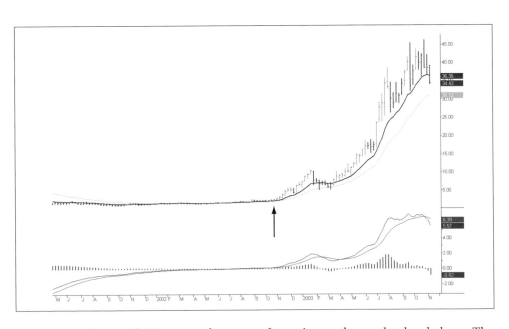

SINA had stopped rising, traced out a top formation, and started to break down. The third bar from the right took prices to a new record high, and that false breakout appears to have marked the top of the uptrend.

## TRADE 2 | BILL'S ENTRY

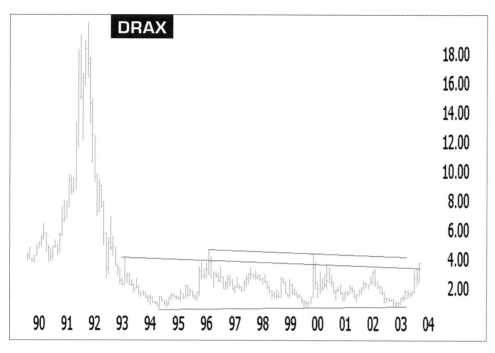

**DRAX**

I love big bases and this looked like a classic—not a two- or three-year base but a 10-year base. I felt convinced this was going to be good and notified several of my clients when the stock was around $3.50.

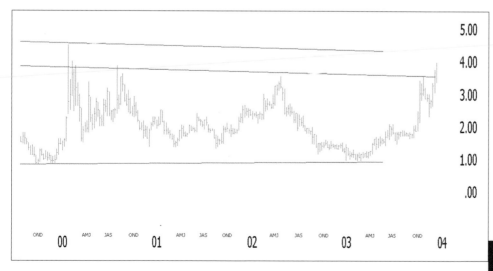

In January 2004, I felt the stock was acting well and was about to begin an uptrend of some importance. It broke above its first downtrendline and was well on its way towards breaking its second.

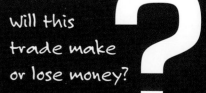

Will this trade make or lose money?

## TRADE 2   BILL'S EXIT

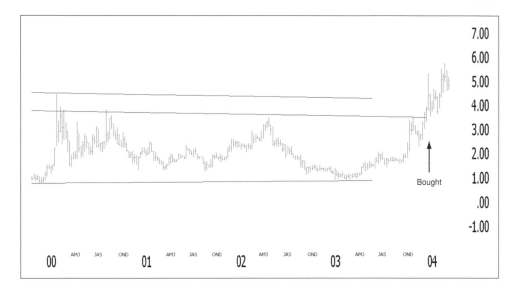

DRAX accelerated after it rallied above its $3.50–$3.60 breakout level. I entered in mid-January, and by late March, had a decent profit as it got up to nearly six dollars a share. But I expected much, much more. I looked at this stock's 10-year base and, knowing that the larger the base, the greater the potential, I stayed with the stock.

This stock may still work out well at some point in the future. Still, it was a disappointment to me that its impressive breakout did not result in an above-average advance. This trade in DRAX is a reminder that a big base is not a guaranteed road to riches and that one must constantly be aware of exceptions. A perfectly clean breakout will, on occasion, fail and pull back into the base from which it emerged. I had not anticipated such a loss of momentum.

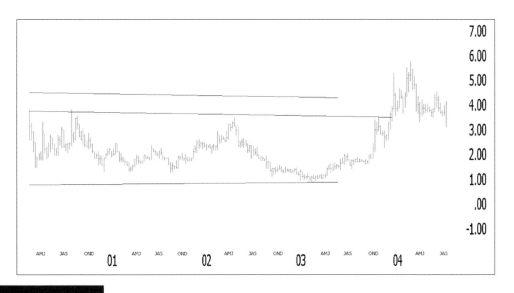

## ▼ TRADE SUMMARY

Long DRAX
Bought 1/14/2004 @ $4.02
Sold 8/10/2004 @ $3.37
Loss = $0.65 per share

The stock suddenly aborted and kind of died on me. It sank back toward its breakout level and then went sideways, with a downward drift. I did not like its action during the break, as it pulled back, and so I cut my loss and got out.

# TRADE 2—ENTRY COMMENT

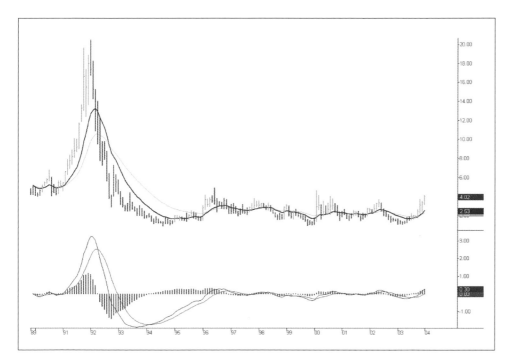

If I were to trade this stock, I'd be more inclined to try and grab it below two dollars, where it declines once every few years. There it becomes a "fallen angel," declining over 90% from $20. Still, I would not try to talk Bill out of his trade. Each serious trader has his method, and Bill's approach is internally consistent and works for him.

DRAX shows a beautiful base, capable of supporting a major upmove. Still, I would like to play devil's advocate and present a bearish case. First of all, stocks have inertia, and that inertia in DRAX is definitely sideways. Secondly, whenever it rose towards five dollars in recent years, it got clobbered and fell back into the range. Now there is a danger of that happening again.

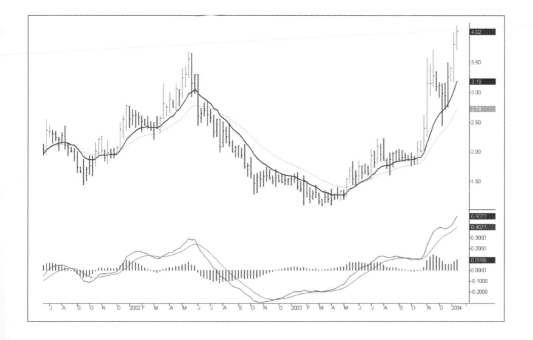

DRAX is accelerating on the weekly chart, rising at an ever steeper angle, high above its value zone at the right edge of the chart. Notice the angle of the uptrend during the first half of 2003 and compare it with the angle of the second half of the year. To me, such acceleration tends to mark unsustainable moves. Still, this is exactly what Bill spoke about in his interview: "A stock erupting from a long base needs a charge to go up. Some people say it is overbought, but I say it is just a beginning."

The Impulse system is green at the right edge of the daily chart, allowing us to buy or stand aside but not to go short. The moving averages tell me that the value of DRAX is somewhere between $2.74 and $3.19, while the stock is trading near four dollars. If I wanted to buy DRAX, I'd be waiting for it with my buy orders within the value zone. Again, Bill has his own methods that work for him, and his entry is fully consistent with his approach.

# TRADE 2—EXIT COMMENT

All serious traders have several features in common. One of them is that they pay just as much attention to exits as they do to entries and sell when they see an exit signal. Once a trade gives them a clear indication that it is not working out, they do not hang around waiting for an improvement.

Bill likes to buy breakouts from long bases, and when a breakout fizzles out, he dumps his stock without giving it a second chance. The Impulse system turned red some time ago, allowing us to sell short or stand aside but not be long. Bill gets out of this trade with a minimal loss and is free to go looking for better opportunities.

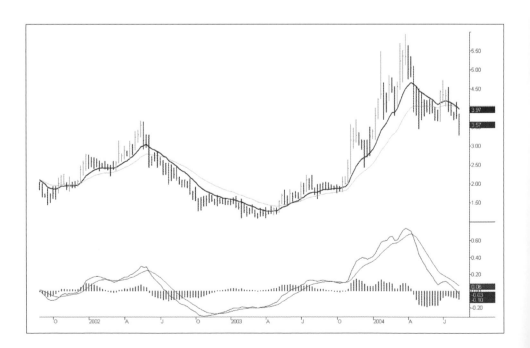

## Application Rejected

My goal is to build my skill in trading using advanced options techniques to enable me to be successful under any market conditions, whether bear, bull, or sideways. An additional goal is to generate $250,000 per year minimum. I also seek to meet a minimum of 10-15%/month ROI trading options. My current capital is $50,000, and I am using Interactive Brokers as my trading desk. I also signed up for Worden to allow myself to carefully search trades and to write algorithms for searches—I'm still in learning mode with this software. I also need software to help track individual trades allowing me to optimize the progress of a trade and fine-tune my exits while simultaneously balancing risk.

*—Trader*

Your goal is totally unrealistic, and looks like a recipe for disaster. No Camp can save you from that. Please be very careful and try not to lose mortgage or rent money. Reaching for such extreme performance is sure to expose you to risks that are guaranteed to prove suicidal—if not on the first trade, then on the second, or third, or fifth. The fact that you have not been aware of that shows a dangerous level of naiveté.

I am being absolutely straight with you, to the level of being blunt, because when I see a man about to jump off a cliff, I yell. But I do not like yelling, which takes a lot of energy, and I have no intention of yelling in the Camp. I wish you well, and please stay in touch.

*—AE*

## Application Accepted

I am a short-term trader (average holding period of half a day) trading futures for myself and for a fund on behalf of my company. I am basically trading 2 patterns:
 a) a continuation pattern aimed at buying/selling in the direction of the daily trend based on momentum indicators and envelopes within intraday charts; and
 b) a reversal pattern based on buying/selling bullish/bearish divergences in daily charts and supported by intraday screens.

I have done over 200 trades in the past eight months, achieving around 65% winning trades, average win/loss ratio of 1.4, and no negative months. I have improved my consistency a lot but still have discipline issues, especially in terms of taking losses. My objective for the Camp is to be able to live for a week with other traders and have the opportunity to observe how you deal with your trading and emotions on a daily basis. I am willing to improve my bookkeeping discipline (diary, etc....), which I don't follow as religiously as I should. I am looking forward to spending some good time with interesting people!!

Saludos, as we say in Spain.

*—Trader*

It is a pleasure hearing from you, and I will be delighted to see you and work with you in Cyprus. Your results are very attractive, and both of us will need to work hard and be inventive to improve them!

Hasta pronto!

*—AE*

# THE ROADS NOT TAKEN

Technical analysts study charts in order to recognize price patterns and profit from them. Each tick reflects a transaction between a buyer and a seller, but it shows more than an agreement between two individuals. The buyer and the seller are surrounded by a crowd of other traders who exert a powerful emotional pressure, making each trade representative of the entire market crowd. Price charts reflect the behavior of all market participants.

Academic economists used to view market participants as rational individuals trying to maximize gains and minimize losses, but that theory is now losing favor. Modern scholars acknowledge the importance of emotions in trading. This view has percolated into the economic mainstream to a surprisingly high degree; recently a Nobel Prize in economics was awarded for work on the emotional basis of making economic decisions.

I've been writing about the emotionalism of the markets for many years, doing my bit to clip the wings of the efficient market theory. While the emotional basis of trading is increasingly recognized, we must focus our attention on the market's emotional pull on us as analysts and traders.

We tend to feel calm when other people tell us about their problems and offer them rational solutions. When we deal with our own problems, we often become more emotional. It is easier to give advice to others than to solve our own problems. As the level of emotion rises, the level of intelligence declines. This is why so many traders make harebrained decisions, buying tops and shorting bottoms.

Bill provides an example of how a mature money manager goes about his work. He clearly knows his likes and dislikes and looks to trade only in situations where he feels comfortable. He can analyze a 10-minute chart just as well as any day-trader, but this type of trading leaves him cold, and he consciously avoids short-term charts. He loves catching breakouts from multi-year bases and scans monthly and weekly charts for such opportunities.

There are hundreds of games in the stock market, and no trader can be comfortable with all of them. Not every girl you see at the club wants to dance with you, and not every trade will work for you either. In a perfect world, every girl in the club would be wild about you, and every trade would be profitable, but that is not how the world works. The sooner you develop a sense of clarity about your likes and dislikes, the happier you'll be.

You do not have to imitate Bill's approach to trading, although you'd be fortunate to develop his self-knowledge and discipline. Out of all the games in the financial markets, you need to find one or a few that appeal to you and concentrate on them. If you're a day-trader, leave breakouts from long bases alone. If you love riding long-term trends, stay clear from catching daily reversals. If you like buying breakouts, forget about bargains. Each and every choice in the markets involves a trade-off, a road not taken. A winner is a mature individual who can choose his road and, just as importantly, calmly and without regret turn away from the roads he passes up. There are many games in the financial markets, and to become a success, you must choose the one that fits your unique personality.

*An e-mail from Bill:*

## BIG BASE PATTERNS

I continue to be fascinated by the multitude of indicators that are supposed to identify buying and selling points. Still, after studying them, I prefer a simple, clean chart with nothing but the price available for analysis. It is very important to me that the long-term picture looks like what I have in the back of my mind. For this reason I like to have a software package that allows me to flick from a monthly chart (long-term), to a weekly picture (intermediate-term), to the daily outlook (short-term).

Anyone can spot a breakout, but the trick is to adjust your lead time. For example, I worked for several decades with mutual fund portfolio managers. Because of the size of their funds, they cannot buy breakouts. If they need two to three months to build a position, then the advisor must adjust his thought process to this reality.

In managing a hedge fund, I can shorten my time horizon. It does my heart good to see a stock begin an upmove within a week to 10 days after I buy it. The rush is similar to birdying a hole in golf or sinking a three-pointer in basketball.

Not all buys result in winning trades. I closely watch the percentage gain or loss for individual issues in my portfolio. I like to cut my losses short and let my profits accumulate. It's not unusual to see some gains in the portfolio to the tune of 100%, 200%, or 300%—or higher. At the same time, I am quick and mechanical about ditching stocks with losses of 4, 5, or 6%. For this reason, my turnover is pretty high. I have found that if a stock is going to be good, it will move out shortly after I purchase it. If it hangs around and cannot get going, then something is wrong. Either my timing is off, or there is a fundamental negative on the horizon.

Stocks or even groups of stocks will often sit out one bull cycle and be ready to go in the next one. I call this "recycling," and it may take six to seven years from the previous price peak to the next breakout of importance. Prior to buying, I want to see a decline of a year or two to a depressed, down-and-out level. Then I want to see four to six years of sideways movement, of base development. I enter after the stock breaks above a significant resistance level, creates outside reversal bars on the weekly or even monthly chart, or when its relative price performance improves, especially during late-stage declines of your traditional once-every-four-years bear markets.

Bottom line? After studying everything under the sun, I settled in and became a specialist in simply "Big Base Patterns."

| | |
|---:|:---|
| Name: | Peter Tatarnikov |
| Lives: | Moscow, Russia |
| Previous profession: | Computer tech support |
| Trades: | Forex |
| How long: | Since 1999 |
| Trading account: | Medium ($250k–$1m) |
| Software: | Rumus |

# CHAPTER 13

# PETER TATARNIKOV

## WE ANALYZE PEOPLE
## WHO ANALYZE MARKETS

In April 2005 I flew to Moscow to conduct master classes in three Russian cities for the country's largest Forex firm. I hoped that my emphasis on the need for discipline and money management would help their clients. I enjoyed touring remote cities and visiting historical sites I'd never seen before. At the company's Moscow headquarters, I met its chief dealer; Peter was involved in day-to-day trading and had the brisk air of a man who lives by practical decisions rather than marketing. I came to his trading room behind a locked door which he shared with two other dealers and a secretary.

I was born in Vladivostok, in the Russian Far East, on September 1, 1980—we call it "The Day of Knowledge" in our country, the first day of school. I started working for this Forex firm at 17, helping with computers, doing the night shift. Our clients trade around the clock, and our software was just being developed (Rumus, which I found very versatile and robust). In 1998 the company moved to Moscow, and they invited me to come and try out to be a dealer. I flew to Moscow, but after testing me, they said I wasn't ready, and put me into tech support. Six months later, in 1999, one of our dealers left, and they promoted me, with a one-month trial period. My job was to take orders from clients and manage our firm's position.

I remember my first shifts as a dealer very well. I was working nights, Japanese yen was going crazy, the Bank of Japan was intervening. So much was happening that sometimes I'd call my colleagues with questions, waking them up in the middle of the night. Everything I know today I learned from Sergey Kovzharov, who was our second dealer at that time. By 2003 he became our chief dealer, and after he left, the firm promoted me to this job. Sergey and I remain in touch, and I can still call him with any questions.

As a dealer, I take orders from clients—they place orders through our software or by calling us. Then we turn around and place a cumulative order in the interbank market; for a large client, we may go there immediately. If the order is small, say under $100,000, we take it ourselves, but we monitor the company's total exposure. We have a limit, and when we reach it, we go to the interbank market to lay off the excess.

We track not only the size but also the volatility, things like the Average True Range of currency pairs. We are the largest Forex firm in the country, and as leaders, we usually do things first. Our competitors keep copying us; they lag behind, but get the benefit of learning from our mistakes. As the leaders in the field, we've made our share of errors. During the 1998 Asian crisis, our system allowed clients to deal at prices that were more than a minute old, and the firm lost money. Our system has been improved, and now it combines quotes from about 70 different banks and dealers. Some banks are better for some currencies, and the system knows that, looking for certain banks. If we get a bad quote—we call such out-of-the-range quotes "boogers" in Russian—our system queries the dealer who provided it.

Clients' orders go through the Internet Dealing System. We were the first company in Russia to show clients how our dealing software works. We also developed an artificial intelligence system to handle routine orders. The maximum margin we offer traders is 100:1, but we recommend limiting it to 10:1. We issue margin calls but allow clients to trade until their equity falls to zero.

Sitting at the dealing desk for months and years, you begin to notice that almost everybody does pretty much the same thing, repeats the same mistakes over and over again. There are well-known rules that traders keep breaking. First of all, they cling to losing positions and keep adding to them until they get hit with a margin call. When people have a loss, they tend to hold, but when they have a profit, they cut quickly. In our trading, we do the opposite.

Other traders take a position, and if the market goes against them, they not only take a loss but also reverse. Then the market turns again, and they lose for the second time. They were right the first time, but instead of winning, took two losses. This happens in every center—in Moscow, Vladivostok, or Yerevan. People are the same everywhere. Traders work in different cities, but they all move at once, like an avalanche.

The market reverses when the mass of traders starts giving up. People place stops at obvious support and resistance levels. The market keeps violating those levels, triggering their stops and reversing, just as you showed in your master class. The market approaches a resistance level and there, 10 ticks above the previous high, is a mass of buy orders. The market triggers them and then goes down. It does the same at the lows, penetrating them by a few ticks before turning up. I used to wonder why it does that. The market doesn't know where our clients have their stops. This means the same stops are placed all over the world. It is some kind of universal human trait.

When psychology kicks in, the amount of money a trader has in his account does not matter—they feel they must act now, this moment! Better capitalized traders simply put on bigger positions. They may use MACD, or Elliott, or RSI, or astrology, but under stress, when support or resistance levels are being tested, they all trade the same way, regardless of their method. People in the crowd use different analyses, but all behave the same way. Their problem is not analysis, but psychology. The majority of market participants act with the crowd, not just in Forex but in any market. A sudden event occasionally allows a crowd to win, but in the long run, the crowd always loses. When

I call my friends at other trading desks or banks, and they all tell me their clients are long the euro, I know the euro must fall.

One of our clients is a famous surgeon. He has been losing money for years, trading a small account without a clue. Once he doubled his money and was very surprised, but then lost it all again. He doesn't have the Internet, doesn't look at charts. Once he called me and said, "Peter, I want to do something, what should I buy or sell? Quick, I need to run to the operating room, will call you for a fill after surgery." I asked him about it, and he said, "My work is to cut people, but in the markets I relax." A trader without a system will lose, and if you trade against him, you'll win.

Successful traders always act differently from the crowd. We had a trader who started with a small account and in less than two years made more than a million dollars. I showed him the indicator I developed for measuring group behavior (see box). He found that most of his losing trades occurred when he traded in the same direction as the mass of traders. He found that when he occasionally traded with the crowd, he lost money.

---

**FOREX CLUB SENTIMENT INDEX**

*Peter says:*  Traders all over the world look for indicators of the mood of the market crowd. Those indicators reflect the fact that most crowd members think alike and are wrong much of the time. Our goal is to track the crowd and do the opposite of what it does. This is why we developed our indicator for measuring the mood of Forex traders—Forex Club Sentiment Index, or FCSI. We calculate it on the basis of open trades by the thousands of clients of our Forex Club.

The indicator's formula is very simple:

$$FCSI = (L/T) \times 100$$

L = the number of long positions in any currency
T = the number of all positions in any currency

FCSI reflects the percentage of long positions in any currency among the clients of our firm, oscillating between 0 and 100. When it rises above 70, it becomes overbought. When it falls below 30, it becomes oversold. Values between 30 and 70 are neutral. Our next step was to develop a mechanical trading system based on FCSI.

---

We are a retail company—we can analyze a large number of trades by real people. On the basis of our data, we created an indicator of mass behavior and called it FCSI—Forex Club Sentiment Index. It reflects traders' behavior worldwide, even though it is based on our dealers' data. FCSI is somewhat similar to what the Commodity Futures Trading Commission does in the United States, publishing summaries of traders' positions in different markets. The difference is that CFTC publishes its data weekly—we do it online and in real-time.

We have built a trading system based on FCSI. Trading against the crowd is not new, but we invented our own system. In developing it, we had no preconceived ideas—we did not know in advance how it would work. It turned out to be an automatic system—we go short, entering the market on close if

## Screening Software

I am writing my own software for daily preliminary stock selection. I am looking for an inexpensive Internet data feed for daily stock updates.
—*Trader*

Do not waste your time trying to reinvent the wheel. For sorting and filtering, look at the inexpensive, but very effective, TC2005. Spend your time analyzing data, making decisions, and documenting them.
—*AE*

FCSI rises above 70. We go long, market on close, if FCSI falls below 30. We cover shorts when it drops below 60 and sell longs when it rises above 40. Our analysis takes 10 minutes per day, we trade on close only and do not look at the computer intraday. We have been testing this system for two years and now we trade it with real money. We are up 12% for the first quarter of 2005. We have clients who use this data, and they trade differently, but this approach works well for us.

We do not analyze money; we analyze the number of trading decisions. We do not look at any individual account while calculating our indicator, only the number of all positions. For us, a $10,000 order to buy the euro and a $100,000 order are the same—together they represent two orders to buy the euro. Yesterday, for example, we had 2,000 open positions in the euro—and most clients were long. The euro went out at 1.2917 last night, but now as we speak, it trades at 1.2875—it fell, and that's how it should be. In trading this system, I am not interested in the price of the euro or the yen. We do not analyze markets; we analyze people who analyze markets.

I told Peter about John Maynard Keynes—the famous English economist was a canny stock picker, successfully managing the endowment of the University of Cambridge. Writing in the days before political correctness, he compared profitable stock-picking to forecasting the results of a beauty contest. To win you did not have to pick the prettiest girl; you had to determine which girl was most likely to be picked by the jury.

Peter spoke about his all-consuming passion for the market: His only other interest is his family. "I married early, over three years ago, and I have no regrets. My wife is a big help. I am always here, in the trading room, away from home. She totally took over our day-to-day lives, our child. She is totally loyal. I can work nights and she does not get angry. I always look forward to going home after work." With two assistant dealers pulling up trade records and charts, Peter selected two trades he wanted to show me and printed them out.

# TRADE 1 │ PETER'S ENTRY

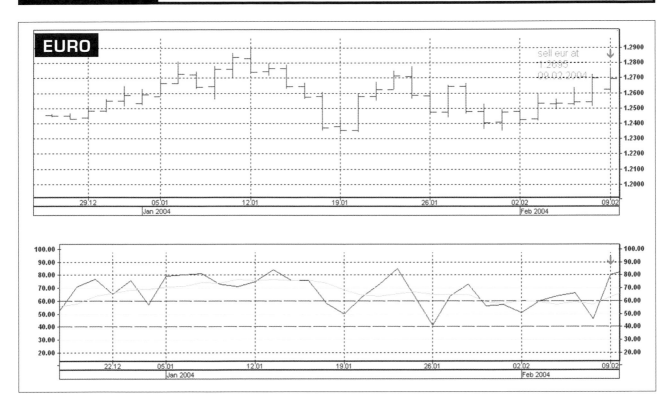

| | |
|---|---|
| **Upper pane:** | Daily bar chart |
| **Lower pane:** | Daily FCSI with a five-day simple moving average |

## Euro

At thc right edge the euro is rising, and we can see in the lower pane of the chart that the crowd likes it. The rising FCSI shows that the crowd is buying into this rally. A few minutes before the close, FCSI rose above 80. My system calls for shorting when FCSI closes above 70, and I followed my system—shorted the euro market on close.

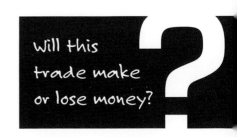

will this
trade make
or lose money?

# TRADE 1    PETER'S EXIT

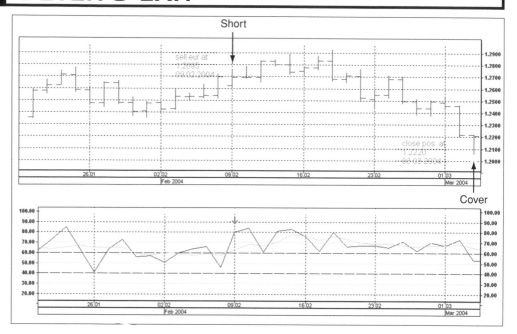

The euro went up for a few days after I shorted. It kept making marginal new highs, but I never covered. According to my system, I have to hold shorts until FCSI falls below 60 percent. It never went below that level; on the contrary, it kept rallying, even rising above 80 on several occasions.

As the euro began to slide, the crowd of traders became less and less bullish. At the right edge of the chart FCSI fell below 60%, nearing 50% just before the close. My system tells me to cover when FCSI penetrates 60%, and I exited market on close—purely mechanical.

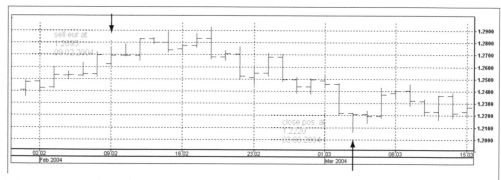

## TRADE SUMMARY

Short Euro
Shorted 2/9/2004 @ 1.2695
Covered 3/3/2004 @ 1.2220
Profit = 475 points

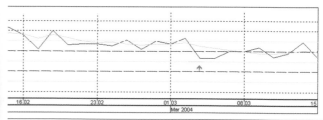

I keep watching my system, measuring its performance, and analyzing its parameters. I allow myself to think about my system, but not violate it. Of course I feel a little more certain if a similar signal emerges at the same time in several currencies and crosses, but I take every signal with the same level of determination. The only thing that can keep me out of a trade is a low number of market participants. If there are fewer than 10 positions in a currency, that signal becomes suspect.

# TRADE 1—ENTRY COMMENT

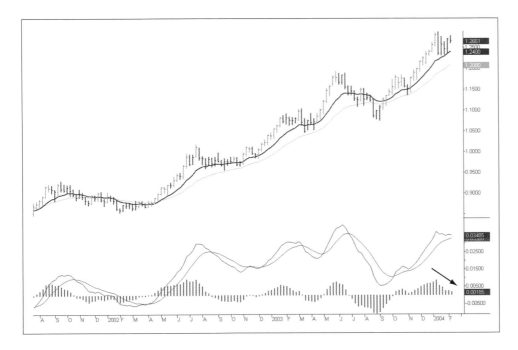

The weekly chart reflects an ongoing bull market in the euro. This chart goes from the lower left corner to the upper right—you do not have to be a technician to recognize an uptrend. Little wonder that public sentiment, measured by Peter's index, is overwhelmingly bullish.

A healthy bull market usually includes several corrections. Some of them are quite deep, knocking out weak holders and allowing the pros to add to long positions at lower levels. The two moving averages reflect the average consensus of value. Occasionally prices rise far above value, but then snap back into the value zone between the two MAs or even lower before resuming their advance. This happened in July 2002, January 2003, May 2003, and October 2003.

Another snapback began in December 2003, and the question now is whether it has run its course and a new rally is under way, or whether the snapback is still continuing. If the first is true, we should be going long, but if the second, short—this is a major choice.

The right-most bar on the chart is above both MAs, in the overvalued zone. The MACD Lines are high and turning flat in the zone associated with tops, while MACD-Histogram is declining from above zero. The Impulse system is blue, permitting both buying and shorting. Shorting appears much more attractive than buying, considering prices are above value and the MACD behavior.

*The daily MACD-Histogram showed a bearish divergence between its November and January peaks. The indicator returned above zero in the past two days and is now in the area suitable for another downward reversal. The daily Impulse is green at the right edge. I would hold my finger on the trigger here, ready to short as soon as the Impulse goes off green.*

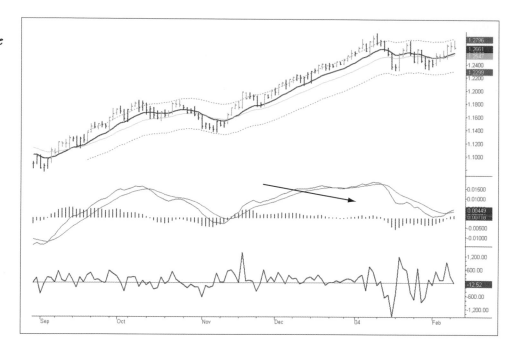

The daily chart shows that the euro has remained essentially flat after bumping its head against the ceiling in the first days of 2004. All that volatility, all that volume for a month—and no progress! When prices go flat at a high level, it is usually a sign that they have run into resistance and a downturn is coming sooner rather than later.

# TRADE 1—EXIT COMMENT

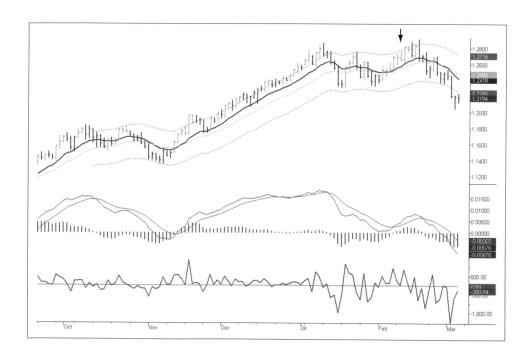

After Peter shorted the euro, it struggled to go higher for a few days, like a bull in a bull-fight with a sword through its heart, still trying to run, not yet knowing it is dead. Prices poked briefly above their upper channel line and took out their January peak by a few ticks, cleaning out stops on short positions and sucking in amateurs who placed buy stops above the January peak. Prices stalled there, the MACD-Histogram turned down, turning the Impulse blue, and the euro plunged to a new low for the year.

At the right edge of the chart, the euro is below its lower channel line, deeply oversold. It is trading near the lows of the year, bears are in control, but a few faint bullish signs are starting to emerge. MACD-Histogram, MACD Lines, and Force Index are at levels normally associated with bottoms. Prices are below the lower channel line and so vastly oversold that it would take a disaster to carry them lower. That would be an extraordinary event—something that amateurs look for, while professionals bet on probabilities. When prices are overbought and near the upper channel line, the pros look to short; with prices near or below the lower channel line, they look to cover, just as Peter did.

## TRADE 2  PETER'S ENTRY

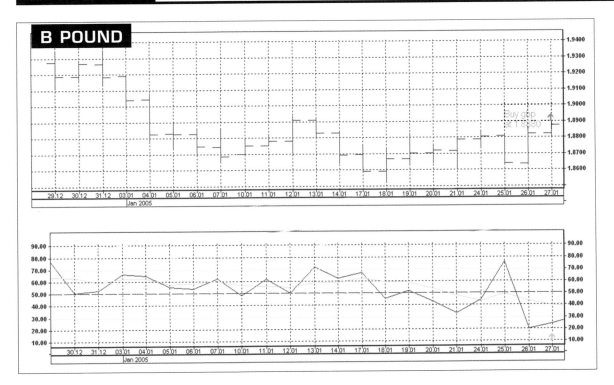

### B Pound

The British pound has been in a trading range. At the right edge bullishness suddenly dropped to almost 20 percent. Since the system tells me to buy when FCSI falls below 30 percent, I went long GBP market on close.

will this
trade make
or lose money?

# TRADE 2 | PETER'S EXIT

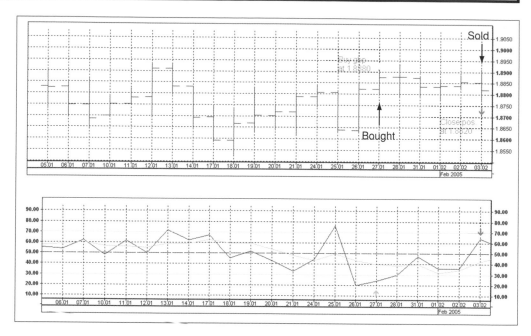

The rally had no follow-through, but as prices hung flat, bearishness began to decrease. When FCSI rose above 40 percent, I sold, taking a loss. My buy signal turned out to be false in this case. Other traders made money here; I lost money.

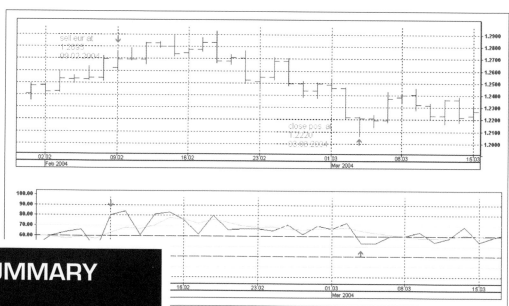

## ▼ TRADE SUMMARY

**Long British pound**
**Bought 1/27/2005 @ 1.8880**
**Sold 2/3/2005 @ 1.8820**
**Loss = 60 points**

It is impossible to make money on every trade. I keep putting on trades and watching the markets, always trying to develop something new. I practically live here, in this office.

# TRADE 2—ENTRY COMMENT

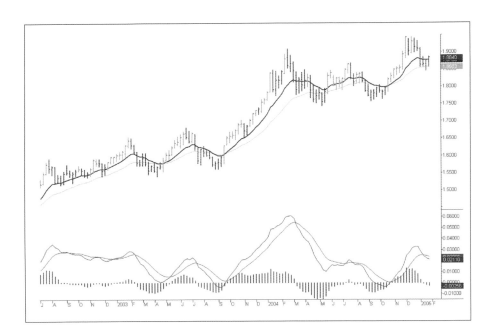

The weekly chart shows an uptrend, with prices marching from the lower left to the upper right corner. This bull market is less orderly than the one in the euro, but the general pattern is the same. The level of value, tracked by the EMAs, keeps rising. Prices occasionally spring above value but then return, as if pulled back by an invisible rubber band.

Near the right edge of the chart, the pound had rallied above value, then pulled back and spent three weeks in its value zone. The rightmost bar is rallying out of the value zone. MACD-Histogram is still declining, but if the rally continues for another week, it will turn up, creating a shallow bottom. Notice that its past three bottoms—May and September 2004 and the current one—are becoming more and more shallow. This is not a divergence because prices are also getting higher, but it is a sign that bears are growing weaker. The Impulse system has turned blue at the right-most bar—by going off red, it removed a prohibition against buying.

The daily chart shows a nice rally that began two weeks ago. Prices fell from their December peak only to find support in the 1.86 area. MACD-Histogram does not show a divergence, which would have been perfect, but other buy signals are present. MACD Lines are turning up, and the Force Index has traced out a bullish divergence. Each downward stab of prices since January was accompanied by a more shallow bottom of the Force Index, showing that bears were running out of steam.

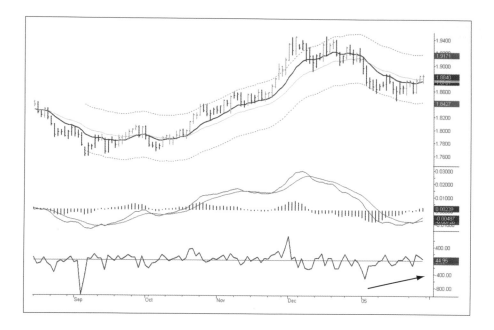

At the right edge of the chart, the Impulse system is green. Buying at this point means chasing prices a bit, but they are not too far away from value.

## Over-optimizing a System

**Q** I recently started using TradeStation to rigorously backtest and optimize the various parameters of a system I believe to have a sound basis. I am concerned that, going forward, the results may not be as good as the tests because of the "curve fitting" issue. How do you backtest properly without curve fitting?                              —*Trader*

**A** The only testing that seems to work for me is manual testing. I open my analytic software and Excel, scroll my stock data to the extreme left, and then look at the right edge, clicking forward one day at a time. When I notice a signal, I write down my orders for the next day and click again, keeping good notes in Excel all along. This is a slow process, but the only one that imitates the surprises and uncertainties of trading.   —*AE*

# TRADE 2—EXIT COMMENT

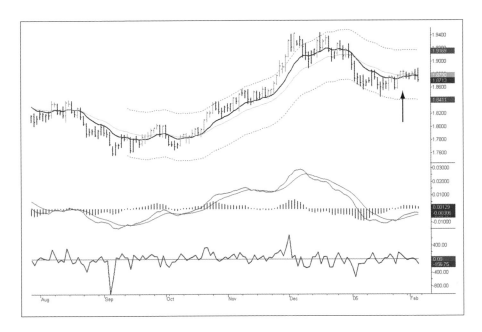

The daily Impulse has gone red on the right-most bar. I would not enter a position against the daily Impulse, but I would hold one even if the daily Impulse turned against it; I would get out only if the weekly Impulse turned against my trade. Each serious trader has his method, and Peter is extremely disciplined; when his system tells him to sell, he gets out without quibbling.

The British pound has not moved much since the day Peter bought it. It made a marginal new high, then a marginal new low, but basically remained within range. Prices are essentially flat.

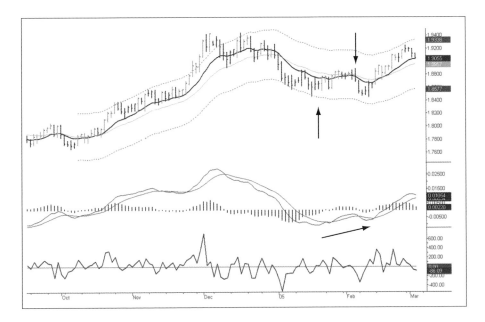

The upmove in the British pound has worked out beautifully. Prices declined into a double bottom, where MACD-Histogram had traced a bullish divergence. The pound rocketed towards its upper channel line. The initial buy signal turned out to be quite good. Still, a professional trader has no regrets. He knows that every individual trade is a bit of a toss-up, and puts his trust in the long-term performance of his system.

### Shaken Out

I often exit trades before they reach my targets because there may have been negative news or the stock seemed to act weak during an up market. Often I notice a trade would have worked out if I had stayed in it and rode it out, but then again, sometimes I've been correct to get out early... *—Trader*

You need to write down your rules and follow them. At an early stage of development as a trader, you have no right to use discretion. You will acquire the right to use it only after a year of profitable trading experience. *—AE*

# TOUGHNESS AND PERSEVERANCE

At the end of the conference, a group of us rented a sauna and went there for a few hours of relaxation, drinking, and singing. There was a steam room, a small swimming pool, and a complex karaoke machine; I took hold of the song list and appointed Peter our chief engineer in charge of karaoke. Even in that boozy, happy group, he looked like a man who would apply himself to a piece of machinery and work its many buttons just right.

Are good traders born or made? Peter was lucky to stumble into a trading firm at 17, but his energy, focus, and perseverance would have served him well in any field. He would have been a success even if he never heard of trading. Markets seem like a natural sphere for him, but it is his toughness and drive that propelled Peter to the position of a chief dealer of the largest Forex firm in the country while still in his mid-twenties.

A casual trader, rising from his couch to glance at the screen, might have a frightening thought: What if the person on the other side of his trade is someone like Peter? He practically lives in his trading room, studying markets, studying other traders, always looking for an edge, for every bit of an advantage. What chance does a casual trader have against him?

Many amateurs crowd into the market, dreaming of a life of ease, an escape from the corporate grind. Lulled by brokerage house propaganda, few newcomers realize how tough the trading game really is. Leaving the corporate cubicle with its moronic boss and nasty coworkers may seem very appealing, but few newcomers anticipate the work that goes into becoming a successful trader. You may chafe under a dumb boss, but in trading you become your own boss—the toughest you've ever had. You must drive yourself harder than any supervisor ever did, and if you cannot do it, don't even dream of trading. Look instead for a larger cubicle and a more reasonable boss.

Peter enjoys working hard. Competence and performance are at the core of his way of life, whether in front of the screen or a karaoke machine. He is a tough professional trader, and when you think of putting on a trade, you have to ask yourself: What have you got that Peter does not have? What will be your edge, your advantage over him in this trade? If you have no answer to this question, do not even start.

By opening his trading room and showing us how he operates, Peter did traders a favor—another example of the openness and generosity of some of the field's best people. The bar over which you have to jump is very high, but Peter shows you where it is.

*An e-mail from Peter:*

## PLAYING AGAINST THE MASS MOOD

People say that the market is 75% psychology and 25% economics. If this is true, then a trader who turns the psychological component in his favor must win in the long run. There are two key reasons why playing against the mass mood can be the cornerstone of a winning trading system.

First, after people have been watching prices for some time they tend to develop a strong subconscious idea of what is expensive or cheap. This is especially pronounced within short timeframes. For example, if the euro was trading at 1.20 half an hour ago and now it's trading at 1.2050, the subconscious says, "It's expensive—sell." The recent range is imprinted on us, and any swing outside of those limits becomes a stimulus to act. Contrary to this, the very concept of a trend, however brief, involves an ongoing price change. Because of this, when we play against the crowd, we position ourselves in the direction of the emerging trend.

Second, the majority of traders have an asymmetrical tolerance for profits and losses. The majority can tolerate much higher losses than profits, which make them anxious to act. If a trader is willing to lose 40 ticks on a trade, he is likely to take profits at a much closer level. If we go opposite to this, we'll be cutting losses short and letting profits run—which is essential for a trend-follower.

Traders all over the world look for indicators of the market crowd's mood. Those indicators reflect the fact that most crowd members think alike and are wrong much of the time. Our goal is to track the crowd and do the opposite of what it does.

Name: Damir Makhmudov
Lives: Riga, Latvia
Previous profession: Cotton purchasing manager
Trades: U.S. futures
How long: Since 2002
Trading account: Small (< $250k)
Software: MetaStock with Elder-disk

# CHAPTER 14

# DAMIR MAKHMUDOV

## TECHNICAL SIGNALS IN THE FUNDAMENTAL CONTEXT

In November 2004 I began receiving e-mails from a trader in Latvia who worked for a cotton company. He was hedging his firm's sizable cotton holdings in the futures markets and becoming increasingly drawn towards technical analysis. Cotton had just made a major bottom at that time. I enjoyed Damir's e-mails in which he outlined some early signs of tightening supply in a market seemingly glutted with cotton. Impressed with Damir's focus on combining fundamental and technical analysis, I invited him for an interview. In June 2005, Damir met me in Amsterdam, where I was spending a few weeks trading from an apartment above a canal.

I grew up in Latvia when it was still a part of the Soviet Union. I was very involved in sports, especially ice hockey. Today some of my childhood friends play on the national team, but I was a bit too small to play at that level. I was drafted into the army and served in special communications. They trained us for 18 months, but probably the most useful skill turned out to be touch-typing.

After the fall of the Soviet Union, I knew I needed to get a Western education. In the early '90s, Concordia University opened a satellite campus in nearby Tallinn, Estonia, and that's where I spent the next eight years, first earning a BA in international business and then an MBA. I needed to support myself while going to school and found a job with a Singapore company that came to Estonia to invest in textile and paper businesses. They put me into the commercial department dealing with cotton, and after six months, sent me to the International Cotton Institute in Memphis, Tennessee. I studied there for two months, and afterwards became involved in buying cotton for the company.

Our factory made fabric, so the price of cotton was one of the key factors in our profitability. While buying physical cotton, I had to deal with price risks. Like everybody, I started with fundamental analysis and studied supply and demand. I developed my own model of price forecasting based on ending stocks worldwide. The cotton business is a small, tight world, and I've been in it since 1997. I wrote my MBA thesis on managing cotton inventory price risk and its impact on a company's market value.

In 2002 I was invited to join a cotton company in Latvia. Some investors bought two cotton factories in Kazakhstan, opened an office in Riga, and asked me to be their senior trader. Now I have to manage price risk from a different perspective. We buy seed cotton from farmers and end up holding physical raw cotton, having to hedge the downside risk. At first I tried using options, but did not like dealing with the delta. So in 2003, I turned to futures. I began by using fundamentals and monitoring the basis—the price difference between physical cotton and New York futures. By holding physical cotton, we make money if prices go up, but lose if they decline. We hedge our long position in physical cotton by shorting cotton futures.

At first I was being fairly intuitive—when to short, when to cover. Then I decided to look into technical analysis and found the Australian Technical Analysts Association site. I read your books and started using MetaStock, bought your Elder-disk. I am a discretionary rather than a systematic trader. A system may give me a signal, but I analyze the fundamental context and may decide to stand aside. I am currently taking two courses at the Australian Securities Institute—one on technical analysis and another on specialized techniques. Afterwards, I want to focus on position sizing and money management and create a speculative fund. Right now, I am involved with both speculating and hedging. Our hedging is pretty large, reflecting our long position in physical cotton. Our firm opened a small $100,000 account to work on our speculative techniques.

## TRADE 1  DAMIR'S ENTRY

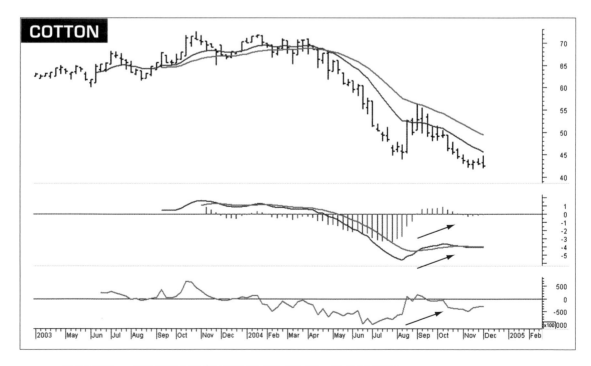

**Upper pane:**  Bar chart with 26-week (green) and 13-week (red) EMAs
**Second pane:**  MACD Lines and MACD-Histogram 12-26-9. Green if MACD-Histogram ticks up, red if it ticks down.
**Third pane:**  13-week Force Index

## Cotton

I could see weekly MACD-Histogram rising from a bullish divergence; furthermore, MACD Lines had traced a bullish divergence, and both were rising, getting ready to cross over. Prices were well below their EMAs, indicating a generally oversold market. There was also a bullish divergence of the Force Index between its July and November bottoms. The combined message of all these signals on the weekly chart was to only look for long trades on the daily charts.

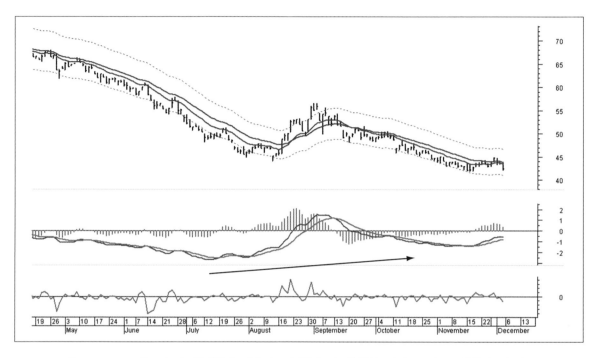

**Upper pane:**  Bar chart with 22-day (blue) and 13-day (red) EMAs. Autoenvelope—2.7 standard deviations around the slow EMA.
**Second pane:**  MACD Lines and MACD-Histogram 12-26-9
**Third pane:**  2-day Force Index

MACD-Histogram was declining after tracing out a large bullish divergence. There was a massive divergence of MACD Lines between the July and December bottoms in cotton. To me, this indicated that prices were going to rise above the recent price peak. The two-day EMA of Force Index was below zero, in its buy zone.

The 13-day EMA of prices was flat to down, but that signal could be ignored as cotton seemed to have entered a trading range between 42 and 45 cents. This relatively narrow range called for a strategy of buying weakness and selling strength. I decided to place a limit order for December 3, 2004, to buy five March '05 cotton contracts at 42.85/lb. I expected to buy on a break to minor support near 42.70–42.80, with a stop-loss at 41.78, slightly below the contract low of 41.80/lb. I had a price target of 44.45, which would capture about 30% of the channel width.

will this trade make or lose money?

# TRADE 1 | DAMIR'S EXIT

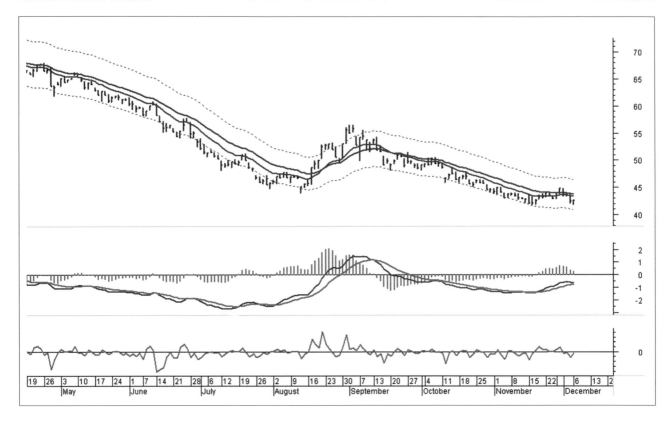

At the time of this trade I was still studying the method. We were just starting to test our discretionary fund, and did not have money management rules in place. I think my weekly analysis was correct, and the entry was basically right.

My mistake was in the poor choice of the stop-loss at the very obvious level just a few ticks below the contract low. I fell into a common trap, and this made my trade the victim of a "fishing expedition" by floor traders.

## ▼ TRADE SUMMARY

Long March 2005 cotton futures

Bought 12/3/2004 @ 42.85¢

Sold 12/6/2004 @ 41.78¢

Loss = 107 points per contract plus six points round-trip commission, for a total loss of 113 points per contract

Entry grade = 63% (relatively poor)

Exit grade = 6% (very poor)

Trade grade = "D" (lost 107 points or −19% of the 550-point channel)

# TRADE 1  DAMIR'S FOLLOW-UP ENTRY

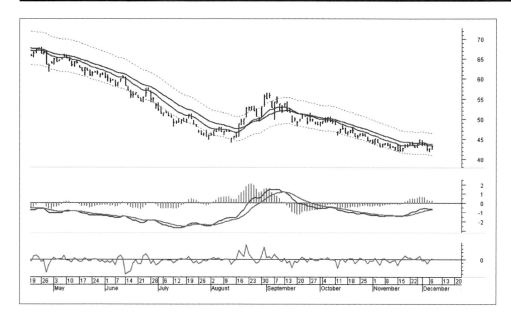

I decided to place a stop order to buy March '05 cotton futures on December 7 at 42.67, slightly above the 42.65 high of the previous day, to capture a possible upside breakout. My stop-loss would be at 41.67/lb, slightly below the contract low of 41.72/lb, and the price target of 44.45, trying to capture about 30% of the channel width.

On the day I got stopped out from my cotton position, I realized that the charts were still bullish and only poor stop placement caused me to get stopped out. The message of the weekly chart was completely unchanged, and this daily chart showed strength. The MACD-Histogram held above zero during the stab to a new low in cotton, and the Force Index was rising.

Taking a look at other indicators, we can see bullish divergence of the 14-day RSI and 5-day Stochastic, confirming the weakness of the bear camp. The price action on December 6 could be called a closing price reversal; it indicates that an upward rather than a downward move is likely in the near term.

Will this trade make or lose money?

# TRADE 1   DAMIR'S FOLLOW-UP EXIT

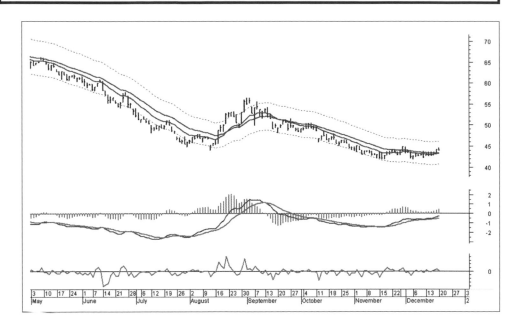

My colleagues questioned my reentry into a long trade just one day after I got stopped out, but I had enough courage to do it. As usual, I had a written plan for this trade because having it helps avoid impulsive trades.

It was a profitable trade, but in retrospect I can see how it could have been better. I got out too early. Now we no longer use the 30% target, but monitor the situation, trying to get more. Also, my money management rules were not yet in place, and my trade size fluctuated. Even though the second trade gained more per contract than the first had lost, I traded five contracts the first time, losing $2,825, and only two contracts the second time, gaining $1,640. Still, such small trades build on each other and train you to trust your system.

## ▲ TRADE SUMMARY

Long March 2005 cotton futures

Bought 12/7/2004 @ 42.75¢

Sold 12/20/2004 @ 44.45¢

Gain = 170 points per contract minus six points round-trip commission, for a total gain of 164 points per contract

Entry grade = 40% (relatively good)

Exit grade = 92% (good)

Trade Grade = "A" (captured 31% of the 550-point channel)

# TRADE 1—ENTRY COMMENT

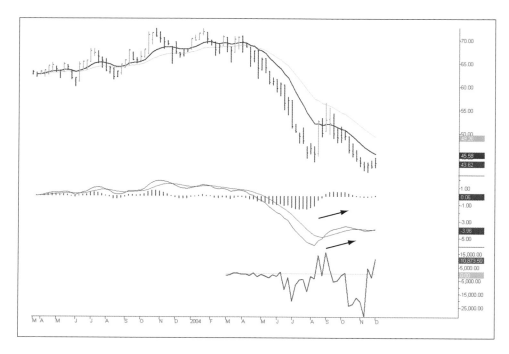

*Near the right edge, cotton is the lowest it has been in several years. Commodities, unlike stocks, have natural floors and ceilings. A commodity, unlike a stock, cannot go down to zero and disappear. There will always be demand for cotton, wheat, copper, sugar, and other basic building blocks of human society. Price floors in commodities depend on the cost of production—if prices fall below that level, the farmers stop growing and the miners stop mining, reducing the supply and arresting the decline. In extreme conditions a commodity may briefly dip below its cost of production, but it cannot stay there for a long time. This is why when I first saw this weekly chart of cotton trading at multi-year lows, it stopped me in my tracks. I no longer recall who drew my attention to it—it may have been Damir. I had not traded cotton for several years, but the moment I saw this screen I knew I had to be in it. If you ever see a chart that looks like this, be sure to trade it!*

If my charts look similar to Damir's, it is because we use similar software. His workhorse is MetaStock while I use TradeStation, but both of us have added Elder-disks to our packages. These are collections of tools from *Come into My Trading Room*, expertly programmed by my friend John Bruns.[1]

Prices usually begin to move before the fundamental data becomes available—technicals precede fundamentals. Approaching events cast shadows ahead of themselves—which is why traders like Damir, surrounded by reams of fundamental data, turn to technical analysis.

I quoted Damir's e-mail in my November 2004 newsletter:

> A combination of expanded area devoted to cotton and favorable weather conditions in the major producing countries resulted in expected world fiber production reaching a record figure in the industry's history. Surprisingly, each higher production figure and higher carryover estimate was first accompanied by panic selling, driving prices close to limit down on the day of the news release, with the market rebounding the next day and posting strong rallies.
>
> I have been in the cotton industry for eight years, first as a raw cotton buyer for a textile mill and now as a cotton trader, but I am a newcomer to technical analysis. Learning the main concepts from your books and applying

---

[1]An Elder-disk contains no secrets—only flawlessly programmed indicators and systems for a specific trading platform. You could program all studies yourself since the formulas are in the book, but the question is how long it would take you and how accurate it would be. As a matter of fact, there are commercial operators running around selling my studies, which they have poorly and erroneously programmed.

them to this market helped me see what I did not even think of before. The market rallied after the most bearish report in cotton's history. Today, the technical picture helps me see the light at the end of the tunnel for cotton despite the majority of industry folks being very bearish; there is definitely something underneath this market that provides support.

In hedging, we are doing relatively large trades that are based on our physical stock position. We sold a fair portion of the stock we accumulated since the beginning of November 2004 to international merchants who had been caught short of physical cotton. We are now replenishing that stock at even lower levels.

The weekly chart is flashing several powerful signs. Cotton reached its peak in October 2003 and remained at that high level until April 2004, making two serious rally attempts but ending up with a major bearish divergence. From there it slid into the low of August 2004, bounced back into its value zone, and then painfully ground its way to a new low in November. There MACD-Histogram and MACD Lines produced massive bullish divergences. Much lower prices were accompanied by much higher indicator bottoms, showing that bears were exhausted and bulls were ready to take control. At the right edge of the chart the Impulse is blue—it stopped being red three weeks ago, allowing us to buy.

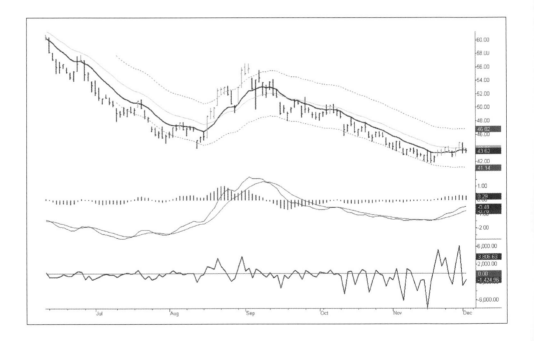

In November cotton broke its August low of 43 cents/lb. It is always instructive to watch what the market does after breaking support—whether the decline accelerates or fizzles out. Here prices chugged down two more cents before completing a bullish divergence in MACD-Histogram, turning MACD Lines up, and crossing above both moving averages.

The downtrend in cotton had started to reverse, and the only sign that would hold me back from buying at this very moment is the red Impulse on the daily chart. The bullish case is very strong, but red Impulse suggests that now is not the best day for buying cotton. It is better to wait until daily cotton goes off red—until the Impulse turns blue, either from an uptick of MACD-Histogram or from price crossing above the fast EMA.

# TRADE 1—EXIT COMMENT

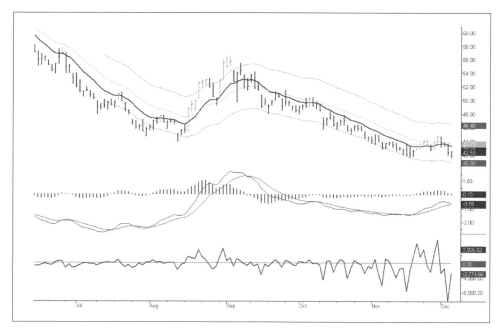

In on Friday, out on Monday—Damir was knocked out of his trade after making the typical beginner mistake of putting his stop immediately below the latest low. Stop orders are always bunched up at those levels, presenting an attractive target for the pros. Their tactic is not necessarily devious: As prices approach support, they simply withhold their buy orders, allowing the slide to continue, then step in and buy when the stops get triggered. They actually provide a public service by buying from frightened holders who want to get out. In effect, they buy at a preseason sale, then sell at the height of the season—not a bad model for running a business!

Technically, little has changed since the day Damir entered his trade. The weekly chart has not changed, and the daily is more attractive than ever. Prices tested a new low, but rejected it and closed higher—a bullish sign. The only bearish sign is the red Impulse at the right edge. As soon as it goes off red, the buy signal will be complete.

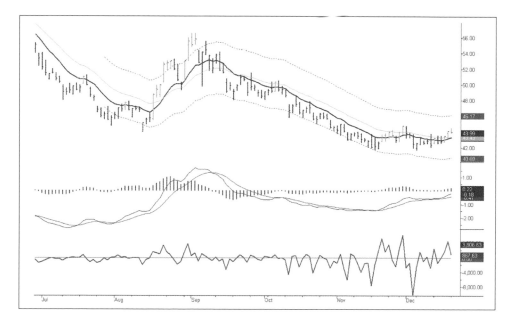

Damir did what very few traders have the emotional strength to do—he re-entered a trade the day after being stopped out. He did it without rancor or some emotional desire to get even.

His technical signals told him this was a good trade and he got back in, like a boxer who gets up after a knockdown. Damir used to be a competitive ice hockey player in his youth; the competitiveness, toughness, and focus continue to serve him well in his trading career.

Damir set himself an attainable goal—to capture 30% of the height of the daily channel, earning an "A" rating for the trade. That is another sign of discipline, but in this case his target seems too modest. In setting up a target, you need to look at both what you want to accomplish and the stage of the market. The early stage of a major reversal can lead to an explosive move, producing much more profit than 30% of the channel.

Damir gave me his statements, pointing out that at the time of these two trades, he did not yet have a good handle on money management. In his first trade, losing $565 per contract, he traded five contracts for a total loss of $2,825. When he bought cotton again, he traded only two contracts, and even though his $820 profit per contract was bigger than the preceding loss, his profit from that trade was only $1,640. This is a typical outcome for a beginner. When people feel confident, they put on bigger trades, and after getting slapped, they become fearful and put on smaller trades. A more experienced trader would not allow the outcome of his latest trade to influence the size of his next one.

## TRADE 2 | DAMIR'S ENTRY

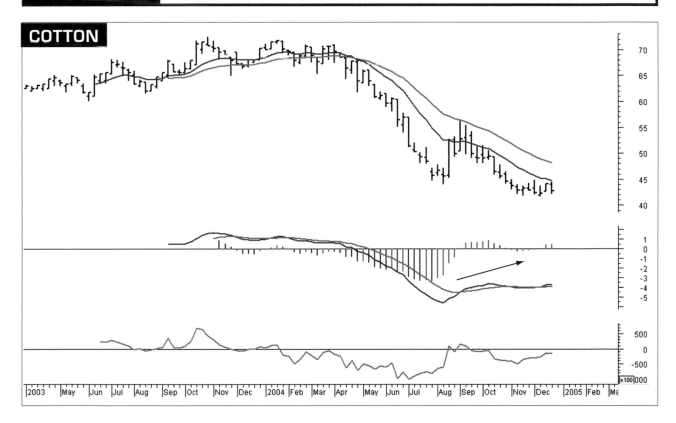

### Cotton

MACD-Histogram was rising from a bullish divergence, with both lines trending higher and the Fast line above the Slow. Prices were still well below their 13-week and 26-week EMAs, signaling a generally oversold market. The 13-week EMA of the Force Index was rising from a bullish divergence but still below the zero line, another bullish sign. The

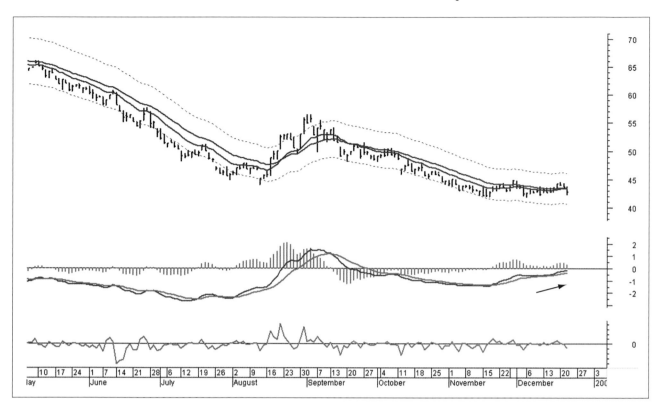

weekly chart suggested looking for a long trade only on a daily chart and trying to reenter cotton below the market.

Daily MACD-Histogram has ticked down, but both MACD Lines are rising, with the Fast line above the Slow. The 13-day EMA is flat to rising, suggesting that the market remains in trading range, calling for buying weakness and selling strength. I decided to place a buy order at the 42.70¢/lb minor uptrend support level and a stop-loss at 41.67¢/lb (still slightly below the contract low of 41.72¢/lb), with a price target of 44.35¢/lb, aiming to capture about 30% of the channel width.

I used money management rules to decide how many contracts to purchase. My risk per trade was $545 per contract, and the 2% Rule allowed me to risk the maximum of $2,000. I placed a limit buy order for three March '05 cotton contracts.

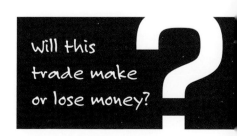

Will this trade make or lose money?

# TRADE 2 | DAMIR'S EXIT

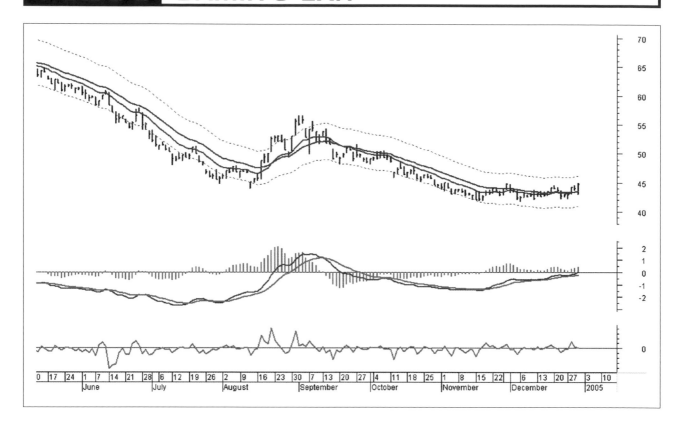

Money management rules have now been established and are being followed. Reentry has been nicely effected even though the original trade with the same strategy resulted in a loss.

## ▲ TRADE SUMMARY

Long March 2005 cotton futures

Bought 12/22/2004 @ $0.4270

Sold 12/30/2004 @ $0.4435

Gain = 165 points per contract minus six points round-trip commission, for a total gain of 159 points per contract

Entry grade = 33% (relatively good)

Exit grade = 69% (good)

Trade Grade = "A" (captured 30% of the 546-point channel)

# TRADE 2—ENTRY COMMENT

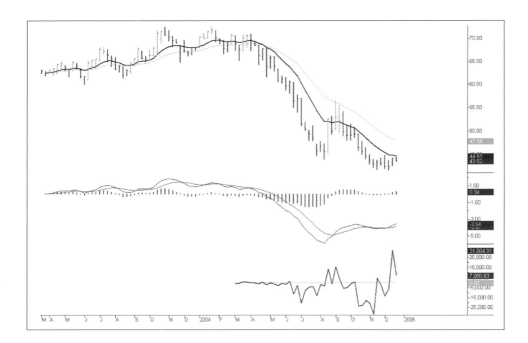

When a major trend changes direction, it rarely turns on a dime. A little boat can turn quickly, but a big ocean liner turns slowly, creating turbulence. Take a look at the previous bottom in cotton, in August 2004—there had been a sharp rally that fizzled out within three weeks. Such sharp rallies are indicative of short-covering: Late-coming amateurs' shorts get squeezed and they cover in a panic, running prices up and triggering more short-covering. Once the panic is over, there is no follow-through to the buying and the downtrend resumes, taking prices down to new lows, much to the consternation of poor shorts who got squeezed out prematurely.

The situation is very different at the bottom that is slowly forming near the right edge of the chart. There is no great volatility, and prices are turning slowly, creating a base that can support a major, lasting upmove. Powerful bullish divergences of the MACD-Histogram and MACD Lines hold out the promise of a major new uptrend. The main difference between this weekly chart and the one we saw at the time of Damir's first trade is a bullish divergence of the Force Index. As it falls in line with MACD, it signals to go long cotton and be prepared to ride a major upmove.

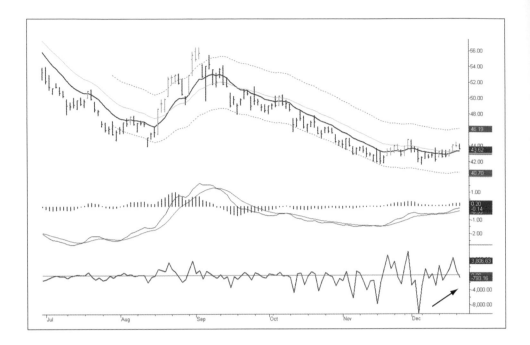

The daily chart confirms that the downtrend in cotton has ended; prices have stabilized and are getting ready to trend higher. MACD-Histogram and MACD Lines have completed their bullish divergences. Notice that while the latest bottom was being formed in December, bears could not even push MACD-Histogram below zero. Markets run on a two-party system: If the bear party is weak, bulls are about to take control.

Notice the downspike of the Force Index in early December—that was the last hurrah for the bears. Every bottom of the Force Index since then has been more shallow and every top higher—another signal of bullish strength. At the right edge of the screen, prices closed above both EMAs, above value, for three days in a row. The last bar is blue, allowing us to buy; the dip towards value creates a good buying opportunity.

# TRADE 2—EXIT COMMENT

At the right edge, cotton is accelerating to the upside, with all indicators bullish and in gear. My only critique of Damir's exit here is that he seems to be getting out too early. He is a highly disciplined man who set himself a target of 30% of the channel. This is a very good target for an ongoing move, but when you're trying to catch a major reversal, it is reasonable to reach for more. In other words, the setting of stops and the placement of price targets depend on the stage of the market you're trading, and your opinion of that stage should be a part of your decision-making process.

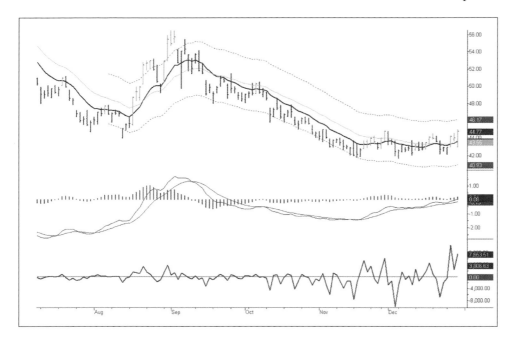

This comment on Damir's exit is a friendly criticism. He is extremely serious and focused on his work, rapidly developing his analytic and trading skills. Having started from a blank slate, he is generating trading profits, keeping terrific notes, and learning from his experience. Damir is scheduled to come to a Traders' Camp three months from this interview, and I look forward to working with him there. My favorite students are serious amateurs and semiprofessional traders coming to improve their performance and reach the next level in their development towards trading for a living.

# GRADING YOUR TRADES

Imagine taking a college class with a friend: Both of you study equally hard and do your homework, but in addition, your friend takes a couple of tests each week. Which of you is likely to get a higher grade on the final exam? Damir buys and sells, makes money on some trades, loses it on others, but after each trade, he grades his performance on three scales—the quality of entry, the quality of exit, and the trade as a whole.

All three measurements have been described in *Come into My Trading Room*. The quality of each entry and exit is reflected in the placement of your trade within that day's bar. Let's say the high of the day was 52, the low 50, and you bought at 51.50. This places your purchase within the top 25% of that day's range—not a good entry, since it shows that you bought near the high of that day's bar. Suppose a few days later you sell at 52, while the high of the day was 53 and the low 51. Now your rating is 50% since you sold right in the middle of the day's bar. Your exit is better than your entry, but still not good enough—the goal is to buy in the bottom one-third of the day's bar and sell in the top one-third. This may sound easy, but is actually very hard to accomplish with any degree of consistency.

Emotionally, the easiest thing to do is to buy high and sell low. Most people buy on the way up and sell on the way down—only the pros do the opposite, as they trade for a living, buying low and selling high. To teach yourself to do the counterintuitive thing, you need to measure the quality of every entry and exit. You need to monitor your trend to make sure you're becoming a sharper trader, and your entries and exits are becoming better. This is why you need to grade every entry and every exit.

There are several ways to grade the quality of each completed trade, but my favorite measure is to do what Damir does—compare the points gained in the trade with the height of the channel on the daily chart. One of the very few scientifically proven facts about the market is that prices fluctuate above and below value. A well-drawn channel contains the bulk of price swings. Comparing the outcome of your trade to the height of the channel allows you to see what percentage of a normal range you were able to capture.

To rate a trade, I divide the points gained in that trade by the height of the channel and express the result as a percentage, with no decimals. Damir, like a true athlete, used to calculate his performance numbers to the second decimal. I told him he was overdoing it—trading is not an exact science, and those decimals only create an illusion of precision. If you capture 30% or more of the distance from the upper to the lower channel line measured on the day you entered that trade, your grade is an "A". If you capture between 20 and 30%, your grade is a "B." Ten to 20% of the channel height gives you a "C," and anything less than that is a "D"—a failed trade.

Years ago, when I developed this grading system, one of my problems used to be that I held profitable trades far too long, waiting for greater gains, but ultimately giving back a major chunk of paper profit when prices reversed. Once I started grading my trades, I began taking profits more quickly, just as Damir is now doing, trying to grab a "B" and later an "A," to raise my grade point average. Trading to get a higher grade taught me useful lessons from which I benefit to this day. Even when I try to catch longer swings, I am quick to grab profits at the first signs of a stall. The habit of grading your trades makes you concentrate on your performance.

If this method is so useful, why do so few people grade their performance? Some may not know this method exists, while others cannot be bothered. Record-keeping is to trading what changing oil is to driving. It is fun to drive but no fun for most people to get under the hood to maintain their car. Trading is a lot of fun, but only good maintenance makes racing possible.

Damir's thorough record-keeping contributes to his rising performance level. He used to be a competitive athlete—and all serious athletes keep score. People who succeed in one field are likely to be successful in another, as long as they handle it with the same level of determination. Failure leads to more failure, and success leads to more success. This is why Damir's long-term plan to get into fund management has a very realistic ring to it.

*An e-mail from Damir:*

# THE MORE EXPERIENCE I HAVE, THE MORE FLEXIBLE I BECOME

Being invited to this interview was a great encouragement for me on this tricky road. Preparing for it became an educational experience, and the meeting in Amsterdam turned out to be a lot of fun.

I am currently applying the Triple Screen trading system to our market (cotton), after learning about it from Dr. Elder's books. I keep modifying the system and techniques to fit my personal trading style, while staying within the framework of the method. The techniques change with the passage of time. For example, having specific targets, such as taking a defined percentage from the channel, was very helpful to me at an earlier stage of development. Many small successful trades gave me much needed confidence in my ability to profit from my analysis, trading system, and plan. Later, the need to grow equity made me realize I had to adjust the system to let my profits run. The more experience I have, the more flexible I become, even though at an early stage, limiting my profit potential with specific targets was essential.

Taking courses in technical analysis at the Securities Institute of Australia has gotten me interested in point-and-figure (P&F) charting. I am trying to use it to supplement the Triple Screen. P&F seems to be very good for detecting congestion areas, support and resistance, while the Triple Screen indicators help determine whether that congestion is predominantly distribution or accumulation. This is a very rough idea at the moment, which I am just starting to test. I also keep in mind that good trading systems tend to be simple. I may end up rejecting P&F, but it feels good to experiment.

I see personal psychology as the key to acquiring an edge in the market. We are all different, with no two identical individuals in the whole world. Since we're all unique, your trading psychology must be firmly rooted in your philosophy of life. For me, positive thinking helps center myself during unprofitable trades. It enables me to calmly face and accept bad trades, analyze the reasons for losses, and avoid repeating mistakes. Bad trades tend to come in strings, one after another, as if the market is throwing you a challenge, testing your emotions, trying to break you. Positive thinking allows me to withstand such difficult periods and move forward by further sharpening my trading skills.

Our life moves forward in cycles, with good and bad periods, ups and downs. The way you manage your bad periods has an impact on how your good periods will turn out in the future. Rising to the stage where trading can support my family, providing a tremendous degree of freedom, is my ultimate goal.

| | |
|---|---|
| Name: | Pascal Willain |
| Lives: | Waterloo, Belgium |
| Previous profession: | Entrepreneur |
| Trades: | U.S. stocks |
| How long: | Since 1998 |
| Trading account: | Medium ($250k–$1m) |
| Software: | Excel, Effective Volume (an Excel add-on), Historical Quotes Downloader from Quotelinks.com |

# CHAPTER 15

# PASCAL WILLAIN

## EFFECTIVE VOLUME

Early in 2005 I received an e-mail from a trader in Belgium. He described his volume-based trading method and wrote: "I believe you will find my work interesting because it is a continuation of what you wrote. It goes in the same line, but with a different set of data, allowing you to get a different view of the market."

The paper attached to the e-mail was written in flawless English but in a style of an engineering report, and I found it heavy going. I asked Pascal whether he traded his system. After receiving a positive reply, I invited him to stop by the apartment I'd rented in Amsterdam that June if he wanted to show me his method. He came to the day-long master class I taught on my first Saturday in Holland, and on Sunday morning walked over to my apartment to show me his work.

His approach was logical and showed good trading results; I also liked Pascal's personal style. We continued our conversation over lunch on a terrace by the canal, and I invited him to be interviewed for this book. A week later he returned to Amsterdam, and we sat down to talk. The micro-computer he brought along belonged to his wife, and in showing me his charts, Pascal flew through Japanese dialog boxes just as easily as if they were in English or his native French.

I grew up in a conservative middle-class family, the second of five children, but became a bad boy at about 12. I had conflicts with my parents, failed two consecutive years in school, started smoking (fortunately, there were no drugs in those days), and shoplifted. After about three years of that, I said to myself, "That's not the way to be, my life is for me, I have to make something of myself." I began to study and haven't stopped since. I love math and studied software engineering, but after graduating did not feel like going to work in a big company. I traveled to Japan, and decided to apply for a scholarship to earn my master's degree there. I had six months of intensive Japanese instruction, then studied for two years for my master's in applied mathematics, while also taking finance and business classes at another Tokyo university. My dissertation dealt with portfolio risk analysis.

I owed a year of military service in Belgium and tried to escape by writing to government ministers who had the right to offer an assistant's position instead of serving in the army. I was looking for something to do with finance and Japan, but no one replied to me. After I completed my service, Philips

Electronics in Amsterdam offered me a job, and there was a bank that invited me to be a trader in Tokyo, but I knew several traders and they were all stressed out. Then one of the politicians to whom I had written a year earlier called and offered me a job. I went to work as a consultant for the minister of technology and traveled between Belgium and Japan for several years.

I was advising Belgian high-tech companies on exporting to Japan, and after a while realized that I could do that as a private consultant. I wrote a business plan, got funding from Japanese friends, and created a company that still exists today. In consulting you can only sell your time, which is limited—and that's why we moved into real business, importing electronic components from Korea and selling Belgian beer to Japan. That's when I met my wife, Michiko. We decided to get married three days after we met—we knew we were right for each other. We got married two years later, but the decision was totally clear on the third day. I recognize things when they're right—I feel when something is happening that the time is now, and I have to take a chance because it will not happen again. I did that when I went to Japan and when I went to work for that minister—when the chance is there, you have to grab it.

I created my second company in Paris where we imported access control components from Korea for a French customer. We developed our own access control systems, subcontracting manufacturing but doing the assembly in-house—it is a high-margin business. I have partners in all my companies because I like to share responsibility and work with people. You have to trust people, and while sometimes it does not work, it usually does because the trust comes back.

In 1997, during the Internet boom, I created a software company to offer database access through a Web interface. After the Internet bubble blew up, we shifted to offering automatic customer care by phone—a dialog between a user and a machine that call centers started to use. There are very few such companies in Europe, and we are becoming recognized. We are small but respected, and big companies buy from us. I used to be the CEO but looked for a replacement because daily business was interfering with my overall focus. Also, I was becoming involved in the markets at that time. I am still a director, working part-time.

I started out as an investor and not a trader. I had some extra money, and in 1998 threw $25,000 into the market on tips from friends. I lost 50% in two months, but was told to have faith and stay long. After a while, my position recovered, but I knew I has been lucky and had to do my own research. During the Internet boom, I picked up a few high-techs that went flying, but after a while I felt I had to sell. A few months later the Internet stocks crashed—and I knew I had been lucky again. As a mathematician, I knew you could not always be lucky and decided to get a professional manager for my portfolio. I asked a friend in the U.S. to manage my money, but he said that would be a bad idea— if you have the ability to make your own decisions, better use it. It'll take longer, but you'll be a bigger winner. In 2001 or 2002 he told me to get two or three books, the first of which was *Trading for a Living*. I worked on it until I "graduated" from its *Study Guide* and then bought *Come into My Trading Room*. I programmed everything from that book into Excel and started trading. I made 60% in six months, but then had a bad month, lost 6% and stopped, following the 6% Rule.

What I did not like about trading was that it took a lot of time. Making many small trades and keeping records was taking time out of my family life. Also, with that method I could not predict big drops, could not see accidents coming. I stopped trading and did research for a year and a half. Luckily,

I could think in a programming language, which got me to the point where I developed my own trading system.

My first objective was to find the trendsetters—people who knew what was likely to happen and who traded ahead of the news. I developed the concept of Effective Volume that tells me when large holders are doing something strange and also when all players are changing their direction, meaning that the price is about to follow.

I divide a stock's daily action into one-minute segments to isolate volume that leads to price changes. If the price has changed from one minute to the next, it means that buying or selling has come in, and I track that volume. If the price has not changed, the volume of that minute is irrelevant. This indicator does not work for stocks priced under a dollar. I also filter out block trades—large trades assembled by specialists for their clients. They buy up stocks, then sell them as a single block, so that in effect they appear on the tape twice. If I see a one-minute bar that has more than 10% of that day's volume, I eliminate it.

**EFFECTIVE VOLUME**

*Pascal says:* To calculate Effective Volume for the one-minute bar, I use only a portion of that minute's volume. I multiply the total by a formula adapted from Larry Williams who divided (close minus open) by (high minus low). I also add a tick to both sides of the equation in order to adjust for one-tick bars:

$$EV = \frac{\text{Absolute value of (Close} - \text{Close}_{\text{prev bar}}) + 1 \text{ tick}}{(\text{High}_{\text{special}} - \text{Low}_{\text{special}}) + 1 \text{ tick}} \times \text{Volume}$$

where

High$_{\text{special}}$ is the highest of the two – the current bar's high or previous bar's close.
Low$_{\text{special}}$ is the lowest of the two – the current bar's low or previous bar's close.
A tick is the smallest permitted price change, normally one cent for U.S. stocks.

My formula is based on the closes because the close of one minute can be different from the open of the next minute. This happens if the last trade of the previous minute took out all the available volume at that price, and the next person buys at a higher or lower price. If I were to use the open price instead of the previous close, I'd lose the influence of that trade and the Effective Volume would become the volume responsible for a price change within one trading minute, giving different results. This is why I use the previous minute's close instead of the current minute's open.

Also, if your formula uses the close of the previous minute, you must modify the high and the low. If the previous close was higher than the high of the current minute and your formula does not account for that, it'll be wrong. Similarly, if the previous close is lower than the low of the current minute, you then need to adapt the low of the formula. This is why I use High$_{\text{special}}$ and Low$_{\text{special}}$ instead of simple High and Low.

Next, I want to find the fraction of Effective Volume that belongs to large traders. Low volume tends to be noise—small retail players who do not have a clue. Large traders tend to be institutions with superior information, and they trade size. I track large players by focusing on bars whose volume is in the top half of all one-minute Effective Volumes for that stock on that day. I find the midpoint for each day—the EV of half the bars is higher, and the other half is lower. It is important to recalibrate this number at the end of each day because the daily volume keeps changing. By adding up the total EV and then the EV for only the top 50% of bars at the end of the day, I get two highly filtered lines—Total Effective Volume and Large Effective Volume. The Large EV shows me whether big guys are buying or selling, which is useful for detecting possible trend changes.

Whenever I look at a trading range trying to decide whether prices are likely to break out to the upside or to the downside, I know they usually move in the direction of the Large EV. I also know it'll take time to prepare for a breakout—days rather than minutes or hours. This is because it takes time for institutions to accumulate or distribute during the trading range. (Compare this with Bill Doane's comment about his experiences at Fidelity in Chapter 12.)

There is a dam, and a reservoir is filling with water. Insiders tend to be big money, and while big money is not necessarily smart, it is better to be on the side of large players than retail. The Securities and Exchange Commission should use my software to detect insider trading—I'm joking, they probably have other methods, but my software gives an individual trader more power against big guys.

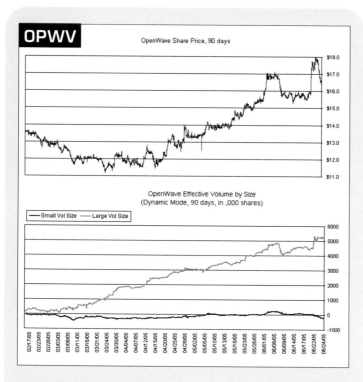

The stock declined in February and went flat in March but Large Effective Volume started picking up, indicating which way the breakout was likely to go. The stock embarked on a healthy rally, with Large EV fully confirming the upmove. The pros had loaded up early and kept adding during the uptrend. The smaller traders fully lived up to Pascal's label of "not having a clue." Their group remained negative through May and went only slightly positive in June, missing the bulk of the upmove.

I use my software to monitor what traders are doing, looking at both the Total EV and the Large EV to see how the crowd and big traders are moving. With the Total EV, I measure the quality of upswings and see whether they are becoming stronger or weaker. I also look for divergences between the Total EV and the price because in an upswing the EV will usually weaken before the price. When the EV becomes weak, the stock is ready to go down fast and may even crash—you have days to buy, but only hours to sell. When the first crack appears in the dam, it is time to run. After developing the EV, I looked at my old trades and said, "Now I have a tool to sidestep catastrophic situations."

This is not a miracle system. It is a tool, but not a complete method. Sometimes it does not work. Life is like that. I do not want to give the impression that this is the ultimate. It works most of the time, but with some stocks it does not, and then I understand this is not a good stock for this method, but there are many other stocks in the market. These days I am working to refine my method, to trade less and take advantage of longer trends. I keep buying uptrends and selling reactions, but need to find whether a reaction is just a pullback within an uptrend, allowing me to hold, and when it is a reversal.

If the Total EV is trending down, I will not buy that stock, whatever the price is doing. I short rarely, and only on the strongest signals—I'd rather pass and look for longs elsewhere. I also do standard technical analysis on the Internet to see what other traders are seeing.

# TRADE 1 | PASCAL'S ENTRY

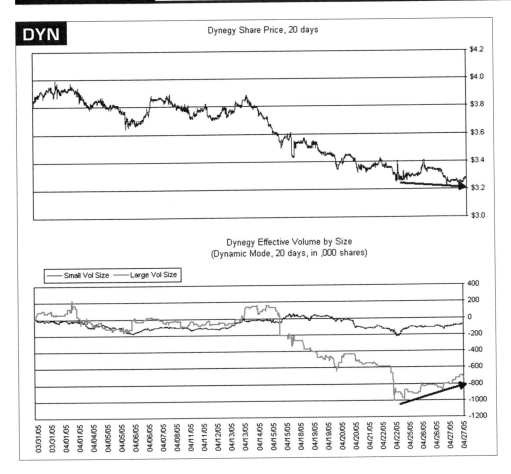

**Upper pane:**  Bar chart (one-minute bars)
**Lower pane:**  Effective Volume (blue—Small, green—Large)

## DYN

Dynegy Inc., is an energy company. This chart shows 20 days of trading, from 3/31/2005 to 4/27/2005—this is the time window at which I like to look. You can see a downtrend, but then the decline slows down, and near the right edge there is a trading range between approximately 3.20 and 3.40.

The bottom pane shows two lines of Effective Volume—one for large traders, the other for small. At first, both EV lines move together with the same tempo and direction, and no clear signal between March 31 and April 14. On April 15 the Large EV went into sell mode, and the price went down—that's normal behavior. On April 22 the Large EV reversed and started trending higher even as prices continued flat and fell to a new low. After several days of this, I said, "Something is happening; I do not know what it is, but big traders are buying, and I also bought."

Will this trade make or lose money?

# TRADE 1 | PASCAL'S EXIT

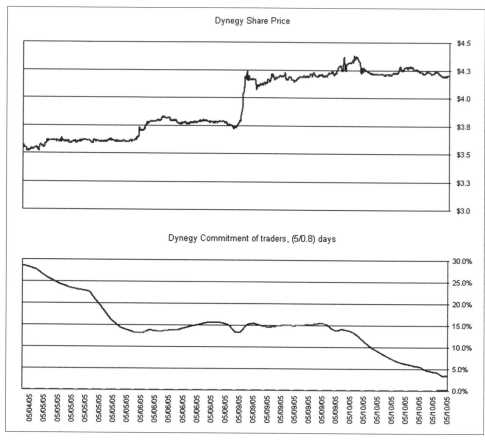

Dynegy Share Price

Dynegy Commitment of traders, (5/0.8) days

**Upper pane:**    Bar chart (one-minute bars)
**Lower pane:**    Effective Ratio (Commitment of traders)

I look at the Large Effective Volume for entering trades, but not for my exits. It is not very useful for exits because it tends to move with the trend, not providing any special signals. What helps me decide when to exit is the Effective Ratio—it is the Total EV divided by the total volume. Since my work is based on one-minute charts, I use a 250-minute EMA of Total Effective Ratio, which covers about one trading day.

When the mass of traders is very committed to a stock, the ratio of Effective Volume to total volume becomes high. When buyers become weaker, the Effective Ratio declines, and it becomes negative when sellers outnumber buyers.

The Effective Ratio confirmed every upleg of the rally, except for the last one. When DYN shot up above 4.30, the Effective Ratio began to decline instead of going up. When it fell below 5%, I could no longer hold. The Effective Ratio was still positive, above zero, but weak—and when I sit on a large profit and the situation is not clear-cut, I'd rather take my profit.

## TRADE SUMMARY

Long DYN
Bought 4/27/2005 @ $3.25
Sold 5/10/2005 @ $4.30
Profit = $1.05 per share

# TRADE 1—ENTRY COMMENT

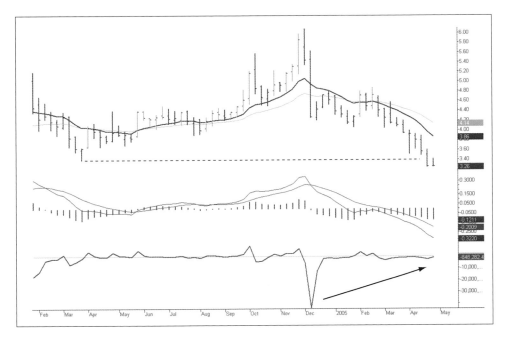

Some bullish signs are starting to appear. There have been 10 weeks of red bars—this downtrend is old and at some point it is going to find support. Weekly Force Index shows a massive bullish divergence. A week ago prices fell to a new low, taking out their 2004 bottom, but this week there is no follow-through to the downside. This could be a false downside breakout, a terrific buying opportunity. Still, the message I get from the Impulse system is to go short or stand aside. I certainly have no interest in shorting here, with all those bullish signs, and so will stand aside.

Since no method for finding trends is perfect, different methods will deliver profits and losses at different times. On this weekly chart of DYN, my system prohibits me from going long. Both the EMA and MACD-Histogram are declining and the Impulse system is red, allowing me to short or stand aside.

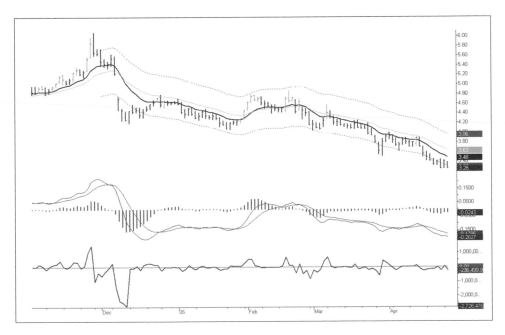

The daily chart shows a slow, painful grind down in this stock. It broke down on a gap in December, fell 20 cents lower in January, a few more in February, 30 cents in March and

20 cents in April. Near the right edge of the chart, most signs are in gear to the downside, with a few bullish exceptions. MACD-Lines have declined to a level where bottoms tend to occur. Prices are below the lower channel line, an oversold area. Force Index is tracing a bullish divergence. Still, the daily Impulse system is red, prohibiting me from buying.

At the same time, had Pascal told me he was planning to buy DYN, I would not have tried to talk him out of it. Different systems have different parameters, and it is impossible to find the one that will satisfy all traders. You have to find the system that appeals to you, test it, and go forward with it.

# TRADE 1—EXIT COMMENT

*At the right edge of the chart, a powerful upswing is underway. The stock shot up above its upper channel line, with indicators rising to record levels. The next-to-last bar is extremely long, indicating a buying panic. Such panic moves are caused by short-sellers caught on the wrong side of the market (regular buyers tend not to feel so urgent). Once the weakest players, the trapped short-sellers are shaken out, the stock is ready to pause or even reverse.*

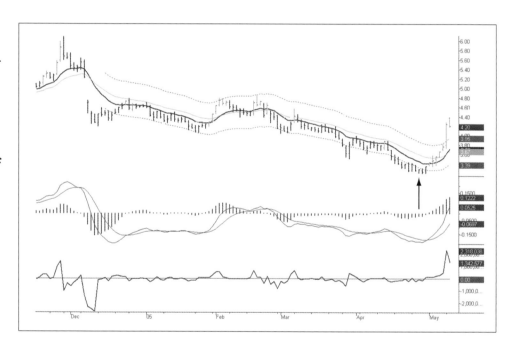

A few days after Pascal went long, prices stabilized at a slightly lower level, and the indicators began to turn up. The daily Impulse system turned blue and then green, as prices closed above the EMA. At the same time, the weekly Impulse (not shown) stopped being red and turned blue, permitting buying.

The last bar is much shorter than the previous one, showing that the buying panic is dying down. The last bar has closed near its low, a sign that bears dominated the endgame for that day. Pascal is totally justified in taking profits. He got in when prices were undervalued, and now they are overvalued—his trade had a logical beginning, a dynamic middle, and now its end. A sensible person recognizes when the party is over and goes home feeling confident there will be more parties in the future.

# TRADE 2 | PASCAL'S ENTRY

## KCS

KCS Energy, Inc., is in the natural gas business. Whenever I trade a stock, I want to know what the company does, its basic fundamentals. This way, if I make a mistake in technical analysis, good fundamentals may provide an additional safety net.

Near the right edge of the chart, KCS is in a trading range, but Large Effective Volume is rising. It tells me that big investors are buying, and the probability of an upside break-out is greater than a break to the downside. I went long and placed a stop at 14.25, just underneath the trading range—if I'm wrong, I'm out.

I did not set a price target—I do not like to have them. The market will tell me when it is ready to turn—when Large Effective Volume starts crashing or the Effective Ratio becomes weak.

Will this trade make or lose money?

## TRADE 2 PASCAL'S EXIT

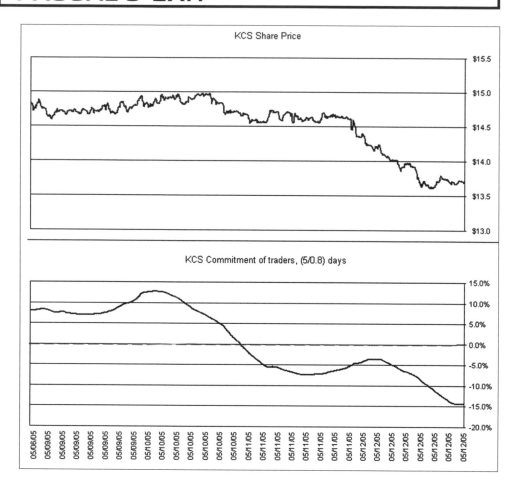

KCS fell two days after I entered, stopping me out. Effective Ratio is trending down, showing that sellers are getting strong. I had bought the top when they were buying—and then they changed their mind, but that did not feel normal to me. I had to analyze why this trade failed.

After taking this loss, I found that KCS would not trade well with my tools because its price is linked to that of natural gas; they are about 90% correlated. My method is based on following the big guys, but it came out that there are much bigger guys who trade this commodity, and they impact this stock more than big stock traders. And so I dropped this stock from my list, stopped trading it because I have no advantage over the competition here.

## TRADE SUMMARY

Long KCS
Bought 5/10/2005 @ $14.75
Sold 5/12/2005 @ $14.25
Loss = $0.50 per share

# TRADE 2—ENTRY COMMENT

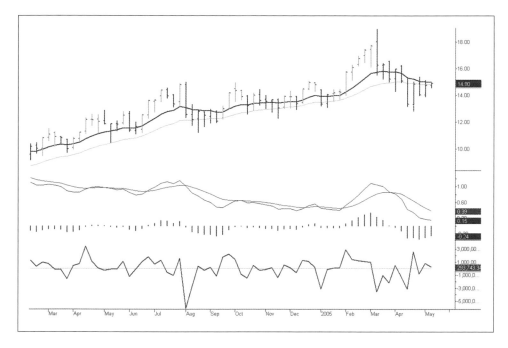

*KCS had a slow and steady uptrend for the better part of two years, but became more volatile in recent months. In March it accelerated and ran up to a new high, only to collapse during that same week and continue to decline into April, when it staged a sharp two-week reversal. At the right edge of the chart, KCS is essentially flat, with very little useful input from my technical indicators.*

The moving averages are flat, MACD-Histogram is rising, but Force Index has traced a bearish divergence. The Impulse system is blue, allowing us to go either long or short. Squint at this chart long enough, and you'll find either a buy or a sell signal. I do not allow myself to squint, believing that a good trade jumps at you from the screen—you can't miss it. If you catch yourself squinting at a chart, move on to the next stock.

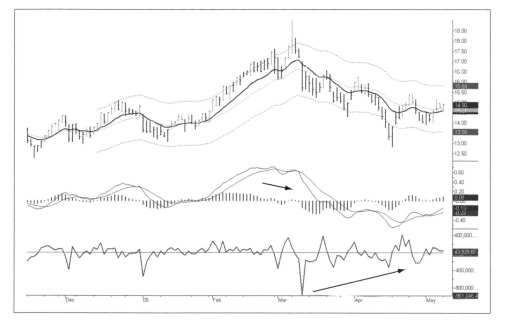

*The daily chart of KCS provides more contradictory signals. The last strikingly clear signal was a sell in early March. Prices shot up and collapsed, leaving a kangaroo tail or a finger pointing skyward. Once the market tested and rejected a higher price, the next test was likely to be to the downside. At the same time MACD-Histogram completed a massive bearish divergence. When two powerful signals come together, you have to put on a trade—it does not really get much better than that.*

KCS slid from above $17, where the sell signal was given, to below $14. There, a similar combination of signals gave a message to buy—a spike below $13 and a bullish divergence of MACD-Histogram. The April buy signals were less clear-cut than the shorting signals that month, and they did not produce such a powerful move either—prices bounced, but then went essentially flat. At the right edge of the chart, the daily Impulse is green, allowing us to buy or stand aside, but not to short. There is no argument against Pascal's decision to go long. The Large Effective Volume is up, his logic is valid, and his stop is in place.

# TRADE 2—EXIT COMMENT

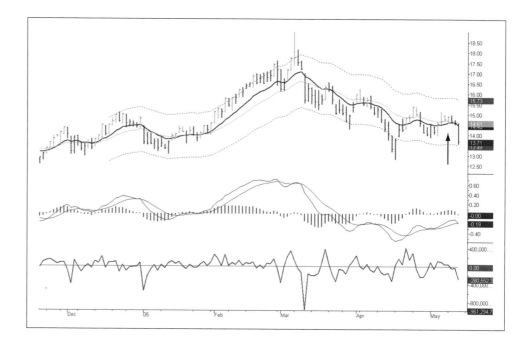

At the right edge, prices collapse, and the trade comes to a quick end as Pascal's stop below the recent trading range gets hit. Characteristically for a serious trader, his research does not end when the trade ends. Where most trades would shrug off a loss and move on to the next trade, Pascal continues to dig, trying to find out why his method failed this time. He comes up with an important discovery—the price of KCS is 90% correlated with the price of natural gas.

Having made this discovery, a trader has several choices. He may start using buy and sell signals in natural gas to trade this stock. He may look for arbitrage possibilities between the stock and natural gas. Finally, he may do what Pascal did—decide he was not interested in futures and cross this stock off his list. A serious trader neither gloats about his wins nor buries his losses. He treats both as the grist for his analytic mill, helping him learn and become a better trader tomorrow than he is today.

# THE TRENDSETTERS

When Pascal first showed me his Effective Volume, I asked what he wanted to do with his concept. He was already trading it and had no interest in managing money, but wanted public recognition. In talking over his desire to share his ideas with the trading public, I thought of those petty individuals who pop up saying, "Why would anyone who knows how to trade disclose his methods?" Here's a good example of how generous a successful person can be. He is a partner in several businesses and makes money in the market, but his main interest today is supporting the foundation he created with his wife for taking care of severely disabled children.

Pascal's method has several more features than described in this chapter. He gave me a thick manual and urged me to include a longer description of several tools that he uses, but I had to draw the line and focus on the essentials for the sake of clarity and brevity. Pascal is planning to write a series of articles or a book detailing his method. He and David Weis are the two traders I interviewed for this project whose future books I look forward to reading; the book by Gerald Appel has already come out to an enthusiastic reception.

With all my respect for Pascal's work, I want to offer a few words of caution regarding his key concept, which could be misinterpreted by some readers. Pascal speaks of trend-setters who act before the crowd and whose buying or selling can send the market into a new trend. Undoubtedly, some market participants are more knowledgeable than others and are more capable of making decisions early. I also agree that more insider trading takes place in the markets than we hear about—that the insiders who get caught violating the law tend to be the greediest ones. The quieter and more cautious ones get away, leaving only their footprints on the charts. Technical analysts look for those footprints in order to recognize trends and reversals early.

At the same time, it is important to realize that no group has a direct pipeline to the truth. Big money is sometimes smart, but not always—just visit money management firms and look at the corporate types managing your investments. When you look for the elusive trendsetters, you must keep in mind that sometimes they are there, but more often they are not. Sometimes people in the know accumulate shares before a rise, but other times insiders are no more present than the Loch Ness monster or the Abominable Snowman. This is why an essential trait of every successful trader is humility—knowing that he does not have a corner on the truth and that his methods do not always work. This is also why serious traders pay a great deal of attention to risk control and money management.

Going a step further, the search for trendsetters, while useful at times, can push impressionable people over the edge and into the conspiracy theory—a view that a vast faceless conspiracy rules not only the markets but the entire world. Such primitive belief is characteristic of emotionally troubled and intellectually challenged persons who are unlikely to succeed in trading.

After I asked Pascal to review this chapter, he added this comment: "I believe that insider trading is linked to the way the company is managed and its type of business. Large contracts involve multiple participants and take weeks to negotiate, creating more chances for information leaks. A company cannot change the way it does business or its management method—if it leaked information in the past, it will leak in the future. Because of this, I like to look at a company's news for the past year to see whether there was a prior signal from Large Effective Volume. If the answer is yes, then the stock is probably a good candidate for my method."    —AE

**A TIGER DOES NOT CHANGE ITS STRIPES**

As I try to visualize the trendsetters, I can see an occasional insider trader, a large fund manager with an unusually keen grasp of a certain stock, and further afield, a person like Pascal who, by his keen attention to a stock, recognizes its potential and gets in early, becoming a trendsetter himself. Other times, there are no trendsetters at all, just a mass of traders stumbling in the dark, buying at the ask and selling at the bid, enriching the dealers. Still, sometimes the trendsetters are present, and now we have Pascal's tools to help us track their actions.

*An e-mail from Pascal:*

## ACTIVE BOUNDARIES

Why didn't anybody else think of these concepts before? This is a question I have been asking myself for some time. My answer is probably similar to what Dr. Elder might say if someone asked how he wrote a book on trading. I think he combined experiences from different fields: psychology, trading, and writing. I came up with these new concepts because of my experience in applied mathematics and writing software, but most importantly I came up with them because I needed them for my own trading.

Suppose this need was recognized by a big financial institution. They would have had to get researchers with different experience: software, math, and trading. Those guys would have had to work together, exchange ideas, write papers, test them, etc.—all the while reporting to their bosses. This would have been quite a task force!

In addition to Effective Volume and Effective Ratio, I would like to describe my second-tier indicator. Active Boundaries show when a stock is overbought or oversold. It differs from all previous measurements of overbought and oversold because it includes volume along with price. Other tools, such as Relative Strength Index (RSI) and Support/Resistance, are based on stock prices alone and ignore volume, even though it is an essential part of market activity.

Support and resistance mark the areas where a trend is likely to reverse. Keep in mind a subtle distinction: Investors buy not because a stock is cheap or sell because it is expensive; they buy because they expect the price to go up and sell because they expect it to go down. Similarly, a stock falls not because the RSI is overbought, but because traders' expectations of that stock become low. These two factors are related: the higher the price, the lower the expectation of a further increase.

I developed Active Boundaries to track the expectations of the pool of traders active in a given stock. An individual's expectation of profit is linked to two factors: where he expects the price to go and the price he has paid. You would expect a trader to make his decision on the basis of fundamental and technical data, not his own purchase price. That price has no influence whatsoever on where the stock is going to go. Still, most people make buy and sell decisions on the basis of their open profits or losses.

Suppose two traders hold a stock currently quoted at $10. Trader A bought it at $8, while trader B bought at $9.95. Both may believe the company has a great future, but trader A is already 25% ahead and more inclined to take his profit. At this point A's expectation for the price increase is lower than B's. This is mainly because A's profit expectation has already been at least partially fulfilled by his 25% paper gain. As a rule, the expectation of any trader at any moment is inversely proportional to his ROI (Return on Investment).

If we knew at what price each share had been bought, we could calculate the ROI for each share at any time. Calculating an average ROI minute by minute is a close enough approximation, allowing us to track the average ROI of the mass of traders. The crowd active in any given stock develops certain behavior patterns and an expectation of returns; when that stock's average ROI reaches that level, the trend is prone to reverse.

Active Boundaries are well-established zones of maximum and minimum average ROIs for the pool of active shares, or what I call Active Float. Estimating the size of that pool is a visual process, somewhat similar to finding the best width of an envelope. When you want to draw a channel around a moving average, you try different coefficients, looking for the best fit to create an envelope that contains the most prices, with only the extreme points sticking out. Some stocks require a 5% channel, others 3.5%, and so on. To determine the Active Boundaries, you have to keep adjusting the Active Float number until you find the one whose average ROI produced the most regular reversal patterns for the past six months or so.

TMR (The Meridian Resources Corp) is a natural gas exploration and production company. The chart on this page shows its average ROI for every trading minute. The plot largely follows the price trend, but is inverse to the average expectation of the mass of traders: the higher the average ROI, the lower the expectation of further increase. Active Boundaries are horizontal lines on the plot of the average ROI. The level of those lines differs from stock to stock because different groups of investors and traders have different expectations for profits and tolerance for losses.

In TMR the average ROI for 50 million shares produces a much more regular pattern than the price. We find 50 million by trial and error—trying 30, 50, 70, and so on in search of the most regular pattern. The average ROI line oscillates between the upper and lower Active Boundaries (UB1 and LB1). When the company announced bad news in November (point A), it changed shareholders' expectations, creating a new set of boundaries (UB2 and LB2) to match the lowered expectations.

As we follow the chart from left to right, we observe the following:

- Between April and November 2004, Active Boundaries were located between the ROI of 0% and 20%. Whenever the average ROI fell to zero, the stock was a buy, and whenever it rallied to 20%, the stock was a sell. Near the upper boundary, the collective expectation for the price increase became very low. The mass of traders considered the stock relatively expensive at that level, reduced their buying, and the stock turned down.
- At point A, in November 2004, the price broke its uptrendline, and the average ROI fell to the lower active boundary (LB1). Taken in isolation, this could have been seen as a buy zone, but a breakdown in Effective Ratio (see chart on page 274) showed that the company was facing momentous difficulties and pointed towards taking a short position.
- After the crash, triggered by a downward revision of the company's reserves of natural gas, the stock developed a very negative set of active boundaries (UB2 and LB2).

An upper boundary below 0% is typical of a strong downtrend, while a lower boundary above 0% indicates a strong uptrend.

- At point *B,* the stock attempted to rally, with the average ROI of the Active Float rising above the upper boundary, into overbought territory. In the absence of positive news, the stock was ready for a downside reversal.
- At point *C,* the average ROI touched its lower boundary, while the Effective Volume showed a very strong upside reversal. Together, they signalled an excellent buying opportunity.
- At point *D,* the price is still very cheap, while the Active Boundaries show that ROI exceeded UB2 and has regained its UB1 level. It tells us that in the short run the stock is overbought; what happens in the long run will depend either on the news being released or on the message of the Effective Volume.

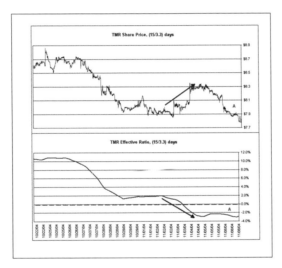

At point *A* in November 2004—the *A* mark is on the same date on both charts (pages 273 and 274)—the average ROI fell to the lower Active Boundary (LB1 in chart on page 273). At that point the mass of traders was viewing the stock as cheap, their collective expectation was high, and the price should have rebounded. It did not because the bad news was already leaking out. Between November 2 and 4, while the share price was increasing, the Effective Ratio turned negative, as shown in this chart. This indicated that sellers were the dominant force even during the price surge, meaning the rally was a fake and calling for price weakness ahead. The combination of the Large Effective Volume, Effective Ratio, and Active Boundaries allows for the best trading decisions, especially for swing trading. This method is not suitable for day-trading or long-term investment. Each of these indicators taken alone could lead to major misinterpretations, and it pays to wait until their signals point in the same direction.

1. *How do you select the pool of active shares?*

This is done by trial and error: I will use different numbers until I find the size that produced the most reliable reversal patterns in the past.

2. *Why does the Active Boundaries indicator produce repetitive top and bottom patterns?*

The honest reply is that I do not know. I think that the pool of traders in any stock tends to be relatively stable. Professional traders do not usually invest in a stock without thorough research, which takes time. Investors prefer to follow the same company for a long time, trading it on different occasions. The Active Boundaries tell us that the average strategy of the pool of active traders remains stable. The study of the ROI of this pool of traders gives us a good picture of how they will react in the future under similar circumstances.

3. *Do Active Boundaries work for any stock?*

Definitely not! They do not work well in the following cases:

- For slow-moving stocks whose float turnover is longer than six months.
- For hyperactive stocks whose float can be turned within a few weeks, because day traders overshadow investors and swing traders.
- For thinly traded stocks, since the trade decisions of a few can have large consequences on the indicator.

I believe that the study of the price/volume relationship is the key to measuring stocks' supply/demand balance. Dr. Elder pointed this out with his Force Index, but to take full advantage of this approach, I had to work on a different set of data—the minute-by-minute information. No method is perfect, and I still make mistakes, usually when I try to anticipate my indicators.

No single market tool works perfectly, but a combination of tools makes success possible. If you are a beginner dissatisfied with your own method, jumping into a more complex method is probably not a good idea. If you are already successful in trading, studying this method can help you improve your results.

| | |
|---:|:---|
| Name: | Martin Knapp |
| Lives: | Vienna, Austria |
| Previous profession: | Personal IT coach |
| Trades: | U.S. stocks, futures, and Forex |
| How long: | Since 1998 |
| Trading account: | Medium ($250k–$1m) |
| Software: | TC2005, TradeStation, Trader's Governor |
| Traders' Camp: | Has taken every Camp since March 2003 and taught in the September 2004 and March 2005 Camps |

# CHAPTER 16

# MARTIN KNAPP

## DO IT RIGHT THE NEXT TIME AROUND

**M**artin rolled into our Camp in the Dominican Republic laughing and smiling, sporting the best computer equipment in the class, and generously helping anyone who needed help with their machines. He ordered good wine for his table at dinners, kissed all the girls, and partied late. He carefully avoided early morning runs on the beach, but was always the first in class, soaking up information, asking questions, and sharing ideas with other campers.

I have a monthly campers' meeting in my apartment in New York—we review markets, share tips, and go out for dinner. Most participants are locals, with the occasional out-of-town camper timing a business trip to coincide with a meeting; it is very unusual to have a camper fly in from abroad. Martin keeps flying in from Vienna, takes part in our meetings, goes shopping for electronic equipment, and hits every party in town.

Martin loves to party, but he likes working just as much. After leaving a party well past midnight one Friday in St. Maarten, I crashed and slept, but Martin went on to a local bar, where he spent hours talking girls into jumping into a pool wearing only a T-shirt. Still, when I woke up before eight, I saw Martin already up on the terrace with his computer, doing his homework.

> During my last year of high school in 1988, the manager of my hometown bank created a fictitious account for our class to trade in the Austrian stock market. Stocks are not popular in my country—people put their money into savings accounts, and only about 4% of Austrians are shareholders. Nobody in my family owned stocks, and I had only vaguely heard of the stock market. Our class started "trading" our "account" of 200,000 schillings (about $20,000) by selecting names that sounded good, buying and never shorting. By the end of the year, we made about a $50 "profit," and the manager gave it to us in cash for our graduation party.
>
> Ever since then, I knew there was a way to get money out of the market. For the next 10 years I did a bit of buying, usually after hearing a tip or reading something in the newspaper. Back then, many Austrian stocks had one fixed price per day, and to buy or sell I would go to the bank, where a clerk would pull out a typewriter to take my order. Then a few days later, you'd know what happened.

I never made or lost much money and never thought of making trading my top priority in life. I was busy at university and with my student jobs, and afterwards co-founded a management consulting company in which I was responsible for the IT department. I consider myself a personal IT coach and work for several top Austrian executives and firm owners, helping them solve their business and personal computer problems. I continue to consult for two clients because I like dealing with them.

In 1998 it became possible to trade stocks on the Internet, and that was a crucial turning point for me. I opened my first Internet account in February 1999 and started becoming interested in technical analysis. I was friendly with an American from Seattle who lived in Vienna, and we started looking at charts on Web sites, very basic. He kept reading *Technical Analysis of Stocks and Commodities* and one day bought a copy of MetaStock to implement something from that magazine. My first software was a pirated copy of his.

Now I realize that what we were doing wasn't real technical analysis. I was painting color lines, but they made me feel good. I was working full-time at my business and looked at charts when the market was going my way, ignoring them when they weren't. In a little over a year, at the top of the bubble in March of 2000, my $3,000 eTrade account had grown to $40,000. I was teaching business management seminars in Eastern Europe, and sometimes showed Eastern Europeans what I was doing with stocks, which they loved because they knew that's where free money came from. I was in Bucharest when Broadvision went from $275 to $285—it was one of the companies that eventually helped return my account from its $40,000 peak back to its $3,000 starting value.

Why did I give back that money? After the loss I felt, as you say, like a dog with a can of food. The dog knows there is good stuff inside, but doesn't know how to open it. I realized I had spent 11 years just messing around.

I always had a life plan—to sit on an island by 35 and not have a job. I was already one of the most successful IT consultants in Austria, but realized that retiring at 35 on fees alone was not feasible. I was a partner in the firm, but far from my goal. Not that I wanted to stop working—I consider myself a workaholic—but I did not want to work for clients; I wanted more freedom. Taking an account from $3,000 to $40,000 in a year seemed better suited to reaching my goal. I decided to give it one more try, and do it right this time around.

At the end of 2000, my then-girlfriend and I went on our first trip to Australia. I love summers in Austria but always wanted to find a place to spend the cold season. We went to check out whether Australia would be a suitable winter destination if and when my goal of sitting on an island was achieved. We went for two weeks—Melbourne, Adelaide, a little wine shopping in the Barossa Valley, then Sydney, and five days on the beach in Port Douglas.

I went on that trip preoccupied with my next step in trading. In Melbourne I stepped into The Investment Bookstore and discovered a copy of *Trading for a Living*. That title rang all my bells. I could see not being tied to my clients in Vienna but making a living from the market, which would allow me to spend six months in Australia if I wanted and not two weeks, like most people on vacation.

I started marking up pages, designing spreadsheets, had great fun programming indicators, and then bought an Elder-disk just to compare my programming with yours. I was happy to see that I had programmed everything supercorrectly. Technical analysis, psychology, and money management started coming together for me.

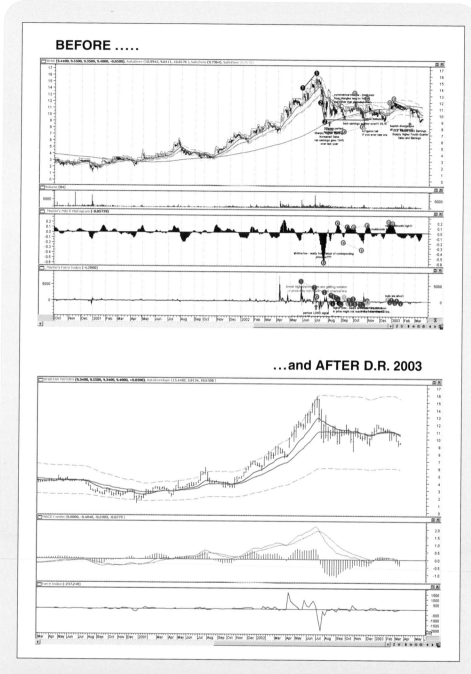

**BEFORE .....**

**...and AFTER D.R. 2003**

**There is less to trading than meets the eye:**  These two images are screenshots of Martin's computer immediately before and after his first Traders' Camp. Putting more lines on a chart can only obfuscate the message of prices. A handful of simple technical tools is more useful than a screen full of indicators.

I was busy implementing the techniques in *Trading for a Living* all of 2001 and was one of the first to buy *Come into My Trading Room* in 2002. I had not met you then, but still have a copy with an autograph—"Thank you for being one of the first readers of my book." Still, my clients had first priority, with no more than 20% of my time dedicated to trading, mostly late evenings and weekends. After reading *Come into My Trading Room* in 2002, about 30% of my time went into trading. I heard of Traders' Camps and knew that one day I'd attend one, but did not feel ready in 2002. I thought campers were highly educated people, and I did not want to come as a complete idiot. I wanted to be able to benefit and even participate in discussions, and switch my focus to trading after that. The day before Christmas in 2002 I was cleaning my e-mails when an announcement came in that an additional Camp had been scheduled for March 2003 because traders who got left out of the January Camp were banging on the door.

The second I read it I knew it was for me. It took two days to coordinate whether my girlfriend could get time off to come with me and then I signed up. I'd read the books, but being in class was no comparison—I had several "ahaa" and "wow" moments, prepared a long list of things I had to do, changes to implement, rules to add, additional software to buy. One of my screensavers is a shot of my standard chart before and after the Camp. It made a huge difference for me, helped me focus on what was important and cut out the crap.

I was implementing what I'd learned, and as soon as my work took the right direction, flew to New York to one of your monthly campers' meetings. I've always been a fan of America, as a student spent a semester at University of Illinois at Urbana-Champaign and had been to one or two computer shows. I worked to improve my trading to be able to fly to New York and say, "Look, I'm not doing too badly." I came in June 2003, and when we met on Saturday morning for breakfast, you mentioned several computer problems which I could easily solve. We spent a couple of hours working on your computer and then I asked you to take a few minutes to look at my trades and charts, receiving wonderful feedback on how to improve. I'd hate to always be on the taking end and was glad to give something back. You told me of your plan to fly to Amsterdam in August to visit friends, then rent a BMW convertible and drive through Germany and Switzerland, returning the car in Milan where your friend would be coaching at an international rowing competition. I volunteered to help but found it was impossible to rent a nice car, let alone a BMW for a one-way rental in Europe. So I said, Look, I have an Audi convertible, let me drive you.

When you came to Vienna, I was trying to organize a network of local trading buddies. Ten people came to our meeting, some even flew in from other countries, but the "network" was a failure. Almost everybody came to listen to Dr. Elder without contributing anything. There were a few exceptions, such as Nic, an Australian camper who came from France. Then a great thing happened—on Saturday morning, you, Nic, and I were looking at market industry groups and indices, and you said, "We have to build a shopping list; this is the time to get long in the market." What followed became the core of our standard weekly homework—review indices and groups, find the most interesting ones, then look for stocks within those groups [see *Seven Days in Dr. Alexander Elder's Trading Room* on page 291].

The three of us worked all weekend and in the end applied risk/reward ratios to select the five most attractive stocks for the week ahead. I remember asking whether you would trade on Monday, and you said, "Of course. Otherwise, why work on a weekend?" I started doing this homework every weekend to establish a better degree of control over my trading.

Today I am striving to become a better trader. Even if I had enough money for the rest of my life, I would not stop trading; it has become a passion. I would not want to sit on the terrace of a villa not knowing what to do with myself all day. Trading is a part of my life. I have not missed a single day in recent years; wherever I am in the world, I always go online every day to study the markets.

My weekend homework is at the core of my trading. I rate about 120 U.S. and international market indices and about 250 U.S. stock industry groups to decide how bullish or bearish I am on the market. I look for any tradeable changes, something that could work for me that has not yet been discovered by other traders. After finding bullish or bearish groups, I look for their most interesting long or short candidates, then put my top choices into Trader's Governor [see Chapter 6] to select the ones I'll trade. I also use a couple of scans—I've programmed a search for bullish and bearish divergences of MACD-Histogram in MetaStock, a scan for Impulse flip-to-green and flip-to-red in TC2005, that sort of thing. I use the "traffic lights" in Trader's Governor to express my degree of bullishness and bearishness.[1] I've developed a weekly routine—the weekend is for analysis, I enter positions on Monday and Tuesday, and start getting out towards the weekend. I do not have to be fully invested and carrying heavy bags—if there are no good candidates, I'd rather stand aside and chase girls that week.

Sometimes being in front of the screen is counterproductive, as I find myself becoming anxious and emotional. I may develop a good plan on the weekend, put on my trades Monday morning, and right then the market starts going against me, making me uneasy and thinking what I did on the weekend was stupid. If I exit, the market usually turns again and does what I expected in the first place, when I was calm and relaxed on the weekend.

I have developed a technique of "doing a martin"—staying away from the screen. After the U.S. stock market opens at 3:30 PM Vienna time, I put on my trades and get into my two-seater convertible and go for a drive with a cigar. Doing a martin works intraday, but also on a longer-term basis. If I feel I have no edge, I'd rather do nothing than trade just to be active and get beaten. In April 2005 I could not decide whether I wanted to be a bull or a bear, and drove to Cote d'Azur with a girl. Had I stayed in Vienna and traded, everything that week would have gone against me. Still, even if I'm doing a martin, I always look at the charts at the end of the day. All I need is my notebook computer, and finding Internet access has become easy in most places in the world. I want to know what's happening, but do not have to be trigger-happy.

---

[1]Martin participated in the development of this software as a very thorough beta-tester.

# TRADE 1 | MARTIN'S ENTRY

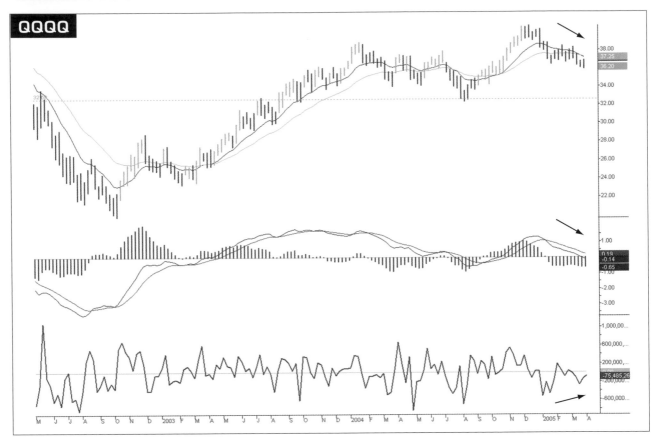

**Upper pane:** Bar chart with 25-week (yellow) and 12-week (red) EMAs and the Impulse system (11-25-8 MACD and 12-week EMA). The green horizontal line is drawn to represent the profit target.
**Second pane:** MACD Lines and MACD-Histogram 11-25-8
**Third pane:** 2-week Force Index

### QQQQ

Both trades I am showing today come from my membership[2] in the Spike group [see Conclusion: Sharing Homework—The Spike Group, page 314]. I've made a commitment to find at least one Spike pick each weekend that I like best and trade it in my account. I will trade a bigger or smaller size, depending on how I feel, but I'll trade at least one pick a week. The group always has longs and shorts, and if I am a bull, I'll choose a long pick, or if a bear, a short one. Here, my own sentiment for the week ahead was bearish, and so I looked for a bearish pick. I found shorts I liked, put them into the Governor, and used the risk/reward ratio to choose this one.

At the right edge of the chart, both EMAs and MACD-Histogram are declining; the Impulse System is red. The last bar has closed almost at the low of the week, a sign of weakness. MACD-Histogram topped out below zero four weeks ago, unable to cross above the zero reference line—also weak. The peaks of Force Index show a downtrend, and if the Force Index ticks down, it will form a top below zero. On the other hand, the bottoms in the Force Index are becoming more shallow, showing a bullish uptrend. This is not the

[2]No longer active.

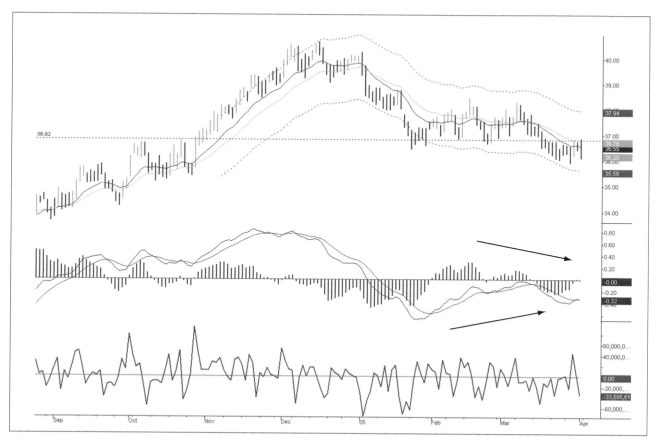

**Upper pane:** Bar chart with 22-day (yellow) and 13-day (red) EMAs and the Impulse system (11-25-8 MACD and 12-day EMA). Autoenvelope—2.7 standard deviations over a 100-day lookback period. The red horizontal line is drawn to represent the stop level.
**Second pane:** MACD Lines and MACD-Histogram 11-25-8
**Third pane:** 2-day Force Index

greatest chart pattern, and I would not have come up with QQQQ as a short on my own, but traded it because of my commitment to trade the picks of our Spike group.

On the dailies, the Friday bar was red and closed at the lows, halfway down from the EMA to the lower channel line. This was a little too far down for my liking, but, as I said, this was the best risk/reward trade from that week's Spike picks. Looking at MACD-Histogram, the peaks are becoming smaller and smaller. The latest attempt at a peak on Wednesday had fizzled out at the zero line, a sign of weakness. The Force Index is not really contributory here. At the same time, there is a bullish divergence of both MACD-Histogram and MACD Lines, but I was bearish for the week ahead and prepared to lean a bit more on the bearish side in my interpretation of the charts.

My risk/reward ratio, as calculated by the Governor, is based on my entry, profit target, and stop. I look at the weekly chart to set my profit target. I expected last August's low to be taken out and had a target of 32.59. I define my stop on the daily chart, drawing what I call "a David Weis line" since I learned it in his class [see Chapter 11]. I drew it across the recent bottoms, where it served as support until about 10 days ago, when it suddenly changed into resistance. My stop was just a little below Friday's high at 36.83. With my intended entry at 36.38, the risk/reward ratio was 8.42. Usually I like to trade when this ratio is above five, and 8.42 felt very good.

Will this trade make or lose money?

# TRADE 1 | MARTIN'S EXIT

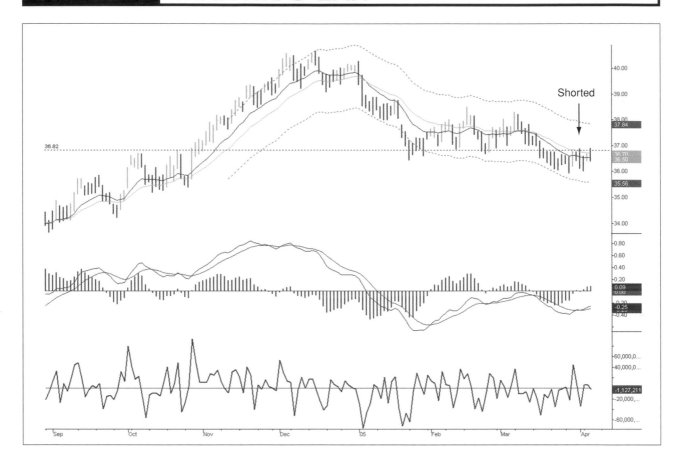

My stop was hit, and I lost money on this trade. I wrote in my diary: "Got scared and covered above my stop, just two cents below the high for the day before it reversed down. It looks weak—a reentry candidate." I do not like using hard stops. I'd much rather use the "Friday Impulse color" rule, meaning that if the Qs would have been green just before the close on Friday, I would have covered just before the close. Having a hard stop exposes you to freak moves. I like to have a real safety net stop in place, but as for my planned stops, I'd rather not give them to my broker, since stops tend to get hit just before the trend reverses.

I exited on Wednesday during a strong rally. I had been calm and thorough in my weekend analysis but was becoming emotional sitting in front of the screen. I covered my short Qs just two cents below that day's high.

My exit was a clear case of not doing a martin. Had I stuck to my rules, I would have been profitable by the end of the week. This was a rich learning experience, but a poor financial experience. Every trade adds to my learning curve, and I am working each day to become a better trader.

## ▼ TRADE SUMMARY

**Short QQQQ**
Sold 4/4/2005 @ $36.34
Covered 4/6/2005 @ $36.88
Loss = 0.54 points

# TRADE 1—ENTRY COMMENT

Martin's charts look very similar to mine, and I will use them for my comments. Also, this interview illustrates an important point—traders often take different trades, even if they look at the same charts.

## Weekly

The Qs had been heading lower ever since topping out in December. Both weekly EMAs are declining, as are MACD Lines and MACD-Histogram. Everything is in gear to the downside, and the weekly trend is definitely down. At the right edge of the chart, a new low of MACD-Histogram indicates that bears are growing stronger, while a bullish divergence of Force Index flashes a contrary signal. Still, the sum of the evidence is bearish, and the red weekly Impulse allows us to short or stand aside, but not go long.

Still, the trade does not look terribly attractive to me because of the position of the price relative to the EMAs. I like to buy low and sell high, and with the Qs closing below their weekly EMAs, below value, they are no longer high. They are low, and that's not where I like to short. I appreciate that Martin made a commitment to trade at least one Spike pick each week. Also, he is not looking for a long-term trade, but a quick entry on Monday, followed by an exit a few days later.

## Daily

Once you identify a downtrend on the weekly chart, the best time to short is during a rally towards value on the daily chart. That's exactly what happened during the second half of last week. The Qs rallied above value—above their 13-day EMA on Wednesday and Thursday and even above the 22-day EMA last Friday. That's where the Qs were an attractive short, and the Friday action confirmed that, as they slid from above the EMA to close sharply lower. The shorting opportunity was definitely there—but it had come and gone. Trying to short after Friday's drop is a bit like running after a train that's already pulled out of the station. It would feel great to hop aboard, but there is a definite risk of slipping on the rails.

The downtrend of the EMAs, the weakness of MACD-Histogram, and the red of the daily Impulse System are bearish. Still, before we enter a trade, we need to ask: Is this trading vehicle cheap or expensive? At the right edge of the chart, the Qs, below value, are starting to look cheap, and that's a dangerous zone for selling short.

# TRADE 1—EXIT COMMENT

On Monday QQQQs fell slightly below Friday's low, then started trending up. MACD-Histogram turned up, completing a bullish divergence. The Force Index failed to penetrate its mid-March low, indicating that bears are growing weaker. It shot up to a new multi-month high by the end of March, showing that bulls were coming in.

One can spend a long time looking at this or that indicator, but it is better to keep things simple. The most important question—Is this stock cheap or expensive?—can be answered in several ways. Martin answers it by rating the stock's position within a channel. Whatever your approach, it is better not to buy a stock that is expensive or short the one that is cheap. Martin, feeling bearish about the market as a whole and given a limited choice, reached out a bit and shorted a relatively cheap stock. He got away with a small loss, and even had a chance to get out at a profit. We all make mistakes, but recording them and learning from them is a hallmark of a serious trader.

# TRADE 2 | MARTIN'S ENTRY

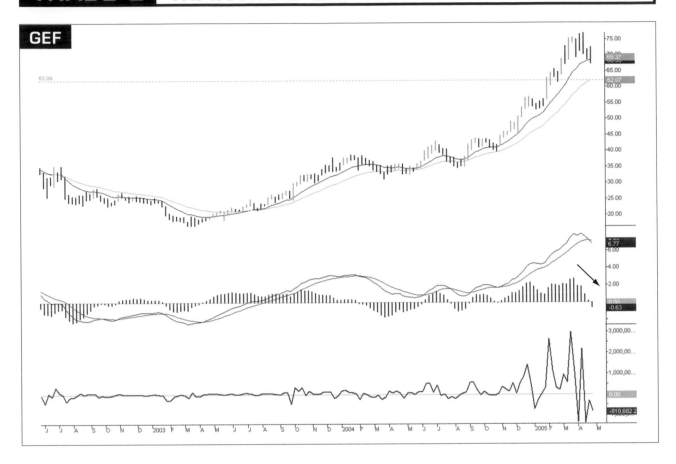

### GEF

GEF was my favorite Spike pick that week, once again in line with my bearish view of the market. The Impulse system was blue, allowing me to short. Both EMAs were still rising, but I was trying to catch a reversal. The Fast MACD line cut below the Slow line at a very high level, with MACD-Histogram going negative—a sign of the bears taking over from the bulls. The latest peak of the Force Index was below zero—the bulls were losing their grip on this stock.

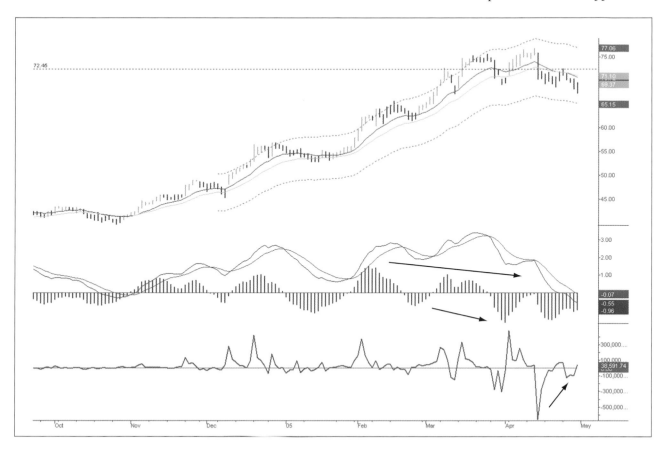

A very bearish sign on the daily chart is the trend of MACD-Histogram peaks since February. In February the bulls were strong, in March weaker, and in April nonexistent, while bears were getting stronger. It was a more powerful sign than the bullish divergence of the Force Index at the right edge. The Friday bar was blue, allowing me to go short. That bar had dipped down to a new low, but closed at a high, which I did not like. Still, when a similar pattern occurred six days before, it was resolved to the downside.

My plan was to short GEF at 70.49 with a stop at 72.50. The red line marking the stop served as resistance during some of the recent peaks and as support when the market was above it. My target of 62.07 came from the weekly chart: The green horizontal line was drawn from the top of the last tall bar and it beautifully coincided with the level of the weekly EMA. These numbers gave me a risk/reward ratio of 4.19. It was less than five but the best of that week's Spike picks and acceptable; the world is not perfect.

Will this trade make or lose money?

# TRADE 2   MARTIN'S EXIT

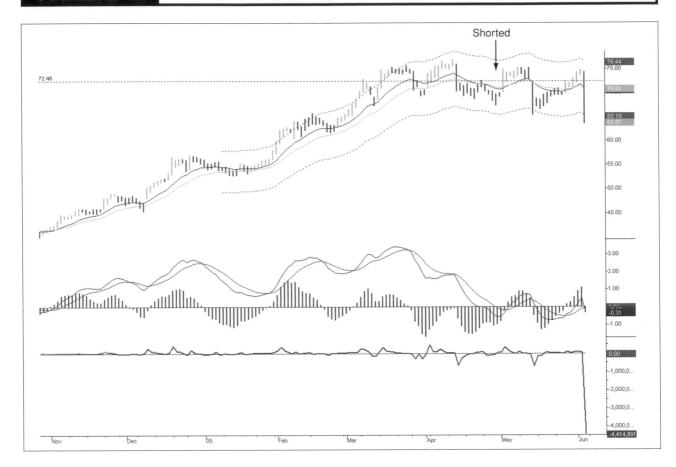

In the course of this trade, I suffered through a major headache, when the stock climbed above my stop level. Even though I was losing money on paper, the charts looked weak. My rule is to hold shorts as long as the weekly Impulse does not go green on Friday. It actually went green on the previous Friday, May 27, but the earnings were coming out the next week, and that gave me an excuse to hold for one more week. I had suffered all this time and saw the chance for this trade to go my way.

The earnings came out on Thursday evening, June 2, and they were bad. The stock opened sharply lower on Friday, June 3. During the previous drop, I failed to take profits at the lower channel line. I wanted to learn from my experience and not let a nice profit slip away. The stock seemed to hold near 68 in the middle of the day on Friday, and I felt tempted to cover. I knew that if I stayed in front of the screen, I'd get excited, so I took out my bike and went for a ride around the island on the Danube, leaving a limit order to cover at 64.99, just below the previous bottom. That was a perfect example of "doing a martin." By the time I returned, my order had been filled at 64.70, with a positive slippage.

Much more than a financial win, this trade was a psychological win for me. I held on to a losing position—the stock kept climbing, but its charts looked weak. I was feeling more and more stressed, but gave GEF time until after the earnings, ready to cover if it rallied or maintained a weekly green Impulse.

## TRADE SUMMARY

**Short GEF**

Sold 5/2/2005 @ $70.49

Covered 6/3/2005 @ $64.70

Gain = 5.79 points

# TRADE 2—ENTRY COMMENT

## Weekly

"Prices are connected to values by a mile-long rubber band," a client once said to me. I believe that a weekly EMA provides a good approximation of value, and that prices in an uptrend keep rallying away from it and then snapping back. That's how GEF behaved for much of 2003 and 2004, but at the end of 2004, it changed its behavior and rallied sharply away from its EMA in 2005. There might have been a piece of fundamental news, or a rumor, or a combination of both—the stock got far away from value and hovered for several months.

Professionals and amateurs often take opposite sides in such situations. Amateurs like to buy upside breakouts, expecting a runaway uptrend, while professionals tend to short, expecting prices to return to value. At the right edge of the chart, MACD-Histogram is declining, showing that bulls are running out of steam. The Impulse has turned blue, allowing us to sell short. MACD Lines have turned down from a very high level and the Force Index is tracing a bearish divergence—both indicators flash important bearish signals. Most importantly, GEF is still above its weekly EMAs, above value. If we want to buy low and sell high, this is a place to sell, or go short, as Martin decided to do.

## Daily

There are two key patterns that tend to occur at the tops of rallies. Sometimes there is a sharp final spike, as weak shorts break and run for cover. That short squeeze leaves a kangaroo tail pointing skywards, as prices reverse and head down. A more common pattern is a step-by-step rise, whose upmoves keep getting shorter and flatter, telling us that bulls are running out of breath.

| Date | High | Increase |
|---|---|---|
| 10/04/04 | 43.64 | |
| 11/11/04 | 45.99 | 2.35 |
| 11/26/04 | 49.09 | 3.10 |
| 12/02/04 | 56.92 | 7.83 |
| 02/15/05 | 65.65 | 8.73 |
| 03/08/05 | 72.79 | 7.14 |
| 03/24/05 | 75.65 | 2.86 |
| 04/13/05 | 76.89 | 1.24 |

Until November 2004, each new peak gained two or three points above the previous peak. After the stock heated up in December, its peak-to-peak gains expanded to seven or eight points. Then the stock began to cool off, with a gain of less than three points in late March 2004 and only a point in April. Those two rallies showed that the rise had become laborious—the stock was breathing heavily, like a runner near the end of a race. The puny rise in mid-April was accompanied by a bearish divergence of MACD-Histogram—a terrific shorting opportunity right near the top.

By the time one of our Spike group members picked GEF as a short and Martin decided to piggy-back that trade, the decline was already well under way. In terms of market seasons, this was no longer autumn with an early morning frost, the best season for shorting; this was a full-blown winter. Both daily EMAs are declining at the right edge, confirming the downtrend. The Impulse System is blue, allowing us to short. The heavy bottoms of MACD-Histogram indicate that bears are very strong and further weakness is likely ahead.

# TRADE 2—EXIT COMMENT

If you short when prices are already low, you face a greater risk of a rally back towards value. Such a rally began the day Martin entered his short. The following day, prices rocketed above both EMAs, with a tall bar indicating it was probably a short-covering rally. Sustainable rallies tend to move more slowly and steadily, while short-covering rallies tend to be sharp and panicky. Martin, unlike many others who had been short, was not shaken out and held as GEF waffled for over a week before resuming its decline. It penetrated the lower channel line, presenting a fantastic short-covering opportunity, which Martin missed.

There was another short-covering signal when the daily Impulse went from red to blue in early May, indicating that the best time for holding shorts was over, but Martin continued to hold. A good rule is to run quickly or not at all. Having missed two chances to run quickly, Martin continued to hold his short.

Martin commented on his own trade: "My rule is to hold shorts as long as the weekly Impulse does not go green on Friday. It actually went green the previous Friday, May 27, but the earnings were coming out the next week, and that gave me an excuse to hold for one more week." Violating one's own rules, whatever the excuse, is a dangerous business. One can get away with a violation now and then, but in the end, breaking the rules will always catch up with a trader who does not stop in time.

The earnings report shoved the stock down again, below its lower channel line. It is okay to make mistakes but not okay to repeat them. Martin missed his first but not the second short-covering opportunity, and got out at a very good level near the lower channel line.

## Working Together

Many traders feel isolated, and if you can find someone to share the work, so much the better. For a collaborative project to succeed, both persons have to be equally motivated, and it has to be a joint effort. If one trader needs to pull the other, it won't work.

For example, several months ago Fred (Chapter 2) came to teach in our Caribbean Camp with Bucky, his partner in a money management firm. Fred is an expert programmer, Bucky a second-generation floor trader with a tremendous feel for the markets. After dinner, the two men returned to the classroom, which had fast Internet, and stayed there past midnight, doing their homework together, preparing for the day ahead. Having two pairs of eyes on their homework helped them focus and avoid mistakes.

While I was writing this chapter my phone rang—Martin was calling from Vienna. I shared with him my concern that for the past several weeks the New High-New Low Index that he updates daily and sends to me has been acting strangely, more like a trend-following, rather than a leading, indicator. I explained to him that in the past Joe Granville used to calculate the number of stocks within a point or two of their highs and lows to find how much potential fuel existed for this indicator. Martin suggested it would be better to count percentages rather than points, and we agreed that he would track stocks within 3%, 5%, and 7% of their highs and lows. He would have to spend several hours setting up the system and then several minutes per day tracking it for at least two months before we could tell whether the indicator was useful or not. He enthusiastically implemented my suggestion.[3]

---

[3]Just as this book went to print, Martin told me that he had suffered a series of crippling losses. He sent me the records for one of his accounts, and the reasons for his severe drawdown leaped at me from the spreadsheet—not using stops and violating the 2% and 6% Rules. This sad development confirmed once again that no matter how good one's analytic skills, without discipline and money management a trader cannot succeed. The absolute necessity of following money management rules is a lesson for all traders.

What follows is a diary of top-to-bottom market analysis, complete with money management and trade executions. Martin sent me this file, describing a joint project I did in 2003 with him and Nic Grove, a camper who was visiting from Australia. We reviewed the market, selected stocks, and traded them.

The project described in this diary grew out of my visit to Vienna in August 2003. Martin had organized a meeting of traders, and afterwards we returned to his penthouse together with Nic, who was living in Paris and had flown in to join us. I had just spent a week on the road, with poor Internet connections. Looking at the screen in Martin's apartment—he had fast wireless Internet, a novelty in those days—I became excited about the state of the market and eager to do some serious work. Martin and Nic jumped at the chance to join me in sifting through the data together, looking for stocks to buy.

Having three pairs of eyes and three computer screens in the same room allowed us to cast the net wider and dig deeper than in the past. We spent the next three days looking for the best stocks and placing trades. Afterwards, Nic flew back to Paris, while Martin and I got into his convertible for a long, meandering drive through Austria and Switzerland.

All three of us made money from our exercise. I chuckle as I look back at what we accomplished; today, with the homework process well established, any one of us can knock out in less than a day what had taken the three of us three full days. We enjoyed working together. Grinding through reams of data can be a little dull; we kept catching each other's mistakes, no one had an ego problem, nobody cared who found this or that stock—we only wanted to make money. The three of us got together again for shared work sessions in October of that year in New York and in November in Cyprus. Nic came to the Camp in October 2004, where Martin was my assistant instructor, and the two of them shared several work sessions on the Cote d'Azur where Nic lived in the apartment of another camper, Angela. Nic had moved back to Australia by the time I started interviewing for this book, but he is a valued member of the Spike group, a winner of multiple contests.

*An e-mail from Martin:*

## SEVEN DAYS IN DR. ALEXANDER ELDER'S TRADING ROOM

Since Martin's e-mail that follows was written in a very brief, telegraphic style, I added some of my own comments along the margins. My reasons for commenting on Martin's diary can be clarified by a phrase from my book *Straying from the Flock: Travels in New Zealand*: "Many professional guilds—lawyers, criminals, physicians, and others—each have their own lingo, allowing them to communicate with insiders at great speed, while being poorly understood by outsiders." Martin wrote his diary in such a lingo—very clear for the three of us who were there, but probably a little cryptic for others. I wrote my comments on the margins of the following pages to help you better understand his text.     —AE

# Saturday, August 16, 2003

## 1.1  First Assessment: Dow Jones, Nasdaq, S&P 500 on a Monthly, Weekly, and Daily Chart. Bullish or Bearish?

**1.1**

I like to begin my homework by approaching the markets from a distance and taking in a broad view. Is the monthly trend rising, falling, or flat? What about the weekly? I rely on the Impulse system to define bullish, bearish, or neutral stages in any timeframe. This section of the homework showed either rising or neutral trends of DJIA, S&P, and Nasdaq in monthly, weekly, and daily timeframes.

—*AE*

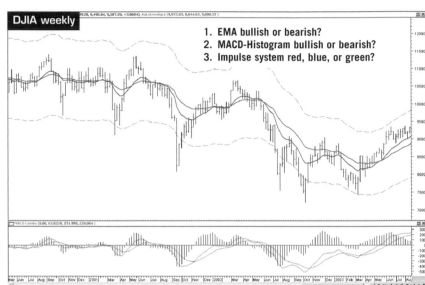

1. EMA bullish or bearish?
2. MACD-Histogram bullish or bearish?
3. Impulse system red, blue, or green?

**1.2**

If the Big Three—the Dow, the Nasdaq, and the S&P—are bullish, do the second-tier indexes support that message? A broad uptrend or downtrend, involving the majority of smaller indexes, is much more likely to persist. This is why it pays to analyze more than a hundred indexes, both big and small contained in many software programs, such as TC2000.

Millions of people glance casually at the big indexes, but how many analyze the lesser ones? Having your hand on the pulse of market components gives you an advantage over the crowd of casual players.

—*AE*

**Analyze NASDAQ and S&P—first monthly, then weekly, finally daily.**

**NASDAQ daily**

**S&P daily**

## 1.2  Scrolling through 126 TC2000 All Indexes (Weekly Charts).

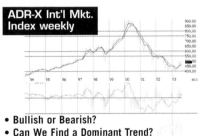

**ADR-X Int'l Mkt. Index weekly**

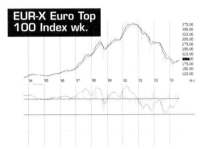

**EUR-X Euro Top 100 Index wk.**

- Bullish or Bearish?
- Can We Find a Dominant Trend?

## 1.3  Scrolling through 239 TC2000 All Media General Industry Groups (Weekly Charts). Bullish or Bearish?

- Bullish or Bearish?
- Can We Find a Dominant Trend?

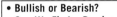

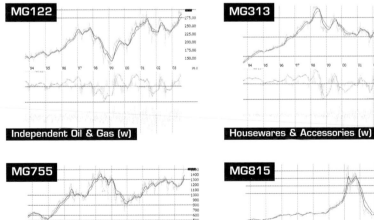

**MG122**

Independent Oil & Gas (w)

**MG313**

Housewares & Accessories (w)

**MG755**

Medical Equip. Wholesale (w)

**MG815**

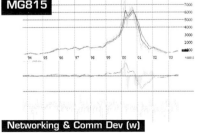

Networking & Comm Dev (w)

- Conclusion: The stock market wants to go up. We should prepare a shopping list.

### 1.3

*Each stock belongs to a subgroup, and it, in turn, belongs to a group. If you begin your analysis on the group level and then proceed to the subgroups, you'll gain deeper insight into the health of the market's trend. There are several group classifications, including a popular one by Investors' Business Daily. I am in the habit of analyzing Media General groups in TC2000 because that software makes it easy to click through well-organized tickers and jump from subgroups to their component stocks.*

*There are two reasons to analyze market groups: to gauge the health of the market and to begin marking the weakest and the strongest groups—a good place to look for stocks to buy or sell short. Two of the four groups shown in Martin's diary—MG122 Independent Oil & Gas and MG755 Medical Equipment Wholesale—are in healthy uptrends, MG313 Housewares is in a downtrend, while MG815 Networking is in an especially sweet spot. This group had fallen from a height of above 7,000 at the peak of the bull market in 2000 to below 100—an over 90 percent decline. This is uncommon even for a single stock, but almost unheard of for a group. The decline ground to a halt in 2002, and for the past year, this group has been tracing a saucer bottom, slowly reversing its downtrend and starting to turn up.*

*—AE*

# Sunday, August 17

## 2.1 The Script: We Want to Build Our Shopping List of "Fallen Angels"

We search for groups and, consequently, individual stocks that have given up most of their previous enormous price and have now started to look up again.

In a first run, we flag all groups that come close to the following chart picture. Doing this exercise with two friends greatly helps to stay focused.

It is interesting to point out that this job is definitely done best by hand and eye. No mechanical scanner could complete this task equally well.

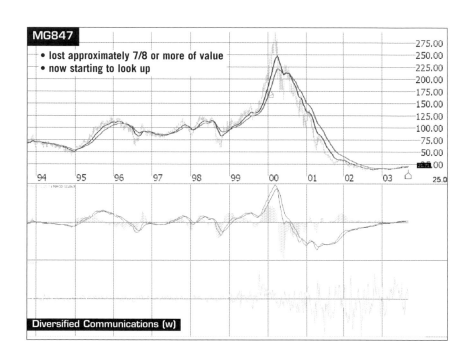

**2.1**

*If the market is financial Olympics, in which event will you compete? You cannot enter weightlifting, track, and diving and expect to do well in all of them. All competitive athletes specialize, and you need to decide what market game appeals to you at this time. Trading the IPOs, inside the channels, breakouts, and fading breakouts are all legitimate approaches, as long as you do not mix them all together.*

*During the time covered in this diary, the market was just starting to come off its panicky bottom, after crashing from its 1999–2000 peak. Many stocks, driven above value in the 1990s, crashed below any reasonable value in 2001 and 2002. My suggestion was to look for stocks that traced a fish-hook pattern—a long decline from a great height, followed by a rounded saucer bottom and a soft upturn.*

**—AE**

The first run yielded 15 groups. In a second run, we limit the findings to the best-looking 5 out of these 15. After intense discussions about which charts were giving us picture-perfect shapes, we agreed on the following groups:

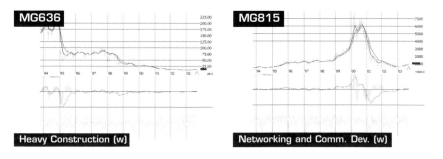

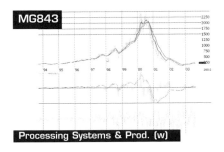

MG843

Processing Systems & Prod. (w)

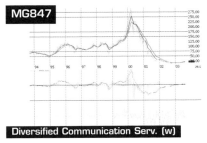

MG847

Diversified Communication Serv. (w)

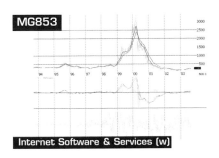

MG853

Internet Software & Services (w)

## 2.2 From Stock Groups to Individual Stocks

The next item on our agenda is to split up the stock groups into their individual member stocks and once again pick out those stocks that best match the "fallen angel" picture.

To help us narrow down the results to really tradeable securities, we apply a volume filter that requires a minimum 50-day average volume of 150,000 shares per day.

Again, we do this process in two runs, always referring to weekly charts. During the first run, we flag all the stocks that appear to be "fallen angels." During the second, we limit the initial findings to the cream of the crop.

This process yields a list of 27 stocks at which we want to look more closely. We collect them in a spreadsheet for detailed evaluation.

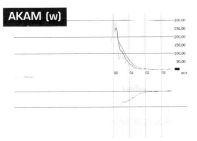

AKAM (w)

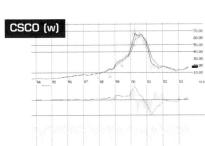

CSCO (w)

| | |
|---|---|
| AKAM | JNPR |
| AMT | LU |
| ARTG | MTZ |
| CAPA | NT |
| CMVT | OPWV |
| CSCO | RHAT |
| DTHK | SFE |
| ETS | SFLK |
| EXTR | SNWL |
| FFIV | TERN |
| FNSR | TMWD |
| HAXSD | VIGN |
| HPOL | VRSN |
| IAO | |

**2.2**

*If you look for fallen angels among groups and subgroups, it makes sense to look for them also among their component stocks. Stay away from thinly traded stocks—they are easy to buy, but hard to sell, often resulting in vicious slippage. Trust your eye more than a computer—no scan will deliver as good results as an experienced eye. I chuckle looking at how it took us a day to generate this list—today it would take no more than a couple of hours. Fortunately, our workday was shortened by a trip to a nearby vineyard, where we did some serious wine-tasting in a centuries-old cellar.*

*—AE*

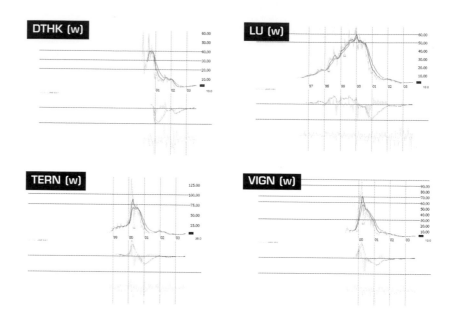

## Monday, August 18

### 3.1 Finding the Most Attractive Stocks: 5 out of 27

On Monday we start with a close look at each of the 27 stocks on our list. We use TradeStation (or Metastock), which also allows us to look at the Impulse system. We add the columns "W" (for weekly), "D" (for daily), and "Comment" to the spreadsheet.

### The Impulse System by Dr. Alexander Elder

Each bar in a monthly, weekly, and daily chart is painted green, blue, or red. The colors have the following meanings:

*Green:* Fast EMA (13 bars) and MACD-Histogram are both in an uptrend. *Consequences for trading:* We are allowed to go long or stand aside; no permission to short.

*Red:* Fast EMA (13 bars) and MACD-Histogram are both in a downtrend. *Consequences for trading:* We are allowed to go short or stand aside; no permission to go long.

*Blue:* EMA and MACD-Histogram are trending in different directions. *Consequences for trading:* We are allowed to go long, short, or stand aside.

## 3.2  What Precisely Are We Looking At?

This is how our spreadsheet looks after checking each stock's weekly and daily chart in TradeStation.

| | W | D | Comment |
|---|---|---|---|
| AKAM | red | | in the sweet zone |
| AMT | green | near top of channel | due for a corr, EMA near 10 |
| ARTG | blue | green | **ready to buy** |
| CAPA | green | green | due for a corr, EMA near 4.50 |
| CMVT | green | green | **ready to buy** |
| CSCO | blue | green | **ready to buy** |
| DTHK | blue | green | **ready to buy—stop near 2.60** |
| ETS | blue | blue | due for a corr, EMA near 4.50 |
| EXTR | green | green | trade range—stand aside |
| FFIV | green | green | too expensive—$18 |
| FNSR | blue | green | **ready to buy** |
| HAXSD | red | | in the sweet zone |
| HPOL | blue | green | starting to roll over? |
| IAO | blue | red | from 10¢ to 120, back to 40 |
| JNPR | green | green | **ready to buy** |
| LU | blue | green | **ready to buy—very sweet** |
| MTZ | green | green | nice chart—up 5x, late in the game |
| NT | green | green | flat, up 6x |
| OPWV | green | green | due for a corr, EMA near 3.60 |
| RHAT | green | green | **ready to buy** |
| SFE | blue | green | **ready to buy** |
| SFLK | red | | below EMA—watch! |
| SNWL | blue | green | **ready to buy** |
| TERN | green | green | due for a corr, EMA near 5 |
| TMWD | green | green | due for a corr, EMA near 2.75 |
| VIGN | green | green | **ready to buy—stop near 2** |
| VRSN | green | green | **ready to buy** |

Evaluation spreadsheet with weekly Impulse, daily Impulse, and comment

3.2
*Even considering the recovery from that tasting, it took us a long time to narrow down our list. The charts of FNSR illustrate what we were looking for at that time. Weekly—a bullish divergence of both MACD-Histogram and MACD Lines, and a slow steady uptrend near the right edge of the chart. Daily—both MACD-Histogram and EMAs are rising; the Force Index showed that bears had no power during the previous week's price dip.*

*—AE*

- We only follow stocks with a blue or green weekly Impulse system.
- How does MACD-Histogram look?
- How far away from the EMAs is the current price? Is the "rubber band" stretched out too far? Is the price in the "sweet zone" between slow (26- or 22-bar) and fast (13-bar) EMA?
- Are there any divergences in MACD-Histogram or Force Index, signaling bearish moves?

We reduce our list of 27 stocks down to 12 that we consider "ready to buy." Below are the weekly and daily charts of FNSR reflecting what we are looking for.

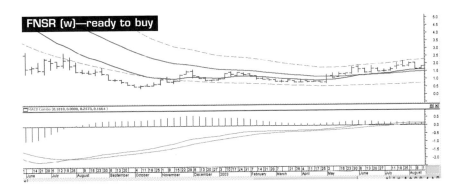

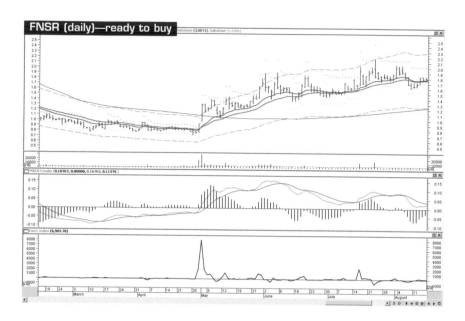

## Tuesday, August 19

### 4.1 Entry Target, Stop, and Price Target

For every "ready to buy" stock, we specify an entry target (from the daily chart), a stop (from the daily chart), and a price target (from the weekly chart).

**4.1**

*The diary shows nicely how a spreadsheet expanded while doing homework. We used daily charts for setting entry levels and stops, weekly charts for setting profit targets. We wanted to go long near value, represented by the moving averages, place stops near recent lows, and set targets near well-established resistance zones. "Sweet zone" refers to the area between two moving averages.*

*—AE*

| | W | D | Comment | Buy | Tgt | Stop |
|---|---|---|---|---|---|---|
| AKAM | red | | in the sweet zone | | | |
| AMT | green | near top of channel | due for a corr, EMA near 10 | | | |
| ARTG | blue | green | **ready to buy** | 2.11 | 5.00 | 1.65 |
| CAPA | green | green | due for a corr, EMA near 4.50 | | | |
| CMVT | green | green | **ready to buy** | too high, too expensive | | |
| CSCO | blue | green | **ready to buy** | <18.35 | minor 22-24 | 17.27 |
| DTHK | blue | green | **ready to buy—stop near 2.60** | 3.01 | 6+ | 2.56 |
| ETS | blue | blue | due for a corr, EMA near 4.50 | | | |
| EXTR | green | green | trade range—stand aside | | | |
| FFIV | green | green | too expensive—$18 | | | |
| FNSR | blue | green | **ready to buy** | <1.88 | 6+ | 1.44 |
| HAXSD | red | | in the sweet zone | | | |
| HPOL | blue | green | starting to roll over? | | | |
| IAO | blue | red | from 10¢ to 120, back to 40 | | | |
| JNPR | green | green | **ready to buy** | 13.95 | 28+ | 12.94 |
| LU | blue | green | **ready to buy—very sweet** | <1.90 | 2.50++ | 1.64 |
| MTZ | green | green | nice chart—up 5x, late in the game | | | |
| NT | green | green | flat, up 6x | | | |
| OPWV | green | green | due for a corr, EMA near 3.60 | | | |
| RHAT | green | green | **ready to buy** | 6.80 | 20+ | 6.10 |
| SFE | blue | green | **ready to buy** | 2.75 | 4.50+ | 2.30 |
| SFLK | red | | below EMA—watch! | | | |
| SNWL | blue | green | **ready to buy** | 5.10 | 10+ | 4.69 |
| TERN | green | green | due for a corr, EMA near 5 | | | |
| TMWD | green | green | due for a corr, EMA near 2.75 | | | |
| VIGN | green | green | **ready to buy—stop near 2** | <2.30 | 4+ | 1.97 |
| VRSN | green | green | **ready to buy** | 13.51 | 25.00 | 21.10 |

Evaluation spreadsheet with entry target ("Buy"), profit target ("Tgt"), and stop ("Stop").

Again, we take FNSR as an example of how we specify Buy, Target, and Stop.

## Entry target

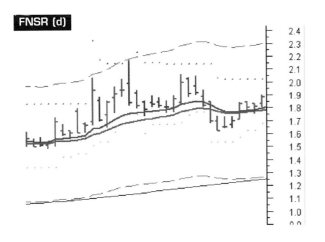

Price bar from Monday, August 18

Open:        1.83
High:        1.90
Low:         1.80
Close:       1.88

Slow EMA (green line): 1.78
Fast EMA (red line): 1.80

→ **Entry target: <1.88**

FNSR (daily) as of close on Monday, August 18

## Stop

We set our stop below the lows of June 18 and June 30 (black arrows in the picture).

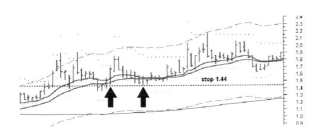

FNSR (daily) as of close on Monday, August 18

## Price target

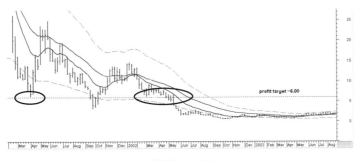

FNSR (weekly)

We look for previous support, resistance, and congestion areas in order to set a price target.

## 4.2  Risk/Return Ratio: Fat or Skinny Rabbit?

Using the numbers from the previous spreadsheet, we add another column to calculate the risk/return ratio ("R/R") for every "ready to buy" stock.

$$R/R = \frac{Tgt - Buy}{Buy - Stop}$$

|  | W | D | Comment | Buy | Tgt | Stop | R/R |
|---|---|---|---|---|---|---|---|
|  |  |  |  |  |  |  |  |
| AKAM | red |  | in the sweet zone |  |  |  |  |
| AMT | green | near top of channel | due for a corr, EMA near 10 |  |  |  |  |
| ARTG | blue | green | **ready to buy** | 2.11 | 5.00 | 1.65 | 6.3 |
| CAPA | green | green | due for a corr, EMA near 4.50 |  |  |  |  |
| CMVT | green | green | **ready to buy** | too high, too expensive |  |  |  |
| CSCO | blue | green | **ready to buy** | <18.35 | minor 22-24 | 17.27 | 4.3 |
| DTHK | blue | green | **ready to buy—stop near 2.60** | 3.01 | 6+ | 2.56 | 8.9 |
| ETS | blue | blue | due for a corr, EMA near 4.50 |  |  |  |  |
| EXTR | green | green | trade range—stand aside |  |  |  |  |
| FFIV | green | green | too expensive—$18 |  |  |  |  |
| FNSR | blue | green | **ready to buy** | <1.88 | 6+ | 1.44 | 11.6 |
| HAXSD | red |  | in the sweet zone |  |  |  |  |
| HPOL | blue | green | starting to roll over? |  |  |  |  |
| IAO | blue | red | from 10¢ to 120, back to 40 |  |  |  |  |
| JNPR | green | green | **ready to buy** | 13.95 | 28+ | 12.94 | 13.9 |
| LU | blue | green | **ready to buy—very sweet** | <1.90 | 2.50++ | 1.64 | 8.1 |
| MTZ | green | green | nice chart—up 5x, late in the game |  |  |  |  |
| NT | green | green | flat, up 6x |  |  |  |  |
| OPWV | green | green | due for a corr, EMA near 3.60 |  |  |  |  |
| RHAT | green | green | **ready to buy** | 6.80 | 20+ | 6.10 | 20.3 |
| SFE | blue | green | **ready to buy** | 2.75 | 4.50+ | 2.30 | 5.0 |
| SFLK | red |  | below EMA—watch! |  |  |  |  |
| SNWL | blue | green | **ready to buy** | 5.10 | 10+ | 4.69 | 14.4 |
| TERN | green | green | due for a corr, EMA near 5 |  |  |  |  |
| TMWD | green | green | due for a corr, EMA near 2.75 |  |  |  |  |
| VIGN | green | green | **ready to buy—stop near 2** | <2.30 | 4+ | 1.97 | 5.2 |
| VRSN | green | green | **ready to buy** | 13.51 | 25.00 | 21.10 | 8.1 |

Evaluation spreadsheet with column "R/R".

**4.2**
*Our expected return is the distance from the entry to the target, and the risk is the distance from the target to the stop. Even though we may adjust these levels later, they provide a useful comparison between various stocks. I call stocks with good ratios "fat rabbits," and those with skimpy ratios "skinny rabbits." If you go hunting, you might as well invest your time, energy, and ammunition in hunting fat rabbits rather than skinny ones.*
**—AE**

## 4.3  The Final Ranking: A Last Look at Weekly and Daily Charts

During our final look at the weekly and daily charts, we grade them "1" (excellent), "2" (second-best), and "3" (something is not right).

| | W | D | Comment | Buy | Tgt | Stop | R/R | W-r | D-r |
|---|---|---|---|---|---|---|---|---|---|
| AKAM | red | | in the sweet zone | | | | | | |
| AMT | green | near top of channel | due for a corr, EMA near 10 | | | | | | |
| ARTG | blue | green | **ready to buy** | 2.11 | 5.00 | 1.65 | 6.3 | 2 | 2 |
| CAPA | green | green | due for a corr, EMA near 4.50 | | | | | | |
| CMVT | green | green | **ready to buy** | too high, too expensive | | | | | |
| CSCO | blue | green | **ready to buy** | <18.35 | minor 22-24 | 17.27 | 4.3 | 1 | 1 |
| DTHK | blue | green | **ready to buy—stop near 2.60** | 3.01 | 6+ | 2.56 | 8.9 | 2 | 3 |
| ETS | blue | blue | due for a corr, EMA near 4.50 | | | | | | |
| EXTR | green | green | trade range—stand aside | | | | | | |
| FFIV | green | green | too expensive—$18 | | | | | | |
| FNSR | blue | green | **ready to buy** | <1.88 | 6+ | 1.44 | 11.6 | 1 | 1 |
| HAXSD | red | | in the sweet zone | | | | | | |
| HPOL | blue | green | starting to roll over? | | | | | | |
| IAO | blue | red | from 10¢ to 120, back to 40 | | | | | | |
| JNPR | green | green | **ready to buy** | 13.95 | 28+ | 12.94 | 13.9 | 1 | 1 |
| LU | blue | green | **ready to buy—very sweet** | <1.90 | 2.50++ | 1.64 | 8.1 | 2 | 1 |
| MTZ | green | green | nice chart—up 5x, late in the game | | | | | | |
| NT | green | green | flat, up 6x | | | | | | |
| OPWV | green | green | due for a corr, EMA near 3.60 | | | | | | |
| RHAT | green | green | **ready to buy** | 6.80 | 20+ | 6.10 | 20.3 | 1 | 2 |
| SFE | blue | green | **ready to buy** | 2.75 | 4.50+ | 2.30 | 5.0 | 2 | 2 |
| SFLK | red | | below EMA—watch! | | | | | | |
| SNWL | blue | green | **ready to buy** | 5.10 | 10+ | 4.69 | 14.4 | 1 | 2 |
| TERN | green | green | due for a corr, EMA near 5 | | | | | | |
| TMWD | green | green | due for a corr, EMA near 2.75 | | | | | | |
| VIGN | green | green | **ready to buy—stop near 2** | <2.30 | 4+ | 1.97 | 5.2 | 1 | 1 |
| VRSN | green | green | **ready to buy** | 13.51 | 25.00 | 21.10 | 8.1 | 2 | 2 |

Evaluation spreadsheet with weekly and daily ratings.

Four stocks (CSCO, FNSR, JNPR, and VIGN) pass the last exam with a double "1". RHAT is added to our shopping list due to its very high R/R of 20.3.

**4.3**

Here we looked for smooth and steady trends with shallow pullbacks. If you have just a few stock candidates, this step might not be necessary, but that weekend we had "an embarrassment of riches"—too many stocks to choose from. We rated the quality of their weekly and daily trends in order to focus on the most attractive candidates.

—*AE*

## 4.4 Money Management Rules

| | W | D | Comment | Buy | Tgt | Stop | R/R | W-r | D-r | | Risk/sh | 2% of... | Cost |
|---|---|---|---|---|---|---|---|---|---|---|---|---|---|
| | | | | | | | | | | | | 106,000 | |
| AKAM | red | | in the sweet zone | | | | | | | | | | |
| AMT | green | near top of channel | due for a corr, EMA near 10 | | | | | | | | | | |
| ARTG | blue | green | **ready to buy** | 2.11 | 5.00 | 1.65 | 6.3 | 2 | 2 | | | | |
| CAPA | green | green | due for a corr, EMA near 4.50 | | | | | | | | | | |
| CMVT | green | green | **ready to buy** | too high, too expensive | | | | | | | | | |
| CSCO | blue | green | **ready to buy** | <18.35 | minor 22-24 | 17.27 | 4.3 | 1 | 1 | buy | $ 1.10 | 1,900 | $ 34,865 |
| DTHK | blue | green | **ready to buy—stop near 2.60** | 3.01 | 6+ | 2.56 | 8.9 | 2 | 3 | | | | |
| ETS | blue | blue | due for a corr, EMA near 4.50 | | | | | | | | | | |
| EXTR | green | green | trade range—stand aside | | | | | | | | | | |
| FFIV | green | green | too expensive—$18 | | | | | | | | | | |
| FNSR | blue | green | **ready to buy** | <1.88 | 6+ | 1.44 | 11.6 | 1 | 1 | buy | $ 0.44 | 4,800 | $ 9,024 |
| HAXSD | red | | in the sweet zone | | | | | | | | | | |
| HPOL | blue | green | starting to roll over? | | | | | | | | | | |
| IAO | blue | red | from 10¢ to 120, back to 40 | | | | | | | | | | |
| JNPR | green | green | **ready to buy** | 13.95 | 28+ | 12.94 | 13.9 | 1 | 1 | buy | $ 1.01 | 2,000 | $ 27,900 |
| LU | blue | green | **ready to buy—very sweet** | <1.90 | 2.50++ | 1.64 | 8.1 | 2 | 1 | | | | |
| MTZ | green | green | nice chart—up 5x, late in the game | | | | | | | | | | |
| NT | green | green | flat, up 6x | | | | | | | | | | |
| OPWV | green | green | due for a corr, EMA near 3.60 | | | | | | | | | | |
| RHAT | green | green | **ready to buy** | 6.80 | 20+ | 6.10 | 20.3 | 1 | 2 | buy | $ 0.70 | 3,000 | $ 20,400 |
| SFE | blue | green | **ready to buy** | 2.75 | 4.50+ | 2.30 | 5.0 | 2 | 2 | | | | |
| SFLK | red | | below EMA—watch! | | | | | | | | | | |
| SNWL | blue | green | **ready to buy** | 5.10 | 10+ | 4.69 | 14.4 | 1 | 2 | | | | |
| TERN | green | green | due for a corr, EMA near 5 | | | | | | | | | | |
| TMWD | green | green | due for a corr, EMA near 2.75 | | | | | | | | | | |
| VIGN | green | green | **ready to buy—stop near 2** | <2.30 | 4+ | 1.97 | 5.2 | 1 | 1 | buy | $ 0.33 | 6,400 | $ 14,720 |
| VRSN | green | green | **ready to buy** | 13.51 | 25.00 | 21.10 | 8.1 | 2 | 2 | | | | |
| | | | | | | | | | | | | | |
| | | | | | | | | | | | | | |
| | | | | | | | | | | | | | $106,909 |

Evaluation spreadsheet complete with money management rules.

**4.4**

*Martin applied the 2% Rule to the account in which he planned to take these trades. That allowed him to risk $2,120 of the account's $106,000 equity on every trade. Knowing his maximum risk per trade and risk per share made it easy to calculate the maximum number of shares he could buy.*

*For example, if he was going to buy CSCO at $18.35 or better, with a stop at $17.27, he was going to risk $1.08 per share. Since his total permitted risk per trade was $2,120, he was allowed to trade 1,900 shares of CSCO.*  **—AE**

Assuming a $106,000 trading account, we apply the 2% Rule to the five final stocks on our shopping list and calculate the order size (e.g., 1,900 shares of CSCO, 4,800 shares of FNSR, etc.).

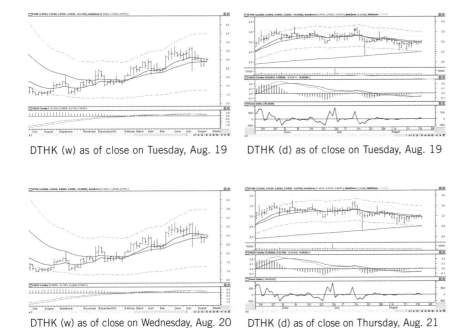

DTHK (w) as of close on Tuesday, Aug. 19    DTHK (d) as of close on Tuesday, Aug. 19

DTHK (w) as of close on Wednesday, Aug. 20    DTHK (d) as of close on Thursday, Aug. 21

## 4.5  Putting in Orders

Tuesday, August 19, the following orders were in before market opening:

    buy 1,900 CSCO @ 18.35
    buy 4,800 FNSR @ 1.88
    buy 2,000 JNPR @ 13.90
    buy 3,000 RHAT @ 6.80
    buy 6,400 VIGN @ 2.30

The orders on CSCO, FNSR, and VIGN were filled. RHAT and JNPR went up too fast and never looked back to fill these orders.

## Wednesday, August 20, and Thursday, August 21

### What to Do If a Trade Goes Against You.
### My Private Learning Curve.

*Looking at this diary in retrospect, it was a mistake to put on this trade. The three existing positions already used up nearly 6% of available risk capital by risking nearly 2% each. Putting on this trade violated the 6% rule.*

*—AE*

On Wednesday, August 20 (before the markets opened), we reviewed our entire list of 27 stocks (looking at their weekly and daily charts) and found that DTHK was looking much better than it had the previous day. The weekly chart looked stronger (blue) and the daily closed above the EMA (green), commencing a fresh uptrend. Following money management rules, we put on a trade to buy 6,800 shares of DTHK @ 3.01. The order was filled.

On Thursday, August 21 (before the markets opened), we reviewed our stock positions. We were not looking for another entry—only managing our four existing positions in CSCO, FNSR, VIGN, and DTHK.

It turned out that DTHK fell back to red on the weekly as well as on the daily chart—which was our signal to get out of this position with a market order at the open that day, taking a small loss before it got bigger.

Not wanting to take a loss (sound familiar?), I tried hard to ask (convince?) Dr. Elder, "Wouldn't it be fine to wait one more day? Maybe the red will go away. What if we wait to exit and maybe get a better price intraday than just putting in a market order at the open? What if the red on the weekly chart goes away until Friday? Do we have to decide intraweek?"

There were probably a few more ideas that would have allowed me to stay in that losing position. In fact, I knew every answer to my questions before I even asked them.

"You stay with your position and do as you please. I'm going to put in my sell order before we leave our hotel this morning."

I argued with myself for another hour and over breakfast, finally deciding to punch in my sell order. And once I was through with it, I really felt relieved and ready for the day's program (which was a three-hour hike up an Austrian mountain path): peace of mind from taking a very small loss in one position and enjoying a bullish performance in the remaining three.

## Friday, August 22, and Going

- Daily review of Dow Jones, Nasdaq, and S&P 500 (weekly and daily charts). Does the bullish trend continue?
- Review of individual stock positions. Weekly Impulse system? Daily Impulse system?
- Is a stock breathing or violating a trend?
- Time to take profits or exit a position?

"Hi Alex,

This morning's markets are beautiful!! The sell-off was not really strong, volume far from dramatic (at least in the stocks I follow), and I think reentry opportunities are ahead.

From our work, CSCO, FNSR, and VIGN netted well over $5,000 :—))

Did you sell your positions today? I took profits on tight stops on many of my positions, waiting to realign my chickens."

# CONCLUSION

## YOUR TRADING ROOM

$A$sk yourself after visiting these 16 trading rooms: "What have I learned?"

What will you do with this information? How will it help you? The answers will depend on your level of development as a trader and your attitude.

I can see three groups of traders reading this book—professionals and semiprofessionals; beginners and amateurs; and those who got hurt in the markets and are trying to come back. Let me address the first two groups and then spend a little extra time talking to the third.

If you're already trading for a living, you have your own style and a method that works for you. You probably picked up this book out of natural curiosity and because you're open to learning. I am sure that some of the ideas from these 16 interviews struck you as worth testing on your own. I do not have to worry about you jumping in with both feet. You will test whatever attracted you—first on your computer and then in your account, starting with a small size and keeping good notes. Several months from now, after researching, testing, and implementing some of these methods, you'll look back and see how your trading has improved as a result of reading this book. When that happens, I'd like to hear from you. If I ever write a follow-up to this book, perhaps you should be in it.

If you're a beginner, this book must have opened some exciting vistas for you. Wouldn't it be great to follow in the footsteps of some of the traders you've met—successful, wealthy, and independent? Before you jump in to imitate them, please stop for a moment and think about one of the headlines in the Introduction to this book—Objects in the Mirror Are Farther Away Than They Appear.

Every trader in this book, including its author, took some serious lumps on his journey to becoming a professional trader. If the methods appear easy and logical, it is because the traders who use them survived their collisions with the markets. These winners emerged with skills—some of which they can verbalize, and others that operate on an unspoken level.

How should you go about implementing these new methods? The only way to master them is through research, testing, and keeping good records. Choose the methods you like and back-test them on your computer. If a method does well on paper, test it with real money. Begin by putting on tiny test-size trades, keep good records, and give yourself plenty of time. Three, five, or even ten trades are not statistically valid. Please reread Mike McMahon's comments on system testing (Chapter 6). If this sounds like a lot of work, that's because it is.

I recently received an e-mail from a beginner—we met at a trade show, and I gave him a ride to the airport. In his e-mail, he asked me about trading the Impulse System without testing because he did not want to spend the time. He went on about his intense desire to be a successful trader, but it sounded to me like he wanted the rewards of trading—the income and the freedom—without the work. Each person in this book is absolutely committed to trading. They love doing research. None of them took a ready-made system, closed their eyes, and ran with it. They test everything. Please follow their example if you're really serious about becoming a successful trader.

# TRADER'S REHAB

The dictionary provides a definition of *rehabilitation*—"The act of restoring to good condition, operation, or capacity." A trader with a damaged account often becomes too fearful to trade; he needs rehabilitation to regain his ability. Most of us need rehab at some point in our trading careers.

Almost all the traders in this book went through at least one severe drawdown. Many, including the author, went through more than one. It is not just the loss of money that rankles. Even worse is the foul mood that goes with it. A person comes into the market, makes a few cautious trades, picks up a few dollars, feels invincible, and tosses a major portion of his capital at a seemingly easy trade. The market turns against him, he fails to take a small loss, and soon finds himself in a deep drawdown. Despairingly, he takes a huge loss, then makes several spastic trades in a desperate push to make back the money, but the more he trades, the deeper the hole he digs.

When people lose a large percentage of their account, they lose something more valuable than money—they lose confidence. Some start acting like a beaten dog: fearful, tail between its legs, jumping back at the slightest movement in the shadows. Many start beating themselves up emotionally, calling themselves names, punishing themselves.

An account is considered damaged if it has lost a third or more of its starting equity. If you take a $100,000 account down to $66,000, there's no doubt your account is badly hurt. I have seen accounts get hurt even worse—down 80 or even 90 percent from their peak equity. People with damaged accounts tend to become gun-shy. They want to put on a trade, but cannot shake off the fear. Pain from recent losses makes people insecure. Most traders who have been hurt wash out of the markets. If you want to trade again, you're more resilient and determined than most people.

The most common complaint of traders who took a beating is "I cannot pull the trigger." A trader does his homework, finds a stock to buy, but cannot bring himself to place the order. He starts tracking it as a paper-trade, and the stock goes his way. The next time he trades it with real money—and loses. He paper-trades again and makes money again, in theory, but as soon as he buys with real money, the stock goes against him. As soon as he dumps it, the stock reverses, as if laughing at him, and moves in the direction he expected. Why do paper trades often turn out "well" while real trades lose money?

Good trades tend to emerge from more unsettled market conditions, with less obvious signals. A fearful trader is too afraid to take such signals. He feels more secure with obvious-looking trades, while in fact, this feeling of clarity is probably a sign that he is late—the trend started without him, and he is running after a train that's already pulling out of the station. The trader's fear prevents him from entering good trades and prompts him to jump into bad ones. He is tripping on his own shoelaces.

My first advice to a fearful trader who got beaten up in the market is to stop trading for a while.

Many traders test indicators and systems by dumping historical data into testing software to obtain the profit-loss ratio, the biggest and the smallest profit or loss, and the average profit and loss. The longest winning and losing streaks and the maximum drawdowns give the appearance of objectivity and solidity.

Those printouts provide a false sense of security.

You may have a very nice printout, but what if the system delivers five losses in a row when you are trading real money? Nothing in your testing has prepared you for that, but it happens all the time. You grit your teeth and put on another trade. Another loss. Your drawdown is getting deeper. Suddenly, an impressive printout looks like a very thin reed on which to hang your future, while your account is being whittled away.

The attraction of electronic testing is so strong that a small cottage industry of programmers test systems for a fee. Some traders spend months, if not years, learning to use testing software. A loser who cannot admit he's afraid to trade has the wonderful excuse that he is learning new software. He's like a swimmer who is afraid of water and keeps himself busy ironing his swimsuit.

Only one kind of system testing makes sense. It is slow and time-consuming, but it's the only method that prepares you for trading. It consists of going through historical data one day at a time, writing down your trading signals for the day ahead, then clicking your chart forward and recording the trades and signals for the next day.

Begin by downloading your stock or futures data for a minimum of two years. Swing to the left side of the file without looking at what happened next. Open your technical analysis program and a spreadsheet. The two most important keys for traders on a computer are "Alt" and "Tab" because they let you switch between two programs. Open two windows in your analytic program—one for your long-term chart and indicators, the other for the short-term chart. Open a spreadsheet, write down your system's rules at the top of the page, and create columns for the entry date and price and the exit date and price.

Turn to the weekly chart and note its signal, if any. If it gives you a buy or sell signal, go to the daily chart ending on the same date to see whether it confirms that signal. If it does, record the order you have to place in your spreadsheet. Now return to the daily chart and click one day forward. See whether your buy or sell order was triggered. If so, return to the spreadsheet and record the result. Track your trade day by day, calculating stops and deciding where to take profits.

Follow this process throughout your entire data file, advancing a week at a time on the weekly chart, a day at a time on the daily chart. At every click, write down your system's signals and your actions.

As you click forward, one day at a time, the market's history will slowly unfold and challenge you. You click—and a buy signal comes into view. Will you take it? Record your decision in a spreadsheet. Will you take profits at a target, on a sell signal, or because of price action? Now you're doing much more than testing a set of rules. Moving ahead day by day, you develop your decision-making skills. This one-bar-at-a-time forward-testing is vastly superior to what you can get from back-testing software.

How will you deal with gap openings, when prices open above your buy level or below your stop? Should the system be adjusted, changed, or scrapped? Clicking forward one day at a time gets you as close to the real experience of trading as you can ever get without putting on a trade. It puts you in touch with the hard right edge of the market, which you can never experience through an orderly printout. Manual testing will improve your ability to think, recognize turns, and act in the foggy environment of the market.

Abridged from *Come into My Trading Room*

Give yourself a reasonable break, stay away from the market for at least two or three months. You cannot make money while feeling hurt and panicky. You need to put some distance between yourself and your loss. It is hard to look at the markets objectively when a loss hurts like an open wound. Taking time off will lower the emotional heat and allow the healing to begin.

Back in the days when I actively practiced psychiatry, I occasionally saw patients who had problems with sexual performance. By the time they got to me, they had been medically cleared, but could not function and dreaded each night. They felt compelled to try to perform, knowing they would fail. I accepted such patients into therapy upon a condition: They had to agree not to have sex until we figured out their problem. They'd always argue with me at first, but then felt relieved. With the pressure off, we could usually solve their problem in therapy.

People under stress tend to make poor decisions. A break from trading allows you to heal your wounds. Your rehab begins with getting out of all positions—go flat, take a total break.

Be prepared for your trading rehab to take at least twice as long as it took to lose all that money. Only gamblers hope for a quick comeback in a short series of brilliant trades. In reality, you'll have to claw your way back, dollar by dollar. Stop beating yourself up. Be kinder to yourself, since you're the one who'll take your account from failure to success. If you go through rehab, you can become a successful trader.

Allow several months to pass during which your equity no longer goes down. As the urgency to make back losses slowly fades away, start getting used to the new, lower level of your account. Once you've become calmer, you'll need to make several important choices. First of all, you'll have to decide whether you want to continue trading.

Trading attracts us with its promise of freedom, but some people find the process too hard. They may not have a natural knack or cannot put in enough energy or time. This is similar to being unable to play a musical instrument or fix a leaky faucet. There is no shame in that. A good friend of mine, after coming to several Camps and losing money on a variety of trading ideas, finally said, "I am not cut out for trading." We are still good friends, since there is much more to life than buying and selling financial instruments.

If you decide that you love trading and want to do it right, your rehab can continue. You notice I said "love trading." Everyone loves the rewards, but do you love research, studying the markets, testing ideas, placing orders? A successful trader loves the process of trading, and the rewards flow in pretty much as an afterthought.

This is no different from any other field, such as medicine, engineering, or law, where the most successful people are those who love their profession. They may live in nice houses and drive good cars, but their goal is competence and accomplishment in their chosen field, not the house or the car. They do not cut corners, take unprofessional shortcuts, or dwell on the rewards. A dedicated professional constantly works to improve himself, respects and follows the rules of his field, and expects rewards to materialize in the long run without focusing on them.

If your sole focus is the rewards, then "get-rich-quick" must appeal to you, with predictably disastrous results. You wouldn't try to get rich quick in medicine or law, would you?

If you love trading, you have a tremendously interesting journey ahead of you. You damaged your account, but now you can turn those losses to your advantage, use your experience to become a more focused, disciplined, and successful trader. In order to come back, you'll need to establish and follow several strict rules. Use your past weakness as a source of future strength, a foundation of trading discipline.

There are few, if any, young geniuses in trading—this is an older person's game. Memory, maturity, and experience matter a great deal. My late great friend Lou Taylor, to whom my first book was dedicated, used to say, "If I get half a percent smarter each year, I'll be a genius by the time I die." You should get better as you grow older.

If you agree with what we've discussed so far, if we're on the same page, I'll recommend several steps for your rehab:

**1.** *Set up and keep good records.* The two main values of record-keeping are accountability and self-education. Only by looking back and learning from your experience can you go forward.

Before you even think of placing your next trade, set up a record-keeping system. Gamblers, curiosity seekers, and get-rich-quick schemers run on adrenaline; they have no use for records. All serious pros keep good records. At a minimum, you'll need a spreadsheet for tracking your homework: one or two lines for each index or stock, a column for each day. You will need another spreadsheet for measuring available risk in your trading account. You will need to set up a diary for your trades. Some of these templates are available from my firm at no charge, others for a fee, and of course, you may very well develop them on your own.

**2.** *Set up and follow money management rules.* It was poor money management that landed you in rehab. Most trading accounts get damaged either by a shark bite—a single disastrous loss—or by piranha bites—a series of losses that together strip the account to the bone even though none is deadly by itself. You are in rehab because you've already had an encounter with either a shark or a pack of piranhas, or both. It was a painful experience, and unless you set up good money management rules, you're guaranteed to have another one, which will feel even worse.

The 2% and the 6% Rules, repeatedly described in this book and *Come into My Trading Room*, are designed to protect you from the sharks and piranhas. You must apply them to every trade.

**3.** *Find a method or methods that appeal to you.* You saw a variety of methods in these 16 trading rooms. Many traders in this book have been to our Traders' Camps and studied with me; had you approached 16 professionals at random, the differences between them would have been even greater. You must be humble enough to realize that you cannot master every single method.

Selecting a method that appeals to you is a personal choice, similar to the choice of a medical student who has to decide whether to train as a surgeon or a psychiatrist, a pediatrician or an anesthesiologist. People are happiest and most successful when they do what they love. Just like a medical student chooses a specialty that appeals to him, you need to choose a trading method that engages you. You can look at many methods, but select the one that makes emotional and intellectual sense to you.

**4.** *Make a time commitment.* Decide how many hours a week you can invest in trading. Do your homework every day, including weekends. A specific commitment confirms that trading is important to you. It shows that research and trading are your priorities rather than just a filler activity when there is nothing better on TV.

**5.** *Start trading a very small size.* You are likely to feel a little shaky coming out of your abstinence period. The pain of your losses is still fresh, your self-confidence a little uncertain. You may set up a record-keeping system and money management rules, find a method that appeals to you, and do your homework. Still, when it comes to putting on a trade, you may be afraid to pull the trigger.

My advice is to begin by trading a tiny size.

Start by putting on trades so small that they are of no financial consequence. Let's say you have only $12,000 left in your trading account. On the day I write this, Google, trading near $300, appears toppy and is flashing sell signals. If I was shorting GOOG in this account during the rehab process, I would short a single share. Another stock, CHTR, is in a buy mode, currently trading at $1.26. Trading it in this account, I would buy 100 shares. The size of these trades is too small to make an impact—a $50 profit or a $50 loss is not going to matter. These trades will not make you tense. The idea is to trade for the experience, not for the money.

You can set up a rule—after five or ten successful trades, depending on the frequency with which you trade, you will double your size. Keep doing that until you increase your average trading size to the point where you start bumping into the 2% and 6% Rules. Remember, you are in rehab. If you had broken a limb, you'd exercise it slowly and gradually before recovering to a full working level.

# HOMEWORK

Several years ago, when I was less aware of my own likes and dislikes, I met a young woman in Europe, and we made a date to meet on a Caribbean island. We settled into one of the nicest hotels on that island, rented a sports car, and went to beaches and restaurants. Several days later, we started bickering, with me taking the lead. It made no sense—we liked each other, and both came to have a good time. Then I figured out my problem—we spent all our time together, and I did not do any work. The more days went by without working, the harder I became on her.

That was an easy problem to remedy—I explained it to my date, and we agreed that every morning after breakfast she would go to the beach alone. She was a very strong swimmer who could swim for 50 minutes straight away from the shore, turn around, and swim back. By the time she returned from the beach, it was time for lunch with perhaps a little roll before it; having worked for several hours, I was in the best of spirits, and we'd have a fabulous rest of the day.

One morning I was sitting in a wicker armchair in the lobby, working on my laptop, when a group of tourists in loud polyester shorts came in from a bus to gawk at our resort. One of them stopped in front of me—"Poor you, have to continue working on your vacation." Vacation?! I hadn't had a vacation since I'd quit my job years ago. That spacious lobby, overlooking gardens and the sea, was my office for the next two weeks.

The point of trading is not to escape work. I love working. By the end of each week, I look forward to reviewing the markets on the weekend. By the end of a weekend, I look forward to Monday morning when the markets will reopen and I can start placing new trades. In recent years, after I began sharing some research projects with a friend, it would have been easy to copy his homework—but it would have been like asking him to go out and eat my dinner or take a woman I've met out on a date. Thank you very much, I'd rather do it myself!

My weekend homework consists of five sections. I rarely do more than two at a time and often take long breaks between them—it is a weekend after all. I often think about the completed sections during the break, and return to my laptop eager to see whether the next section will confirm or contradict what I've already seen. I may begin my homework as early as Friday evening after the markets close if I do not have any social plans that night. I do the bulk of my homework on Saturday and Sunday, but if pinched for time, I may do the last session as late as Monday morning before the markets open. The order of these sections is always the same:

1. Indexes
2. Groups
3. Futures
4. Current positions
5. Prospective positions

In recent years I've been using TC2005 for the first two sections of my homework. Their database contains over 100 market indexes, which I exported into a spreadsheet, one index per line. I use three columns per week—one for the weekly Impulse, a flag column whose cells change color if the Impulse stops being red or green, and a comments column for jotting down my remarks.

Even though TC2005 does not allow me to color price bars depending on the Impulse, it is handy for a quick review of multiple tickers. My weekly template includes moving averages and MACD-Histogram, allowing me to see what color the Impulse would have been if I could color the bars. I sort indexes alphabetically and tap on the space bar, going down the list and recording my findings in the spreadsheet.

International Market Index and S&P Bank Index, CBOE Gold Index and PHLX Housing Index, all the way down to World Platinum Index and North American Telecom—I record their weekly Impulse, while Excel keeps a running tab of green, red, and blue groups. A few years ago, this section of my homework used to take a long time and did not seem very useful. What did it mean that 39 indexes were green, 81 blue, and 11 red? I found that by rating these indexes each week I picked up speed; I also discovered several important patterns, such as what levels of green and red tend to indicate market tops and bottoms.

I like doing this homework by hand. Several programmer friends have offered to automate it for me so that the numbers for all indexes could pop up at the push of a button, but I have declined. Seeing each index once a week and recording its changes gives me an almost physical feel for the market. No amount of programming can deliver that.

In the second section of my homework, I go through 239 Media General industry groups and subgroups in TC2005. They include chemicals, durable goods, aerospace, Internet, and many others. Each group has several subgroups, and each of those has a number of stocks. The work is similar to rating Indexes—mark the Impulse for every subgroup, pay special attention to color changes, jot down notes on the most promising groups. The first section of my homework helps me decide how bullish or bearish I am on the market overall. The second section helps me find groups in which to look for buy and sell candidates.

In looking for the strongest subgroups, I am not interested in those making new highs. I look for groups that got beat up but stopped declining and started to turn up, tracing a sort of fish hook. I look for the opposite pattern in shorting candidates, keeping in mind that tops are slower than bottoms. Fear, the dominant emotion of bottoms, is sharper and stronger than greed, which is why prices tend to turn faster at bottoms.

For the third section of my homework, the review of futures, I turn to TradeStation and another Excel spreadsheet. Futures have their own groups: For example, the Energy group includes crude oil, heating oil, unleaded gasoline, and natural gas. There are two reasons to review futures: to look for trading opportunities as well as for connections with the stock market. If you become interested in gold stocks, it is only logical to analyze gold futures, and if oil drillers look overvalued, it is useful to know the current trend of crude oil.

Much of market research involves a search for connections, some fairly obvious, others more obscure. You may see that interest rates are rising while housing stocks are going through the roof. Knowing that rising interest rates should be bearish for real estate, you can start watching that group for signs of slowing down, preparing to short as soon as those signals appear. Good trades usually take time to come together, and your homework prepares you to look for signals in advance, ready to act as soon as they flash on the screen. This puts you well ahead of amateurs who casually "follow trends" and hop aboard too late.

The fourth and fifth sections of my homework, analyzing open and potential trades, follow well-established steps that must be familiar to you from reading my comments on many trades in this book (see also *Seven Days in Dr. Alexander Elder's Trading Room* in Chapter 16). I am interested in buying the strongest stocks in the strongest groups and shorting the weakest stocks in the weakest groups (strong means starting to turn up and weak means starting to top out). Put up a weekly chart, compress it until the entire history fits into a single screen in order to see whether it is cheap or expensive, then uncompress it to see approximately two years of history. What is the price trend, what are the messages of the fast- and slow-moving averages, MACD-Histogram and MACD Lines? Are there any divergences? What is your conclusion? Are you a bull or a bear on this stock, or do you see no advantage either way?

Drop down to the daily chart and look for entries and exits in the direction of the weekly trend. Do you see an attractive entry point, a realistic profit target, a close enough stop? Put those numbers into a spreadsheet, calculate your risk/reward ratio, and decide whether the trade is worth taking. Make sure that the 6% Rule allows you to trade and verify the maximum size permitted by the 2% Rule.

All this homework makes for a busy weekend, but doing it gives me an advantage in the battle for market profits. Doing your homework week after week and month after month, keeping good records, and documenting each step can lift you above the crowd of amateurs and gamblers. The job of losers is to provide money to winners, but they're not in a hurry to mail us their checks. You need to find those turning points in the markets where losers fold and run, leaving their money on the table for us.

What are the alternatives to doing homework? You could beg for tips, listen to financial news, perhaps subscribe to an advisory service. Do you think they will give you much of a chance of winning the trading battle? The only viable alternative would be to give your money to professional managers, but even that choice is far from work-free. Most money managers underperform market averages, and you need to split your money between several of them, closely monitoring their performance and moving your assets. The discussion of how to choose, rate, and use money managers is outside the scope of this book. Just keep in mind that there is no free money in the financial markets.

An amateur who has a few dollars burning a hole in his pocket buys himself a couple of market books and dreams that if he sets Stochastic just right, the money spigots will open. Soon he'll be able to move to Easy Street, never work, and sip piña coladas on the beach, while that Stochastic or some other indicator continues to bulk up his account. Let him dream. You have better things to do with your time. You have homework.

# SHARING HOMEWORK— THE SPIKE GROUP

In 2004 I began sharing some homework with a group of traders. We have found a way for our group to pool resources, while each member remains responsible for his or her own workload and performance. We look for new trades and compete on the quality of our picks.

The roots of the story go back to 1993 when I wrote in *Trading for a Living* that the New High–New Low Index was one of the best leading indicators of the stock market. The New Highs are the leaders in strength, and the New Lows are the leaders in weakness; their shifts of balance provide useful clues to the future path of the stock market. Oddly enough, while NH–NL data is easily available from the *Wall Street Journal* and other newspapers, most financial databases present it in a user-unfriendly way, making the index difficult to track.

A couple of years ago, I asked Martin (Chapter 16) to set up a system for tracking NH–NL. He began sending a nightly e-mail to me and several other friends with the weekly and daily charts of NH–NL. That index had recently spiked down, clearing the air for a fresh upmove, and we started referring to his nightly chart as the spike chart. During the 2004 Traders' Camp in Cyprus, Martin showed an updated spike chart to the class each day. When campers asked to be added to his Spike mailing list, Martin readily agreed, but said he was not interested in feeding passive users; anyone who did not respond to his e-mails with comments would be off the list after two weeks.

The group quickly shrank as noncontributing members were eliminated. At the same time, members' feedback started to produce useful stock tips and insights. Around that time, I read a book called *The Wisdom of Crowds* by James Surowiecki, who argued that groups were smarter than individuals. That went against the common view that crowds were basically dumb. Surowiecki showed that groups were stupid when members fed off each others' and their guru's emotions, parroting the same line and creating financial bubbles. Smart groups had a different structure—independent input from all members, uncontaminated by others' opinions, with the leader simply maintaining the group structure.

My recent experience of running webinars for small groups of traders led me to agree with this novel view. I was struck by the high quality of tips coming out of those classes. Webinar participants, using different methods and acting independently of each other, generated a cascade of tips from which we could pick favorites. The Surowiecki model seemed to work well.

That is how it all came together: Martin's daily NH–NL mailings; the high quality of group feedback; the Surowiecki model; and the cascade of good tips from my webinars. I e-mailed the NH–NL group suggesting we set up a system: Each member should e-mail me their best pick for the week ahead, and I'd collate all the tips into a spreadsheet and send that file to every group member. Most people agreed, and we went ahead, naming our project the Spike group.

Each member is obligated to send his or her best pick accompanied by a brief text explaining his choice by no later than 3 PM on Sunday every week. In return, he receives a spreadsheet and a text file on Sunday afternoon containing the picks and comments of all group members. All tips are rated at the end of the week, with three points awarded for the #1 pick, two points for #2, and one point for #3. At the end of each quarter, group members are rated by their total number of points and equity gain. The gold, silver, and bronze medal-winners in both categories receive prizes, with grand prizes at the end of the year.

The members of Spike receive access to research by a group of serious traders, but accept certain obligations; failure to abide results in expulsion or fines. Members are expected to contribute each week, with four absences permitted per quarter. Members are free to share their own work with anyone they like, but sharing group files with outsiders results in immediate expulsion.

Looking at the results of the Spike group competition, it is easy to be dazzled by the winners' performance—22% gain for the first quarter of 2005, 55% for the second quarter, 16% for the third. Those are results for betting the entire account on paper, starting with the initial $1,000, on each week's pick. Trading real money, you wouldn't bet your entire account on a single pick, and the results would be less spectacular, but more real. Most group members report an improvement in their real-money performance. They become sharper and more focused on their homework, knowing that their best picks will compete with the picks of their friends. I asked group members to self-report whether they traded their own and other members' picks. The rate of trading their own picks runs at about 60% each week and the rate of trading other picks is about 30%, with some members trading both and some none.

There are about 20 traders in our group, with a small turnover each quarter. Most of those who left could not keep up with the workload. Membership in the group is by invitation only, and we usually have a pool of candidates waiting for openings. The system continues to function as a strong generator of trading ideas. One of the key lessons of our group is that traders can work together as long as each does his own research and shares only the result. Also, these results have to be submitted simultaneously, to avoid influencing one another.

# GEOGRAPHY AND TIME

If you know how to trade, you can do it anywhere in the world—but once you begin traveling, you quickly discover that some locales are better suited to trading than others. Fast Internet is of paramount importance, but the next most important factor is the time zone from which you trade.

The U.S. financial markets are located mostly in New York and Chicago, their trading hours set for the benefit of floor traders. The New York Stock Exchange is open from 9:30 AM to 4 PM EST, the NASDAQ keeps the same hours; bond futures trade in Chicago from 7:20 AM to 2 PM (8:20 AM to 3 PM EST), and so forth. The farther west you go, the earlier you have to get up to watch the markets in real-time. For example, if you want to trade the opening in bonds from California, you'll have to be up by 5:20 AM, and three hours earlier if you trade from Hawaii.

A couple of years ago, I spent two weeks in Sydney, Australia, when the U.S. stock market was very active. I needed to manage my positions and traded almost every day. The U.S. market opened at 1:30 AM local time. I'd go to sleep before midnight, wake up for the opening, then go back to sleep, get up in the middle of the night, go back to sleep again, then wake up for the closing at 8 AM and afterwards catch another hour of sleep before getting up for a run around Darling Harbor, breakfast, and homework. I had bags under my eyes and hated that schedule.

Going east, on the other hand, is an entirely different story. The local time in much of Europe is six hours later than in New York. When I trade, say, from Vienna, the U.S. stock market opens at 3:30 PM and closes at 10 PM. I can sleep late, go for a long bike ride, have a leisurely lunch, then return to the computer and do homework to get ready for the opening. After the market closes, there is enough time for dinner because you can sleep late the next day.

What about the markets that trade around the clock, such as stock index futures? Do not imagine you'll be able to trade them actively whenever you want. Their volumes dry up after the main markets, in New York and Chicago, close for the day. You may be able to bang out of a bad position or even open a new trade, but expect to face heavy slippage due to thin after-hours volume.

Currencies, which actively trade almost around the clock, have their own problems. In trading, you're trying to pick other people's pockets while they're picking yours. It is hard enough to protect your pockets while you're awake, but how about having your pockets picked while you sleep? Stops alone will not solve this problem. Trading 24-hour markets sounds good in theory, but presents just as many problems as opportunities for active traders.

A beginning or intermediate trader is unlikely to have much choice where to trade, but he can certainly decide which markets to trade. It pays to concentrate on stocks and futures that are actively traded in your own time zone. Trading is a hard game, and you are better off working when you are fresh and alert. The grass may seem greener on the other side of the septic tank, but believe me, it is not. I have Australian friends who keep trying to hit U.S. stocks, and Americans who try to trade in Europe. It is one thing to take on a long-term position that you do not have to monitor intraday. It is quite another to actively trade a market while trying to stay awake. A comfortable and well-rested trader is more likely to win.

# TRADERS' SPOUSES

As I began interviewing traders for this book, I was surprised how many of them wanted to talk about their love for their wives. One after another talked with great feeling and without any prompting from me about the trust, support, and encouragement he felt at home.

The intellectual demands of the markets are not very high. In this game we only have to deal with five factors: open, high, low, closing prices, and volume. Why then do so many people who are successful in their professional lives fail in trading? This is because trading places immense emotional demands on all of us. It evokes powerful feelings—fear, greed, and so on, making it very easy to make bad decisions. A person with a happy personal life has an advantage, while the one with a stormy personal life finds himself doubly stressed.

This is not to say that every trader in this book lives in marital heaven. Some are single, and at least one is currently going through an unpleasant divorce. Curiously enough, he is also in a drawdown this year, although as a professional trader, his losses are minimal, and I am sure he will pull out of his slump. I still remember the deep slump I had at the time of my divorce many years ago.

A person who goes home to a smiling, loving spouse and does not need to spend an ounce of mental energy on figuring out the angles of a tense personal relationship is in a much better position when he sits in front of the computer to analyze charts and make decisions. While most traders in this book conformed to this pattern, it is difficult to translate it into a specific recommendation. What you do with this insight is entirely up to you. I can only share with you my surprise at discovering this factor in the lives of many successful traders.

# TRADING—MORE THAN MONEY

I enjoyed writing this book. Towards the end, racing to meet the deadline, I stopped trading for two months during which stocks, currencies, and several futures staged fantastic reversals. I saw those moves coming; the money looked as available as it ever gets, but I stayed away, knowing I could not fully focus on both tasks at the same time.

Why write if you can trade? Probably for the same reason 16 traders in this book gave their interviews and opened their trading rooms to you. There is more to life than money, even to a trader's life. This is what tight-fisted and narrow-minded folks cannot understand. They have asked before and undoubtedly will ask again: Why would anyone who knows how to trade talk about it? Why not close the door, pull down the shades, and grind out profits? When those folks were kids in summer camp, they probably ate their food packages from home at night under a blanket. Some people are a little more tight, others a little more generous.

Success in trading does not stem from knowing "the secret" because, as I said before, there is no secret. There is hard work, focus, attention to detail, being careful with money, being oriented toward the long term, and having a bit of flair. Why do prominent physicians, actors, and engineers teach classes, bringing up the level of the competition? Because they feel comfortable in their success, love their craft, and enjoy sharing with like-minded people. Why does someone like Steven Spielberg give master classes on filmmaking? What if someone learns his method, improves upon it, and makes a better movie? I am sure he'd feel energized if that happened, see that movie, and then move on to make an even better one himself.

Clayton Seitz, a camper and trader at whose house I like to stay when visiting Boston, recently said to me: "I used to race cars when I was younger. If after a race you came up to the winner and said, 'Wow, today you blew the doors off my car—what did you do?' He would say: 'Well, last time I was racing I had a little problem with this or that, so I made this adjustment and that adjustment.' If you came up to the last man in that race and asked the same question: 'Wow, towards the end you were really gaining on me, what did you do?' he would say, 'I cannot tell you, that is a secret.'" Trading is not the only field in which winners and losers behave differently.

This is not to say that successful traders walk around freely dispensing wisdom and good trading tips. They seldom do. All have had too many experiences with people trying to sponge off of them. When someone asks them for advice, their first reaction is similar to how many people react to beggars—make no eye contact and quickly walk away. You have to know how to approach them, and the best way is by sharing your work. Have nothing to share? Well, that's a problem. How can you put yourself into a position in which you will have something to share? Work, perhaps?

For me, one of the nicest aspects of trading, in addition to the freedom it provides, is that it puts me in contact with so many interesting people. Serious traders develop independent minds, and I find being with them very stimulating and a great deal of fun. Looking at the faces on the cover of this book reminds me that during the past two months, I discussed life choices with Pascal, went bicycling with Damir, toured Dutch canals on a motorboat with Martin, went to a museum with Andrea, and had a long talk about terrorism with Sohail, who stopped by my apartment for a cold beer on his visit from the United Kingdom. Last weekend I went canoeing at Jerry's summer home, and next week I am going to Washington, D.C., where I want to take Peter, visiting from Moscow, to the Smithsonian Air and Space Museum.

All of us are busy studying the markets and trading for ourselves or managing other people's money. Still, there is more to life than money and what it can buy. I think of this book's dedication to Eddie, who, stuck on a high floor in a burning building, called his family members and his fiancée, telling them he loved them. He did not call his bank on that day.

Trading can give you money, which can buy many good things—freedom from having a boss, the ability to travel wherever and whenever you like, and much more. Still, when the chips are down, it is not money that determines the quality of your life. Your goal in trading should be to become the best professional you can be. Your success will be measured largely by money, but not by money alone. This is why, once again, I want to thank the 16 traders who opened their trading rooms—helping all of us become better traders, and serving as examples of kindness, generosity, and drive.

# BIBLIOGRAPHY

These are the books mentioned by the author or 16 traders in the course of their interviews:

American Society of Mechanical Engineering. *Unwritten Laws of Engineering.* American Society of Mechanical Engineers, 1944.

Appel, Gerald. *Day Trading with Gerald Appel* (video). Financial Trading Seminars, 1989.

———. *Technical Analysis: Power Tools for Active Investors.* Financial Times-Upper Saddle River, NJ: Prentice Hall, 2005.

Crabel, Toby. *Day Trading with Short-Term Price Patterns and Opening Range Breakouts.* Greenville, SC: Traders Press, 1990.

Dominguez, Joe, and Vicki Robin. *Your Money or Your Life: Transforming Your Relationship with Money and Achieving Financial Independence.* New York: Penguin Books, 1999.

Douglas, Mark. *Trading in the Zone: Master the Market with Confidence, Discipline, and a Winning Attitude.* Upper Saddle River, NJ: Prentice Hall Press, 2000.

Elder, Dr. Alexander. *Come into My Trading Room: A Complete Guide to Trading.* New York: Wiley, 2002.

———. *Straying from the Flock: Travels in New Zealand.* Hoboken, NJ: Wiley, 2005.

———. *Trading for a Living: Psychology, Trading Tactics, Money Management.* New York: Wiley, 1993.

Hutson, Jack K., Carl F. Schroeder, and David Weis. *Charting the Stock Market: The Wyckoff Method.* Technical Analysis, 1991.

Kiyosaki, Robert T., and Sharon L. Lechter. *Rich Dad, Poor Dad: What the Rich Teach Their Kids about Money—That the Poor and Middle Class Do Not!* Warner Business Books, 2000.

Lefèvre, Edwin. *Reminiscences of a Stock Operator.* New York: Wiley, 1994.

MacPherson, Malcolm. *The Black Box: All-New Cockpit Voice Recorder Accounts of In-Flight Accidents.* New York: William Morrow, 1998.

Murphy, John J. *Technical Analysis of the Financial Markets: A Comprehensive Guide to Trading Methods and Applications.* Upper Saddle River, NJ: Prentice Hall Press, 1999.

Sperandeo, Victor, and T. Sullivan Brown. *Trader Vic—Methods of a Wall Street Master.* New York: Wiley, 1993.

Surowiecki, James. *The Wisdom of Crowds: Why the Many Are Smarter Than the Few and How Collective Wisdom Shapes Business, Economies, Societies, and Nations.* New York, NY: Doubleday, 2004.

Watts, Dickson G. *Speculation as a Fine Art and Thoughts on Life.* New York: Fraser Publishing Company, 1965.

Weis, David. *Trading with the Elliott Wave Principle.* Chicago, IL: Probus Publishing Co., 1989.

Wyckoff, Richard Demille. *Studies in Tape Reading.* Traders Press, 1964. [Also known as *Studies in Tape Reading* by Rollo Tape, Richard Wyckoff's pseudonym.]

# Reading Lists

After these interviews were completed, I asked each trader for a list of books they would recommend.

## Chapter 1  Sherri Haskell

1. *Reminiscences of a Stock Operator*, Edwin Lefèvre.

   My favorite: This book brings trading down to earth, as narrated by a real trader. Its timeless lessons should be revisited every few years.

2. *The Visual Investor: How to Spot Market Trends*, John J. Murphy.

   A great book on technical analysis—comprehensive and to the point.

3. *Market Wizards: Interviews with Top Traders* and *The New Market Wizards: Conversations with America's Top Traders*, Jack D. Schwager.

   These books have interviews with several different traders. You learn about individual approaches and the value of tenacity.

4. *Come into My Trading Room: A Complete Guide to Trading* and *Trading for a Living: Psychology, Trading Tactics, Money Management*, Dr. Alexander Elder.

   Loaded with great information, innovative trading concepts, and wit.

5. *The Candlestick Course*, Steve Nison.

   A text- and workbook by the man who introduced candlestick charting to western traders.

## Chapter 2  Fred Schutzman

1. *Trading for a Living: Psychology, Trading Tactics, Money Management*, Dr. Alexander Elder.

2. *Technical Analysis of the Financial Markets: A Comprehensive Guide to Trading Methods and Applications*, John J. Murphy.

3. *Reminiscences of a Stock Operator*, Edwin Lefèvre.

4. *Elements of Successful Trading: Developing Your Comprehensive Strategy through Psychology, Money Management, and Trading Methods*, Robert Rotella.

5. *Market Wizards: Interviews with Top Traders*, Jack D. Schwager.

6. *The New Market Wizards: Conversations with America's Top Traders*, Jack D. Schwager.

### Chapter 3   Andrea Perolo

1. *Trading for a Living: Psychology, Trading Tactics, Money Management*, Dr. Alexander Elder.

   Along with the two classics—*Technical Analysis of the Futures Markets* by John Murphy and *Technical Analysis Explained* by Martin Pring—this book is clear and complete with the two golden rules of money management (the 2% and the 6%).

2. *Martin Pring on Market Momentum*, Martin J. Pring.

   This is the book for a deep understanding of how and why oscillators and indicators work.

3. *Pring on Price Patterns: The Definitive Guide to Price Pattern Analysis and Interpretation*, Martin J. Pring.

   How to trade different price patterns and where to put stops and take profits for each.

4. *Schwager on Futures*, Jack Schwager.

   A good book on technical analysis, but I especially appreciate "Real World Chart Analysis" in Part 2—a trading practice with 210 pages of charts. You read about a trade based on a particular pattern, then turn the page to see how it would have worked.

5. *Technical Trader's Guide to Computer Analysis of the Futures Markets*, Charles LeBeau and David Lucas.

   Another complete book on technical analysis. The "Set-Up Pattern," p. 75 and pp. 138–139, works well in real trading. The authors describe this pattern for Slow Stochastics, but I found it works even better for RSI.

6. *Japanese Candlestick Charting Techniques*, Steve Nison.
   The main book on candlesticks.

7. *Charting Commodity Market Price Behavior*, L. Dee Belveal.
   This 35-year-old book proves that quality has no age! Still the best for volume and open interest in the futures markets, with a very interesting chapter on COT reports.

8. *Precision Trading with Stevenson Price and Time Targets*, J.R. Stevenson.
   A very smart tactic for confirming valid trendline breaks.

9. *Technical Analysis for the Trading Professional*, Constance Brown.
   I recommend it for the chapter on RSI.

10. *Trading in the Zone: Master the Market with Confidence, Discipline, and a Winning Attitude*, Mark Douglas.

    Last but not least—much easier to study than his first famous book, *The Disciplined Trader: Developing Winning Attitudes*, Chapter 11, on taking profits, has a valuable trade-management concept.

### Chapter 4   Sohail Rabbani

I have tried hard to list as few books as possible and still cover the trading spectrum.

The list for traders:

1. *Trading for a Living: Psychology, Trading Tactics, Money Management*, Dr. Alexander Elder.
   A must-read do-it-yourself guide for new traders.

2. *Starting Out in Futures Trading*, Mark J. Powers.
   A logical introduction to financial futures.

3. *The Investor's Quotient: The Psychology of Successful Investing in Commodities and Stocks*, Jake Bernstein.
   Trader styles and psychology.

4. *The Disciplined Trader: Developing Winning Attitudes*, Mark Douglas.
   Trader's case history and psychological introspection.

5. *The Visual Investor: How to Spot Market Trends*, John J. Murphy.
   An introduction to technical analysis.

6. *Winner Take All: A Top Commodity Trader Tells It Like It Is*, William R. Gallacher.
   Criticism of market gurus and technical analysis.

7. *Options as a Strategic Investment*, Lawrence G. McMillan.
   An encyclopedic review of options.

8. *The Bear Book: Survive and Profit in Ferocious Markets*, John Rothchild.
   Defensive advice for turbulent markets.

Second list, for big-picture perspective:

1. *Against the Gods: The Remarkable Story of Risk*, Peter L. Bernstein.

2. *The Dollar Crisis: Causes, Consequences, Cures*, Richard Duncan.

3. *Running on Empty: How the Democratic and Republican Parties Are Bankrupting Our Future and What Americans Can Do about It*, Peter G. Peterson.

4. *Bull's Eye Investing: Targeting Real Returns in a Smoke and Mirrors Market*, John Maudlin.

5. *Financial Reckoning Day: Surviving the Soft Depression of the Twenty-first Century*, William Bonner and Addison Wiggin.

6. *Tomorrow's Gold: Asia's Age of Discovery*, Marc Faber.

7. *The World Is Flat: A Brief History of the Twenty-first Century*, Thomas L. Friedman.

8. *Wealth and Democracy: A Political History of the American Rich*, Kevin Phillips.

9. *The Case Against the Fed*, Murray N. Rothbard.

10. *The Creature from Jekyll Island: A Second Look at the Federal Reserve*, G. Edward Griffin.

11. *Crossing the Rubicon: The Decline of the American Empire at the End of the Age of Oil*, Michael C. Ruppert.

## Chapter 5    Ray Testa Jr.

1. *Come into My Trading Room: A Complete Guide to Trading*, Dr. Alexander Elder.

2. *Reminiscences of a Stock Operator*, Edwin Lefèvre.

3. *How to Trade in Stocks*, Jesse Livermore and Richard Smitten.

4. *Stock Market Wizards: Interviews with America's Top Stock Traders*, Jack D. Schwager.

5. *Trend Following—How Great Traders Make Millions in Up or Down Markets*, Michael W. Covel.

6. *Seven Habits of Highly Effective People: Powerful Lessons in Personal Change*, Steven R. Covey.

### Chapter 6    Mike McMahon

These books had the most impact on my trading, in the order that I read them:

1. *Trading for a Living: Psychology, Trading Tactics, Money Management*, Dr. Alexander Elder.

    My first awakening from "online/short-term investing" to real trading.

2. *Come into My Trading Room: A Complete Guide to Trading*, Dr. Alexander Elder.

    Greatly expanded my record-keeping and money management.

3. *Trading in the Zone: Master the Market with Confidence, Discipline, and a Winning Attitude*, Mark Douglas.

    Improved my trading psychology and confidence.

4. *Trading Rules: Strategies for Success*, William F. Eng.

    50 common sense rules—I focus on one of them each week as a reminder during the trading year. (This week is #32: Never permit speculative ventures to turn into investments.)

5. *Riding the Bear: How to Prosper in the Coming Bear Market*, Sy Harding.

    An author who believes in bear markets and sees the fallacies of "buy and hold."

6. *Trading Classic Chart Patterns*, Thomas Bulkowski.

    I don't use patterns a lot, but this works well as a "pattern encyclopedia" and I especially like his method of scoring patterns.

7. *Technical Analysis: Power Tools for Active Investors*, Gerald Appel.

    A great book from the creator of one of my favorite indicators, MACD.

### Chapter 7    Gerald Appel

1. *Technical Analysis of the Financial Markets: A Comprehensive Guide to Trading Methods and Applications*, John J. Murphy.

    Fine, broad coverage of technical indicators; a good foundation and reference source.

2. *Stock Trader's Almanac*, published annually, Yale Hirsch and Jeffrey A. Hirsch.

    The 38th edition was published in 2005. Probably the best source of information on seasonal factors in the stock market.

3. *Profit Magic of Stock Transaction Timing*, J.M. Hurst, 25th anniversary edition.

    A classic discussion of stock market timing cycles and ways to profit from them.

**Chapter 8   Michael Brenke**

Books in order of importance:

1. *Trading for a Living: Psychology, Trading Tactics, Money Management*, Dr. Alexander Elder.

   Useful information that helped me get started, with rules that limited my losses during the early years. Without this book I would probably still be struggling and more than likely would have had to consider another line of work.

2. *How I've Achieved Triple-Digit Returns Day-trading: 4 Hours a Day*, David Floyd.

   I learned a very valuable lesson about staying in tune with the market.

3. *The Master Swing Trader: Tools and Techniques to Profit from Outstanding Short-Term Trading Opportunities*, Alan S. Farley.

   I learned to watch daily and intraday charts together, and this, combined with the Impulse system from *Come into My Trading Room*, had a serious impact on my results.

4. *Technical Analysis of the Financial Markets: A Comprehensive Guide to Trading Methods and Applications*, John J. Murphy.

   A good book for learning the basics of chart patterns.

**Chapter 9   Kerry Lovvorn**

1. *Trading for a Living: Psychology, Trading Tactics, Money Management* and *Come into My Trading Room: A Complete Guide to Trading*, Dr. Alexander Elder.

   These are must-reads for any trader looking to pursue the trading profession. They cover the entire game in a very enjoyable way. *Trading for a Living* gave me a jump start on my path to trading.

2. *12 Habitudes of Highly Successful Traders*, Ruth Roosevelt.

   Preparedness is essential in any profession. Successful traders have a habit of being prepared.

3. *Exceptional Trading*, Ruth Roosevelt.

   I believe knowing yourself has the biggest impact on your trading.

4. *Investor Therapy: A Psychologist and Investing Guru Tells You How to Out-Psych Wall Street*, Dr. Richard Geist.

5. *Trading in the Zone: Master the Market with Confidence, Discipline, and a Winning Attitude*, Mark Douglas.

6. *The Trading Game: Playing by the Numbers to Make Millions*, Ryan Jones.

   Money management is exceptionally important, second only to the understanding of one's self.

7. *Market Wizards: Interviews with Top Traders* and *The New Market Wizards: Conversations with America's Top Traders*, Jack D. Schwager.

   Schwager writes: "I am frequently asked whether writing this volume...helped me become a better trader. The answer is yes, but not in the way people expect. No trader revealed to me any great secrets...The single most important lesson provided by the interviews is that it is absolutely necessary to adopt a trading approach precisely suited to one's personality."

8. *Studies in Tape Reading*, Rollo Tape.

    I keep this classic in my briefcase for regular rereads.

9. *Technical Analysis: Power Tools for Active Investors*, Gerald Appel.

10. [Title Yet Unknown], David Weis.

    David, you must complete your book; I am convinced it will be a classic.

### Chapter 10    Dr. Diane Buffalin

1. *Trading for a Living: Psychology, Trading Tactics, Money Management*, Dr. Alexander Elder.

### Chapter 11    David Weis

Influential books directly or tangentially related to trading (in no particular order):

1. *Technical Analysis of Stock Trends*, Robert D. Edwards and John Magee.

2. *Studies in Tape Reading*, Rollo Tape (Richard Wyckoff's pseudonym).

3. *Tape Reading and Market Tactics*, Humphrey B. Neill.

4. *Prices*, George F. Warren and Frank A. Pearson.

5. *A History of Interest Rates*, Sidney Homer and Richard Eugene Sylla.

6. *Market Wizards: Interviews with Top Traders*, Jack S. Schwager.

7. *Profits in the Stock Market*, H.M. Gartley.

8. *Freedom from the Known*, Jiddu Krishnamurti.

9. *The Wisdom of Insecurity*, Alan W. Watts.

10. *Siddhartha*, Hermann Hesse.

### Chapter 12    Bill Doane

1. *How Charts Can Help You in the Stock Market*, William L. Jiler.

    A much easier read than *Technical Analysis of Stock Trends* by Edwards and Magee, which is the bible of technical analysis.

2. *Jesse Livermore Speculator King*, Paul Sarnoff; and *Reminiscences of a Stock Operator*, Edward Lefèvre.

    Anyone wishing to become a successful trader must read about the life of Jesse Livermore.

3. *Trading for a Living: Psychology, Trading Tactics, Money Management*, Dr. Alexander Elder.

    On the top-10 list of any experienced investor or trader.

4. *The Crowd*, Gustave LeBon and *Extraordinary Popular Delusions and the Madness of Crowds*, Charles Mackay.

    These two classic books on crowd psychology can help one understand the manias of the Japanese market in the '80s, the run-up of gold to $880/ounce, and the bubbles of Internet stocks and house prices.

5. *The Battle for Investment Survival*, Gerald M. Loeb.

   An investment primer that has withstood the test of time; chock-full of helpful observations gathered from hands-on experience.

## Chapter 13   Peter Tatarnikov

1. *Intraday Trading System: Five Points for Success*, V.I. Safin.

   A manual by the chief trading instructor of our firm, rating each trade on a five-point scale; the book is being translated into English.

## Chapter 14   Damir Makhmudov

1. *Trading for a Living: Psychology, Trading Tactics, Money Management* and *Come into My Trading Room: A Complete Guide to Trading*, Dr. Alexander Elder.

   These books cover all the major aspects of trading the markets. Their study guides test you and provide feedback on your understanding of the material.

Recommended courses:

Technical Analysis and Specialized Techniques in Technical Analysis, Securities Institute of Australia, *www.securities.edu.au*

Technical analysis is covered in a very organized way, with lectures, assignments, examinations, Q&A, etc. Optional certification in Technical Analysis from the Australian Technical Analysis Association is possible after completing these courses.

## Chapter 15   Pascal Willain

I suggest reading the following books in the proposed order:

1. *The Four Pillars of Investing: Lessons for Building a Winning Portfolio*, William J. Bernstein.

   First, you need to understand the very large picture: asset allocation. This book is a great help in deciding what percentage of your assets to put in cash, stocks, real estate, etc. It advocates diversified index funds instead of specialized, managed funds, particularly addressing the bad returns of the former compared to the latter.

2. *How to Make Money in Stocks: A Winning System in Good Times or Bad*, William J. O'Neil.

   You need a good stock-picking strategy for the money you decide to put in the stock market.

3. *Fire Your Stock Analyst: Analyzing Stocks on Your Own*, Harry Domash

   The third step is to analyze stocks you select for investing. This is a must-read for those who are not accustomed to reading balance sheets; enables you to perform your own fundamental stock analysis.

4. *Trading for a Living* and *Come into My Trading Room*, Dr. Alexander Elder.

   Then come Dr. Elder's technical analysis books that show how to build your entry/exit strategy and money management policy.

5. *Portfolio Management Formulas: Mathematical Trading Methods for the Futures, Options, and Stock Markets*, Ralph Vince.

   Finally, for math lovers and those who have already developed a winning strategy, this book on money management will help you optimize your method and maximize your capital growth while reducing your risk.

### Chapter 16    Martin Knapp

1. *Trading for a Living: Psychology, Trading Tactics, Money Management*, Dr. Alexander Elder.
   My all-time favorite, without which I would not be where I am today.

2. *Come into My Trading Room: A Complete Guide to Trading*, Dr. Alexander Elder.
   No book in my library has more mark-ups.

3. *How I Found Freedom in an Unfree World: A Handbook for Personal Liberty*, Harry Browne.
   Great views on living a life of freedom.

4. *Jesse Livermore: The World's Greatest Stock Trader*, Richard Smitten.
   I prefer it to the more famous *Reminiscences of a Stock Operator*.

5. *The Inner Game of Tennis*, W. Timothy Gallwey.
   A different approach to "doing a martin."

# ACKNOWLEDGMENTS

I feel grateful to the 16 men and women who opened their trading rooms to me. Thank you for being open and generous, showing me your trades, and reviewing your chapters. I look forward to staying in touch with you in the years ahead.

My initial plan was to approach three dozen traders and ask each to show me one trade. My friend and a repeat camper Peter Cameron pointed out a flaw: "Everyone is going to show you a successful trade, and some poor guy who reads your book will see three dozen profitable trades and not a single loss; he may think that trading is easy." Peter declined to be interviewed for this book because he makes a lot of money, lives in a tax haven, and keeps a very low profile, but his comment changed my project. I started asking people to show me two trades—a winner and a loser, knowing from my own experience that I learned more from losing trades than from winning ones.

Thanks to dozens of traders who came to my Camps each year and kept me on my toes with their questions. I feel grateful to Kim and Charles Githler and their capable staff, whose invitations to Traders' Expos and Money Shows gave me valuable opportunities to meet hundreds of traders. Thanks to Jack Schwager, whose *Market Wizards* created a new genre of market literature. In writing this book, I started out on a trail laid out by Jack.

Thanks to Joan O'Neil at John Wiley & Sons, who leaned on me to initiate this project and move it forward. She took the risk of publishing *Entries & Exits* in full color and encouraged me to create a *Study Guide*. My old friend Ted Bonanno served as an agent for this book. Ted and I work out together several times a week, and our gym sessions were punctuated by his practical and innovative advice. Paul diNovo was my top choice for an art director; I have tremendous respect for his artistic judgment and taste. Joanna Pomeranz and her staff for converting a plain text file and a folder of charts into the book you hold in your hands. Carol Keegan Kayne made sure that the final version met her purist English standards.

All three of my children, Miriam, Nika, and Danny, pitched in with editing the manuscript. In addition, Nika helped oversee many issues of design. Inna Feldman, my manager of more than 10 years, ran the office alone for weeks at a time, while I had my face in the word processor. She relied on Oleg Andryyets and Konrad Krupinski, two trusted associates, to keep the office humming. Last but not least, many thanks to Patricia Liu, who helped create a happy emotional background against which this book was written.

Dr. Alexander Elder

# ABOUT THE AUTHOR

Alexander Elder, M.D., is a professional trader, based in New York City. He is the author of *Trading for a Living* and the *Study Guide for Trading for a Living*, considered modern classics among traders. First published in 1993, these international best-sellers have been translated into Chinese, Dutch, French, German, Greek, Japanese, Korean, Portuguese, Polish, Russian, and Spanish. His *Come into My Trading Room* was named a 2002 Barron's Book of the Year. He also wrote *Rubles to Dollars: Making Money on Russia's Exploding Financial Frontier* and *Straying from the Flock: Travels in New Zealand*.

Dr. Elder was born in Leningrad and grew up in Estonia, where he entered medical school at the age of 16. At 23, while working as a ship's doctor, he jumped a Soviet ship in Africa and received political asylum in the United States. He worked as a psychiatrist in New York City and taught at Columbia University. His experience as a psychiatrist provided him with unique insight into the psychology of trading. Dr. Elder's books, articles, and software reviews have established him as one of today's leading experts on trading.

Dr. Elder is the originator of Traders' Camps—week-long classes for traders. He is also the founder of the Spike group, whose members are professional and semi-professional traders. They share their best stock picks each week in competition for prizes among themselves. Dr. Elder continues to trade, conducts webinars for traders, and is a sought-after speaker at conferences in the US and abroad. Readers of this book are welcome to request a free subscription to his electronic newsletter, as well as a template of Trader's Diary by contacting his office:

elder.com
PO Box 20555, Columbus Circle Station
New York, NY 10023, USA
Tel. 718.507.1033; fax 718.639.8889
e-mail: info@elder.com
website: www.elder.com

# INDEX